SPENDING SMARTER
AND
SPENDING LESS

POLICIES AND PARTNERSHIPS
FOR HEALTH CARE IN CANADA

RALPH SUTHERLAND, M.D.
JANE FULTON, Ph.D.

CANADIAN CATALOGUING IN PUBLICATION DATA

Sutherland, Ralph W.
    Spending smarter and spending less: policies and partnerships for health care in canada

Includes index.
ISBN 0-9693537-1-5 (bound) —
ISBN 0-9693537-2-3 (pbk.)

    1. Medical policy—Canada.   2. Health planning—Canada.   3. Medical care, Cost of—
Canada.
I. Fulton, M. Jane   II. Title.

RA449.S89 1994   362.1'0971   C94-900313-1

PRICE —   Soft cover $39.00
                Hard cover $47.00

There may be shipping and handling charges.

Published by: The Health Group, Ottawa   and   The Health Group, Pacific
                 445 Piccadilly Avenue   9065 Lochside Drive
                 Ottawa, Ontario   **MAIN LIBRARY**   Sidney, B.C.
                 K1Y 0H5   V8L 1N1

Printed by MOM Printing, Ottawa

Distributed by: The Health Group, and by

                  Ralph Sutherland   The Canadian Public Health Association
                  Box 129   700-1565 Carling Avenue
                  Plevna, Ontario   Ottawa, Ontario
                  K0H 2M0   K1Z 8R1
                  1-613-479-2325

                  Canadian Hospital Association Press
                  17 York Street, Suite 100
                  Ottawa, Ontario
                  K1N 9J6

Acknowledgements

It is once again a pleasure to acknowledge the manager of the production of this book, Diane Fontaine. Diane worked with us on *Health Care in Canada: A Description and Analysis of Canadian Health Services* and she brought the same dedication and accuracy to *Spending Smarter and Spending Less*. Diane is also able to read the hand writing of doctors, both academic and medical, an amazing feat.

We also wish to acknowledge the many colleagues in governments, the health professions and in Canadian communities who generously provided information for us. We wish to particularly thank the Ontario Ministry of Health for permission to use documents and information associated with work done in the Ministry in 1991 and 1992.

Dedications

RALPH SUTHERLAND

This book is dedicated to all of my family and friends, but in particular to Jean Taylor, my only sister, to her husband Cle and to their children and grand-children, and to some special rural Ontario friends.

The special friends are all part of the Lucy Gorr family, including her children, grand-children and great-grand-children, but in particular Bill and Glenna Gorr and all of their family and Joan Murphy and all of her children and grand-children. I wish everyone could have the pleasure of having such neighbours and friends.

JANE FULTON

For Jim Fair who walks the talk.

Table of Contents

LIST OF FIGURES

LIST OF TABLES

Preamble to the Book

WHY THE BOOK WAS WRITTEN

Most people know health care consumes one quarter to more than one third of all the money spent by provincial governments, and that spending levels have risen steadily for 30 years. Most people know that all provinces are trying very hard to control spending on health care, and many support these efforts.

Health care is only one of the many things which affect our health. If too much is spent on health care there will be less left for all of the other things which also matter to our health, such as education, safe roads, safe communities and healthy environments. There may not be agreement on how much should be spent on health care, or which health care spending should have highest priority, but there is broad agreement that government spending on health care does need to be controlled.

Less spending means fewer health care services delivered at public expense. Fortunately spending less on health care need not threaten the safety of the ill, the injured or those who wish health care to protect them against illness or injury. The solution is to combine fewer dollars with better spending. This book describes policy options available to those who wish to control health care spending and spend the available dollars better.

Unfortunately, neither the provinces, the health care institutions and programs, the health care professionals nor those who rely on health care are giving a great deal of attention to the elimination of unproductive health care. Attention to this problem is urgently needed. Continuing to provide all Canadians with necessary health care will be possible only if we spend our health care dollars better.

This book reviews the policy options available, puts forward some ideas and predicts some effects. Perhaps most importantly, it suggests ways to start, including ways to mobilize the immense energy, initiative and creativity that exists in every health care delivery situation and in every population. Canadians are anxious to contribute to the better use of scarce health care dollars.

In the face of fewer resources the system must downsize, and it is doing that. The cut-backs are stressful to managers and caregivers, and occasionally unpleasant or even dangerous to those in need of care. The stresses and dangers will be intolerable unless all players, working together, identify, and stop, bad spending.

This book explains why cut-backs are unavoidable and even desirable, and looks at the ways in which decisions can be improved. It invites everyone to work together towards greater social benefit per health care dollar spent. It will hopefully acquaint users and providers with both the complexity and the manageability of the health care system and its problems. Change can be managed and directed, and good management of it will benefit all Canadians.

1

The managers, planners and providers of health care were for several decades dominated by the idea that more health care was always a good thing, and that the public purse should pay for it all. The theme was *do everything for everyone, and if it can't be done now plan to do it as soon as possible*. The theme has now changed; cut-backs are the name of the game. Changing our health care habits and learning to live with cut-backs in health care spending will perhaps be easier, and will certainly be more tolerable, if the reasons for the changes are understood and if realistic participative processes are described through which changes can be explained and guided.

The future will be woven with many threads from the past, but it will also contain much that is a complete break from the past. This book may help users, payers and providers move more easily from the old rules to the new ones. Setting out the options may help everyone prepare for a future which will be difficult even if understood, and chaotic if it is not.

THE CHALLENGES OF TERMINOLOGY

Health care issues are often described in technocratic jargon. Jargon can hide things that are ordinary behind a smokescreen of the incomprehensible. Jargon cannot be completely avoided, but ordinary english will be used as much as possible.

The terms effectiveness, efficiency, cost-effectiveness and relative cost-effectiveness will be used. They are all part of the vocabulary of economic evaluation. They say something about performance.

An efficient person or program uses fewer resources to carry out specified activities, or reach specified goals, than do others who perform the same activities or attain the same goals. Efficiency will, in this book, always mean cost-efficiency. This book will not use the term allocative efficiency, and we wish no-one else would either. Allocative efficiency is a term which, when it was created, was not needed. It refers to the wisdom with which resource allocation decisions are made. The resource allocation process can be adequately discussed through the use of already well established terms such as policy analysis, optimal policy selection, strategic thinking, strategic planning, cost-effectiveness, cost-benefit and operational planning. Allocative efficiency was created by academics who came to realize that doing things right was not enough; doing the right thing was even more important. So they invented a new term to describe a process and outcome for which others had long before created quite suitable terms.

An effective program or person can be described as one which, or who, accomplishes desired goals such as *to make sick people well*. If the goal is accomplished at reasonable cost then the program is not just effective, it is cost-effective. If two programs or processes both attain a particular goal, but at different costs or with different degrees of perfection then one will be more cost-effective than the other.

The terms cost-benefit and cost-utility will be used very little, although cost-benefit is a superb term. Cost-benefit has unfortunately come to be considered appropriate only when the effectiveness of what is being measured can be expressed in dollars, a rather silly restriction on the use of a very sensible term. Cost-utility is used in the literature when the benefits are expressed in terms of quality of life or wellness. This term would, if vocabulary was more logical, just disappear. The fact that impact or effectiveness can be expressed in a variety of ways, and that this variety led to confusion for academics, should not have led to the terminological rigidity which now exists. Benefits can, and in certain circumstances should, be described in dollars. In other circumstances benefits should be described in terms of years of life lost or changes in quality of life. In all cases, regardless of the measures used to describe the benefits, the term cost-benefit is appropriate. Unfortunately the literature and the experts are so locked in to the current definitional quagmire that one dare not completely ignore it. Cost-effectiveness will therefore be used instead of cost-benefit.

The terms input (structure, resources), process (throughput) and output will occasionally be used, but impact and outcome will dominate in use and importance.

Input has in the past been given far too much attention, although the costs of inputs must be known if one is to determine efficiency and cost-effectiveness. Inventories of inputs (ambulances and gas masks and health care workers) are performed regularly and ritualistically as if they were useful (and they usually are not).

Process is important when examining the adequacy of the decisions and performance of individual health care providers and consumers. It therefore is important to cost control and better spending at the micro level.

Output carries the idea of production. Hospital output may be expressed as the days of care produced. The output of ambulances can be expressed as the number of trips made, and the output of a physician or social worker can be expressed as the number of patient contacts per week.

Outcome and *impact* refer to the effects of decisions and services on a person or population. (These *effects* could also be called outputs, but output will be reserved for use when products rather than effects are being considered.) The products (the visits and the trips) of the hospital, ambulance or health care worker must not be assumed to be of value. The desirability of continuing to produce these products cannot be estimated until one knows both effects and costs.

Cost will throughout this book almost always refer to the direct financial cost of health care. Chapter 3 offers brief comment on indirect economic costs and on social costs.

Cost control and better spending have spawned many a new term and many a successful consultant while the subject was hot, as with Management by Objectives, Quality Assurance, Total Quality Management and Continuous Quality Improvement. The habit will continue and new terms will appear whether they are useful or not.

THE SEQUENCE OF THE PARTS OF THE BOOK

Part One (chapters 1-3) provides background information. Chapter 1 describes the indirect factors and techniques which affect health care expenditures, demand and need. Chapter 2 describes the evolution of those health care characteristics which are of particular relevance to the current need for cost control and better spending. Chapter 3 describes current patterns of spending on health care in Canada.

Part Two (chapters 4-14) explores health care policy options. Discussion of the basic policy options is followed by a review of options pertaining to organization, planning, evaluation, cost control, physician's services, the role of consumers, human resources and research.

Part Three (chapters 15-20) looks at the policies and processes associated with policy implementation as well as at some of the policy options associated with specific health care sectors.

Part Four consists of only Chapter 21. Chapter 21 summarizes the policy options supported by the authors and takes a very brief look into the future.

Chapter 1

Factors Which Affect the Demand for, Need for and Expenditures on Health Care

INTRODUCTION

Later chapters will look at options which directly affect what is spent on health care, and what is bought. They will consider such questions as `how much can this province afford to spend on health care this year, or, how many of the health care dollars should go to hospitals?`. Such questions are immediate, operational and cannot be avoided, but behind these questions are many forces and events which indirectly affect or determine the answers. Chapter 1 describes some of these factors which indirectly affect health care.

The impact of these indirect factors on policies is often difficult to measure, difficult to understand and quite unpredictable, especially when the factors are rooted in culture. Cultural changes require behavioral readjustment, a process which in an open and democratic society is not easy to build into public or private policies.

One point must be made strongly. These indirect forces seldom, especially in the short term, affect the amount spent on health care. Health care will spend all it can get, just as will all other public sectors such as education, pollution control, job creation, income redistribution and community security. The indirect forces will, however, alter the number of persons requiring and/or seeking health care, alter the care they will need, alter the services they will receive, alter the extent to which the services will be of benefit and alter the policies of governments and of institutions and programs. Through these effects they will affect public perceptions of the importance of health care, of how much should be spent on health care and of how that money should be spent.

These factors which indirectly affect health care are not given attention in later chapters. The failure to follow up these issues is not a reflection of their importance. They are central to long term changes in utilization and costs, but are not the subject of this book. Our subject is constraining health care spending and spending the available dollars well, but because the background factors are fundamental to the protection and improvement of the health status of Canadians they are introduced in this first chapter.

The discussion of factors which indirectly affect our health care use and costs is a reminder to all readers that the health care system is almost entirely a system which responds to what has happened, and what happens is usually not under the control of those who deliver health care. Regardless of the amount spent on health care, and regardless of how well our health care dollars are spent, the state of health of Canadians will be determined largely by individual and collective decisions made in all corners of society, by each person and by all levels of government.

An understanding of the factors which indirectly affect health care will help governments, agencies and associations to write policy, and will help individuals to make choices which best protect and improve community and individual health. These factors include wealth, perceptions of health, societal priorities and expectations, lifestyles, public policy in departments other than Health, new (non-health care) technology, demography, patterns of illness and injury and the state of the many environments.

THE INFLUENCE OF WEALTH ON HEALTH STATUS

It has been estimated that at least three quarters of the increases in life expectancy in the developed countries in the 1800s and 1900s was due to increased prosperity and the improved nutrition, housing, sanitation and work safety which came with the increased prosperity. (McKeown, T., The Modern Rise of Population, 1976)

It was once thought that the poor would become as healthy as the more well to do if there was equal access to health care, but experience has shown that this does not occur. In Britain, after almost 50 years of the benefits of the National Health Service (which is much more comprehensive than our universal programs in Canada), the health status gap between rich and poor has widened instead of narrowed. Health inequalities between the manual and nonmanual employment groups in Britain were greater in the 1980s than in the 1970s. (Whitehead, M., The Health Education Council, London, U.K., 1987, as reprinted in Chronic Diseases in Canada, Nov 1988) The health status disparities are found whether the comparison is of males, females, smokers, nonsmokers, infants or other groups. Income, and the privileges and self-image associated with it, is a major determinant of level of health. Wealthy populations and countries are healthier than poor populations and countries.

Throughout the early 1980s Canada became more sharply divided into the *haves* and the *have nots*, and the recession of the early 1990s reinforced the trend. Average family income in 1991 was $53,131, approximately the same (in actual dollars, unadjusted for inflation) as 12 years earlier. (Statistics Canada) Income in constant dollars has therefore fallen, and purchasing power fell even more due to increases in taxation.

The recession in the early 1980s increased the number of Canadians on social assistance from 1.5 million to 2 million, and 3 million were supported by unemployment insurance (UIC). The surprise was not in these figures; it was in the failure of the figures to return to prerecession levels when the recession ended. The recovery was not a recovery for the unskilled or the skilled whose skills were outdated, it was a recovery for the professionals, those with international skills and those with knowledge needed in the new economic milieu. Unemployment became structural, rather than cyclical.

In the recession of the early 1990s the pattern was repeated but more strongly. The hundreds of thousands of jobs lost were permanent jobs, and many of the families on unemployment insurance, or eventually on welfare, were formerly middle class families who considered their economic future to be secure. The last two recessions have decreased the size of the middle class, a class to which most health care workers belong and the class which pays most of the taxes which support social programs.

The 1980s and 1990s produced a pessimistic population. An Angus Reid survey in late 1992 found that 2/3 of Canadians expect their standard of living to either worsen or stay the same in the future, and over half of the middle income earners thought their children would be worse off than they (the parents) now are.

In the midst of this depressing picture the elderly and the wealthy have improved their financial position. In Ontario only about one quarter of the elderly qualify for the supplement to the federal old age pension. An increasing percentage of retirees in Canada have substantial private incomes to supplement their OAS and CPP pensions. It is predicted that within the next decade or two the average wealth of the elderly will begin to decrease as more workers reach age 65 without having had the benefit of secure long term employment, but for the moment the incomes of many seniors are more adequate than the incomes of seniors in earlier decades.

THE INFLUENCE OF CULTURE

Canadian culture affects the health of each of us. If our peers think violence is natural, entertaining and the best way to resolve disagreements there will be lots of it. The number of youths under 18 charged with violent crimes doubled in the five years 1986-1991 (Statistics Canada), and in some high schools 10-15% of students carry weapons. (Ottawa Board of Education, 1993) It is not only war which produces battle injuries; they can be a product of culture.

Culture plays a major role in determining whether women are thought to be inferior to men or the property or playthings of men. If men are considered to be superior and dominant, then women will not be treated fairly at work, in the home or in the courts.

The impact of culture on health is both good and bad. If our peers and friends approve of regular exercise, good eating habits and learning to manage stress we are more likely to also approve of them. Similarly, if it is usual to smoke, drive too fast, abuse alcohol and be personally abusive (physically and/or psychologically) then more of us will have these habits. Role models do matter. If being skinny is thought to be sexy there is more anorexia.

A study of the British civil service showed that lower level civil servants died much younger than higher level civil servants. (Wilkinson, R., ed., Class and Health, Tavistock 1986, as quoted by the Ontario Premiers Council on Health Strategy in Nurturing Health, 1991) All levels of British civil servants have stable employment, but only 29% of the top level workers were smokers compared to 68% of the lower level workers. Smoking incidence is not the only cultural difference in these worker groups, but it will have played a role in creating the different life expectancies. Other factors which will have contributed to the differences include job satisfaction, other lifestyle choices and the level of individual support in the workplace and the community, all of which are affected by culture.

The changes in the use of tobacco in Canada have been a response to peer pressure as well as a response to information, although the peer pressure originated in the information. The percentage of Canadians over age 15 and using tobacco fell from 49.5% in 1965 to 31.0% in 1990. (CJPH, Nov-Dec 1992, p. 405) In 1989 the life expectancy of a 45 year old male smoker was 7 years less than a nonsmoker. Later studies have reported that the impact of tobacco use is even greater, with life expectancy differences perhaps being as high as 15 years. A decrease in the incidence of tobacco use from 31% to 10% would result in the temporary avoidance of 21,000 Canadian deaths annually.

Culture affects the frequency with which families stay together and the extent to which social units are emotionally supportive and forgiving versus being critical. Cultural attributes contribute to the self-image, coping skills and confidence of everyone, but especially the young. Networks of supportive friends and family lead to longer lives as well as better ones.

Culture determines the importance assigned to winning. If winning is everything then the losers are losers in every respect, and there is a clearly established link between the immune system and levels of depression, social deprivation and self-image.

It is not always easy to relate cultural attributes to health status. It is often unclear, for example, whether, and in which circumstances, competition has a positive versus a negative effect on societal or individual health.

Expectations also have implications for psychosocial health, and expectations are largely cultural. Unrealistic (unattainable) expectations in terms of owning a house, getting a job, taking two holidays (or even one holiday) each year, going to university or having a summer cottage or a bigger boat, or in terms of what constitutes a decent place to live or a decent income, will lead to anger, frustration, depression and a poor self-image, and these in turn contribute to (or represent) inadequate mental and psychosocial health.

When expectations and demands routinely and continuously exceed what is possible optimal mental health becomes impossible. When failure to get what one wants is routinely blamed on the bad intentions or the incompetence of someone else, rather than on the inability of the world to satisfy everyone's needs and/or demands, there is inevitable anger against those considered to have the bad intentions or the lack of competence. Governments and leaders in almost all countries face this anger, an anger rooted in our cultural expectation of continuous personal economic growth.

Culture includes attitudes to risk. It may not be wise to try and tell Canadians how much risk they should calmly accept, but it is possible to quantify some risks and comment on public reaction to them.

More young people die on the highways during a bad long week-end than die all year from meningococcal disease. (Every year Canada reports 50-150 cases of meningococcal disease with 5-20% mortality.) The hazards at work and on the highways are a greater risk to our young people than meningococcal disease, and prevention of meningococcal disease is more difficult than prevention of many accidents, but it is meningococcal disease which produces public hysteria and public policy response. Society is willing to spend much more freely to save the life of a teenager who will die from meningococcal disease than it is willing to spend to save the life of a teenager who will die on the highway.

There is media and public anger whenever someone dies due to a real or apparent imperfection in health care availability or delivery. Canadians appear to be more willing to expose healthy individuals to injury and death than they are willing to expose unhealthy people to risk. Deaths from preventable highway accidents, snowmobiles going through the ice, suicides, work related accidents or abuse of hazardous substances receive a few lines in the media and the news item is gone. The possibly preventable death of a sick or seriously injured person who has entered the arms of health care may merit months of headlines, inquiries and inquests.

Culture affects the use and cost of health care in many ways. There is evidence that the health beliefs of a population or a person affect the extent to which that population or person seeks or accepts health care. (Dollard, C., and J. Trudel, "Medicaments: La surconsommation chez les personnes âgées", Montreal, Editions du Meridien, 1990) Health beliefs therefore are factors which affect health care costs and demands, and as the beliefs change so will the demand for, and costs of, health care.

Culture also affects health through its effects on food preferences. North Americans have a love of red meat, which increases the intake of saturated fats, which increases the incidence of coronary artery disease.

Culture determines the vigor with which death will be delayed, especially when that death is close and inevitable. In Holland the number of cases of assisted suicide (voluntary euthanasia) had by 1992 approached 3% of all deaths. Physicians were involved in perhaps half of these cases. In 1993 the Dutch Parliament approved voluntary euthanasia/assisted suicide, and the number of such cases will almost surely increase. These suicides are partly culturally determined.

STATE OF MIND

Optimism and tolerance are signs of good health and are also health producing. Depression and anger are health damaging. Women with breast cancer were found to live, on average, one and one half years longer when they participated in group psychotherapy, a form of social support. ("Can Psychotherapy Delay Cancer Deaths", Science, October 1989, as reported in Nurturing Health, Ontario Premiers Council, 1991)

PATTERNS OF ILLNESS AND INJURY

The incidence and mix of illness and injury has an obvious effect on the demand and need for health care and on the ability of the health care network and other social systems to deliver services to those in need. The extent to which illnesses and injuries have changed is startling. Some of the changes have decreased the need for health services; others have increased the need.

8

The prevalence of diabetes is increasing. It has been estimated that 10% of persons over 65 years now suffer from it, and that by early in the next century the 10% figure may apply to the total population. The prevalence of dementia is also rising steadily, primarily because of the increasing very elderly population. Eighteen percent of males in Manitoba over age 85, and 33% of females, have moderate to severe mental impairment. (Shapiro, E., Manitoba Health Care Studies and their Policy Implications, 1991). AIDS has appeared as a major new disease while other diseases such as chlamydia have become better understood.

Other diseases and conditions are becoming less common. The prevalence of disease of the arteries of the heart (ischemic heart disease/coronary artery disease/arteriosclerotic or atherosclerotic heart disease) has fallen steadily for a quarter of a century, as has the incidence of strokes, some cancers, most infectious diseases, occupational injuries and diseases, highway accidents and sports injuries. Despite the decrease in the prevalence of coronary artery disease it is still estimated that if Canadian volumes of this hazard were equal to the levels in Japan Canadian deaths from heart attacks would fall by 80%. (Health Promotion, Spring 1992). Injuries and deaths from motor vehicle accidents are lower than in previous decades, but about one third of all Canadian accidents still involve an automobile, with 20-25% being sports related and one fifth work related. (Adams, M., Can. Soc. Trends, Summer 1990, p. 22-24)

A number of diseases which caused significant expense 30-40 years ago, including rheumatic fever, rubella, measles, mumps and poliomyelitis, have largely disappeared.

The incidence and prevalence of other common conditions may be stable. The 1978-79 Canada Health Survey reported that one quarter of all Canadians had a health problem severe enough to warrant attention. The common problems included anxiety, joint pain, dental trouble, skin conditions, stomach problems, headache, family conflict, allergies, the common cold, gynecological problems, insomnia, high blood pressure, birth control and addiction to legal substances. Few of these are a threat to life but many are a threat to quality of life and all affect health care. The Canada Health and Disability Study of 1983-84 found almost 13% of all Canadians with some level of disability. Seven to eight percent suffered from reduced mobility, 2 to 3% had a hearing disability and 1 to 1.5% were living in some form of institution.

The prevalence and significance of a particular disease does not always determine the amount of attention it receives. About 1% of the population suffers from a significant dissociative disorder, primarily schizophrenia. Improved ability to predict, prevent or treat schizophrenia, especially prevention, would significantly alter population health status, but a major disease such as schizophrenia may receive less attention then the disease or treatment of the year, e.g. Reyes Syndrome, genital herpes or heart transplants.

It is evident that many, and probably most, of the conditions which lead to the use of health care are not life threatening. The offices of physicians, chiropractors, social workers and nurse practitioners are full of the walking worried and the slightly ill. Changes in the extent to which individuals understand chronic conditions (for which self-care can often be as good or better than professional care) and short term self-limiting conditions (those which will go away no matter what is done), and changes in the skill with which individuals and families learn to identify and manage stress and conflict, could significantly affect the use and cost of health care.

DEMOGRAPHY

When discussing demography and effects on health care the aging of the population is the feature which usually receives the most attention, but health care has also been affected by other demographic changes including the lowered birth rate, the increasing number of one person households, the increasing number of single parent families, the urbanization of the population, the rise of females to almost half of the labour force and the increasing number of children in households below the poverty line.

Aging brings new demands for social support, primarily in those over age 75, but there is little reason to panic about these new requirements. About 19% of the Swedish people are over age 65, and that country is handling the demands comfortably. In Victoria B.C. over 20% of the population is 65 or over, and seniors comprise 25% or more of the populations of many small Canadian villages and small towns. (Expression, Newsletter of National Advisory Council on Aging, Winter 1993) Canada will face its most serious challenges from the seniors population in the years when the first of the baby boomers reach age 75, at about the year 2025. The pressures will begin to fall by the year 2045 when persons over 65 are likely to stabilize at about 20% of the population.

It is no longer reasonable to consider age 65 to be of medical significance. Health care demands change very little in the decade after age 65. Sweden in 1992 raised its retirement age to 66, a recognition of the capacity of individuals in what has been thought of as their post-retirement years. Canada will almost surely gradually raise the age at which persons will be classified as old and at which they qualify for a variety of special programs.

Despite the likelihood that the crisis of aging is being overstated, aging does bring new demands. The percentage of seniors with significant disabilities increases from 20% in the age group 65-74 to 49% in the age group 85 and older. (Statistics Canada, Health and Activity Limitation Survey, 1990) Persons 65-84 use hospitals about three times as much as persons 25-64, whereas persons 85 and over use hospitals five times as much. (Mustard, F., in Aging and Health: Linking Research and Public Policy, as quoted in the Porter Report)

Age should not be seen to be the only factor increasing the use of health care by seniors. In British Columbia. in the period 1975-1986 visits to specialists by persons over 75 years more than doubled. Physician supply, new approaches to medical care, user expectations and superspecialization (which leads to referrals to multiple specialists) also play a role in the use of health care.

TECHNOLOGY (OTHER THAN THE TECHNOLOGY OF HEALTH CARE)

The technology of modern society, including the technology of cybernetics, resource industries, communications, recycling, food processing, residential construction, warfare, drug synthesis (licit and illicit), pest control, energy production, transportation and environmental protection, constantly alters the mix of persons seeking or requiring health care. The importance to health of various technological advances outside health care is not well described, but these advances definitely affect quality of life, length of life and the hazards being faced during life.

THE ENVIRONMENTS

Environments can be categorized as physical, emotional, social, intellectual, political and economic and they can be described as a series of locations, including workplaces, homes, classrooms, play places, uteri and institutions. All types of environments and all of the specific locations bring their own psychosocial as well as physical health hazards and protections.

The role of the sun in skin cancer and of smog in respiratory diseases is well established. The importance of the *climate* within houses and places of work is becoming more understood as the sick building syndrome becomes documented. Noise, dust, temperature, radiation, pests, rodents, unsafe machines, hazards of transportation, poor visibility and polluted food, water and air can contribute to injury and ill health. Concerns regarding the ozone layer, deforestation, pollution of the oceans and the subterranean water reserves, desertification, global warming and destruction of the diversity of the natural gene pool include concerns about effects on physical and psychosocial health.

Population density and geographic features affect the costs of attracting and retaining health care professionals, of transporting patients to other centres, and of heating and cooling health care facilities.

Evidence clearly supports the indirect effects of the psychosocial environment on health care costs and needs. In the psychosocial environment the threats include isolation, loneliness, fear (of failure, of being left alone, of abuse, of loss of income), inadequate social support, guilt, insecurity, rejection and other experiences which lower self-esteem and quality of life.

The negative and positive effects of various general or special environments on health are widely discussed and documented, but conclusions often are contradictory. What is known is that certain extremes are bad for our health and certain general environmental factors are good for it. Many excellent documents on the environments and our health have been produced by the World Health Organization and its regional offices, for example, Gro Harlem Bruntland, World Commission on Environment and Development: Our Common Future, Oxford University Press, 1987.

GENETICS

Genetics is the major determinant of how long we live, which organs survive or don't in the face of various threats and how well humans recover from injuries and illnesses. It is also becoming increasingly accepted that genetics may be the single most important determinant of not only the likelihood of developing many illnesses such as cancer but also the greatest determinant of how rapidly diseases will progress.

PUBLIC POLICY OUTSIDE OF THE MINISTRY OF HEALTH: PRIMARY PREVENTION

Policies outside of Ministries of Health act positively on health status almost entirely through primary prevention.

Primary prevention includes all those actions and decisions which keep us healthy. Primary prevention devices include child-proof medicine bottles, roll-bars on tractors, helmets on motorcycle riders, support for single parents, sewage treatment plants, communication aids for the isolated and disabled, low fat diets and a milieu in which speed and violence are replaced by moderation and caring. Most of these actions and decisions are outside of the domain of health care.

The payoff from primary prevention can be immense. About 200,000 Canadians die annually. Of these, about one half die from diseases of the circulatory system and 20-25% die of cancer. Within diseases of the circulatory system, heart attacks (coronary artery disease) are the biggest killers. Prevention can significantly lower the likelihood of having a heart attack and the incidence of some cancers.

The potential impact of prevention on life expectancy is seen even more clearly if one looks at when people die as well as at the cause of death. A death at age 45 represents, on average, almost 30 years of life lost for a male and 35 for a female. Using Potential Years of Life Lost (PYLL) to measure the importance of various threats to life shows that the effects of cancer and of heart disease are still important but no more important than accidents and suicides.

The five biggest causes of loss of potential years of life of Canadian males are coronary artery disease, automobile accidents, suicide, lung cancer and perinatal mortality (death within the first 28 days after birth), in that order. In the Yukon and the Northwest Territories suicide moves to number one. The picture for females is much the same as for males except that breast cancer joins lung cancer in the top five and suicide drops off the list. Lung cancer passed breast cancer in 1993 or 1994 in terms of number of female deaths. (McCann, C., "Potential Years of Life Lost, Canada, 1982-1986", Chronic Diseases in Canada 1988; 9: 98-100, and Balram C., "Impact of Chronic Diseases on the Health of Canadians", Chronic Diseases in Canada, May, 1989)

An understanding of the causes of premature death and of PYLL is useful when considering what decisions will most improve the length and quality of life of Canadians. It becomes evident that most of the major causes of loss of potential years of life are much more able to be prevented than treated. Breast cancer is the only hazard in the top five for which there is at this time no generally accepted method of prevention, although breast feeding appears to reduce hazard in premenopausal years and estrogen may do the same in postmenopausal years. For lung cancer and suicide there is no satisfactory treatment but prevention is possible; for victims of coronary artery disease, perinatal mortality (mostly from prematurity) and automobile accidents there are good, improving and expensive therapies but proven and often much less expensive methods of prevention.

A Report on the Health of Canada's Children which was released in 1989 by the Canadian Institute on Child Health supports greater emphasis on prevention. The Report states that 6% of babies born had a low birth weight. As many as 20% of premature low birth weight babies have long term disabilities with resultant personal and social as well as economic costs. (Chance, G., Fourth National Conference on Regionalized Perinatal Care, Ottawa, 1988) Statistics are particularly unfavorable for native populations. Many of the low weight births are preventable through reductions in smoking and alcohol exposure and improved prenatal care. Children born to teenagers or into poverty are more likely to have a low birth weight.

More American children die each year of preventable injuries than from all diseases combined. (Can. Fam. Phys., October 1988, page 2326) In Canada over 60% of deaths of persons aged 1-24 are due to intentional or unintentional injury, many of which are preventable. (Statistics Canada, 1992; Mortality Reports)

Sixty to seventy percent of persons who are diagnosed as having lung cancer are dead within a year, and survival rates for the more malignant types have changed little if at all in recent decades. Almost all of these cases of cancer were preventable. When early diagnosis makes little difference, when treatment is ineffective, when prevention is possible and when the hazard is a major killer it becomes sensible and cost-effective to spend seriously on prevention.

Treating a case of lung cancer may include any combination of surgery, chemotherapy, radiotherapy and palliative care. The first three of these often do very little to extend the length of life and often decrease quality of life. The greatest positive impact on the tragedy of lung cancer has come from less smoking. The increase in lung cancer in females is entirely a product of increased smoking.

In the years 1969-1987 age adjusted cancer mortality rates went down in 5 industrialized countries and rose in 11 others. There have been some treatment success stories, but in general the expectations of the 60s and 70s have not materialized. The war against cancer is far from won, and in fighting this war it is clear that prevention, when prevention is possible, should receive major emphasis. The promises of those delivering cancer treatment are the same as those of 20 years ago, and even more expensive. Unfortunately the improved results which are so often predicted do not tend to be supported by the statistics of later decades. The five year survival rate of all cancers (excluding skin cancers other than melanoma) is only about 50%. (Chronic Diseases in Canada, Nov-Dec 1992) The brightest spot in terms of treatment outcomes is in children, where there has been an almost across the board improvement.

Primary prevention is initiated through policy selection and personal choice, through both collective and individual action. Governments and agencies use regulation and education; individuals use wisdom and willpower.

Regulation can be the most important tool. Research proved tobacco was a threat to health, but taxes (a form of regulation) are the most successful instrument in the war against the use of tobacco. Seat belts, even when their value was known and the public was well informed, were used by a minority of drivers. The threat of substantial fines made use much more universal.

Education alone may also be effective, as with programs to reduce spinal cord injuries and programs to reduce teen-age pregnancies. A combination of education (including social marketing) and regulation, and subsequent cultural change, offers the best hope of reducing child abuse and wife assault, two of the major pandemics of our day for which prevention is much more attractive than treatment.

The best primary prevention approaches have not been identified for all problems. For example, it is accepted that poor parenting increases the likelihood of children with problems, but what is good parenting? There would at times even be disagreement as to the desirable outcomes of parenting. Even when there is agreement as to what constitutes good parenting, and there probably is agreement that all children benefit from love and caring, there will be disagreement as to how to accomplish what is desired. What kinds of programs improve parent skills? Diverse values and/or inadequate information make it difficult to practice primary prevention in some areas.

The linkages between societal stresses and health status are becoming clearer although many of the mechanisms by which social stresses affect health are still not clear. The multifactorial nature of the interactions makes understanding difficult and remedial action rather random. There is, however, strong support for the belief that experiences in early life are very important in determining levels of both psychosocial and physical health in later life. These beliefs suggest that spending on the psychosocial health of children will, even if the techniques used are imperfect, produce major pay-offs in future health.

Decisions which determine which primary prevention programs will be financed affect the need for, and the nature of, health care. Major expenditures on road safety reduce pressure on emergency services and rehabilitation programs; expenditures which reduce use of tobacco and saturated fats reduce future pressure on cancer treatment centres and cardiovascular surgical units. All of these programs reduce premature deaths and move care to an older age group. The persons who would have needed cancer treatment, emergency care or surgery on their coronary arteries will live longer and need a different mix of health care.

Public policy will both shape and respond to public perceptions of the importance of the physical environment. In a 10-15 year program Quebec and Ottawa will spend $6-10 billion upgrading sewage treatment plants. When complete the St. Lawrence basin will be largely clear of raw sewage. This will, it is assumed, improve the habitat of the fish and other wild life in the basin and, less directly, improve the health status of the residents of the shores of the basin.

POVERTY AND HEALTH

Unemployment definitely can have a very detrimental effect on health, and it is affected by public policy. The loss of middle income jobs in Canada in the 1980s and 1990s may decrease health status more than any other recently introduced factor. These losses transform families from viable financial and social units to families on social support or with inadequate employment incomes, and without prospects for reasonable incomes family health goes down. Employment becomes an instrument of primary prevention.

The relationship between poverty and both illness and premature death has been extensively reported (The Black Report, U.K.; Chronic Diseases in Canada, Sept/Oct 1991) In 1986 over 20% of children in Canada were living in poverty and the percentage was, and still is, rising. (Chronic Diseases in Canada, Sept/Oct 1991, p. 91) Public policy is one of the important tools available to reduce the impact and incidence of child poverty.

Public policy often determines level of income, especially for those members of the population who do not work. In Canada in 1991 50% of the income of males 65 and older was from government pensions. For females the figure was 72%. For many of these the public pensions are the only source of income. (Statistics Canada, 1992) The future holds a very significant likelihood that governments will be unable to sustain present levels of income support for the elderly and others in need of social assistance. The impact of the falling incomes on the health status of these populations is difficult to estimate.

Public policy is at times the only tool for support of primary prevention, as with the dividing of highways and guaranteeing the quality of drugs. In 1992 the federal government in cooperation with film producers and TV channels aired a 60 minute special on drug use by youths. In the same year a six part series called Degrassi Talks dealt with such topics as sex, drugs, sexual preference, household abuse and mental health. These types of programs are unlikely to be produced and aired unless governments are the sponsors, although churches and charitable foundations and societies also do excellent work of this type.

Some healthy public policies such as pasteurization of milk have been the direct product of efforts by health care professionals. In other instances pressure from health care professionals and agencies has contributed to the passage of new policies, as with the many laws affecting the price, purchasing, use and advertising of tobacco. Health care professionals opposed the lowering of tobacco taxes in 1994.

JUDICIAL RULINGS

The courts have an influence on health care through their interpretation of the Charter of Rights and Freedoms and their rulings in independent cases. In 1992 and 1993 the courts rejected a request from a British Columbia patient for a physician assisted suicide. Other rulings and recommendations, especially of coroners juries, have also led to changes in health care, changes which often are unreasonably expensive. Coroner's juries have frequently ignored, and probably not even been aware of, the concepts of cost-effectiveness and opportunity cost. In response to single cases they have at times promoted standards which were not sensible. Fortunately their recommendations are no longer routinely followed.

THE LABOR MARKET AND LABOR LAWS

The price of labor for health care institutions and programs is influenced by prices in the private market and in other public systems, and also by labor legislation regarding gender equity requirements, job safety, visible minority hiring requirements, mandatory employee benefit packages and minimum wages.

OTHER FACTORS

Factors not yet understood also affect health care. AIDS, for example, burst onto the scene as a new clinical syndrome with unfamiliar processes and from an uncertain source. It is the first known example of a human infection which appears to be universally fatal within a few years. Only time will tell whether other life forms with their own unpredictable consequences will in a similar fashion challenge the skill and life of the human species.

FACTORS WITHIN HEALTH CARE WHICH INDIRECTLY AFFECT HEALTH CARE DEMAND, NEED OR COST

Most of the factors which indirectly affect the need and demand for, and the costs of, health care are outside of the health care network, but factors within health care are also important.

Many health surveys have been conducted to measure health status, and many hospital and other data are routinely collected for the same reason. These data influence health care priorities and spending. To the extent data concentrates on physical health then health care may tend to do the same, and, to the extent that physical health services dominate health care systems then physical health statistics will dominate. It is a *Catch 22* situation, but to the credit of society and its leaders the preoccupations of health care providers with physical health have not prevented an emerging and strengthening interest in mental and psychosocial health.

Health care has a culture of its own quite separate from the larger societal culture, and this health care culture affects utilization and costs. The culture of health care has, in the past, included a paternalism in which users and other health workers deferred to physicians on clinical matters, but that deference is decreasing. The culture of the medical model has been perpetuated by most medical schools, most medical practitioners, all medical associations and most health care legislation. But the culture is changing. Consumers, governments and health care workers other than physicians have become more dominant, and the era of relative cost-effectiveness is at hand.

Health care culture is not consistent from country to country. Canada is closest to the aggressive and expensive American style, a similarity which has implications for those who write policy.

The medical culture also has historically been steeped in technological naivety in which the latest and most expensive technology is assumed to be better and therefore must be used. This latest technology continues to be used, whatever the cost, until it is found not to be nearly so useful and/or safe as it was thought to be, at which time it is replaced by the latest untested new technology. There is an underestimation of risks (a product of technological naivety), an overestimation of outcomes (professional expectations commonly exceed actual results), a slowness to change unless new technology is involved (if new information doesn't fit the mythology the information must be wrong) and a certainty of wisdom. Fortunately one can safely say that all of these features are either decreasing in prevalence or will do so as new health care cultures emerge.

Both users and providers still retain a significant attachment to slogans of the past. (Figure 1.1) These slogans are an impediment to setting the priorities and making the resource allocations which will best protect and improve the health of Canadians.

Figure 1.1

HEALTH CARE ASSUMPTIONS AND SLOGANS
THAT ARE DEAD (OR SHOULD BE)

1. Everyone should, at public expense, receive the best health care that money can buy.
2. Nothing is as important as health care; health care is the first line of defence against poor health.
3. Money is not important when lives are at stake: we can't let people die just because we are short of money.
4. When it comes to deciding how to protect our health, doctors know best.
5. Only physicians should be allowed to diagnose and prescribe.
6. Health care professionals can only be evaluated by their peers.

The attachment of health care users and providers to the above slogans and principles is still affecting, and sometimes driving, public policy. Rejection of these outdated slogans by users, administrators, policy makers and providers will eventually contribute to the emergence of a new health care culture.

The attitudes of both providers and users of health care towards risks associated with health care are also part of our health care culture, and these attitudes are quite unpredictable. Health care is full of well documented and avoidable risks such as inappropriate prescribing, persons kept too long in the inherently dangerous hospital environment, and surgery performed in circumstances in which the surgeon would be unable to convince his confreres of the need. These risks are routinely ignored, and yet in other circumstances both providers and users refuse to accept even minute avoidable risks associated with the delivery of health care.

Physicians in particular have a tendency to underestimate the risks of health care, to feel obliged to do something even if there is nothing sensible to do, to have almost infinite faith in the pronouncements of the marketers of new drugs and technology and to complicate simple things such as a normal pregnancy. Some of the lottery mentality of providers (*'Let's give this a try, perhaps it will work'*) is also present in users who prefer having something done to them whether or not it is worth doing. (*'Just give me a prescription and I'll leave'*.)

Medical decisions reflect, among other things, the norms (the culture) of the educators in universities and in teaching hospitals. The frequency with which physicians recommend coronary angiography varies, for example, with the age of the physician and the level of training. Cardiologists and younger family physicians have lower rates of recommendation. (Young, M.J. et al., Health Services Research, 22:623-35, 1987)

The gender of health care professionals may also influence health care costs. Male physicians, for example, have been found to be twice as likely to recommend hysterectomy as female physicians. (Roos, N.P., American J. of Public Health, 1984, 74.327-35)

Accessibility and acceptability of health care also affect demand and cost. Consumers use less health care if they must travel significant distances to get it, or if they do not like the environment or manner in which it is delivered. (Acton, J.P., "Nonmonetary Factors in the Demand for Medical Care", The Economics of Health, 1992, p. 239-258)

SUMMARY

The indirect factors which influence health care demand, need and costs are innumerable, and their relative importance is often not known.

Health status, in particular psychosocial health, is directly affected by those parts of our lives which are usually seen as political and economic, and by those social characteristics which are called cultural. Later chapters will provide only passing comment on the political, economic and cultural features which are beneficial or damaging to health status, but this lack of attention does not suggest that the issues involved are unimportant.

The amount of publicly financed care a person seeks or receives (or which is sought or received when other third party payers are paying the bills) may be reduced by regulatory devices such as user fees, but it can also be reduced by less direct techniques such as preventing ill health or injury or by altering user expectations or perceptions.

Reducing the volume and cost of care provided per person may not directly reduce expenditures by government on health care, but it makes it easier for governments to maintain ceilings on costs. Waiting lists are likely to be shorter, immediate access easier and unfriendly headlines less frequent.

The extent to which primary prevention is implemented has a great deal to do with who arrives at the hospital emergency department, the jail, the group homes or the morgue, and it influences the use of all health services. It includes many actions and decisions which are discussed throughout many chapters but under other headings.

The objective of Chapter 1 was not to describe the impact of the many factors which indirectly affect demand for health care; it was merely to establish that these indirect forces are important. Awareness of the presence and importance of these forces may decrease the likelihood that simplistic and unrealistic expectations will develop in those who wish to alter the patterns of health care utilization.

Chapter 2

The Evolution of Canadian Health Care: How We Got to Where We Are

INTRODUCTION

Chapter 1 looked at many of the external factors which have shaped, and which continue to affect, Canadian health and health care.

Chapter 2 carries on with the examination of the forces and events which have produced modern health care, with special emphasis on those which have contributed significantly to the current need to control costs and improve spending. Understanding the origins of modern Canadian health care, and of its problems in the 1990s, will make it easier to visualize the relevance and appropriateness of policies being considered for the future.

THE CHANGES WHICH HAVE OCCURRED

The last few decades have brought new definitions of health, a broadening of social objectives and an improved understanding of what keeps us healthy and makes us ill. There is increasing evidence of the inappropriateness of many of the decisions of health care professionals, and a disintegration of the medical model has led to new competition for power, patients and health care dollars. There has been a growing transfer of power from providers to consumers and a new emphasis on community based care. This last decade has brought an awareness that no country can afford to provide at public cost all of the services that health care professionals will order or that users will ask for, and an end to open-ended public spending on health care.

Chapter 2 introduces these changes. Examination continues throughout later chapters.

THE CONSTITUTIONAL CONTEXT

The *British North America Act* of 1867 (BNA Act) (now incorporated into our constitution as the *Constitution Act* 1867) made no specific mention of health care. Jurisdiction over this important social service was claimed by both the provinces and the central government. The dispute was eventually won by the provinces, and as a consequence each of the 10 provinces can design and control health care in whatever way they wish.

This is no such thing as a Canadian Health Care System. There are eleven health care systems in Canada, one for each province and another under federal jurisdiction. The constitution gives the federal government responsibility for health care in those parts of the country which are not provinces (the Yukon and the Territories) and for the aboriginal peoples, the armed forces, the RCMP and a few smaller classes of persons. (Ottawa has delegated responsibility for health care to the governments of the Yukon and the Territories, but because these do not have the status of a province the constitutional authority of the federal government is unchanged.)

CHANGES TO THE MEANING OF 'HEALTH'

Pericles (495-429 B.C.) said *"Health is a state of moral, mental, and physical well being which enables a person to face any crisis in life with the utmost grace and facility."* In the 1970s and 1980s *health* became a broader term than it had been a few decades earlier, although obviously no more broad than 2400 years ago. *Health*, which had meant *physical health*, came to encompass physical, mental and psychosocial health. It was seen as a *resource for daily living* rather than merely *the absence of disease*. The new perceptions of health gave attention to wellness as well as sickness, to the presence of positive as well as negative factors. There was acceptance of the idea that absence of physical and mental disease does not assure optimal health, it merely assures the absence of some of the hazards to optimal health.

The broader perceptions of health changed what people wanted from health care. Canadians became interested not only in how long they would live but in how well they would live. The singular preoccupation with avoidance of death was replaced by a dual effort aimed at avoidance of premature death while also enriching the remaining years or days of life.

NEW PERCEPTIONS OF THE DETERMINANTS OF HEALTH

Universal hospital insurance and medical care insurance were introduced in Saskatchewan, and later across Canada, on the belief that good health care was the key to a healthy population and that physicians and hospitals were the most important components of health care. These beliefs are now gone, and partly as a result of the 1974 book *A New Perspective on the Health of Canadians*. This book was internationally acclaimed as the first time a government had formally proposed major new approaches to the preservation and improvement of the health status of an entire population. Health care was not said to be unimportant to health, but it was said to be less important than other factors.

There is not always agreement as to the order of importance of the determinants of health, but there is general agreement as to what those determinants are. They are wealth (collective and individual), the environments, the individual choices of each individual (including lifestyle), the genetic endowment given to each of us by our parents, the decisions made by our governments, and health care.

National comparisons support the proposition that health care is not a dominant determinant of health status. Japan, whose per capita expenditures on health care are only half of those of the United States, (6.8% versus 14% of GNP spent on health care in 1993) has the worlds best health status as measured by such classical indicators as length of life and infant mortality. Japan sets high standards in terms of equitable income distribution, job satisfaction and levels of employment, factors now recognized as important to health status. (`Nurturing Health: A Framework of the Determinants of Health', Ontario Premiers Council on Health Strategy, 1991.)

These international comparisons illustrate the extent to which health care can siphon off public and private expenditures which would produce more health if spent in other social sectors. In the United States, and probably also in Canada but to a lesser extent, expenditures on health care have begun to reduce the ability of the nation to allocate sufficient funds to such things as a national economic strategy, industrial research and development, the production of skilled workers and the avoidance of children raised in poverty.

To the extent that Canada, or any other nation, allows its wealth to be unreasonably concentrated in small portions of its population and allows social or other spending to saddle the future with excessive debt, the overall health status of the population will fall. Sensible allocation of public resources combined with a publicly influenced private sector agenda can bring the highest level of population health possible with the national wealth available.

The importance of factors other than health care has been confirmed by health surveys. These surveys have produced many new findings, some of which were not expected. They have shown, for example, that the difference in life expectancy and life quality between the lower and upper income populations has not been narrowed by the availability of publicly financed health care. National health insurance cannot compensate for the differences in social, physical, economic and domestic environments that go along with differences in income.

The aboriginal peoples in Canada also provide a comment on the importance of health care to health status. These populations have always had access to a full range of traditional health care services at federal expense, but their health status indicators (infant mortality, suicide rates, life expectancy) compare very poorly with those of other Canadians.

Doctors, hospitals, nurses and pills are often crucial to the care of the sick and injured, but they are not primary determinants of average life expectancies or of the quality of life of total populations.

THE RISE OF CONSUMERISM: A DISPERSION OF POWER

In the 1960s North America exploded with Ralph Nader, community groups, advocacy groups, grey power, black power and rioting throughout the United States. The extra-parliamentary process arrived with its consultation processes, community development, opinion polls and all of the other elements of people power. The small band of business and financial interests which had for centuries been the dominant government advisors had to share their power with others. Governments became increasingly unable to act unless they had allies (or at least no organized enemies) in the general population. Consumer protection and a social safety net rose to prominence in Canada.

Health care moved from an era in which providers were in charge to one in which users may be in charge if they wish to be. Consumers may now, if they wish, be active rather than passive participants in the preparation and implementation of their health care plans. Patients now have the right to be told, in language they can understand, about the benefits and the hazards of all health care alternatives available to them, to select the treatment option that they prefer and to refuse treatment regardless of the consequences of the refusal. Caregivers must honor patient wishes as expressed directly or in other ways such as a card refusing blood transfusions or a medical directive refusing resuscitation. To act against the patient's wishes is assault.

A Supreme Court ruling in 1992 established the right of patients to access to all of their medical record including all reports on file from other providers of care. Professionals who do not wish to reveal all or portions of a file must obtain a court order supporting the nondisclosure. New legislation in most provinces assures greater public access to information held by professional colleges. Discipline hearings are open and there are public representatives on complaint review committees.

The role of consumers in policy selection has been increased by the weight given by governments to opinion polls and by the extensive public consultation which is now almost a routine part of policy development. Governments no longer seek advice only from health care professionals, and the opinions of the public often carry more weight than the opinions of the experts.

The consumer era brought a dispersion of power, a situation in which everyone has some power but no-one has a great deal of it. This dispersal of power provided an opportunity for everyone to affect events. Openness replaced secrecy, and simple processes became complex. The major winners were the communities and the organized users/consumers/citizens. The losers were those groups and persons who had historically been the advisors to governments. In health care the major losers were the physicians and hospitals.

Advocacy groups and self interest groups rapidly refined the art of networking, consensus seeking and single issue pursuit. These groups, whether advocating on behalf of the physically handicapped, abused spouses or persons with Alzheimers disease (to mention only a few) became, and will continue to be, a force in health care.

With an increase in the number of players and the dispersal of power, tactics and weapons have changed. The most important new weapons are skill, evidence and allies. The most important new skills are those through which the available evidence can be arrayed, allies found and messages delivered to the right people at the right time and in an effective manner. Coalitions, demonstrations of public support and the backing of influential groups and individuals will, in the future as now, be powerful weapons.

The allies who will be most vigorously sought will be the users of health care and their advocates. The public, or specific parts of it, will increasingly decide whose services they wish to use, and competing health care professionals will need to sell themselves to the public. The public will seek and use information about the value of various elements of health care and the consequences of alternative policies and actions.

All of these changes in the policy development process are desirable, but they bring considerable insecurity. Not many planners or administrators have much experience with them.

One fundamental right is still not available to Canadians. They cannot buy hospital and physicians services at home with their own money. The services of hospitals and physicians remain perhaps the only completely legal product which is produced in Canada but cannot be bought at home by Canadians with their own money.

ACCEPTANCE OF THE SKILLS OF NON-PHYSICIANS

History clearly records the ability of a variety of health care professionals to acquire special skills. The obstetrical outcomes of midwives have been proven to be as good as those of physicians. The care provided by nurse practitioners has been shown to be just as good as care provided by physicians. It is now clear that pharmacists can significantly improve on the safety and efficacy of the prescribing patterns of physicians. Nurse Case Managers can improve the outcomes and lower the costs of patients in hospital. Within the Saskatchewan children's dental program the dental work done by dental therapists was found to be superior to the work done by dentists. The ability of an increasing array of health care professionals to provide services formerly in the realm of physicians and dentists is fully established, and this ability will be increasingly noticed as health care dollars become more scarce.

The list of professionals with direct access to patients, and with the legal right to diagnose and treat patients without physician approval, has lengthened. The list now includes (in at least one province) chiropractors, physiotherapists, psychologists, social workers, optometrists, midwives and podiatrists/chiropodists. The list will in all probability soon include nurse practitioners, clinical nurse specialists, ambulance attendants and others.

EVIDENCE REGARDING COST-EFFECTIVENESS

When public hospital insurance and medical care insurance were introduced everyone assumed health care professionals, and especially physicians, routinely knew what advice was best with respect to personal health and health policy. Massive, expanding and scientifically sound evidence has now established that professionals regularly make inappropriate health care decisions. (see Appendix 1) This evidence has shown that health care professionals are as human as everyone else. They regularly are wrong, and they often are wrong even when they are sure they are right.

The mythology of modern medicine encompasses a belief that physicians always know what to do, what to prescribe and what not to do. If physician fallibility is accepted then the patient-physician relationship changes, but this is as it should be. Advisors on important public and personal matters ought to be questioned if the consumer and payer so wish. Users increasingly know that medicine is not an exact science.

The mystery of medical care will decrease as diagnostic and therapeutic alternatives are described to patients and as the risks associated with care are more fully discussed. Many patients will continue to wish all decisions to be made by their physicians or other health care professionals, and this is their right, but even for these individuals there will be less certainty that the decisions made will be the best ones that could have been made. Increased insecurity of some patients will be a by-product of the demystification of health care.

Objective evidence has not only allowed much more reliable and useful evaluation of health care; it has allowed this evaluation to be carried out by almost anyone. In the past it was commonly accepted that a physician could only be evaluated by other physicians, a nurse by other nurses, etc. This was a sensible belief when the evaluations were based on professional judgment. But evaluation is often now performed by comparing professional performance to objective standards, and the ability to make this comparison is growing steadily. The role of judgment is sharply reduced, and comparisons can, therefore, be made by persons other than peers. This change has produced a situation in which every health care profession may, if it wishes, continue to be involved in the evaluation of its work, but governments, user groups and other health care professions may also be involved if they wish.

The new importance of evidence will change the rules. Evidence which proves the cost-effectiveness of a service will improve the chances of that service being funded, as will evidence which confirms community support. Evidence which shows that the services being delivered by someone else will not bring improvements in health status at reasonable cost may protect one's own funding. Evidence well presented will have greater value than the same material handled poorly.

THE DISINTEGRATION OF THE MEDICAL MODEL

In the 1950s and 1960s physicians were the team leaders, the bosses and the gatekeepers. They, and only they, decided, with a very high degree of individual control, whether or not a patient would have access to prescription drugs, physiotherapy services, laboratory investigation, X-rays, pulmonary function tests, a hospital bed, or surgery. Their orders were not questioned. Physicians had complete or almost complete control over the training of various health care technologists and technicians and they determined which duties would be delegated to nurses and other health care professionals.

In all provinces a statute such as *The Medical Act* established *diagnosis* as almost exclusively a physician function. No one else was allowed to *practice medicine* unless specifically authorized to do so by some other statute, as with chiropractors and dentists.

The physician in charge of the medical team was not only autocratic with other health care professionals, he was paternalistic in his dealings with patients. It was accepted that the physician knew what was best for the patient, and that there was need for little if any patient input into the medical care decisions being made. Patients signed a global consent form on admission to hospital and physicians proceeded to deliver care largely as they saw fit.

In this medical model *health* meant *physical health*. Death was the enemy. Hard sciences dominated research. Medical schools emphasized biochemistry, anatomy and physiology rather than the social sciences. Geriatrics, public health, family pathology, palliative care and wellness promotion were either unheard of or given minor attention. Caring could not compete with curing. Procedures often mattered more than patients. The Medical Research Council allocated 99% of its money to research into physical health problems (a pattern which still exists).

In these years physicians (MD only, not osteopathic physicians) dominated macro and micro health care decisions, including resource allocation. They were the professionals given, by law, the task of defending the public interest during the delivery of almost all health care. In matters pertaining to health they were accepted as the experts, and their opinions were routinely accepted, often without question, in court and elsewhere. They were the profession with *private* patients and a provider-patient *relationship*. Other professions within the medical model provided services only with the authorization of an individual physician or within an authority delegated by physicians.

Health care professionals not protected by special legislation were persecuted and/or prosecuted by physicians and physician organizations if they (the other professionals, such as midwives) were thought to be *practicing medicine*.

Physicians had been given these sweeping powers and such broad jurisdiction because it was believed that they, and only they, were capable of accurate judgment regarding almost everything affecting health. They were thought to know the implications to health of a broad range of activities, factors and experiences such as exercise, alcohol, nutrition, the environment and work. The physician was thought to know whether a patient would live or die, how long he or she would live, whether a person was able or unable to work, and when persons were a public menace. Most of the public, most of the politicians and most of the physicians fully believed that physician advice could be relied upon in virtually all situations.

Almost none of the elements of the medical model have stood the test of time. There has been a steady decline in physician power and privilege, a decline due to a combination of centralized financing, centralized planning, new objective evidence regarding the quality of professional decisions, the rise of consumerism and the militancy and proven competence of other health care professionals.

The financial world of Canadian physicians has changed as much as their clinical world. Prior to public medical care insurance physicians set their own fees and could bill for as many services as they wished. With government insurance in place government fee schedules replaced fee schedules written by physicians. When control over fees did not lead to acceptable levels of cost control, governments capped the amount which would be spent on physician services, capped the billings of individual physicians and began to restrict access to billing numbers. Physician incomes began to fall, especially the incomes of high earners.

The time when physicians could pack up and go to another province if the income at home wasn't large enough, or the place wasn't attractive enough, is almost gone. The United States may still be attractive to some but many of the most attractive States now discourage the arrival of more physicians. In addition, there is greater intrusion into professional decision making in the United States than in Canada.

It has not been easy for physicians to lose control over what they do, what they charge, and what they earn. It has not been easy for physicians who were formerly able to almost ignore their clients to have the power picture reversed, and equally difficult to move from endless provision of self selected services to limited provision of services influenced or controlled by others. But these are the changes to which physicians must adapt, and other health care professionals face some of the same changes. Figure 2.1 brings together some of these changes.

NEW COMPETITION FOR POWER, PATIENTS AND DOLLARS

Within health care there has always been some degree of competition between sectors and between individual hospitals, programs, researchers, private laboratories, and providers. Competition will increase as provider groups struggle to preserve incomes. Competition between health care sectors such as emergency health services, hospitals, long term care, and physicians, will also probably increase. Government policy has led to hospitals, physicians and emergency health services no longer being able to assume they will get whatever new money is available. There is now greater policy emphasis on community health services, palliative care, long term care, health promotion and mental health services. As evidence which demonstrates impact becomes more important in policy selection all sectors will become more aggressive in presenting evidence in support of their claim for more money, and more aggressive in refuting the claims of others.

There will also, for many reasons, be more competition between health care and other publicly financed sectors such as education, police and highways. Governments are broke. The pool of avail-

Figure 2.1

THE CHANGING WORLD OF HEALTH CARE PROFESSIONALS

1. From evaluation based on professional judgment to evaluation based on objective evidence.
2. From evaluation by peers to evaluation by everyone.
3. From high levels of professional autonomy to increasing outside control of, or influence over, professional decisions, including at the time the decision is being made.
4. From being seen as special people who put their clients first to being seen as much like all other special interest groups.
5. From the medical model to increasing competition for power, patients, function (turf) and public dollars.
6. From telling patients what would be done to them to asking patients what they want done.
7. From deciding how much information to give patients to being obliged by law to be certain patients have sufficient information to make choices and give informed consent.
8. From patient faith in professional judgment to greater public awareness of the frailty of professional decisions.
9. From guaranteed employment to possible unemployment.

---

able public dollars is unlikely to grow in the near future. If publicly funded health care or any other public service is to grow the growth can only be at the expense of other publicly funded services, and health care services have lost much of the special status they once had. Education, highway safety, community safety, income maintenance and other services are all known to be important to health status, and they are now much more able to compete for the money that is available. The funding imbalances of the past which favored health care are now likely to be redressed.

Competition between health care professionals will increase. More professions will deal directly with patients and be able to prescribe and order investigations. They will be able to compete with physicians on a much more level playing field. Alternative therapists who have been outside of the public insurance umbrella will wish greater recognition, and they will be supported by the expanded nonwestern constituencies which have become important in the Canadian cultural mix.

Consumers will make choices, evaluate professionals and make resource allocation decisions, and these will create competition for the support of consumers.

The rules governing the competition for patients, resources and power are at times quite brutal. If you win someone loses. Factors which most determine success will be political, tactical and technological. Good evidence, well presented, will beat shouting and whining. Winning is more likely if you have good data, good presentation and many friends. (Consumers, powerful leaders and favorable opinion polls are powerful friends.)

The increased competition will demand a new mix of techniques and skills. There will be more advertising and lobbying, and greater development of tactical and strategic planning skills. Everyone will search for allies and will look for the win-win situations which encourage the creation of alliances and networks. There will be increased criticism by everyone of everyone, and a greater need for someone to broker disputes. All competitors should, by now, be beginning to see the need to provide proof of positive outcomes from their activities.

As it becomes more and more accepted that not all services can be provided to everyone at public expense the various user groups will, inevitably, to at least some degree, come into conflict. Will the winners (or the losers) in the competition for resources be the elderly, the young, the rural, the employed, the unemployed, those with healthy lifestyles, those with the ability to produce, the younger disabled, those unlikely to survive, those unable to conceive, the visible minorities, or others?

Outcomes per dollar spent (cost-effectiveness) are on the verge of being seriously considered as the primary measure of the desirability of competing policies. This will require new skills, new data and new approaches by those who are competing for resources. Every sector, program and profession will struggle to prove it can provide greater value-for-money than can its competitors.

The battles will be in a war that will never end. To win it will be helpful to understand the rules and the forces at play.

DECREASING PERSONAL, PROVINCIAL AND NATIONAL WEALTH

The real after tax incomes of Canadian families fell 4.3% in the period 1980-1991. (Statistics Canada, 1993) The fall will have continued in 1992 and 1993, and with the costs of carrying our public debt continuing to mount there is little chance of early relief. The hey-days of endless increases in our material standard of living are gone, and with them have gone our ability to endlessly publicly fund social services including health care. *"Canada spends more on health care (on a per capita basis) than any other industrialized country with national health insurance"* (Nurturing Health, Ontario Premiers Council, 1991, quoting from `Health Care Financing Review: International Comparison of Health Care Financing and Delivery', USDHHS, 1989)

A Burns Fry report in early 1993 identified Canada as having the largest external debt, compared to Gross Domestic Product, of any industrialized nation. This growing debt has led to a lowering of the credit rating of several provinces. The majority of recent borrowing has been from sources outside Canada, and the outflow of interest payments worsens Canada's balance of payments. The percent of every federal tax dollar which goes to pay interest on the national debt has risen from 13% in 1968 to 33% in 1992. (1994 Report of The Federal Auditor General)

The problems of debt and the ensuing interest are made worse by a decline in economic prospects. The 1990-1993 recession led to major reductions in provincial and federal revenues. Personal and corporate tax revenues fell. This fall in revenues, when combined with continuing shrinkage in federal transfer payments, led to a 10% reduction in Ontario revenue in 1991-92, 1992-93 and 1993-94. Lower provincial income combined with much higher social service and income support payments (caused by increases in unemployment) and larger payments on debt made large deficits difficult to avoid and made increased spending on health care unlikely as well as undesirable. Health care, which had barely been affected by earlier recessions, became a place where governments looked for dollars.

A combination of increasing debt and increasing levels of taxation have made it financially imperative that health care costs be controlled. The health care system must expect minimal growth in its funding when times are good, and must, when provincial revenues fall, expect health care spending to also fall.

Out of country expenditures by Canadians demonstrate one of the serious causes of the economic disequilibrium between Canadian tax revenues and social expenditures. In 1992 Canadians spent about $8 billion more outside Canada than foreign visitors spent in Canada. If that $8 billion were spent at home it would, when the economic multiplier effect was taken into consideration, eliminate a significant portion of the deficits of Canadian governments. Canadians want to have their cake and eat it to. They wish to buy cheap goods and gas across the border, to spend their winters in the south, and also to get free health care at home.

Japan, with the best health status statistics in the world, has low health care spending. Canada borrows the money the Japanese save, and the interest payments make it more and more difficult to meet our social expectations and to remain economically competitive.

The economic restructuring which has characterized the 1990s was unexpected. Economic recessions were routine but eventual return of economic growth was always expected. The idea of a permanently reduced material standard of living was not part of the perceived future of Canadians, but it has arrived.

FEDERAL SPENDING ON HEALTH CARE

In the 1940s the federal government became a supporter of a national plan of publicly financed health care, but without constitutional jurisdiction over health care it could not introduce national health (care) insurance. It therefore sought a device by which it could control policy in a field in which it had very little constitutional jurisdiction.

Federal wealth was the device chosen. The constitution had given the provinces jurisdiction over the very expensive public service fields of education, social services and health care but had given the provinces limited taxation opportunities. The federal government had the money and the provinces had the expenses. Ottawa offered money in return for policy control.

In 1957 *The Hospital Insurance and Diagnostic Services Act* was passed by the federal parliament. This *Act* guaranteed approximately half of the cost of *necessary hospital care* to any province which met certain conditions. The *Act* came into force on July 1, 1958 and within 2 years all provinces were participating. Similar federal legislation authorizing federal cost sharing with respect to provincial medical care insurance programs was passed in 1966 and implemented in 1968. By 1971 all provinces were participating.

In return for federal cost sharing the provinces committed themselves to programs which would be universal (initially 95% of the population was acceptable, later 100% was required), accessible (no exclusions on the basis of health status and no unapproved patient payment at the time of service), comprehensive (covering all physician services), portable (guaranteed continuous coverage for persons who move within Canada), and publicly administered. Physicians were to be reasonably remunerated, a condition which has never been clarified.

Provincial acceptance of the federal cost sharing proposals was not immediately universal, but financial realities rapidly led to full provincial participation. The cost sharing opportunity not only helped the provinces tolerate the rapidly rising costs of open-ended health care programs, it meant that if any province opted not to participate in the federal program then the federal taxes collected in that province would be spent on health care in other provinces.

Besides sharing in hospital and physician costs the federal government in 1966 established the Canada Assistance Plan (CAP). This program offered 50% federal funding for a broad mix of new community based and social support programs including income maintenance, home care, rehabilitation, care in long term care institutions and a variety of work related programs. The federal treasury contributed half of the costs so long as the services were delivered. The provinces made all decisions regarding administration of the programs, the levels of coverage and how the remainder of the money would be raised. There was no requirement that the other half of the costs had to be financed by the province. Some provinces handed out the federal money as if it was theirs and left municipalities or voluntary agencies to find the other half of the money.

The Canada Assistance Plan was one of a number of federal programs designed to provide support for vulnerable populations. Other programs were directed towards veterans, the unemployed, the blind, children and disabled persons.

Throughout the 1970s and 1980s everyone became increasingly concerned about the rising costs of health care. The policy makers and the funders became aware that the costs associated with endless access to health care would rise indefinitely, and they became increasingly certain that additional spending brought very few benefits. Discussion moved on to questions such as how much care was worth buying, which care should be given priority and how costs could be controlled.

By the mid-1970s the federal government had a serious problem. It was in a no-win cost-sharing situation. More health care spending was not thought to increase the health status of the population very much, if at all, and the federal treasury was facing rapidly rising expenditures. Obviously health care spending should be constrained, but the provinces had few if any incentives to reduce their health care spending. Ottawa had a contract to provide half the money and no way to control the spending. Ottawa either had to revise its financial commitment or keep providing more money.

Ottawa bit the bullet and in 1977 cancelled its open-ended contributions to health care costs (along with a cancellation of its similarly open-ended contributions to the costs of post-secondary education). Federal hospital and medical care insurance legislation (1957 and 1966 respectively) was replaced by the *Federal-Provincial Fiscal Arrangements and Established Programs Financing (EPF) Act*. The federal contributions became tied to changes in the Gross National Product rather than to provincial expenditures. Provincial spending which exceeded the federal commitment would be 100% provincial dollars.

In return for cancellation of unlimited cost sharing the federal government gave the provinces a direct payment based on a per capita formula, provincial access to an additional 13.5 personal income tax points and one additional corporate income tax point, an equalization payment to provinces which suffered the most under the new formula and new money to help finance *extended health care* services such as home care. These terms were guaranteed for five years. The terms were somewhat different for Quebec, with less cash but more tax points.

The provinces cried *foul* when the funding formula was changed, but the federal government made the right decision when it cancelled the cost sharing arrangements. The new financial agreement gave provinces an incentive to control health care costs, and they responded with many measures which probably would not have been put in place if the open pipe-line to federal money had remained. The new arrangements gave provinces the opportunity to reallocate funds from institutions to community health services, and most provinces soon began this reallocation.

In 1986 the limitations on federal contributions became more stringent. Federal contributions as a percentage of provincial expenditures fell from 44% in 1979-80 to 35.8% in 1989-90. (Provincial Government Health Expenditures and Related Federal Contributions, 1974-75/1990-91, Federal Department of Health, 1993). Federal expenditures as a percentage of total public and private expenditures on health care fell from 32.9% in 1980 to 24.4% in 1991. (Health Expenditures in Canada Summary Report 1987-1991, Health and Welfare Canada, 1993).

The later restrictions on federal transfer payments had a tremendous impact on provincial revenues, and the process by which they were introduced can be seen to be less fair than the original federal cut-backs. By the late 1980s it appeared likely that by the end of the century the federal government would have withdrawn from direct funding of health care.

THE CANADA HEALTH ACT

When the federal hospital and medical care cost sharing arrangements were replaced by the EPF legislation in 1977 there was a fear that the federal government was no longer adequately protecting the five principles of Medicare. In response to these concerns Monique Begin, federal Minister of Health, introduced the *Canada Health Act* in 1984.

This *Act* defined the penalties that would apply if the Medicare principles were not honored by a province. The penalties were financial. For example, if user fees were considered to be a threat to accessibility the federal payments to the provinces would be reduced by the amount spent by patients. At the time the *Canada Health Act* was introduced a number of provinces were allowing physicians to extra-bill. By the end of the three years of grace allowed in the *Act* all provinces had outlawed extra-billing rather than lose substantial amounts of federal money.

The *Canada Health Act* penalties apply only to the delivery of physician and hospital services. There is no requirement that other health care (home care, long term care, ambulance services, outpatient prescription drugs, optometry, chiropractic care, dental care) be universally insured or accessible, nor are there penalties for user fees associated with these services when they are publicly financed.

THE END OF OPEN-ENDED PROVINCIAL SPENDING

Provincial governments may have wished to reduce spending in the early 1970s, but each of them faced a dilemma. Spending less saved the provincial treasury only half of each dollar of reduced health care spending (the federal treasury saved the other half) but the provincial economy lost a whole dollar. The contribution of the provincial residents to the federal treasury (in taxes) remained unchanged but the money flowing into the province from the federal government went down. On the other hand, each additional dollar of health care spending cost the provincial treasury only 50 cents but $1 was added to the gross domestic product of the province. The federal money created jobs, increased provincial tax revenues, was thought to protect the health of the population and helped win elections.

The end of open-ended cost sharing by the federal government provided provinces with an incentive to control the rate of growth of health care spending. Provinces began to experiment with capping, alternative payment systems and additional reductions in hospital beds. With the economic downturn of the 1990s the attempts at cost control ceased to be tentative. Cut-backs were applied everywhere.

Like all publicly financed programs (education, police, income support, job creation) health care has an endless appetite for resources. Health care, as all other public programs, contributes to health. Optimal public benefit from the full mix of public programs cannot occur if any sector or program receives a disproportionate portion of the available public funds. Open-ended spending on health care is now, and for good reason, almost fully gone.

MAJOR INSTABILITY IN HEALTH SERVICES

Throughout health services there is an unease which began in the 1970s but which has become more marked in the 1990s. The status quo as it existed in the 1960s has been discredited. Health services have been shown to be overvalued, and professional domination is incompatible with the consumer era. Preoccupations with physical health are incompatible with the current emphasis on quality of life (QOL). The almost religious faith of patients in the *priests of medicine* is being challenged by evidence of the inappropriateness of many professional decisions. New professional alignments, new organizational options, new payment options, new social objectives, new distributions of power, new roles for government, new partnerships, new forms of scrutiny of professional decisions, new levels of personal responsibility for health, new approaches to evaluation and monitoring of health care and shrinking public expenditures on health care have left health care providers and users with a pervasive sense of insecurity.

Vestiges of the old are mixed with the new. Providers, users, administrators and policy makers are at varying levels of agreement with, and understanding of, what is happening. Simple solutions are being sought for poorly understood complex problems, and anger has sometimes replaced common sense.

The emotional and structural upheaval which began in earlier decades will continue for the foreseeable future. It will wax and wane until a new status quo is in place, and that will not occur for some time.

THE CHANGING POWER STRUCTURE

In this period of transition from the old status quo to a new one the power picture is fuzzy.

Provincial governments can legislatively control almost any aspect of health care, but constitutional power is not a substitute for public permission and it operates poorly in the absence of bureaucratic competence and leadership. Provincial ministries of health have at times failed to appreciate the need to complement their formal power with the power of planning, consensus, alliances and the marketing of rationale.

Physicians are no longer in charge but remain powerful, primarily because patients hold their personal physicians in high regard but also because some of the skills of physicians are unique and essential and because cultural change usually occurs slowly. The power of nurses should be considerable and should be increasing, but they are not seizing the opportunities of the moment. Other health care professionals, including physiotherapists, nurse practitioners, pharmacists, midwives and ambulance attendants, tend to be in the early stages of adaptation to the changes going on around them. All of these professionals have new opportunities for expanding their roles and their independence, and success will vary directly with the skill and energy of each group and its advisors.

The power of hospitals appears to have declined. Hospitals for too long relied on blackmail of Ministries of Health and perceived public support as weapons in the emerging power struggles. Public support for more dollars for hospitals decreased when it became clear that public service did not suffer significantly when hospital spending was controlled. Hospitals also have learned, and appear to have accepted, that they cannot directly challenge the authority of the Ministry of Health (a lesson they learned the hard way after they decided to spend according to their wishes rather than as instructed by the Ministry). Hospitals in their response to cut-backs may also have failed to appreciate the extent to which physician interests often differ from hospital interests. Physician interests require maintenance of service even as hospital resources are decreased, and physician interests therefore reduced the public impact of hospital cut-backs.

The public health sector is an enigma. It should be riding a wave of growth and increased power as prevention, health promotion, user empowerment, community programs, health education and healthy public policy are given greater emphasis, but it does not appear to be. Some of the explanation may lie in the retention within public health of a physician dominated and often authoritarian structure and philosophy.

Mental health services, including their preventive components, have achieved new levels of importance as family violence, child abuse, emotional disturbance in childhood, violence in the schools and a general milieu of public anger become daily topics for discussion. Whether the mental health services and personnel will increase their influence by developing the community based alliances which could occur remains to be seen.

THE COMMON FEATURES OF FUNDERS AND PROVIDERS

Governments, institutions, agencies and some individual providers, most of the major players, are struggling with the same set of problems. (Figure 2.2). Everyone is in the same boat. No-one is having an easy time of it. The problems don't get smaller just because everyone else also has them, but the knowledge that other parts of the system are faced with the same impossible challenges should encourage tolerance and provide an incentive for everyone to work together to find ways to reduce the urgency and magnitude of the problems.

Figure 2.2

COMMON FEATURES OF GOVERNMENTS AND PROVIDERS
1. A limited and relatively fixed income.
2. Demand which exceeds capacity to deliver.
3. A limited ability to change.
4. A lack of outcome data.
5. A public mission.
6. They spend public money.
7. Difficult resource allocation decisions to be made.

On the positive side, all health care players are in a system with a high degree of public acceptance. Two polls in 1991 (Angus Reid and CBC/Globe and Mail) reported 86% of Canadians satisfied with their health care system.

SUMMARY

Only 25-30 years ago the control of public expenditures on health care was considered to be undesirable and unnecessary. Health care was seen as crucial to the health of the population. Governments were committed to equal access for all Canadians to all of the care that physicians thought necessary. Physicians were thought to know what was necessary. Health care costs were expected to eventually stabilize as health status improved, and it was believed that economic growth would routinely provide the revenues needed to pay for the health care considered necessary. All of these assumptions are now known to have been incorrect.

By the end of the 1980s the idea of underfunding had been largely discredited and there was acceptance that better spending and less spending were needed, but there was little evidence that the major players had a clear idea of what to do. Public concern over the loss of one of their most treasured social programs was making change difficult, and physicians were struggling with a gradual erosion of a special status which was no longer appropriate.

These changes were not merely the product of a shortage of money, although bleak economic times accelerated some of them. Most of the changes also were not part of any master plan. They were also neither anti-doctor nor anti-health care.

To a very large extent the changes have been evolutionary and rational. They have tended to be congruent with the new social, cultural and technological age. Although individual events have on occasion been unplanned, emotionally induced, media driven and counter-productive the general trends have been both predictable and desirable. They arose from fundamental changes in society, and health care cannot ignore changes in society.

The health care changes have sometimes been perceived to be radical and revolutionary, especially to those whose comfortable past was being disrupted, but the changes have been usually slow, usually introduced rather timidly and almost always incremental. (Figure 2.3)

The reasons for the changes were philosophical, cultural, political, technological, organizational, educational and economic, and all of these forces will continue to be important in the future. (Figure 2.4)

Times have changed, and they will continue to change, but some things remain. Canadians continue to seek collective solutions to individual problems. They are not afraid of government leadership. They support strong consumer protection, and they support user influence and control over health care policies and decisions. They support good access for all people to a broad range of health care services, and they oppose user fees for physician and hospital care (but not as strongly as earlier).

The dominance of the physician is steadily declining. Consumers and cost-effectiveness will drive health care in the future. The medical care safety net is wanted by the public but the inclusiveness and open-endedness of the past are disappearing. The volume of health care known to be inappropriate is becoming of great concern. Wasteful spending has become the biggest threat to a reasonable level of universal and publicly financed health care for everyone.

The reactive nature of health care is becoming recognized. Primary prevention is known to occur mostly in other social policy areas.

Institutional services are being deemphasized. Mental health, long term care, health promotion and community based care are areas which are growing or surviving at the expense of spending on institutions, physicians and drugs.

Cost control is in place. Greater value-for-money will be the next big emphasis. Public management of health care will increase but in a model dominated by partnerships rather than a central bureaucracy. Regional systems and budgets will continue to evolve in patterns consistent with provincial variations in size.

Changes in health services are only partially understood by the leaders of the system, but they are even less clearly understood by the public. The users and taxpayers have not yet been systematically and routinely involved and therefore have not yet been heard from in an adequate fashion.

Figure 2.3

THE EVOLUTION OF THE HEALTH CARE PARADIGM

1950s AND 1960s
Uncontrolled expansion
Open-ended funding: do everything the doctor orders
National principles
Promotion of a one tier system
Physical health dominant: save life at any cost

1960s AND 1970s

Worries about cost
Global budgets and attempts to control growth
Greater attention to MH, QOL AND CHSs
Medical model still the king

1980s

Aggressive top-down cost control
Beginning attention to micro resource allocation decisions
Efficient delivery of both appropriate and inappropriate care
Increasing emphasis on Health Promotion and Healthy Public Policy

1990s

Reallocation rather than new dollars
Greater emphasis on value-for-money
Sectoral, program and individual capping
Greater ministry management of the system
Interest in regional budgets
A de facto two tier system: a one tier myth
Continued public support for medicare principles
Rewards for cost-effective spending: penalties for the reverse
Tighter control of physician supply
Disintegration of the medical model
Increasing external intrusion into professional decision making
Less federal money and control
Limits on physician billing numbers

Figure 2.4

THE RATIONALE FOR PRESENT AND FUTURE CHANGES

1. Response to the consumer era.
2. Acceptance of the importance of Quality of Life.
3. Health care is a minor determinant of population health
   — primary prevention mostly outside of health care
   — health care expenditures do not correlate with health status
4. Professional advice and decisions have been shown to be inadequate or uncertain
   — professional consensus can be wrong
   — individual professional decisions often inappropriate
   — major differences in health care patterns may produce no noticeable change in health outcomes
   — physicians disagree regarding what care is indicated
5. Physicians demonstrated the need for regulation
   — they used regulation to reduce physician freedom
   — they used billing profiles as a basis for reduced fee payment
   — they demonstrated the inappropriateness of many physician decisions
   — they used economic reasons to reject applications for hospital privileges
6. Practices and decisions often don't change even when evidence indicates they should.
7. The adequacy of the skills and outcomes of other health care professions has been proven.
8. Agency independence is not conducive to good spending.

The arguments driving change are powerful. Even if national and provincial budgets were balanced and revenues were high it would still make sense to wish to spend our health care dollars better. It would still be wise to reduce public expenditures on health care when spending elsewhere brings greater health status improvement per dollar spent. Both national and provincial debts are out of control, which adds an economic dimension to the other arguments for control of the costs of health care and for spending health care dollars more wisely. Some parts of health care are now a bit like a 2% or 0% investment. Investments which bring such low return should be abandoned in favor of other investments which bring more health status protection and improvement per dollar spent.

The problems of the moment, and those still to come, could leave the impression that the past 40 years were a period of inadequate political leadership. To a large extent this is not true. Political leadership in Canada (with respect to health care) has often been innovative and often courageous. Any country should be proud of its wish for compassionate and equitable care for the sick and injured and be proud of the leaders who in the 1950s and 1960s sought that end. In more recent years political leaders were among the first to accept the need to limit spending on health care, and it is to be hoped that they will lead the search for more value-for-money.

Leadership has not always been ideal. Failures include the lack of development of processes to bring the public into the discussion of how best to spend the public dollars available, a very serious lack of attention to reduction of the volume of inappropriate professional decision making in health care and a failure in some provinces to develop leadership and competence in the public service.

The dilemma is simple. If the public purse is used to pay for all the health services physicians and other health care workers wish to provide or prescribe, and all the services users wish to receive, there will be few dollars left for other social programs. If the romance of health care wins the day then sickness and imperfection will be attacked with great vigor and at great public expense but the health status of Canadians will be lower than it might be. If some health care dollars are reallocated to support appropriate environmental, economic, social and cultural decisions Canadians will live slightly longer and better lives. The downside of this reallocation is that perhaps, but not necessarily, some sick and injured persons will fail to receive cost-effective health care at public expense.

The evolution of the new milieu has been tumultuous, as is said to be the case with social change. Conflict, confusion, insecurity, anger and unreasonable expectations are everywhere, and are likely to remain features of the health care system throughout the foreseeable future. But there can be no turning back of the clock.

The rules of the game, the players in the game, the powers of the players, the prizes being sought and the tools and strategies being used would be incomprehensible to someone arriving unprepared from even 25 years ago, and the changes will continue.

Chapter 3

Where The Health Care Dollars are Spent

INTRODUCTION

The focus of Chapter 3 is economic costs, and primarily direct economic costs. To control costs one must know where money is being spent, by whom, for what and for whose benefit. There can be no major payoff from examining sites or activities which represent only a very small proportion of total expenditures, although good spending is desirable everywhere. There is less likelihood of payoff if those affected are powerful and they object to the lower spending, or if the activities being considered for cut-backs are favored by those who control spending.

Chapter 3 does not examine all spending. There is, instead, the reporting of only selected figures and examples. The objective is to provide perspective, illustrate the ways in which information on expenditures can be reported and illustrate some of the ambiguities which characterize financial data.

Comments on a few of the factors causing costs to rise will show that the importance of many of the factors is unclear. The impact of some factors, such as population growth and inflation, is much more measurable than the impact of others such as aging and unemployment.

The direct and indirect costs arising from ill health, injury and premature death are both economic and noneconomic. Economic costs arise from health care, income maintenance, social support, public housing, lost productivity, future income loss and special education. Nonmonetary costs include pain and suffering, family stress and breakdown and loss of the opportunity for individuals to realize their personal potential.

The 1986 economic costs of illness and injury in Canada have been estimated at $97 billion, of which slightly over half ($50 billion and 9% of GNP) were direct costs. (Table 3.1) These data and their analyses, now dated, are more important in their relationships than in their absolute numbers.

When considering the economic costs of ill health and injury it is desirable to acknowledge the costs which are not in the health care system and also are not in the social support systems, including costs to other public services such as the police and the courts. For example, community based treatment of a group of chronically mentally ill in Wisconsin was costed in 1988. It was reported that the costs of a community mobile treatment program was about $3,700 per year per patient, and other related mental health programs added a further $650. During the same period the law enforcement services costs associated with the same users were about $900 per year per person and court costs were $300. There was no costing of other social costs such as housing and income maintenance. (Wolff, N., T. Helminiak, et al., "A Case Study of An Assertive Mental Health Community Treatment Program", in Restructuring Canada's Health Services System, 1992, p. 263-270)

PROBLEMS WITH DATA

Data on costs by health care sector are often reported in ways which defy sensible interpretation and which make comparisons difficult. Emily Friedman reports that "Health care data are hard to

Table 3.1

DIRECT AND INDIRECT COSTS OF DISEASE
AND INJURY IN CANADA, 1986
(in billions and percent)

	Billions	Percent
INDIRECT		
Future loss due to premature death	25.6	26.3
Lost time due to chronic disability	19.0	19.5
Lost time due to short term disability	2.4	2.4
DIRECT		
Hospital care	17.1	17.6
Professional services	10.0	10.3
Other health care	7.7	7.9
Pensions and benefits	6.9	7.1
Nonhospital inst. care	4.4	4.5
Drugs	3.6	3.7
Research	0.5	0.5
Total	97.2	100.0

(Economic Burden of Illness in Canada, 1986, Chronic Diseases in Canada, Supplement to Volume 12, No 3, May-June 1991)

understand, the methodologies are strange (and often dishonest), key variables are missing and even relatively simple indicators like hospital mortality rates are suspect." (Health Management Quarterly, 1993, v.4, p. 19)

Assume one wishes to know the per capita cost of inpatient care in acute treatment hospitals to provincial beneficiaries. Hospital costs as usually reported tend to be either the total operating budgets of hospitals or the operating funds allocated to hospitals by Ministries of Health. These are not useless figures, but neither of them provide the cost of providing care to provincial beneficiaries who are admitted to hospital. Total operating costs include costs unrelated to provincial beneficiaries and costs unrelated to inpatient care, and they do not include the capital costs and physician payments which also contribute to the cost of inpatient care.

The operating budgets of acute treatment hospitals represent about 40% of health care dollars, and this is sometimes referred to as the cost of acute hospital care. But the total cost of this care is much higher than 40%. The total cost includes the cost of hospital care provided by physicians and the hospital capital costs, minus the cost of care to out of province persons. Hospital costs as customarily reported do not include the costs of psychiatric hospitals. The costs of chronic hospitals may or may not be included.

A 1983 study in Saskatchewan reported that, on average, 64% of patient costs were directly related to hospital care. This dominance of hospital costs explains why delivery arrangements which lower hospital utilization can so markedly lower total per capita health care costs.

Estimates of the costs of care in the home are even less well known and much more confusingly reported. The costs of individual programs are usually adequately reported, but many users receive services from many programs. Total costs are seldom known.

HEALTH CARE COSTS IN PERSPECTIVE

The Gross National Product (GNP) of Canada in 1989-90 was about $540 billion. Forty-six to forty-eight per cent of this sum, about $250 billion, was generated in the public sector, a proportion higher than in Japan and the United States but lower than most European countries.

The major components of the public portion of the GNP are pensions, education and health care, in that order. Health care expenditures have until the 1990s risen steadily regardless of the health of the national or provincial economies. Health care costs rose whether the GNP rose or fell. (Figure 3.2)

"The OECD estimates that member countries devoted, on average, 6.5% of Gross Domestic Product (GDP) to health in 1975 and 7.3% in 1987." The comparable figures for Canada were 7.3 and 8.6%. (The Health Care System in Canada and its Funding: No Easy Solutions, Standing Committee on Health and Welfare, Ottawa, 1992, p. 2) Canadian per capita public expenditures on health care were second only to the United States and were therefore the highest of any country with a national program of health care insurance.

Insulation from economic downturns causes a rapid growth in percentage of GNP spent on health care when there is little or no growth in the economy. In the recession of 1978-82 the percentage of Canada's GNP spent on health care rose rapidly from just over 7% to over 8.6%. In 1991 when the GNP rose only 1% the per capita health care expenditures grew 5%. The increase in health care expenditures as a percentage of GNP would have been even greater in the early 1990s if health care costs had grown at the previous rate. By 1991 all provinces had begun serious control of health care costs. 1993-94 total Canadian public spending on health care was projected to increase about 0.15%, with the only major increase being in British Columbia (at 4.1%). (Group Healthcare Management, Oct/Nov 1993)

The economic downturn of the early 1990s was so severe and prolonged, the loss of permanent jobs so great and the governmental deficits so high that health care costs were not allowed to grow at their earlier rates. Even physician incomes became recession sensitive, although physicians retained insulation from the hazard of unemployment.

Table 3.2

CANADIAN HEALTH CARE EXPENDITURES — SELECTED YEARS 1960–92		
Year	Expenditures (in millions)	% of GNP
1960	2,142	5.5
1965	3,415	6.0
1970	6,253	7.1
1975	12,267	7.2
1980	22,703	7.5
1982	31,150	8.6
1985	40.407	8.8
1986	44,285	9.0
1990	62.700	9.7
1991	66,800	10.2

Source - Health Expenditures in Canada Summary Report, HWC 1993

FEDERAL SPENDING ON HEALTH CARE

Federal spending on health care has two components, transfers to the provinces and expenditures on services which are constitutionally within federal jurisdiction. In the period 1979-1993 federal transfers for health care fell from 11% of total federal expenditures to about 8%. (The Porter Report, 1992, p.17)

Expenditures on those populations which are constitutionally the responsibility of the federal government represent about 3% of the total national public and private expenditures on health care. Despite a stated conviction that health promotion (HP) deserves increased support Health and Welfare Canada in 1991-92 spent only slightly over $85 million on it.

SPENDING BY THE PROVINCES

Provincial spending on health care is partly money transferred from the federal government and partly money from provincial taxes or borrowing. Provincial spending on health care varied in 1987 from 7.7% of provincial GDP in Alberta to 12% in Prince Edward Island. (The Porter Report, 1992, p. 7) Health care spending as a percentage of total provincial spending varies from a low of about 25% to a high of 36%. These expenditures have been increasing for decades at several times the rate of inflation. In Manitoba in the years 1979-80 to 1989-90 the population grew 6%, the Consumer Price Index (CPI) grew 71%, the Gross Provincial Product grew 124% and health care costs grew 178%. The pattern is similar in most other provinces. Hospital operating costs and payments to physicians are the largest cost centres. (Tables 3.3 and 3.4)

Provincial fee-for-service (FFS) payments to private practitioners are predominantly, but not exclusively, to physicians. (Table 3.5). The number of claims per year from practitioners on FFS in Ontario is in the order of 5000 per physician, 6000 per optometrist, 3000 per chiropractor, 18,000 per chiropodist and 6500 per physiotherapist.

EXPENDITURES BY SOURCE AND SERVICE

Public spending (all governments) on health care as a percentage of total spending on health care in Canada stayed around 74-75% for most of the 1970s and 1980s, but by 1991 had fallen to 71.5%. (Table 3.6) This is a lower public spending level than is found in most European countries, where the public percentage is close to 80%, but is higher than the 41% in the United States in 1987. (The Porter Report, 1992, p. 3) Increasing control of public spending in 1992 and 1993 will have lowered the percentage of health spending from public sources even further. Private expenditures will probably have risen to close to 30% of total spending by 1994.

About one quarter of the private expenditures are for dental services, one quarter for institutional services, one third for drugs and appliances and most of the rest for nontraditional health care. Private expenditures represented 70% of total spending on drugs (prescription and nonprescription) in 1991. Private spending was 4% of total expenditures for physicians services, hospitals 11% and *other institutions* 23%. (Health Expenditures in Canada Summary Report 1987-1991, HWC 1993)

EXPENDITURES ON DRUGS

Public expenditures on drugs for nonhospitalized patients vary from $10-100 per capita (total population) depending on the province. Most of these expenditures are incurred by the major provincial drug programs. The cost of these programs varies primarily with the percentage of the population which is covered and the extent to which user fees apply. In Ontario in recent years over 50% of all prescriptions filled have been paid for by a public plan covering 20% of the population. Expenditures on prescription drugs have shown the highest rate of growth of any of the mature health care sectors.

Table 3.3

PROVINCIAL EXPENDITURES PER CAPITA
FOR SELECTED HEALTH SERVICES, 1990-91

The Service	Provincial expenditures per capita
Acute treatment hospitals	$700-900
Long term care institutions	60-130
Physicians services	300-500
Community health services (including Home Care and Public Health services)	25-100
Emergency health services	40-60
Mental health services	50-100
Prescription drugs	30-100
Nonprescription drugs	0-10
Dentistry	less than $1
Nontraditional therapies	nil
All health care	1800-2100

Note: These estimates and ranges are an aggregation of data from several provincial annual reports and from a number of federal reports. They should be used only to obtain a general perspective of the expenditures per category of service. There are major provincial differences in many categories of service.

In addition to the major programs, all provinces support some of the costs of very expensive diagnostically specific drugs. These drugs can cost $15-20,000 per person per year or more, and the number of these expensive drugs is increasing each year. The cost of these expensive drugs now exceeds $100 million annually in Ontario, or more than $10 per capita.

Prior to 1987 a drug patented by one company could be manufactured by other companies if issued a permit by the federal government. The companies producing the copies (the generic drugs) were obliged to pay a royalty to the company holding the patent. This mandatory licensing arrangement, which was at that time in place in many countries, saved Canadians hundreds of millions of dollars. In 1987 the patent protection period of drugs was extended by the federal government to 10 years, and in 1992 (retroactive to 1991) the protection was extended to 20 years and mandatory licensing was eliminated.

MENTAL HEALTH SERVICES

In 1983/84 the Ontario Ministry of Health spent $783 million on mental health related activities, or about $85 per capita. These expenditures were 38% on psychiatric hospitals, 20% on medicare payments, 22% in general hospitals, 11% on Homes for Special Care (residential care), 4% on community mental health services and 4.5% on alcohol and drug programs.

During the last decade there has, in Ontario as elsewhere, been a stated intention to increase emphasis on mental health services, but the percent of total Ontario health care spending allocated to mental health services fell from 7.71% in 1979-80 to 4.59% in 1989-90. Community mental health services, the main focus for expansion, rose (for those same years) from 0.71% of total Ministry of Health spending to an estimated 0.78%. The percentage of health care dollars spent on community mental health services rose, but total spending on mental health services fell by 40%. (Lurie, S., "Mental Health Policy and Expenditure Analysis", Canada's Mental Health, March

Table 3.4

HEALTH CARE EXPENDITURE BY MAJOR COST CENTRE 1975, 1987 AND 1991, IN PERCENT			
Category	**1975**	**1987**	**1991**
Hospitals	44.4	39.3	39.1
Other institutions	9.7	10.1	10.0
Home Care	0.3	0.8	
Physicians*	15.7	15.8	15.2
Other professionals**	6.0	6.7	6.9
Drugs (Rx and non Rx)	8.9	12.2	13.8
Capital Expenditure	5.0	4.6	3.6
Health care research0.8		0.9	
All other categories	9.2	9.6	11.4***

* Does not include costs of physicians on payrolls of hospitals, public health agencies, etc.
** Includes dentists, chiropractors and optometrists
*** Includes research and home care

Ref: Health Expenditures in Canada, HWC 1993

1992) These figures may be somewhat unfair to Ontario; they do not reflect significant new spending on community mental health services since 1990 nor do they reflect spending in other departments for care for the chronically mentally ill within the community. The figures do not, however, suggest a correction of the long standing imbalance between attention to mental versus physical health. Only about 0.2% of mental health spending in Ontario goes to support self-help, mutual aid, advocacy groups or sheltered economic development programs. (Lurie S., see above)

Expenditures on persons with mental disorders were, in Quebec in 1988-89, about $1 billion, or about $150 per capita. In 1984-85 65% of the Quebec expenditures on mental health services were on psychiatric hospitals. (Morin, P., "Quebec's Mental Health Policy", Canada's Mental Health, March, 1992)

Many mental health related costs are not included in the above figures. If an anxious patient develops a peptic ulcer the costs of the care will not be included in calculations of the cost of mental or psychosocial ill health. The same applies to injuries arising from family or other violence, to accidents at work or elsewhere which have their genesis in stress, or to many of the other sequelae of emotional or psychiatric illness.

COMMUNITY HEALTH SERVICES

In 1987 Home Care programs were costing $10-25 per capita in those provinces with mature and universal programs. The programs were serving between 1000 and 3000 clients per year per 100,000 population, with case-loads at any one time being 300 to 1500 per 100,000 population. Cost per person served was $1000-1500. (Richardson, B.G., "Overview of Provincial Home Care Programs in Canada", Healthcare Management Forum, Fall, 1990) Home care has also been reported to consume 2-4% of provincial health care budgets. (Shapiro, E., Proceedings of the First National Home Care Conference, 1989 p. 23) Discrepencies in data are a reflection of their inadequacies. Over half of the expenditures for services delivered to the home were for organized Home

Table 3.5

FFS PAYMENTS BY PROVIDER CATEGORY IN ONTARIO AND SASKATCHEWAN AS % OF ALL FFS PAYMENTS*		
	Ontario 1990/91	**Sask.**
All physicians	84.5	91.0
Private laboratories	10.5	N/A
Dentists	0.2	0.6
Optometrists	1.9	3.2
Chiropractors**	2.0	5.2
Chiropodists	0.1	N/A
Physiotherapists	0.7	N/A

   *Excluding out-of-province FFS payments.
 **There were in 1990-91 no co-payments or ceilings on chiropractic services in Saskatchewan whereas in Ontario there were user fees and provincial limits on total cost per person per year.

Care to persons over age 65. (Richardson, B.G. — see above) For persons on Home Care homemakers are the most commonly used service and may represent 60-70% of cost.

Community Health Centres are less than one percent of provincial spending in most provinces. In Quebec the CLSCs represent about 5% of the provincial health care budget (1990). This percentage will rise to as much as 10% if CLSC functions are expanded in accordance with the policy announcements of 1990. In 1991 Ontario had 35-40 Community Health Centres in operation but they represented only about 0.25% of the Ministry budget.

SCREENING PROGRAMS

Screening programs search for presymptomatic disease or precursors to disease. Costs of different screening programs can be compared by use of such measures as cost per quality life-year saved.

A 1991 report by the Technology Evaluation Council of Quebec estimated that biennial breast screening of all Quebec females 50-69 years would cost $27 million, or $30-40 per capita for the population being screened. The program was predicted to be able to reduce breast cancer mortality by 40% and save 230 lives annually for a cost of $3,400-5,700 per year of life saved. (These figures are predictions, not experience.)

COSTS BY MAJOR DIAGNOSTIC CATEGORY

Estimates of costs by major diagnostic category offer only a very vague picture of relative magnitude. (Table 3.7) This information does indicate that there are many diagnostic categories in which expenditures are large, and therefore there are many diagnostic categories which offer major potential for savings.

A comment on pension costs will illustrate the weaknesses in the data in Table 3.7. Social costs met through social assistance, which are a common sequelae of mental disorders, are not included, whereas a disability pension arising from an injury at work is included. This discrepancy inflates the apparent social costs of disabilities due to injuries and undervalues the social costs arising from mental illness.

Table 3.6

TOTAL HEALTH CARE EXPENDITURE BY SOURCE, 1975, 1987, 1990 AND 1991				
Sector	**1975**	**1987**	**1990**	**1991**
Federal Government	30.8	29.5	27.7	24.4
Provincial Government	43.3	42.6	43.4	46.0
Local Government	1.1	1.4	1.1	1.1
Workers Compensation	0.9	0.8	0.8	0.9
Private	23.6	25.8	27.5	27.8

Ref: House of Commons Standing Committee on Health and Welfare

Potential for savings (or for increased costs) can be best estimated if specific diagnoses, rather than diagnostic groups, are examined. Benign prostatic hypertrophy, for example, has been estimated to affect over 75% of men over age 50. (Johns Hopkins monthly Newsletter - Health After 50, 1993) Such a high prevalence of a chronic condition known to produce demands for health care automatically identifies this clinical entity as one worthy of surveillance.

Some general interpretations of the information in Table 3.7 may be safe. Prevention of injuries will lower physician, hospital and pension costs. Cancer control will have its greatest effect on reduction of premature death. Control of musculoskeletal disease will have its greatest effect on pension costs. The main message is that costing is complicated. Reliability will have to be improved if the data are to be safely used to predict the impact of various policies.

Costs by disease category have a great deal of overlap. For example, the Canadian Diabetes Association estimates the cost of health care arising from diabetes to be $2.5 billion annually. Some of these costs will be caused by coronary artery disease or blindness secondary to the diabetes, and these costs will also be reported by some other agency or researcher as the costs of coronary artery disease or of blindness.

The cost of many common surgical procedures in the United States has been estimated, for example, cholecystectomies - $6.8 billion, hysterectomies - $4 billion, caesarian sections - $3.2 billion. ("For the Health of the Nation: A Shared Responsibility", Report of the National Leadership Commission on Health Care, Ann Arbor, Michigan, 1989, p. 129) These figures allow estimation of the financial impact of lowering utilization by 5% or some other selected figure. Reductions in the volume of surgery can either lead to reduced spending by government or allow hospitals to allocate more of their global budgets to other health care activities.

SPORTS INJURIES

The volume of sports injuries has been significantly decreased by better equipment such as helmets, mouth protectors, safety glasses and safer skiing footwear. Despite these reductions sports related injuries in Quebec in 1987 were estimated to have cost the province $187 million or $25-30 per capita. About 20% of the costs were for direct medical care. (Report of the Regie de la securite dans les sports du Quebec, 1990) Approximately 250,000 persons (3-4% of Quebec residents) received sports injuries which led to medical attention. These figures are about half the magnitude of injuries suffered at work.

One hundred eighty-six persons were killed, with cycling being the major killer (46), swimming next (41), fishing-hunting (including related drownings) (29), all terrain vehicles (ATVs) (27), other drownings (24) and snowmobiles (10). The message is that water kills, and usually obviously

Table 3.7

COSTS ARISING FROM SELECTED CONDITIONS, IN PERCENT*						
	Drugs	**Phys's**	**Hosps (excl drugs)**	**CPP/QPP**	**Loss due to prem. death**	**Loss due to chr diability**
C/V Disease	20.9%	8.9%	20.7%	26.1%	31.9%	17.4%
CAD (in CVD)	5.3	–	4.9	–	20.8	–
Respiratory	14.9	9.1	7.0	5.3	5.1	5.8
CNS & sense org	7.8	8.2	6.9	7.8	2.0	4.3
Genito-urinary	2./0	7.6	5.0	0.7	0.9	–
Mental dis's	6.7	6.9	10.7	10.5	1.0	5.1
Injuries	4.0	6.8	7.9	7.7	19.0	7.0
Musculoskel.	3.8	6.2	5.3	29.0	0.3	31.9
Pregnancy	–	3.8	5.7	–	–	–
Cancer	2.8	3.7	8.9	5.0	28.0	–
Digestive dis's	8.0	6.6	8.1	2.0	3.8	2.4
Endocrine	2.2	2.8	2.6	3.1	2.9	1.8
Well pt care	9.2	10.6	3.5	–	–	–
Total	100.0	100.0	100.0	100.0	100.0	100.0
Total cost	3.6B	7.0B	17.1B	2.7B	25.6B	19.0B

Ref: Chronic Diseases in Canada, Supplement to May-June 1991

*These data are at best only general indications of the costs associated with specified diagnostic groups. The data were taken from varied sources, were not always known to be comparable and were often incomplete. The table should be interpreted with these deficiencies in mind. In 1986, for example, Quebec estimated mental disorders accounted for 18% of provincial health care costs, a figure considerably higher than those in Table 3.7.

without leading to major demands on medical services. Some sports cause many injuries and few deaths. There were 37,000 hockey injuries in Quebec in 1987

Spinal cord injuries are low in incidence but very expensive. Each year, for each million persons, there are about 15 spinal cord injuries which lead to permanent serious disability (paraplegia and quadriplegia). Traffic accidents cause over 50% of these cases. The costs arising from these injuries is increasing due to the ability to prevent complications which formerly caused death secondary to the spinal cord injury.

RENAL DIALYSIS

Haemodialysis costs $25,000 to $50,000 per year. Peritoneal dialysis is less expensive. The costs of dialysis may rise with the introduction of new anti-anemia drugs which cost $10-20,000 per person per year. There will be offsetting savings in blood use and some hospital costs, but the savings may accrue to the institutions involved whereas the new drug costs may be open-ended and in a different program.

INCONTINENCE

Ontario in 1991 estimated a cost of $300 million annually if incontinence products were insured, and $20 million if coverage applied only to those with severe incontinence. These figures are based on Alberta experience with insured incontinence products.

Australia in 1987 reported $465 million of laundry costs in nursing homes. Much of this cost was caused by incontinence. Studies have established that much of the incontinence of mentally competent persons can be eliminated with proper training, but changing the laundry still is often the response.

IMAGING TECHNOLOGIES

In 1985 expenditures on all imaging, including X-rays, angiography, ultrasound and newer sophisticated machines, represented 3.5% of all health care costs in the United States. Similar equipment in Australia represented 2% of public expenditures on health care, and the figure was 1.5% in Finland, with the biggest item being conventional X-rays. (Figley, M.M., and A.R. Margulis, American Journal of Research, Dec. 1987, p. 1112).

THE COSTS OF CARE FOR SPECIFIC POPULATIONS

As with other parts of this chapter, only a few illustrative populations will be described. Costing of publicly funded social support and health care for various populations tends to be incomplete, but such costing, even imperfect, is at times useful to planners and resource allocators.

Health care and social support for the dependent physically disabled have markedly prolonged their lives. This is a triumph, but the ability to prolong these lives adds to the costs of health care and other social programs. In 1984 the annual cost of care of the seriously physically disabled was estimated by Dr. David Symington to be $11 billion per year. This estimate included residential care and institutional health care. An additional $2 billion was spent on income support. About 250,000 Canadians (almost 1% of the total population) live in long term care institutions or in chronic beds in acute care short term hospitals. (Symington, D., "Integrating Disabled Canadians", Dimensions, Nov 1984) Symington estimated in 1990 that total expenditures on institutional care and income support for disabled persons had risen to $20 billion annually. (Symington, D., Dinsdale Memorial Lecture, Dinsdale International Conference in Rehabilitation, Ottawa, 1990)

Terminology can lead to misunderstandings of data and of the health status of the persons being described. It has been estimated that 80% of all health care resources are consumed by persons who are chronically ill or disabled. (Neifing, T., in Chronic Illness: Impact and Interventions, 2nd ed, 1990, Ch. 19) For most of these persons the chronic illness or disability does not lead to dependency. Most persons with diabetes, arthritis or hypertension lead normal lives but they can quite properly be classified as having a chronic illness. To the extent health care is required it is not sought within the chronic care system.

Despite the current emphasis on community care much new money still goes to long term care institutions. In 1993, Ontario, in the face of severe cut-backs everywhere, committed an additional $300 million to improve institutional care. Not one more person was to be served (the beds were already full). Quebec in 1992, as part of its proposed restructuring of the health care system, said it would build another 7000 long term care beds. Capital costs, considering inflation, will be in the order of $500-700 million, with annual operating costs of $300-500 million. This proposed new expenditure dwarfs the funds committed to new community services.

THE ELDERLY AND THE COST OF DYING

In any year one half of the elderly use very little health care, 45% receive care representing significant costs, and 5% consume very large volumes of care. Health care in the last year of life drives expenditure patterns. (The Millbank Quarterly, Vol 67, Nos. 3-4, 1989)

As with other factors, the impact of demographic changes on costs is unclear. Higher health care expenditures on the elderly arise from the higher incidence of diseases and disabilities and from the high health care costs commonly incurred in the last year of life. More of the elderly are in the last and most expensive year of their life than any other age group. If the public costs associated with non-cost-effective health care can be reduced and if unavoidable deaths are accepted the effects of the aging of the population on costs will be minimized.

The process of dying is expensive at all ages. Premature infants who do not survive, children with fatal chronic diseases, persons who die of AIDS, persons who reach hospital alive after a car accident but who later die, and persons with Alzheimer's disease, all represent high health care costs. The only low cost deaths are those which are sudden and unexpected.

It has been estimated that as much as 40% of all health care is consumed by persons in the last three months of life. (Lubitz and Riley, New England Journal of Medicine, 1990)

EXPENDITURES WITHIN HOSPITAL BUDGETS

The distribution of expenditures within hospitals in 1979/80, as reported by Statistics Canada, was nursing 41%, general administration 8%, dietary 10%, pharmacy and drugs 4%, medical supplies 4%, laboratory 6%, radiology 2%, laundry 2%, education 2%, plant operation 8%, health records 2%, social work 1% and other 10%. These data are out of date, but the overall general distribution of total costs of all hospitals is probably still much the same. The distribution of costs in tertiary care hospitals is quite different from that in a smaller community hospital.

Intensive Care Units can account for as much as 15% of the operating costs of a hospital. (Linton, A., Medical Post, August 8, 1989) Intensive care includes neonatal intensive care and the coronary care unit. Other expensive units include renal dialysis, cardiovascular surgery, cancer treatment units and high technology imaging devices.

COSTS OF ADMINISTRATION

The cost of administration of Canadian health care is usually estimated at 2-4%, which compares very favorably to the estimated 15-20% in the United States. If operating funds are used to fund much greater attention to evaluation and improved delivery of care, and they should be, it is likely that 4-6% will be a more appropriate level of expenditure on administration.

Administrative costs should also rise to prevent the issuing of insurance cards to ineligible persons. Ontario has estimated that as many as 600,000 cards may be in active use by ineligible persons at an annual cost of between $10 and $100 million per year. (Ontario Medical Review, Dec 1992) New Brunswick has estimated that 18,000 cards might have been issued to ineligible persons. (Fraud in health care is not unique to Canada. Fraud of over $400 million has been identified in mental health services in United States federal programs.)

FINANCIAL IMPLICATIONS OF THE SUPPLY OF
HEALTH WORKERS, IN PARTICULAR PHYSICIANS

Payments to physicians represent 15-20% of all expenditures on health care (20-25% of public expenditures on health care) but the extent to which physicians dominate health care spending is only seen when the payments to physicians are combined with the costs of services which are only available on the order of a physician. Generated costs which happen only on the order of a physician include almost all diagnostic investigations (X-rays, ultrasound, laboratories), almost all hospital based health care, almost all prescriptions for medication and assistive devices and almost all referrals to other physicians or to other health care professionals in the medical model (such as physiotherapists and respiratory technologists).

Physicians are seldom responsible for 100% of the costs in any category of service but their dominance is immense. With respect to laboratory tests, for example, physicians are responsible for all such ordering except for tests able to be performed at home by the user, those ordered by dentists, those ordered by public health personnel (such as stool samples of restaurant workers) and a few other equally minor exceptions.

The phenomenon of generated costs is one of the two main reasons for the financial impact of an increasing physician population. Most physicians bill in the range of $150,000 to $350,000 per year for personal services but the average physician produces at least the same amount of additional expense through secondary or generated costs.

The frequency with which Canadian family physicians refer to specialists varies. One study of three urban family practice units reported that 5% of visits to a family physician led to a referral to a specialist. (Hines, R.M., and D.J. Curry, "The consultation process and physician satisfaction: review of referral patterns in three urban family practice units", CMAJ, 1978; 118: 1065-1066)

A referral can lead to many specialist services over an extended period. A 1984 one month study at the Sunnybrook Medical Centre family practice clinic (a clinic financed on capitation) reported that 21% of patients on capitation were seen by a specialist during the month, and that the services of the specialists represented 61% of the total physician costs. Some specialists see patients without referral and the volume of care given by specialists is therefore not fully the product of referrals, and all referrals would not be from family physicians. (Norton, P.G., W. Nelson, H.L. Rudner, and E.V. Dunn, "Relative costs of specialist services in a family practice population", CMAJ, Oct. 15, 1985)

SUMMARY

The intention in this chapter has been to produce images rather than precise photos. Precision may be wanted but will not always be available. Perspective is more important. Discrepancies in the figures within this chapter illustrate the difficulties inherent in attempting to base policy on data which often are produced from many sources and based on different definitions and terms.

Data on costs have shown that physical health care dominates despite our cultural acceptance of the importance of psychosocial health, that expenditures on institutional care are falling but still dominant, that private expenditures on health care are growing as a proportion of total expenditures on health care, and that Canada spends considerably more on health care per capita than many countries with better health status than we have.

Rising health care costs are not due to a failure to practice more prevention and live healthier lifestyles. More attention to prevention will lengthen life and improve its quality, but it will not lower the demand for health care dollars.

Preamble to Part 2

The three chapters in Part 1 examined information important to an understanding of the issues associated with control of the costs of health care and with better spending of health care dollars. The eleven chapters in Part 2 describe and discuss many of the policy options available as governments wonder where to control health care costs, how tightly to control them and what cost control techniques to use.

Cost control has the single objective of lowering or limiting government spending on health care. Improved spending is much more complex both in its intentions and its implementation. How to improve the manner in which health care dollars are spent will often be mentioned in Part 2 but will be discussed more fully in Part 3.

Policy makers must review many options, and making choices is often difficult. Many factors must be considered, and many principles which are important must often, in the end, be fully or partially abandoned. Some policy options will bring benefits, but only far in the future. Some options will help only certain populations and will not be very attractive to other populations. It will not be easy to find policies which are acceptable, sustainable, understandable, tolerable and implementable, and which reduce costs while preserving the principles which are dear to Canadians, but that is the objective.

Part 2 will be most acceptable to the reader who has accepted the need for control of expenditures on health care, or has at least accepted that control is inevitable and will continue.

Part 2 assumes there will be no major changes, if any, in the role of the provinces in health care. They will remain dominant and probably become more so. The federal government role will continue to decrease.

Evaluation of policies will often rely on principles and theories associated with economics, research, behavior modification, policy analysis, community development, organizational behavior, social change, crisis management, public education, planning, management, information systems and finance. There will be no prolonged consideration of these theoretical bases, but a few of the contributions of theory are worth noting.

CONTRIBUTIONS OF ECONOMICS

Economics contributes the concepts of opportunity cost, diminishing returns, critical mass, economies of scale and cost-effectiveness.

Opportunity cost reminds us that when a home care visit or a surgical procedure is carried out there are two costs: first, the actual financial costs of the activity and, second, the consequences of not being able to use those resources for other activities. Visits made or surgery performed must bring more benefits than the activities which were (because the visits or surgery used up the resources) not carried out, or the opportunity cost was too high. Hospitals, for example, should be certain that the persons in hospital have a greater need for hospital care than those persons who are waiting. If the benefits of hospital care for someone not in hospital would be greater than the benefit being gained by someone who is in hospital then the wrong person is in hospital and the opportunity cost is too high.

The law of diminishing returns tells us that the benefits per dollar spent on a particular activity often decrease as more of those activities are performed. For example, performing a PAP smear every two years is considered adequate when screening for cervical cancer in females who have previously had normal smears. Doing a PAP smear every year would identify a small number of precancerous lesions one year earlier but the benefits would be very small compared to the doubling of the cost.

Similarly, immunizing the first 80% of the infant population may cost $3 per child. (These numbers are not real; they are merely used to illustrate a point.) Immunizing the next 10% of the children may cost $5 per child (the higher costs could be caused by many factors such as the need to make special efforts to find the children) and the next 8% of the children could cost $10 per child. The benefit obtained from one immunization is the same whether the immunization costs $3 or $10. There are diminishing returns per dollar spent as immunization levels climb towards 100%.

Anesthesia offers another example. With good basic anaesthetic practices there will be very few poor outcomes. The great majority of patients will survive their anaesthetic and not be damaged by it. A modest increase in costs per case will avoid the majority of the few undesirable outcomes that occur with only the good basic practices. Major extensions in cost will eliminate almost all of the remaining undesirable effects. Many people benefit at low unit cost when the service is adequate but not as perfect as it can be. Very few persons benefit from the last round of improvements and the costs are very high. The diminishing returns per dollar spent lead to very high opportunity costs.

The above examples also illustrate the concept of cost-effectiveness. As the unit costs of services or activities rises their cost-effectiveness almost always goes down. At some point it may not be reasonable to continue to spend. It may not be reasonable to search for the last few children who remain unimmunized, or not reasonable to try and make anaesthetic services any more perfect, at least not at public cost.

The cost-effectiveness of health care increases when:

- both costs and benefits go down but costs go down more than benefits. An example could be homemaking hours in a home care program. If the hours and the costs go down 30% but there is only a 10% drop in benefits to the person(s) receiving the services then the reduced level of care is more cost-effective than the higher level of care,
- both costs and outcomes go up but outcomes go up more than costs. This could be the case if a new more expensive anti-cancer therapy produced longer remissions for breast cancer, or if a new schizophrenia treatment cost more but sharply improved the quality of life of the users,
- total costs go down and benefits increase. This is the happiest of all situations. Examples would include a program to prevent spinal cord injuries. The costs of the prevention program might be only one tenth of the savings resulting from reduced expenditures on the care of persons with spinal injuries, and the individuals would have all of the benefits that go with not having a broken neck or back. Discontinuing drugs which should not have been prescribed or which are no longer needed is another example,
- costs go down but outcomes/benefits remain the same. This occurs when prices go down (as with group purchasing of drugs, with the use of generic drugs, and when a different therapy produces the same results at lower cost) or when efficiency increases, (as with economies of scale, a shorter hospital length of stay, or the elimination of unnecessary diagnostic tests),
- costs stay the same but benefits increase. This would probably happen if a complete physical by a physician on fee-for-service was expanded to include lifestyle counselling but the fee stayed the same.

Cost-effectiveness is decreased when the cost of a product or service is increased, or the frequency of a service is increased, without improving outcomes or with an improvement in outcomes which is smaller than the increase in costs. This occurs when a CAT scan or MRI (which will produce a better picture) are used when an ultrasound or X-ray provides all that is needed, or when routine hypertension is monitored monthly in a physicians office when the patient could monitor it equally well at home and be seen less often.

The concepts of economies of scale and critical mass are important in situations in which unit costs are high if volumes are low. *Critical mass* refers to the number of people or things or events that are necessary if unit costs and/or quality are to be reasonable. In laboratories and in emergency departments quality tends to go down and unit costs go up when service volumes are too low. Economies of scale may occur when larger equipment can be justified (as in regional laundries), as volumes rise (as in group purchasing) and when idle time is reduced as caseloads increase (as in obstetrical units).

THEORIES OF PARTNERSHIP AND SHARED POWER

The consumer era is here, but the understanding of shared power and the processes of consensus seeking is weak. The concepts inherent in community development are seldom known about. The art of assisting communities to identify and promote their priorities is only very slowly being refined. Some of the stated goals of governments cannot be fully attained until governments learn to be partners at least as much as regulators.

THE CONTRIBUTIONS OF POLICY ANALYSIS

Policy can originate in the field as well as within government, and from consumers as well as technocrats. It can emerge through complex and formal processes or can move quickly from the extra-parliamentary process to the halls of power. Sound policy is most likely to follow a process in which alternatives are identified and methodically evaluated.

The identification and ritualistic evaluation of alternatives is the heart of good decision making. It is a part of policy analysis, strategic planning, operational planning, strategic management, administration, problem solving and good government. The terminology is rather unimportant but the concept is not. It is difficult to select the policy which is best for governments and for populations if the alternatives are not first identified and evaluated.

The preferred policy option(s) will seldom be innovative. The actions which will preserve universal access to a reasonable level of necessary health care at public cost while avoiding continued increases in public spending on health care will usually already have been tested somewhere.

Policy analysis should usually include consideration of at least culture, political implications, impact on other policies and programs, legality, feasibility of implementation, cost and impact.

THE IMPORTANCE OF THEORIES OF
BEHAVIORAL AND ORGANIZATIONAL CHANGE

Social and organizational disruption are a feature of this decade. The literature on organizational behaviour, crisis management, organizational transformation and social change can help explain what is happening, what is likely to happen next and how agencies and governments can perform best in unstable environments.

THE RELATIONSHIP BETWEEN COST CONTROL AND BETTER SPENDING

Part 2 introduces the proposition that there is little if any relationship between how much is spent on health care and how well the available money is spent. Whether one has lots of money (1970) or a definite shortage of it (1994), that money can be spent well or poorly. When one goes to the grocery store the purchases made can be sensible or wasteful regardless of the money supply, and buying health care is no different.

Many of the policies, tools and techniques discussed in Part 2 will affect only the amount of money spent. There will be no expected change in the wisdom with which the dollars are spent. Some policies, tools and techniques will both control costs and improve spending, and often the two effects are inextricably linked, but the concept of two quite separate objectives, processes and outcomes should be kept in mind.

Policies, tools and techniques which deal primarily with how to spend wisely are discussed in Part 3. These tools and techniques which improve spending should be used regardless of the generosity or frugality of provincial or private allocations to health care.

Chapter 4

Social Priorities: The Fundamental Choices

INTRODUCTION

Chapter 4 describes broad and often value-dominated policy options, almost all of which affect cost control and the quality of health care spending. These first level policy choices are of primary importance. No government or governing body should deal with day-to-day issues until the general themes and directions considered to be consistent with social and political values, and with realities, have been identified.

Examination of the basic policy options, and selection of those most consistent with provincial, regional or program values, functions and resources, will assist in the preparation of precise goals, objectives and mission statements by Ministers and others who create policy. Clarification of these basic policy preferences makes it easier for public servants and other advisors to provide useful advice.

The first level choices are not easy. Many values that are thought to be sacred will be sacrificed in the face of trade-offs which are unavoidable. Choices will have to be made between alternative outcomes and between populations. These choices will often reflect the preferences of democratic leaders, or of populations, more than technocratic evidence. Clarification of which options are compatible with values and objectives, and which are not, can reduce the likelihood that operational planning will be unacceptable or inappropriate.

In a consumer sensitive society the first level of options faced by strategic planners and policy makers is a level at which the choices of the users should dominate if possible. The opinions of the consumers should be seen as more important than the opinions of the technocrats, subject to unavoidable legal or economic constraints.

Social priorities are not black and white. Almost all choices are affected by many factors, and factors change in importance from situation to situation. It is easy to be in favor of economic growth, a strong social safety net and protection of the physical and social environments, but it is also easy for two or more of these to be in conflict. Similarly, most of us would like to have both better health now and better health in the future, but when resources are in short supply the costs of prevention compete with the costs of health care to-day. Choices often establish emphases rather than exclude one option.

This chapter avoids issues which have few financial implications. Ethical and cultural conflicts in these issues may be extreme, as with consent to treatment or appeal processes for mentally incompetent persons, and these issues are not unimportant, but they are of minor importance to cost control and better spending.

There has been no attempt to label issues as *left* or *right* on the political spectrum. The performance of various provincial governments as they legislate and fund health care indicates that political stripe has little to do with how health care will be organized, funded or delivered, or with who will most innovatively control health care expenditures and inappropriate spending. No party, whether right or left, should spend more than a country or province can afford, and all should wish to spend the taxpayers money well.

There is at times significant and unavoidable overlap between the headings in this chapter.

PRESERVING LIFE VS IMPROVING QUALITY OF LIFE
(QUANTITY VS QUALITY OF LIFE)

The protection and preservation of life has always been a primary objective of health care, and this continues to be true, but in the 1980s the protection and improvement of quality of life was increasingly seen as a second and equally important primary objective. This duality will, hopefully, continue to apply in the future.

Quality of life is something which can only be evaluated by the individual involved, and it can seldom be sought without the participation and direction of that individual. The emergence of quality of life as an objective of health care has, therefore, been inextricably tied to the emergence of user control and users rights.

Health care is, for most of the population at any point in time, not very important to quality of life. The important factors are our personal relationships, our self-image, our personal wealth and the personal rewards received from work and play. Health care is, however, important for quality of life and/or length of life at those times when it can assist in protection, recovery or support associated with illness or injury. Health care can improve and protect quality of life by either curing or avoiding illness and by providing care and support.

Policy makers may seek any level of balance or imbalance among the impacts and outcomes that can be produced by health care. These health care impacts range from complete cure to completely no effect on the disease, and from minimal attention to factors important to quality of life to major emphasis on care and support. Optional outcomes include elimination or reduction of threats to the lives or health of a population (primary prevention for a population) and elimination or reduction of threats to the life or health of an individual (primary prevention one person at a time). Health care may cure a life or health threatening condition, cure a non-life threatening condition, relieve a long term symptom or disability seriously interfering with the life of an individual, provide assistance with the essential activities of daily living (such as eating, toiletting and transferring) of a cognitively intact person, relieve a short term symptom or disability associated with a self-limiting condition, provide services which demonstrate caring and/or provide support services to someone who does not demonstrate the responses which differentiate humans from less developed life forms.

Society should assist government with the question of when there should be limits put on the types and volumes of services which will be provided at public expense. (It is assumed that expenditures at personal expense should be as determined by the individual(s) involved.) Some of these questions relate to the acceptance of human mortality, for example:

- when should there be no further attempt to cure or attempt to cure?
- when should there be no further attempt to lengthen life?
- when should there be no further provision of support services, including caring?

Both care (aimed primarily at improving quality of life) and cure or control (aimed at avoidance of premature death and at improved quality of life) are legitimate objectives. Health care will, without doubt, always give attention to both care and cure, and the choices are therefore choices of emphasis rather than exclusion.

Should the degree of emphasis given to protection or improvement of quality of life versus the lengthening of life increase as the age of the consumers increases? There are optional positions that can be argued.

- Elderly persons should have reduced access to curative health care at public expense because they are approaching inevitable death and the resources should be more generously allocated to younger people.
- All age groups should be treated equally when public funds are being spent.
- Publicly financed health care resources should, as persons age, gradually be moved from avoiding premature death to improving quality of life. (Callahan, D., Setting Limits: Medical Goals in an Aging Society, 1987) Within this principle activities directed towards lengthening life would be much more vigorously pursued when death would be considered premature. This statement is not as helpful as it appears to be. The avoidable death of a cognitively intact and physically well 95 year old is a premature death, and quality of life is of special importance to children and youths.
- Allocation of public dollars to health care should be on the basis of the cost per year of life saved or the cost per year of quality life saved. This would mean that an elderly person whose life of reasonable quality might be extended 3 years for $5,000 would have the same opportunity to receive health care at public expense as a 25 year old whose life also might be extended three years for $5,000, and also with a reasonable quality. Older persons would often have less likelihood of receiving care because of their shortened life expectancies, but they would be treated no differently than others whose lives are also expected to be short. A day of high quality life would be considered to be of relatively equal value at all ages. Within this practice the extent to which a death would be seen as premature would depend on more than just the age of the person.
- Allocation of resources to the preservation of quality of life should be independent of age and vary with the short term cost-effectiveness of the intervention, whereas allocation of resources to the protecting of life should vary with the cost per year of life saved.

This last option accepts quality of life as something which is especially relevant in the short term and which, therefore, must constantly be protected, whereas the protection of life can have long term dividends. The biggest exception to this general statement is with respect to children, where protection of quality of life pays very large long term dividends.

As with many of the choices discussed in this chapter, everyone favors preservation of both life and quality of life. Preferences and priorities only becomes visible when resources are being allocated to competing programs. Common sense and culture will continue to be more important than formulas, but organized information can provide guidance.

PHYSICAL VS PSYCHOSOCIAL HEALTH

Health for decades meant *physical health*. Mental health services were a poor second in image and funding. Psychosocial health was not yet being discussed.

Policy makers have the option of continuing the historical definitions of health, or of following the lead of provinces who as early as the 1950s (Saskatchewan) and the 1960s (British Columbia) moved to give mental health the status it deserves. Fortunately the moves are all in the direction of a balanced interest in physical, mental and psychosocial health.

DELAYING DEATH VS AVOIDING PREMATURE DEATH

Society and health care professionals still often define life in physical terms. Presence of a heart beat no longer is considered proof a person is alive, but the heart beat has been replaced by the presence or absence of brain waves. The criteria are still physical.

If life was defined in terms of the presence or absence of the cognitive, social and communicative characteristics which differentiate a human from an amoeba or a tree there would be less care given to the permanently vegetative organisms who are now routinely cared for because they have a few brain waves. Changes in the criteria which define life would alter the costs associated with care of some persons without altering the actual end of the life of those persons.

If death is seen as the enemy then it is fought to the last even although it always eventually wins and the cost of the war becomes greater as the end becomes more difficult to delay. Failure to accept the mortality of man leads to massive and unrewarding emotional and tangible investments which would be better assigned to avoiding deaths which are premature and to improving and protecting the quality of lives.

Those who work in hospitals are especially aware of the many times heroic care is delivered when death is inevitable. This pattern is probably not as pronounced as it was 10-20 years ago but a rational acceptance of unavoidable death is still not fully here.

PREVENTION VERSUS RESPONSE: HEALTH VERSUS HEALTH CARE

Should one concentrate on staying well or on being well cared for if one does not stay well? Countries, provinces and people can choose to practice allegiance to the Goddess Hygeia (the Goddess of Health) or the God Aesculapius (the God of Medicine). The choice is important. There are times when the choice is between care and cure for those who are ill and injured to-day versus expenditures to-day to avoid injury and illness both to-day and in the future. Expenditures on protection will reduce the amount of public money available for care and cure to-day, and much of the money spent on prevention will be spent in social systems other than health care.

There is a special need for protection of the mental health of children. Disturbed children become disturbed adults, who tend to require high levels of social support or may cost $52,000 per year in prison. On the other hand, children who are psychosocially stable become stable adults. Children who feel good about themselves become parents who respond well to parenthood and are most likely to raise stable children. Violence and disturbed behavior among children and youth is now pandemic with resultant costs in property damage, social support and law enforcement budgets, and these are only the monetary costs. It has been estimated that 6% of children and adolescents display clinical levels of socially unacceptable behavior. (Offord, D., Ontario, 1992)

The Canadian Mental Health Association has stated that the gifts to give young people are a sense of self worth, a repertoire of problem solving skills and connectedness with family and community. (CJPH Supplement 2, Nov/Dec 1988) Programs to support these goals are not cheap, but their payoff is likely to be greater than the payoff from many of the aggressive clinical habits routine in North American medicine.

There is renewed awareness that eliminating hazards or strengthening the ability of people to manage hazards plays a larger role in protecting and elevating health status than does treatment of disease and injury. This does not mean that health care is unimportant. It is desirable that health care react to the events and processes which shorten life and reduce its quality, but health care is a reactive system. Head injuries provide an example. The Hospital For Sick Children studied head injuries caused by bicycle accidents. It concluded that additional expenditures on ambulance services and medical care would have minimal effect. The hospital therefore designed a program to prevent accidents and to reduce head injuries when accidents did occur. The care and rehabilitation of head injury patients helps patients and families but smaller sums spent on prevention will bring greater social benefit.

Most primary prevention is not under the aegis of health care professionals or the health services network. Very few of our modern epidemics and pandemics (those things we would like, in the interest of our health, to prevent or control) can be prevented or controlled by our health care system. Health care professionals and institutions are unable to do much to prevent depression, isolation, fear, a poor self-image, unemployment, cancer, coronary heart disease, traffic accidents, suicide, addictions, family violence (and other forms of abuse), unreasonable expectations, accidents (at work, at home, on the highway or during recreation) or dangerous environments.

Responsibility for primary prevention rests primarily with programs and personnel who deal with the environments (all of them), with education, with job retraining, with law enforcement, with income redistribution, with transportation and all other areas of social and economic activity. The health services network remains responsible for immunization and a number of smaller primary prevention programs, but most of the responsibility for primary prevention rests outside of health care with either an individual, a family, a community, an employer or a government.

The conflict between prevention and response is not just a conflict between health care spending and other social spending. The same conflict exists within health care. Most of the problems seen by almost any health care professional are not life threatening nor are they usually a serious threat to health. Many of them are also preventable. When health care providers do not have the time to see everyone who might benefit how should their time be assigned? Should a high priority be assigned to the prevention of poor health and of injuries, or should attention be given to treatment. If the latter is chosen there may be little time left for those types of prevention which do fall within the domain of health care.

Where can society find the money for all of the desirable prevention programs that will improve the quality and length of life of present and future generations and which are not the responsibility of the Ministries of Health? One possible source is health care. The transfer of health care dollars to preventive activities in the fields of transportation, the environment, education, employment, and others is difficult for many health care users and providers to consider, but the option should be kept open.

If half of the inappropriate health care which is currently being delivered was stopped Quebec alone would save $1 billion or more per year. This is considerably more than the costs of a major antipollution program currently underway in that province. Nationally $5-10 billion could be made available annually for health protecting activities if a major portion of public expenditures on inappropriate health care or on health care of low cost-effectiveness could be avoided.

A second source of funds for increased attention to cost-effective prevention is the budgets of other government departments. If Health Impact Analysis is made a part of all policy analyses, that is, if the Healthy Public Policy concept is implemented, the spending of all governments and all departments may contribute more effectively to an improved health status for Canadians.

INDIVIDUAL HEALTH VS POPULATION HEALTH

Health care is usually of primary benefit to only one person at a time. The traditional medical model is based on the evaluation of individuals and the delivery of whatever services are considered to be appropriate for each person.

Some health care services, however, and many services provided outside of health care, do not identify the individuals they are protecting. This is the case with work safety legislation, divided highways, sewer and water systems, programs which protect the physical environment and income maintenance. The socio-political model of health maintenance emphasizes these collective tools.

The product of expenditures on one individual are usually easy to see, either in the form of activities or in terms of improved health. The product of the expenditures on population health is much less personal and may be difficult to see even when impact has been greater per dollar spent.

ACCESS ON THE BASIS OF RELATIVE NEED VS ABILITY TO PAY

There are several options along the spectrum from access on the basis of need to access on the basis of ability to pay. Access to health care based on ability to pay could apply to the entire population for all services, in which case the poor would receive very little care and the middle class would receive whatever they could afford. This model does not exist in a developed country.

Access can be publicly financed for low income persons (to a prescribed level of care, which can be minimal or excellent or anything in between), with access for all or some of the rest of the population being a personal responsibility. This is the United States pattern.

In another model everyone has access to health care from publicly financed outlets and they also may, if they choose and are able, purchase more health care with private funds. This is a common model, with the adequacy of the publicly financed system varying immensely from country to country. In Canada access to most publicly funded health care is good and the care is of good quality. In Israel the care is of good quality but access is not very convenient, and in many less developed countries neither the access nor the care is very good. When access to the publicly financed sources of care is difficult and/or the services are of questionable quality, persons with disposable income will regularly use that income to seek privately financed care.

EQUITY VS INEQUITY

Should only a limited number of people be served very well by publicly financed health care, or should all people be served to approximately the same level of adequacy? Policy choices determine whether there will be inequities based on age, the type of services needed, the productivity of the user, the type of provider involved or the ability of the consumer to pay part of the cost.

Policy makers regularly struggle with the fact that populations with a high level of access to publicly funded health care want to keep it, whereas populations with poor access to publicly funded care would like better access. The elderly are often a privileged group. In 1991 in six provinces the elderly, including the well-to-do elderly, received prescription drugs at no cost while the rest of the population who were not on social assistance had to buy their drugs. Some provinces have, since 1991, introduced user fees for the elderly or have reduced coverage in other ways, but the elderly tend to retain a higher degree of financial protection against drug costs than is granted to nonelderly persons.

In Ontario in 1991 there were approximately 3 million persons with no public or private drug insurance. Most of these were low income workers and their families. At the same time about one million seniors had very comprehensive first dollar coverage for a broad range of pharmaceuticals. User fees for the seniors who did not qualify for the federal Guaranteed Income Supplement would have generated enough savings to provide coverage for the entire uninsured population (assuming there would also be user fees for this uninsured population). The Ontario policy reflected a low priority for equity.

Persons with health care needs of similar importance may have quite different degrees of access to publicly funded services. In all provinces a middle income person who needs physician services receives them without direct cost, whereas a similar person who needs equally important and expensive dental care must pay for it from disposable income. Inequities may arise from supply rather than legislation. If the problem is chronic pain public support is theoretically available but there are few services, whereas if the problem is cancer or allergies there is easy access to highly specialized services.

Inequities can occur because of political sensitivity. Twenty-seven thousand abortions were performed in Ontario in 1986, but 5000 women had to go to free standing clinics in the United States and elsewhere and meet significant out of pocket expenses to receive an established and legal medical service. In addition, many patients faced delays which resulted in the abortion being performed later than was desirable.

Access to abortion is strongly supported by Canadians (Table 4.1) in every major sector of the population. The majority in favor of personal choice is approximately the same regardless of income class, occupation, community size, education, language, gender, age or employment sector. Private and rapid access to abortions should be more assured.

Table 4.1

	Tot	Atl	PQ	ON	MB	SK	AB	BC
SUPPORT FOR FREEDOM OF CHOICE (in percent)								
Agree	79	76	80	81	74	67	78	82
Disagree	16	18	17	15	17	25	19	13
Do not know	5	6	3	4	9	8	3	6
Environics Poll, June 1992								

Canadians who choose to receive their medical care from nontraditional therapists are also treated inequitably. Persons who prefer ethnic medicine must pay all practitioner and medication costs, whereas those who are willing to use western style health care pay much less, if anything. Those who use uninsured nonwestern and nontraditional care are likely to eventually begin to object to paying taxes to buy medical care for those who prefer, or are prepared to use, western medicine.

Inequities also arise from preferential treatment of some providers. Physicians are the most well protected. Almost every service they choose to provide is insured, including services which are also provided by chiropractors, midwives, nurse practitioners, physiotherapists, social workers, herbalists, psychologists, dietitians and counsellors. The services are often not insured when provided by the other professionals, and users quite logically seek the provider who can provide no-cost or low-cost access. This choice will often mean receiving services from a physician whether or not the physician is the most appropriate provider, is the least expensive one or is the one the consumer would prefer to use.

Inequities can be rooted in social class and consumer characteristics. Prevention programs, for example, often miss the highest risk persons because they are the most difficult to find. (Schabas, R., Ontario Medicine, Dec 1990) This applies to Pap smears (14% of eligible females in Ontario had, in 1990, never had a Pap smear, and many of these were females at high risk of cervical cancer), prenatal care, protection against AIDS, and hepatitis B immunization.

As provinces identify their high priority and low priority groups it is likely that not all jurisdictions will make the same choices. They will see equity differently. There are many populations who are likely to be treated differently in different provinces, including:

- babies under 1000 grams
- persons who have lost, or who never had, the characteristics which identify humans as different from other living organisms, and who will not recover these characteristics or develop them
- persons who are unable to be productive and who will not become so in the future, as with many of the elderly and the permanently severely physically or mentally handicapped
- couples unable to conceive
- persons able to afford to pay for their care
- persons who will not benefit from additional attempts to cure
- persons whose chosen lifestyle is responsible for their injuries or ill health such as smokers with lung cancer or emphysema, alcoholics with cirrhosis of the liver, drivers injured in accidents caused by them, person injured while not wearing their seat belts
- persons who contribute inadequately to their recovery from illness or injury.

UNLIMITED ACCESS TO PUBLICLY FUNDED HEALTH CARE REGARDLESS OF THE CAUSE OF THE NEED VS INCREASED USER OBLIGATIONS AS THE NEEDS/COSTS ARE INCREASINGLY SELF-GENERATED

The question is the degree to which there should be public funding of health care regardless of the extent to which lifestyle or other choices of the users caused the need for care. Should public funding be contingent, in whole or in part, on user cooperation and user efforts to avoid the costs? The decisions of individuals do affect how much health care they may need. Should public and/or private health care insurance plans reward users who protect their health and/or use health care wisely and frugally, and, conversely, penalize users who endanger their health or use health care inappropriately. Private life insurance rewards individuals who do not drink or smoke, and who exercise regularly. These individuals pay lower premiums. The same practices are in place in the car insurance industry.

To date the cause of ill health or injury has not been a factor in access to health care at public expense. Addicts or reckless drivers are given the same quality of care and the same relatively unlimited quantity of care as a newborn or the victim of reckless driving. Similarly, cooperation with health care regimens has seldom been a factor in access to health care. Cholesterol levels can, for example, be significantly lowered in most persons by changes in diet and lifestyle. If these lifestyle changes are not tried, or are not sustained, the patient may be advised to take long term medication to lower the cholesterol levels. Should a public drug plan pay for medication which reduces a risk which could have been avoided if the user had followed recommendations for a healthier personal lifestyle? Requiring patient compliance or cooperation as a condition for receipt of health care at public cost, or at complete public cost, would represent a major change in philosophy.

If user choices are to be a factor in determining access at public cost, then policy makers must identify the grounds for reduced public financing, and public advice will be needed. When resources for publicly funded health care were considered to be endless the impact of user decisions was not considered, but discussion may be desirable now.

There are a few instances in which consumer lifestyles and/or lack of compliance have altered access to publicly financed care. Some centres will not provide a liver transplant to someone who has said they will not make the lifestyle changes necessary for the transplant to be a success, and a stated intention to continue smoking may lower the access of a patient to coronary artery by-pass surgery. These decisions have been justified by the argument that the therapy will, because of patient choice, either not be successful, or will be less likely to be successful.

SANCTITY OF LIFE VS THE RIGHT TO DIE (WHOSE LIFE IS IT ANYWAY?)

This conflict has, in the last decade, been resolved. Patients may, when they are mentally and physically able to do so, choose to die. They may reject life saving health care or they may, if able, end their life. If physically unable to end their life, they cannot legally obtain assistance to implement their choice.

There are situations in which the wishes of the user are not known and will not be known in the future, the care required is expensive and potentially long term, and the quality of life of the consumer is considered to be low. What should be done? Relevant policy options include to write no policy. In this case providers may be obliged to sustain *life* indefinitely regardless of the knowledge that a positive outcome cannot occur. Policy may also define a hierarchy of agents who may rule on whether or not care at public cost is to be continued. Policy may also promote early identification of user wishes regarding therapy or the withholding of it.

WORKERS RIGHTS VS USERS RIGHTS

These rights come into conflict when the delivery of care places the worker at risk, as when dealing with psychopathic or emotionally disturbed persons or persons with AIDS or hepatitis B.

The conflict also exists when the volume of care to be delivered is greater than can be reasonably provided in the time available or with the equipment available, when the worker wishes to strike as a part of the collective bargaining process, or when the services required are incompatible with the religion or culture of the worker, as with abortion.

Issues include whether workers should have the right to refuse to work in the face of risk and whether religious beliefs take precedence over job descriptions. Policies can require worker protection but cannot always eliminate risk. Policies can also, if so desired, identify situations in which risk must be accepted as an inherent part of the job.

WORKERS INCOMES VS TAXPAYER PROTECTION

Issues inherent in the conflict between workers incomes and taxpayer protection include whether to promote affirmative action aimed at gender equity and the hiring of visible minorities, the relationship between salaries in the private versus the public sector, the extent to which historical income relationships are to be maintained, whether the incomes of professionals on FFS should be capped and whether professionals should be able to make a profit from services they order.

Incomes in female dominated occupations have not kept up to male dominated occupations. Policies to accomplish income equity are expensive when the technique is to bring everyone to the highest common denominators, as was discovered by Ontario in the early 1990s. Ontario made pay equity a priority in 1991, a policy which led to a 29% pay increase (over time) for nurses at a time when public sector pay increases were being held to approximately zero. There appear to be few if any examples of equity being accomplished through the lowering of some incomes and the raising of others, or the freezing of some incomes until payment to less advantaged workers catches up.

Incomes in the health care sector compare favorably to incomes of other equally educated and trained workers, and job security has been high although not complete. The health services sector has not faced the degree of job loss and income reduction that has occurred in much of the private sector, and taxpayers could be expected to believe that incomes in jobs which are fairly secure should fall more than incomes from more uncertain employment.

Significant income disparities exist within health care, with physicians being very much at the top. As public funds become more scarce every jurisdiction will have to decide whether to reduce or maintain the income disparities which have existed. Physicians will be the major losers if taxpayers are protected by bringing the average incomes of physicians closer to the incomes of other professionals working within the publicly funded system.

Professional regulations prevent physicians from receiving income from referrals for diagnostic services, eyeglasses and the equivalent. Chiropractors financially benefit from X-rays they prescribe, and this may be unavoidable until chiropractors are able to have their X-rays taken in medical and hospital X-ray departments. Optometrist relationships with providers of eyeglasses, and pharmacist relationships with drug manufacturers, are relatively unregulated.

PROTECTING EMPLOYMENT VS PROTECTING WORKER INCOME LEVELS

This issue, as with a number of other issues, is no different within health care than within other public and private employment sectors. It is an issue for employers, employees and health care users. Public sector employees have often accepted contracts with no wage and salary increases but seldom have accepted a negotiated decrease, whereas in the private sector wage roll-backs have been common among both unionized and nonunionized workers. Income reductions have been accepted in the private sector both to avoid layoffs and to avoid plant closures.

In times of decreasing public revenues and the need to restrain health care expenditures governments can choose to protect jobs or protect income levels. They cannot protect both without increasing either taxes or debt or both. Wage roll-backs are attractive in that they may avoid adding to unemployment while also avoiding reductions in levels of service. There is also the intermediate option of reducing incomes without lowering the base wage rates. Ontario and Manitoba used mandatory days of unpaid leave and other devices to reduce payroll costs without altering the wage and salary structure. In 1994, Alberta rolled back all public sector salaries and wages while also reducing public sector employment.

Selection of the expenditure targets which are to be reached through the use of income freezes or roll-backs is a policy decision which will vary with one's ideology, the state of the province's finances and the date of the next election.

PROTECTION OF CONSUMERS OF PRIVATELY FUNDED AS WELL AS PUBLICLY FUNDED HEALTH CARE VS PROTECTION ONLY WITHIN THE PUBLIC HEALTH CARE SYSTEM

Governments enact consumer protection legislation in many fields and are unlikely to ignore the protection of populations and individuals who are vulnerable because of ill health or injury. The issue is not whether to protect consumers, but how much to protect them, and against what. Should protection include price as well as quality?

Governments either set or influence the prices of the health care they pay for. To what extent should they protect the pocket books of other payers? In Ontario the province establishes the prices of drugs in its provincial formulary, and those prices are, by law, the prices which must be charged to persons who are not beneficiaries of the provincial plan. Governments could also require predelivery evaluation of the appropriateness of privately and publicly purchased elective health care.

Consumer protection in the private health care market could be the responsibility of a Ministry of Health or of whatever ministry is responsible for consumer protection in other service areas.

PRESERVE MEDICARE, IMPROVE IT, OR LET IT GO

Canadians love medicare. They heavily support collective rather than individual responsibility for health care costs. To the average Canadian the key characteristics of medicare (meaning hospital and physician services) are universality, comprehensive coverage, portability and accessibility (meaning no user fees). There are policy options with respect to each of these characteristics, although some provincial options will be largely unavailable so long as the *Canada Health Act* is in force and the federal government is prepared to apply financial penalties to provinces which offend the requirements of the *Act*.

There is a perception that Canadian medicare is comprehensive, but it is not. It covers only hospital care and physicians services. To be truly comprehensive (as is the British National Health Service) coverage would have to be extended to include drugs, dentistry, ambulance services, community health services, nontraditional health services and income maintenance. In the present fiscal climate publicly financed health care will not become more comprehensive. Most provinces are reducing coverage.

There is also a belief that health care is accessible in the sense that there are no financial obstructions to access, but this is also not true. Ability to pay is a substantial determinant of access to many health care services in all provinces, with the amount of private payment varying considerably among the provinces.

The concept of universality is strongly supported by the public, although the public has not voiced serious opposition to drug programs which cover only a part of the population or to special housing options for seriously disabled persons which have been available almost exclusively to only the nonelderly population.

Portability (guaranteed continued coverage for persons who move to another province) exists for most hospital care and most physician services. Public coverage of most other services is not uniform from province to province and therefore portability often cannot be assured.

With respect to administration the Canadian pattern conforms closely to the principle defined in the Medicare Act. The original federal-provincial cost sharing arrangements for hospital and physician insurance assured public administration of these programs. History had already assured that there would be public administration of public health and of institutional mental health services. Evolution has placed most home care under public or nonprofit administration. Community health services, dentistry, nontraditional health care, ambulance services, long term care institutions and a variety of specialty services have no uniform administrative pattern.

Public policy in each province will determine the future of publicly funded health care in that province, especially if the federal government abandons its role as a major funder. Public funding and public or private nonprofit administration will continue to be dominant in health care in Canada, but provincial policy choices will vary regarding which services will be fully or partially insured and under what conditions. Provincial policy choices will determine the degree of security which is to be provided by the social safety net, and will determine how dominant health care will be as part of that net.

RISKS IN HEALTH CARE VS RISKS ELSEWHERE

Canadians treat death quite casually so long as the death cannot be blamed on an imperfection in the health care system. They regularly report, but only modestly note, deaths on the job (800 per year), deaths on the highways (4000), drownings (700), deaths by fire (700) and suicides (3000). There is a very different reaction to a death while waiting for coronary by-pass surgery or while travelling an extra 15 minutes to an emergency department. It is unfair to spend a great deal of public money to try to save the life of someone already seriously ill or injured and at the same time fail to spend smaller sums to protect the lives of healthy individuals, but that is often our current practice.

Health care professionals and the public both demand very high levels of safety in health care. Illness and injury which are the product of carelessness, or of exposure to risks, in other social or economic systems, risks which could have been reduced by public spending, usually receive little public attention. After entry into the health care network, however, no risks are considered to be acceptable and no degree of failure is tolerated. There is an irrational ambivalence which caters to excessive spending on health care, and one of the policy options which governments should consider is the search for an acceptance by the public of risks in health care as well as everywhere else.

CONTROL BY USERS VERSUS PROVIDERS

Issues of control pertain to diagnosis, treatment, control of public funds and influence on policy. Diagnosis has, until recently, been almost exclusively the prerogative of physicians, dentists, chiropractors and optometrists. They were the only professionals legally authorized to diagnose and prescribe. Consumers became important diagnosticians when they began to take their own blood pressure and test their urine for sugar. Now blood sugar levels are tested routinely at home, pregnancy tests are performed either at the pharmacy or at home, and kits for the diagnosis of everything from strep throat to sexually transmitted diseases are either on the market (especially in the United States) or will soon be.

Federal policy will determine which diagnostic kits will be approved for over-the-counter sales throughout Canada. The manufacturers of the kits will press for their approval, and in this age of consumer responsibility it can be argued that individuals should decide whether or not to use them once a reasonable level of safety and accuracy exists. Few of the kits are 100% accurate, and professionals, led by physicians, will ask that the public be protected from the hazards of diagnostic error, but when evaluating public protection it will be sensible to note the frequency with which health care professionals misuse technology and miss a diagnosis. The hazards associated with direct public access to diagnostic aids should become tolerable as soon as they are no greater than the hazards associated with professional decision making.

Provinces do not have the constitutional authority to approve the sale of diagnostic kits, or to overrule federal approval, but they can decide whether to encourage or discourage use once a kit has been approved. Access to these kits will alter the use and cost of formal health care. If patients buy a diagnostic kit the patient is likely to have to bear the cost, whereas if the patient goes to a physician or other health care professional the costs of the diagnostic tests are likely to be borne by the public. If the patient sees a professional the patient will save money, but the public cost will have been expanded to include the test and a professional visit or visits. Provinces should encourage the most cost-effective option.

Fortunately Canada will have the advantage of observing events in the United States. Their experience will help us determine what is most consistent with our culture and with our wish to spend health care dollars wisely. Discussions of these policy choices should be open and continuous. If they are not it is likely that the professions will dominate and will preserve for themselves choices which should be also available to users.

Consumers became important in determining treatment when the principles of informed consent and user control were accepted. Neither is, as yet, fully implemented, but the principles are in place. Policy determines the extent to which users of long term care, for example, have control over the development of their care plan and the delivery of services. Research has shown that user priorities usually are quite different from those of providers; users are more likely to emphasize quality of life factors. When user priorities are implemented the mix of delivered services changes, but in most provinces professional choices still dominate when care delivery decisions are being made. Sweden allows clients to formulate the goals of chronic care, and their experience indicates that user control brings higher levels of user satisfaction and lower costs. (Fernow, N., "Swedish Elder Care in Transition", Current Sweden, The Swedish Institute, Nov 1992)

Delivery arrangements in which users control the money strengthen the ability of the users to see their priorities respected. The user control can be absolute (meaning the money is given to the consumer to spend) or anywhere along the spectrum to full provider control. In current practice the consumer usually has few if any financial tools with which to influence care.

Consumers, through opinion polls, community development processes or other participation options, can indicate what they would like the health care system to emphasize. They might, for example, indicate that user control and the opportunity for regional differences are desired. If these preferences are expressed and are acceptable to government then it becomes the responsibility of technocrats to devise systems which increase user control and the opportunity for regional pluralism. This process clearly increases the influence of users rather than professionals.

When the Ontario Premiers Council on Health Strategy went through a priority setting exercise in 1990/91 they gave highest priority to three policy areas; healthy child development, labour market adjustment and the environment (presumably the physical environment, but it could mean more). These choices were the product of an elitist process in which senior bureaucrats from many ministries ranked a series of options. Other more user dominated processes will be commonly used in the future. The general trend is towards greater respect for user priorities.

OPTIONS FOR RATIONING

If one accepts the proposition that there is not enough public wealth to afford all of the health care which providers wish to give and consumers are prepared to receive, then some form of rationing must occur. The main options are price versus nonprice rationing, and implicit versus explicit rationing. All rationing leads to some users receiving less health care at public expense than they would otherwise get.

Health care is price rationed when user ability to pay determines access. Health care which is not publicly financed is price rationed unless completely paid for by workers compensation or some other insurance, such as an employer financed plan under a collective bargaining agreement. A limited form of price rationing occurs when the user must make a limited direct payment, as with user fees.

When the user does not contribute to cost through payments at the time of service, rationing, if it is to occur, occurs through nonprice rationing devices. Common nonprice rationing devices include inconvenience, cultural insensitivity and limited availability.

Rationing which is not easily seen, which occurs when professional discretion determines who gets care, is *implicit rationing*. This form of rationing occurs when providers choose to serve some patients ahead of others, or to limit the amount of care that a user will receive. This is the form of rationing which occurs within global budgets. (Naylor, D. and A. Linton, "Allocation of Health Care Resources", CMAJ, Feb 18, 1986) Waiting lists are a form of implicit rationing. The desirable rules are *first on, first in*, with adaptation, when indicated, to conform to *worst off, first in*. These rules may be ignored when the prerogatives of physicians (who also are in queues for beds and operating space) take precedence over the needs of patients. Implicit rationing occurs when spaces are limited. In Alberta the government will pay for only 16 cochlear implants per year and a special committee chooses the adults and children who will receive the implant. (Ontario TV program, Sept 17 1993)

Rationing which openly identifies the kinds of services that will not be paid for with public funds has been referred to as *explicit rationing*. When governments chose to remove financial barriers to physician and hospital care and not insure dentistry or outpatient drugs there was explicit rationing of the use of drugs and dentists. In Oregon a public participation process was used to rank the importance of a broad range of health care services, and on the basis of this ranking some services were not offered within public funding. This also is explicit rationing.

Explicit macro level identification of which health care is to be fully or partially available at public cost (the explicit rationing decisions) should continue to be determined by public policy. Allocation decisions at the micro level, allocations currently made almost exclusively by health care workers, should more often be the product of user preferences and public policy, acting with the assistance of professional advice.

It is likely that all rationing devices will continue to be used in Canada, although if health care dollars are more effectively spent there may be, for at least a few years, no need to deny anyone access to health care of reasonable cost-effectiveness. At such time as the supply of public funds is inadequate to provide all health care of reasonable cost-effectiveness then it is to be hoped that Canada will opt for rationing on the basis of public priorities guided by cost-effectiveness. Rationing of cost-effective services for the ill and the injured should be no more or less strict than the rationing of a variety of other cost-effective publicly financed services also important to health.

OPTIONS RE ACCOUNTABILITY

Society and its policy makers can require accountability, or hope for it, or ignore it. Accountability, if required, may be of providers to users, providers to payers, providers to evaluators, users to payers, users to other users, payers to providers, and/or the recipients of delegated responsibility to those who delegated the responsibility.

Providers can be accountable to users for the quality and appropriateness of the services provided, for the confidentiality of information, for referral when indicated and for provision of information necessary for informed user choices. Users can be accountable to payers for participation in prevention and treatment. Providers should expect to be accountable to payers for responsible use of resources and for appropriate reporting and billing.

Users could be accountable to other users for responsible use of public dollars. Users may wish to be aware of the extent to which the choices of some users limit the access of others to health care. Payers are accountable to providers in the ways that all employers or contractual partners are accountable. Payers should be open and honest, encourage safe working environments and appreciate the rights of workers. Legislators and persons with executive powers are, or should, be accountable to consumers for equitable access to services, appropriate opportunities for appeals, opportunities for involvement in decisions and spending in accordance with regulations and goals.

Professionals will continue to be accountable to their professional bodies. Hospital boards should become more accountable to their communities. Professional leaders will be accountable to their constituencies and to taxpayers and users. Almost no-one will be accountable to only one group, person or task. Divided loyalties will be, as they always have been, the norm.

SUMMARY

The choices made with respect to the options described in this chapter will seldom affect the need for control of public spending on health care. There must be control or the costs of health care will overwhelm all governments. The choices made will also seldom change the amount of public money available for health care. That amount will be arbitrarily selected by governments. The choices will, however, certainly affect the way in which available dollars are spent.

Very few, if any, of the options can be considered in isolation. In the end policies will reflect the way a whole series of factors are seen, and no matter what choices are made there will be many who will say the choices are wrong.

Chapter 5

The Powers and Functions of the Major Players

INTRODUCTION

The major players are the consumers and their agents, the two senior levels of government, the Ministers and Ministries of Health, the nongovernmental policy makers, planners and administrators, the private for-profit sector, the researchers, the educators, the professional associations, the voluntary agencies and the international forces. Other players include local and regional governments, consultants, the pollsters and the media. Each player affects the way in which public dollars are spent on health care, and each can contribute to the wisdom with which the available dollars are spent.

THE ROLES OF ALL GOVERNMENTS

Although different levels of government have different functions in health care, there are some functions and responsibilities which belong to all governments.

Leadership

Health care leadership within the public sector can come from the politicians and the senior bureaucrats. Leadership can be charismatic or technocratic or both. It can be intellectual or emotional or both. It is best accepted if actions support rhetoric.

Governments should honor the themes and principles they ask others to accept, such as resource allocations on the basis of cost-effectiveness, user and community empowerment, reallocation of current funds rather than a search for new money for new tasks, no deficits and support for partnerships with users, communities, advocacy groups, providers, educational institutions, research funders and the private sector. Ministries should be accountable for spending less and spending smarter. They should be as accountable as, but no more accountable than, every other player in health care.

Governments should encourage creative and intellectual discussion and assure opportunities for productive rather than defensive thinking.

Leadership can be reinforced or impeded by organization. If better spending is desired strategic planning units which promote, coordinate, monitor and illustrate cost-effectiveness can help. In Britain the Department of Health has created a Clinical Outcomes Group to recommend ways to achieve greater cost-effectiveness. Such a unit sends the message to all players that better spending is not only an important governmental target but an area in which the government intends to provide leadership.

Leadership is also enhanced when leaders and their senior advisors possess the appropriate skills. Skills needed include those which support strategic planning, networking, joint decision making (partnerships), information dissemination, identification of community priorities and health impact analysis.

Financial control

The total level of public spending on health care is largely determined by cabinet, acting with the advice of the financial and technical experts within government (the Ministry of Finance, Department of Revenue, Treasury Board, the Ministry of Health), universities and private think-tanks. The players and processes vary from province to province. The cabinet decisions are authorized by, or are eventually legitimized by, the appropriate legislature.

The financial watch-dogs within government, whatever their name(s), estimate government revenue for the coming year (primarily taxes plus transfer payments), comment on how much new debt the province can stand, and give advice to the cabinet regarding the amount the province can afford to spend (revenue plus new debt). Once the total sum available to the government is known the cabinet can then allocate money to the various departments and agencies, including the Ministry of Health. These allocations are then approved by the legislature as part of the estimates.

The use of regulatory powers

Governments and some quasi-public bodies can limit funding, can require or prohibit certain actions, can establish priorities, can include or exclude selected costs from the health care allocation, can set standards, can determine what services will be insured and can directly intervene in the professional decisions of health care providers. All of these are accomplished through use of regulations. In the past, regulations which reduced the decision options available to physicians were introduced more commonly by hospitals than by Ministries of Health, but such central decisions are becoming more common.

Regulation is used at the federal, provincial, municipal and institutional/program level. Regulatory power is exercised through statutes and their regulations, orders-in-council, by-laws passed by the boards of agencies, institutions and local governments, and directives from the Minister of Health, ministry officials or others with the necessary authority.

Regulations are often inflexible and always top down. They reflect the constitutional power of provincial and federal governments, powers which can, within limits, be delegated to an agency such as a College of Physicians and Surgeons, a hospital board of trustees, a Minister or a lower level of government. The regulations with the widest impact in health care tend to be written by provincial governments, but in a specific situation the dominant regulations might be written by local boards, by municipal governments, by the federal government or by special purpose bodies to whom a government has delegated the necessary authority.

Regulations which place limits on spending may or may not be designed to also alter the way in which money is spent. Global budgets of many health care institutions and programs, for example, are a top down technique to control costs. They do not tell the institution or program, or the professionals who work there, how to treat individual patients, and they do not necessarily lead to better spending, but they do put a ceiling on expenditures.

Promotion of Healthy Public Policy

Only governments and public boards, councils and quasi-public agencies with executive powers can write public policy; only they can make it more healthy. Others can influence it, and should, and others can be essential to successful implementation of policies, but the dominant role of those who can actually approve policy is clear.

The World Health Organization (WHO) has stated that the first responsibility of every government is the health of its people, and that all governments should use all of the tools available to them to protect, improve and restore that health. Individual choices, including lifestyle choices, are important to health, but there has been increasing recognition that individuals have little or no control over many of the factors which are important to health. These factors can, however, almost always be influenced or controlled through public policy.

Public policy is a powerful tool for improvement of population health regardless of the level of wealth of the nation or community involved, as was demonstrated by changes in Cuba after the revolution. Failure to effectively use this tool has led to the failure of the United States to produce a national health status commensurate with its great national wealth. Appreciation of the importance of public policy to health status has led to adoption by many governments of the concept of Healthy Public Policy and has led to the endorsation by many local governments of the Healthy Communities theme.

Public policy affects almost everything which is of consequence to health, including safety at work, at home, on the highways and elsewhere, the quality and cost of what we eat, the distribution of wealth, consumer financial and other protection, the availability and quality of work and the access to and appropriateness of health care. Genetics is the only determinant of health status which is almost unaffected by public policy.

Public policy can have a positive or a negative influence on health. In 1992 a California earthquake measuring 7.4 on the Richter scale killed one person. The cost of disaster proof buildings, expressed as cost per year of life saved, is not known, but the buildings are partly a product of healthy public policy. The minimal loss of life is a tribute to the California construction standards (and to the wealth of America). (In other parts of the world where heavy roofs on mud-brick walls are standard residential construction there would have been thousands of deaths from an earthquake of this magnitude.)

The impact of public policy is also seen in the damage caused by tornadoes. Fifty to sixty percent of casualties from tornadoes in the United States are in trailer homes but only 5-15% of the population live in them. Public policy could require better built and better anchored trailer homes, and these would be safer, but public trade-offs demand that trailer homes be inexpensive to build and locate.

Seat belts, collapsible steering columns, collapsible front ends, power steering, air-bags, roll-bars and new braking systems have reduced highway accident volumes and reduced their sequelae, as has the dividing of highways, the separation of level railroad crossings and more attention to drunk drivers. The murder and mayhem on busy undivided highways between major Canadian centres such as Toronto and Montreal, Saskatoon and Regina, Calgary and Edmonton and Ottawa and Montreal ended suddenly when the highways were divided. Investments in seat belts and in the dividing of busy highways are investments in health, as are air traffic control systems and new vaccines or antibiotics. Most of these are the product of Healthy Public Policies.

The promotion of Health Impact Analysis (HIA)

HIA is the process by which the impact of policies on health status is estimated. This process is a prerequisite to the selection of health supporting decisions by agencies and individuals.

Policies under review in all governments are almost always assessed in terms of economic impact (employment, tax revenues), environmental impact (usually physical environment only), constitutionality and compatibility with existing legislation. There may also be assessment in terms of ethnocultural acceptability, impact on female issues and impact on other specific sectors or factors. The addition of health impact analysis would require examination of information regarding health effects (outcomes). The health impact information would be combined with the political, financial, cultural, economic, environmental and other data to allow a full policy analysis.

Health impact analyses are made difficult by deficiencies in information and skills. There is increasing acceptance by all levels of government of the influence of all departments, all budgets and all policies on health status, but few governments have extensive experience at estimating the impact on health of the many policy alternatives. Communities are being asked to become *Healthy Communities*, but inadequate information plus lack of skills make it difficult for communities and local governments to act. Employers have been asked, or instructed, to improve the safety of the workplace, but the necessary evaluations of action alternatives are often not yet done. Information is also important to individuals who wish to select lifestyles which promote good health. Selection of these healthy lifestyles is only possible when there is a documented and valid understanding of the impact of various lifestyles on health.

The most beneficial personal and collective decisions cannot be made if there has not been some estimation of the positive and negative impacts of the options. The task is immense, but there have been successes. Governments should assign resources and develop permanent organizational units to participate in refinement of Health Impact Analysis skills so that whatever information is available will be wisely and routinely used.

The marketing of health care change

All governments have the incentive, the resource control and the mandate needed to lead a public information and participation program in which everyone becomes aware of health care policy options, their implications and the role of the public in cost control and better spending. This marketing activity has barely begun. (See Chapter 17)

Removal of obstructions to better policy

One of the responsibilities of all governments and bureaucracies is to identify statutes and regulations which obstruct desirable change. Such legislation may have been on the books for decades. Examples include legislation which requires routine laboratory testing when testing is necessary in only selected situations, which places unnecessary limits on local discretion and prevents implementation of local priorities, which prevents governments from paying for only part of the cost of insured services or drugs, or which places limits on the use of a variety of health care professionals and prevents sensible reallocation of function.

THE FEDERAL GOVERNMENT

Federal roles are established by the constitution and are unlikely to change. Federal responsibility for the health care of all Canadians would require a major constitutional amendment, which is not about to happen. The provinces will retain full control over most health care regardless of its cost and problems.

Federal influence over national health status

The federal government has at various times developed strategies to stabilize and equalize the opportunities of Canadians. These strategies have affected employment, education, social services, health care, recreation and individual incomes. All of these federal initiatives have affected the health status of Canadians.

Income has been identified as a major determinant of health status. The federal government has stabilized incomes of individual Canadians through the old age pension, unemployment insurance, the Canada and Quebec Pension Plans, the Canada Assistance Plan, legislation increasing the portability of many private pensions, the family allowance program (now discontinued) and the tax rebate programs in which low income households receive rather than pay when their income tax forms are submitted. These income maintenance programs have contributed directly and significantly to the health of many Canadians. The federal government has also indirectly protected individual incomes through the use of provincial equalization payments.

The federal government has many other options for alteration of national health status. It could, for example, promote and implement health impact analysis of federal policies as part of its commitment to the concept of Healthy Public Policy. Problems of social pathology such as family violence, disturbed youths, suicide and addiction could be made part of a federal emphasis which would bring to these problems the kind of leadership shown 35 years ago when the national health care insurance programs were begun. Federal initiatives with respect to AIDS have shown that Health and Welfare Canada (now Health Canada) can respond to a modern epidemic. It remains for the same department to address epidemics of social as well as cellular pathology.

The federal Ministry of Health performs tasks which have a national impact and in which the federal government has been a leader. Examples include the Laboratory Centre for Disease Control, the national virology laboratory, the encouragement of health promotion, the compilation of national health and health care statistics and the funding of research. The list could, if the federal government wishes, become much more imaginative.

The federal government could expand already established activities aimed at assisting communities to understand the sources of health and ill health and act together to improve the length and quality of life. It could coordinate national examinations of delivery of care to specific high cost populations such as the dying. It could fund education and information programs needed to acquaint consumers with the rationale behind the control of the costs of health care, and with the potential for better spending. In addition, health and health care spending on aboriginal populations could show increased sensitivity and flexibility, which would be likely to increase the impact of federal spending on the health status of that population.

Federal reductions in contributions to provincial health care costs have unfortunately not been accompanied by federal identification of more constitutionally legitimate spending on health. In 1991 federal support for the Healthy Communities movement was largely eliminated, which may or may not be a signal of even greater federal withdrawal from an interest in national health status.

The federal government should become more interested in national standards of health and less interested in national standards for health care. Health inequities are much more important than health care inequities. Health inequities require attention to income, environments and lifestyles much more than health care.

Federal influence over provincial health care policy

Federal influence over provincial health care policies is currently being exercised largely through financial incentives and disincentives associated with three statutes and programs, the *Established Programs Financing* (EPF) legislation (1977), the *Canada Health Act* (1984) and the *Canada Assistance Plan* (1966).

The *EPF* provides funds to the provinces in partial replacement of the cost sharing associated with the original national hospital and medical care insurance legislation. The *Canada Health Act* demands provincial compliance with the principles spelled out in the 1966 *Medicare Act*.

The Canada Assistance Plan (CAP) is a cost sharing program in which the federal government shares in the costs of a number of provincial programs including some health care. Without this cost sharing there would be reduced provincial ability to provide selected long term care, rehabilitation, home care, welfare and other programs. In recent years the federal government has placed limits on CAP contributions to the three richest provinces, Alberta, British Columbia and Ontario. The CAP transfer increases were capped at 5% per year, an increase which barely began to acknowledge the increased provincial social assistance costs associated with the major recession. The CAP will be vigorously reexamined during the review of federal social programs which was begun in 1994. It is likely to undergo major changes.

Some of the currently most controversial options facing the federal government relate to the future of the *Canada Health Act*.

Policy options regarding the *Canada Health Act*

The *Act* could be left in force as is. The federal government would continue to financially penalize provinces which offend its principles. Preservation of the *Act* can be defended on the basis of public wish. There is widespread concern that the national program of universal and comprehensive coverage for hospital and physician services will fall apart if the provinces are not forced to honor the basic principles in the *Act*.

The *Act* could be repealed and not replaced by any other mechanism for federal control over provincial health care policy. There would be no federal penalties when provinces chose health care policies which differed from federal preference.

Federal funding of provincial hospital and physician costs is now shrinking and provincial autonomy is rising. Provincial health care differences are becoming more marked and more defensible. The provinces have constitutional jurisdiction over health care, and for reasons which can include culture, politics and provincial wealth a particular province may choose not to approach health care with the same priorities, organization, expenditures or philosophical preferences as other provinces. The appropriateness of national requirements for publicly financed provincial health care programs has been questioned by provinces and others.

The *Canada Health Act* can be seen to be flawed in that it gives special attention to minority determinants of health status. The *Act* obliges continued emphasis on hospital and physician services, services which, in terms of positive effects on population health status per dollar spent, do not merit the special status they have. This emphasis in the *Act* is inconsistent with the policy priorities expressed by most jurisdictions. The emphasis within health care is now on community services and on a broad network of independent professionals, and beyond health care the emphasis is (or should be) on the Healthy Public Policy concept.

The question of revisions to the *Canada Health Act* may be becoming academic. There has for the last 10 years been a steady and substantial reduction in direct federal contributions to health care costs. It has been estimated that cash transfers to Quebec in support of health care will, under the current payment restraints, end in 1995, with payments to all other provinces ending by 2002. (Rachlis, M., Healthbeat, Summer, 1991)

Canada does not have universal federally enforced standards for child day care, highway safety, occupational health and safety, environmental protection, nutrition or education but all of these are important to the health of Canadians. (Table 5.1) It is time to either abandon federal constraints over provincial health care policy, significantly revise the constraints, or apply similar federal constraints to other provincial policies relevant to health and partially financed through federal dollars.

The *Act* could be significantly amended. New terms and conditions could become the basis for federal rewards or penalties. These rewards and penalties to provinces could, for example, be tied to specified health status changes. There could be rewards or penalties for the attainment, or failure of attainment, of identified levels of improvement in a mix of health status indicators. The *Act*, as amended, could encourage provinces to seek federal funds through the implementation of provincial policies (in any department) which lead to more *"equitable access to the basic conditions which are necessary to achieve health for all Canadians"*. (Taken from the Mission Statement of the Canadian Public Health Association.) This option would emphasize the move from individual health status to population health status. It has been suggested that the federal government should give special attention to the health and the opportunities of children and leave care of adults to the provinces.

Table 5.1 compares a number of policy areas important to health. The comparison applies the principles protected by the *Canada Health Act* to the various policy areas. The table confirms the

Table 5.1

APPLICATION OF THE CANADA HEALTH ACT PRINCIPLES TO A MIX OF DETERMINANTS OF HEALTH

Across the country, is the service

	Universal*	Comprehensive+	Portable	Accessible**	Public admin.	Penalty for noncompliance
Hospitals	Yes	Yes	Yes	Yes	Yes	Yes
Physicians	Yes	Yes	Yes	Yes	Yes	Yes
Dentists	No	No	No	No	No	No
Home care	Yes	No	No	Partly	Partly	No
Long Term Care	Yes	Yes	No	No	Partly	No
Grades 1-12	Yes	Yes	Yes	Yes	Yes	No
Day care (children)	No	No	No	No	Partly	No
Police	Yes	Yes	Yes	Yes	Yes	No
Employment	No	No	No	No	Partly	No
Income support	Yes	No	Partly	–	Partly	No
Community Mental Health Services	Yes	No	No	No	Yes	No
Safe workplace	No	No	No	–	No	No
Road safety	No	No	–	–	Yes	No
Healthy physical environment	No	No	No	–	Partly	No
Healthy psycho-social env't	No	No	No	–	Partly	No
Housing	No	No	No	No	Partly	No
Adequate Quality of Life	No	No	No	No	No	No

*Meaning all persons are eligible to receive it at public expense
+Meaning all significant components of this service are included in the publicly funded services
**Meaning the services are available to those who need them with no direct charges at the time of service

special status of hospitals and physicians services. They are the only ones for which there are federal penalties when provincial policies do not meet federal preferences.

The demand for accessibility, portability, universality and comprehensiveness of publicly financed physician and hospital services coverage was justifiable when physicians and hospitals were considered to be the crucial components of health care and health care was considered to be the main determinant of health status. Both of these assumptions are now known to be incorrect. There is widening acceptance of the fact that the protection and improvement of health occurs mostly in the schools, workplaces, executive offices, communities, highways and homes of the nation, and that community health services, health promotion and primary prevention are less adequately funded than hospitals and doctors. In the light of these changes it is no longer rational for the federal government (through the *Canada Health Act* or any other device) to give special status to health care, let alone hospital and physicians services.

If the population of a province wishes the maintenance of medicare there is no need for federal rules. The residents of all provinces have universal primary and secondary education, and universal police protection, because the residents of all provinces wish these services to be universal. It would be reasonable and consistent to let the residents of each province decide the amounts and types of hospital and physician services which should be available to everyone without direct charge at the time of service. At the moment the residents of each province, through their elected provincial government, cannot, without risking federal penalties, decide that there should be limits to access to physician and hospital care at no direct cost. This is an unjustifiable limit on the opportunities of provincial governments and populations to exercise choice.

Licenses and patents

The issuing of licenses and patents for drugs and health care equipment, and the evaluation processes which precede and follow licensing, are federal responsibilities. Pre and post-marketing evaluation, and the standards for approval, have an impact on the costs, safety and quality of health care.

The federal Health Department also governs dangerous drugs. In 1992 a new *Act*, the *Psychoactive Substance Control Bill*, updated the controls formerly in the *Narcotic Control Act* and the *Food and Drugs Act*. This new legislation expanded controls over mood altering drugs including anabolic steroids.

The federal government could be more proactive when considering drug approvals. The use of RU-486, a drug which causes abortion, should be approved. Costs of abortion are reduced and user control is increased. The licensing and distribution of the drug should, if necessary, be under federal rather than company initiatives. Company concerns over boycotts should be recognized as legitimate but not be allowed to prevent rational use of a cost-effective product which increases the choices available to females who wish greater control over family planning. In 1992 the Society of Obstetricians and Gynecologists of Canada supported immediate testing and approval.

In France, where RU-486 has been in widespread use since 1989, and where women are routinely given the choice of RU-486 or a surgical abortion, two thirds choose RU-486. In Britain, where RU-486 was approved in 1991, 20% of females were choosing RU-486 within 6 months of its introduction.

THE PROVINCIAL GOVERNMENTS

Provinces have the authority to be as dominant as they wish in health care policy. Either by action or inaction they repeatedly determine who should or may do what, and to whom, and at whose cost. Provincial governments, if they wish, regulate data collection, data use, the evaluation of professional decisions, the form of regional planning, the availability of resources, the functions of agencies and professions and the disclosure of information to users. The payments to physicians and other health care professionals, and the professional choices they have, can be determined by, or affected by, provincial governments, subject only to constitutional limitations.

Thirty years ago governments provided money and the professionals, primarily the physicians, decided how to spend it. To-day provincial governments are major players, and often *the* major players, in determining how, and how much, health care money is spent, and where and on whom.

Provinces may be responsible for any or all aspects of health care, whatever is their wish, but they also may, if they wish, delegate functions and responsibilities to other agencies. Delegation can be to a special purpose body, a consumer group, a professional association, a local government or any other agency or group. Functions which have been delegated to a special purpose body include responsibility for licensing and assessment of members of a professional College, operation of a laboratory quality review program, defining standards for diagnostic and therapeutic facilities outside of a hospital and monitoring pharmacies to assure practices and prices which conform to legislation.

In the immediate future governments will need to decide the extent to which professional monitoring and evaluation are to be delegated to professional groups who wish to be in control of these activities. Both physicians and pharmacists, for example, wish to be responsible for province-wide drug use improvement programs. The best choice is likely to be the use of a process in which all players (professionals, consumers and government) are active participants. The pattern should be multi-party cooperation rather than delegation to only one party.

The role of the premier and cabinet

The cabinet makes decisions about raising money and spending it. Ministers, including the Minister of Health, are, as with health care providers, people who spend money which is raised by others.

Provincial premiers and their cabinets dominate in the preparation of all provincial policy. Until a decade ago most of them would have felt that health policy was being discussed only when health care was being discussed, but now it should be hoped that all have accepted all of their policies as *health* policies. *Health care* policies are amongst those *health* policies.

In 1989, on the advice of the Ontario Health Review Panel (Evans Commission) Ontario established the Premier's Council on Health Strategy, later renamed (by a succeeding government, in keeping with the idea that no previous government ever does anything quite right) the Premier's Council on Health, Well-being and Social Justice. The establishment and continuation of this committee, with the Premier as Chairman, acknowledged the Healthy Public Policy proposition that the first responsibility of all governments is the health of their people, and that in the search for optimal health each government should use all of the departments and tools at its disposal. Other provinces have since established similar committees.

The role of the Minister of Health

The role of the Minister of Health is to manage public expenditures on health care and be responsible for legislation and activities pertaining to both public and private health care.

The definition of what services are health care, and therefore within the purview of the Minister of Health, is not easy, nor is definition necessary. There appears to be no pay off in arguing about whether marriage counselling, the teaching of cardio-pulmonary resuscitation (CPR) or the delivery of Meals-on-Wheels or geriatric day care should be considered part of health care. Every province will do as it pleases or as history dictates. Having said this, it is fair to note that there has at times been a tendency to move activities into the domain of the Ministry of Health merely because they were of consequence to those who are sick or may become sick. This is usually a mistake.

The primary functions of Ministries of Health are the regulation, provision or purchase of health care for the sick and injured and the protection of health when that protection can be delivered best by traditional health care workers. Ministries of Health are not well equipped to be responsible for transportation, employment, housing, job safety, education (including special education), lifestyle modification or general support in the home. These functions are best left to departments whose areas of expertise are transportation, employment, housing, labor, education, and social services. Ministries of Health should oppose attempts by providers of health care, especially hospitals, to deliver an expanding array of community services merely because they are publicly funded and have a relationship to health status.

Ministers of Health are responsible for the allocation (budget, or envelope) of the Ministry of Health (or equivalent — not all provinces use the title Ministry of Health). Once this allocation has been determined by cabinet, the distribution of that allocation to various health care sectors and programs is made by the Minister of Health within instructions from the Cabinet and as detailed in the estimates.

Distribution of the budget of the Ministry of Health to the various health care sectors (public health, hospitals, physicians services, emergency health services, mental health, community health, long term care) is largely predetermined for any given year. Most of the available funds are required for the continuation of established programs. These programs cannot usually be altered quickly. When money is scarce very few new programs, if any, are established. `Them that has, keeps'.

Besides the funding of established and new programs the Ministry of Health must be prepared for unanticipated demands. The Ministry must retain contingency funds with which to respond to unforeseen and unavoidable expenditures. In past decades Ministries of Health assumed that additional funds (supplementary estimates) would be made available to respond to what was not planned for, but the Ministers of Finance of to-day have very limited ability to produce additional funds for any department. Every Ministry of Health should, therefore, be prepared to finance, from the original ministry allocation, the costs of an unpredictable epidemic, disaster or cost increase. Each program or sector within the Ministry should also, for the same purposes, retain contingency funds within their budgetary allottment.

Fiscal realities in all provinces, and in Ottawa, have altered the criteria for a good health minister. It now is at least as important to be able to hold the line on spending as it is to keep everyone happy. The current shortage of money is not temporary. Even if government revenues increase as the economy improves the new money is unlikely to be spent on health care. New money, if any becomes available to government, should go towards reducing deficits and expanding expenditures in areas other than health care.

Provincial Ministers and Ministries of Health are responsible for a long list of statutes including those governing the health care professions. These statutes determine the degree of self governance and the activities which are legal. They change over time, as illustrated by changes in the roles of chiropractors, denturists, and midwives, and by the altered mechanisms for disciplining professionals.

The province as paymaster vs planner vs manager of the system

In the 1988-89 Annual Report of the Ontario Ministry of Health Dr. Martin Barkin, Deputy Minister, wrote as follows:

"During the 1960s and the 1970s the focus (of the Ministry of Health) was on funding doctors, hospitals and an expanding array of programs. But now the economic pressures of the 1980s and the demographic projections of the 1990s demand that we manage the system. This means we must provide more imaginative leadership, establish goals, achieve measurable improvements in the health status of our citizens and ensure that standards of care are maintained."

This was not a declaration of a dictatorship in which the Ministry would rule. It did mean that the Ministry would no longer fully delegate to any other party full responsibility for the operation of, the cost-effectiveness of, or the measurement of the cost-effectiveness of, health care.

The term *manage* when referring to provincial roles in health care may be a misnomer. It does not infer a provincial wish to administer the sources of health care. It refers instead to a wish by Ministries of Health to have a greater and more direct influence over the way services are delivered. It means an extension of the intrusion of politicians and public servants into the delivery and local organization of health care. These extensions are not new trends, they are merely the continuation of previously established trends.

Changes in provincial government roles are shown in Figure 5.1. Many of the changes are substantial, and some completely reverse a former position. Managing the system, for example, is very different from merely financing it. To question professional practice patterns and be prepared to change them is a complete rejection of the historical sanctity of professional freedom. New partnerships between Ministries of Health and providers are a major departure from past practice.

Ministry dominance vs partnerships and delegation

Policy makers can, as a matter of principle or ideology, favor centralization of the financing, planning, evaluation, administration and information systems of all, or of major sectors, of the health care network. On the other hand, governments may, if they so wish, opt for decentralization to a greater or lesser degree.

The common practice of expecting the public service and the politicians to provide the ideas and the leadership, and then to be criticized endlessly by the field, was never productive and is now a recipe for substandard care and spending. The field has many more professional leaders, has higher incomes, has vast experience and has a direct opportunity to alter care. Health services must now compete with other sectors for public money and they must provide necessary care with steadily shrinking resources. Success will require all of the talents of both the field and the Ministries of Health.

Shared responsibility is the desirable and contemporary way to make many health care decisions. It is particularly necessary when dollars are scarce and when better spending is the goal. Planning decisions should usually be the responsibility of a mix of politicians, other representatives of the public, planning and administrative professionals and health care professionals. Decisions about the care, protection or diagnostic investigation of individuals should reflect user choices made with professional help and be within relevant local, program and/or provincial policies.

The limited manpower and experience of government must be supplemented by and supported by, and at times led by, the immensely greater numbers and experience of policy makers and care providers in the field. There is a tendency for the field to be reactive rather than proactive, or to be proactive but only with ideas which are dominated by self-interest and which are unacceptable to other players. Leaders in the field need to accept new roles in public service, roles which will frequently require a greater willingness to see the larger picture.

Figure 5.1

THE CHANGING ROLE OF PROVINCIAL GOVERNMENTS

FROM	TO
Insurance company	Planner, manager and funder
Financial protection of patients	Quality protection as well as financial protection
Open ended spending (1960s)	Control of spending (1990s)
Professional decisions unquestioned	Professional discretion limited by public policy
Health care as the top priority	Health status as the top priority
Health status protected by the `Health' department	Health status protected by all departments
Emphasis on hospitals and doctors	Emphasis on community care and health promotion
Support for the medical model	Abandonment of the medical model
Sickness policy	Health policy
A bureaucratic authoritarian Ministry	Partnerships with consumers and providers
Everything for everybody	What can be afforded

The political and public service leaders, for their part, must stop trying to solve every problem with a new regulation. They must work more with the field. In Ontario there was in the late 1980s and early 1990s a four year public consultation process leading to reform of the long term care system. A number of general directions emerged from the public consultation, but the partnership approach then largely ceased. The Ministry proceeded to produce numerous long and cumbersome documents describing relationships and organizations which should have been developed in partnership with the agencies and regions who had to implement the plan.

The province needs partnerships not only with users and health care professionals but also with regional and local planners and administrators. These local and regional decision makers do not just control resources. They have many years of cost control experience and, especially in the teaching hospitals, have tested many approaches to greater value-for-money.

Better spending can be promoted by the province or be left to the initiative of others. If a province chooses to promote better spending there are several organizational options from which to choose. Promotion can be centralized within a ministry, centralized within some legislatively created body such as the College of Physicians and Surgeons, centralized within a private nonprofit agency such as a Public Health Association, a professional association or a consumer association, decentralized to regional or municipal government or decentralized to regional or district agencies. Decentralized functions will usually be carried out within provincial guidelines and with ongoing provincial support and surveillance.

Government can, and should, provide leadership, encouragement and resources to promote partnerships both in the field and between the province and the field. Partnerships are desirable because they use the wisdom of many different players, they promote sharing of experience and information, the solutions will be better, the field is more likely to willingly implement solutions which it helped identify than solutions imposed from the top, and win-win situations are more likely to be found. Partnerships create the equivalent to self-help groups in which people and agencies with similar problems support each other as the problems are tackled. The formalization of the partnerships between physicians and ministries (through such vehicles as Joint Management Committees) has been described as a great improvement over the former unstructured guerilla warfare. (Evans, R., Journal of Health Politics, Policy and the Law, 1990, 15(1):101-128)

Limits on the professional discretion of physicians and other health care workers should be the product of multiparty discussions. Current provincial limitations vary from alterations in the list of insured services (which does not in theory restrict professional choices but which in practice affects them significantly) to direct government examination of professional decisions and outcomes and direct intervention when desired. Governments must select the extent to which they intend to dominate, participate in or delegate an immense array of evaluative functions including interpretation of data, assessment of practice profiles, development of, or adoption of, clinical practice guidelines, and evaluation of billing patterns.

There are a number of vehicles for multiparty participation. Professions can be represented on committees which operate within the structure of the ministry, such as drug evaluation committees. This example is toward the central or government end of the spectrum. The professional representatives can be appointed by the Minister on ministry advice, appointed by the Minister with the advice of the body to be represented, or named by the profession, but in all instances the committee and its activities are within the ministry structure.

Professions and Ministries can be represented on joint bodies such as the physician/government Joint Management Committees that exist in several provinces. The mandates and memberships of these committees vary but the objective is to allow physicians, through their provincial medical associations, to participate more fully in policy development. Similar committees have been established with hospital associations. These committees represent an extension of the long standing practice of regular meetings by Ministers of Health with hospital, medical, nursing and other health care associations.

LEGAL ISSUES ASSOCIATED WITH
CUT-BACKS AND GREATER VALUE-FOR-MONEY

There is concern in the health care professions, in particular by physicians, that reduced investigation, treatment or protection of patients will lead to charges of negligence. Governments can respond to these concerns by assisting in the creation of professional consensus on the limitations on service, and at times specifically requiring specified patterns of care when that care is at public expense.

Concerns also arise from increased monitoring of practice patterns. Peer review of the quality of the professional decisions of colleagues will be more open and useful if there is assurance that opinions will be confidential in most circumstances. Governments should work with the professions to protect both those doing the evaluating and those being evaluated. Improvements in the quality of care could be jeopardized by lack of protection of those who are participating in the review and improvement processes. These defence mechanisms are routinely built into legislation requiring the release of patient information by providers of care.

THE PUBLIC SERVANTS

Public servants are major players in health care, as they are in all social services and all public sectors. They advise governments, prepare statutes and regulations and convert the general instructions of Ministers and legislatures into programs. They manage programs and deliver services. They directly and massively affect and create policy.

As monitors of activities in the field, and as writers of rules which others must follow, they can assist with or interfere with the activities of providers of service. They can, and often have, demanded levels of performance from the field which exceed the levels of performance met or demanded in their own world. They can fail, and often have failed, to master new skills such as those required for public participation, participatory decision making and trade-offs based on impact per dollar spent.

THE PRIVATE FOR-PROFIT SECTOR

There is little support in Canada for a health care system which is entirely in either the public or private sector. The free market option is not acceptable to Canadians, but neither is complete government funding, planning, administration and delivery of health care. A mixed system is therefore inevitable and it is the nature of the mix which is to be decided by each province.

When considering roles for the private for-profit sector there must be acceptance of the need for profit if this sector is to be involved. The requirement therefore is to identify the situations in which profit is possible and is also acceptable to the public and the government of the day.

The private for-profit sector can participate in the financing, administration and/or delivery of health care. It can be a source of capital, a contract manager, an insurer, a deliverer of health care services or a provider of hotel or other non-health care services. It can be part of an integrated or coordinated public/private system or operate quite independently of the public system. It can provide the same services as the public system (a second tier) or provide only services not offered by the public system (as is the current situation with respect to hospital and physician services).

Private capital

Private capital has been used in a variety of lease-back arrangements in which there is private purchase of radiology or other expensive hospital equipment or facilities and the equipment or facilities are then leased back to the hospital for an annual fee. These arrangements were welcomed in some provinces and fully rejected in others. Private capital was a factor in private management arrangements in Hawkesbury, Wetaskiwin and elsewhere. Access to capital may be tied to contract management. The private management option appears to have lost favour and is likely to be of even less importance in the future.

Private housing capital has been used to assist young disabled persons to remain in their own accommodation while receiving institutional levels of care twenty four hours a day. The health care and support services are provided by a publicly financed program based within, or adjacent to, the privately financed and privately owned residential spaces. The users and their families remain together in accommodation they control. User control over service delivery is increased and public sector costs are lowered by the use of private housing capital. To justify the twenty four hour on-site service the residential units are aggregated into groups, usually of at least ten units. Private capital is also commonly used for group homes which operate with public global budgets. To date, the model of public/private cooperation has unfortunately not been widely used to serve the elderly disabled who require institutional levels of care and who could, with appropriate support, receive their care in private but aggregated units.

Private sector insurance programs can protect public funds, and this can be done without losing the universality which is so important to Canadians. On the other hand, private sector withdrawal from the financing of health care can increase pressures on the public system. A survey conducted in late 1992 found that over half of Canadian employers wish to reduce their contributions to employee health care benefits such as drug programs, dental care and supplementary health care. If these reductions occur there will be new pressure on governments to fill the gaps. (Ottawa Citizen, Nov 28. 1992, survey done by Foster Higgins, Consultants)

For-profit service delivery

The private sector provides many community based services such as home care, ambulance services, laboratory services, pharmacy services and consulting, and also operates long term care facilities.

The role of private for-profit agencies in home care varies greatly among provinces. Ontario is a major user of for-profit agencies with as much as 50% of home care being provided by them, but in 1993 the government announced that the percentage would be reduced to 10%. The preference for nonprofit management of home care agencies can be defended. Nonprofit agencies have the objective of community service and have been shown to do a better job of equitably distributing scarce resources than do profit based agencies.

Through Workers Compensation Boards, which are quasi-public agencies, the private sector finances health care for injuries and illnesses arising from employment. The costs of this health care and related income maintenance and pensions have grown quickly and some countries have begun to implement measures for control of costs and of abuse. (Huber, E. and J.D. Stephens, "The Swedish Welfare State at the Crossroads", The Swedish Institute, Jan 1993) Control devices include waiting days before sick pay begins, lower income replacement rates and altered rules regarding pensions and pension continuance.

Private industries often operate their own occupational health services. These are well developed in many larger firms, but largely absent in smaller enterprises. There appears to be a role for public/private cooperation in the development of cooperative or regional programs which would bring basic occupational health services and protection to all workers.

For-profit weaknesses and strengths

There are things the private sector does not always do well. They sometimes do not appreciate the inevitability of government regulation, appreciate the complexity of public sector decision making (which is often much more complex than private sector decision making), defend the public interest, appreciate the presence in the public sector of many people with skill, intelligence and commitment, and differentiate between private ownership and free market competition. Profit seeking providers often are paid on fee-for-service; there is no price competition. When competition does not affect price or quality the basic components of free enterprise are missing. Private ownership does not automatically bring competition, and without competition there is no reason to believe private ownership brings benefits.

The argument most commonly put forward in support of private sector involvement is that the private sector can do things more efficiently and less expensively than the public or the private nonprofit sector. This argument is only valid when there is competition which is helpful to the buyer and/or the consumer.

Hospitals operated for profit represent a policy alternative for Canada but not one that will be seriously considered until a second tier of hospital care is approved. Profit hospitals do not provide care any more efficiently, or with greater public benefit, than do nonprofit institutions, and they definitely distort service delivery patterns. They siphon off high revenue patients and vigorously avoid providing care to patient populations who are a financial risk.

Privatization has become a buzz-word in the 1990s. It is seen by some as the cure for all ills and by others as the cause of them. It is neither. Private sector health care has both strengths and weaknesses. It is characterized by an ability to stay within budget, seize opportunities, pay workers less and manipulate services and users to optimize profit. In its first report on health care in 1993 the World Bank expressed concerns about the ability of the private for-profit market to deliver cost-effective health care.

THE PRIVATE NONPROFIT SECTOR

Within the private nonprofit sector there are agencies which raise money, fund research, administer health care programs and institutions, license professionals, evaluate health care, collect and analyze data, operate educational programs and advocate for various causes and populations. There are also national or provincial umbrella organizations which coordinate local or provincial organizations.

The hundreds of boards, councils, associations, community groups, advocacy groups and special purpose bodies in the private nonprofit sector both write policy and dominate those who do. Special purpose bodies include professional colleges, regional planning agencies and Workers Compensation Boards, and community boards include those responsible for hospitals, CHCs, and community mental health programs.

Hospitals and their boards were at one time dominant in the health care network. They had the highest priced help, the biggest budgets and the ear of everyone. They still have the high priced help and the big budgets, but their position is less dominant. Their position has been weakened by a shift in emphasis to community based care, but hospitals have also weakened their own position by believing they are the hub of the health care system rather than an important link in the health care chain. Hospitals have squandered precious staff and trustee time and energy trying to be major players in such areas as health promotion, long term care and mass screening, and in trying to find new money instead of concentrating on spending the available money as wisely as possible.

Private nonprofit administration (by Blue Cross Life Insurance Co. of Canada) has been chosen by New Brunswick, Newfoundland and the Department of Veterans Affairs for management of drug and other programs.

TRUSTEE FUNCTIONS

Trustees of hospitals were historically concerned primarily with the financial viability of their institution or program and with being certain that resources were available for physician use.

Trustees raised money and arranged for the delivery of services chosen by physicians. Boards are now responsible for priorities, resource allocation, participation in regional networks and the appropriateness of clinical decisions. These new responsibilities mirror the new roles being assumed by provincial governments as they move to management of the system rather than merely the funding of it.

Hospital trustees should decrease their attention to financial matters, stop trying to find more money, and concentrate on being certain that the community is being as well served as possible with whatever money and other resources are available. Emphasis should be on such things as being certain that the clinical and administrative decisions are consistent with current knowledge, that the institution is contributing appropriately to the regional network of services, that there is proof that funds are being spent cost-effectively (that the budget can be defended if necessary), that the community is aware of and involved in priority setting and that services are offered in ways which are culturally sensitive and in accord with the values of the community.

Boards of some other agencies should also be giving attention to new tasks. Boards of Community Health Centres in most provinces should be examining the place of their institutions in the networks which will dominate in the future and be planning for the day when all funders will ask for proof that money is producing positive effects on health status. To the extent boards in the publicly funded private nonprofit sector are inadequately preparing for the future the blame must rest largely with their senior staff. It is quite unfair to be very critical of the part-time and unpaid board members.

The trustees of voluntary agencies, such as the Cancer Society and the Canadian Red Cross, also have important roles and considerable power. The Cancer Society finds its power in its cause and its supporters. The Canadian Red Cross has an important role because of the importance of services it controls, especially the blood transfusion service. For many voluntary agencies, power and role are as great as the fervor and size of their supporters, which can be considerable, as demonstrated by the success with which the Alzheimer's society and the advocates for the physically disabled changed public and government perceptions, policies and spending.

Nonprofit agencies and groups will continue to be major players in the planning, delivery, evaluation and evolution of Canadian health care.

THE REGULATION OF HEALTH PROFESSIONALS

The *Regulated Health Professions Act* (RHPA), and related *Acts*, in Ontario represents one policy choice as governments redefine professional relationships, functions and independence. The RHPA identifies thirteen *controlled acts*. Each profession is only authorized to perform those acts which are included in its scope of practice. Activities which are not controlled acts can be performed by anyone. Some controlled acts are the reserved domain of a single profession; others are approved for more than one professional group. Physicians are authorized to perform all controlled acts except dentistry. The new *Acts* expand the independence of a number of professionals and make it more likely that many professionals will be given new functions and greater authority in the future.

The professions with their own legislation in Ontario are audiologists and speech-language pathologists, chiropodists and podiatrists, chiropractors, dental technicians, dental hygienists, dentists, denture therapists, dietitians, massage therapists, medical laboratory technologists, midwives, naturopaths, nurses and nursing assistants, occupational therapists, ophthalmic dispensers, optometrists, osteopathic and allopathic physicians, physiotherapists, psychologists, radiological technicians and respiratory technologists. The new act gives full physician status to osteopathic physicians.

The *Acts* establish a mechanism (a committee) through which professions can seek revisions to their powers and roles. This Committee is an agent of the Ministry of Health, not of the medical profession, and therefore as of January 1994 physicians do not control the allocation of new functions or powers to other health care professionals. As an agent of the Ministry of Health the Committee will operate in a political rather than a physician dominated atmosphere.

The new procedures for defining the appropriate range of practice of health care professionals will be much more likely to expand the area of legal practice of nonphysicians than the old process which was under the control of physicians. Ambulance attendants, for example, will surely seek the right to perform defibrillation and use life saving drugs without physician approval, and although physician advice will play an important role in determining what changes will take place (physicians may even support the changes) the changes themselves will be the product of a public policy process rather than the former physician controlled process.

The new legislation replaces many former statutes, including the *Act* which established the supremacy of physicians and gave them a monopoly on the *practice of medicine*. Diagnosis (within the medical hierarchy) is no longer the sole prerogative of physicians. Nonacceptance by physicians (as was the case with midwives) was a serious obstacle when the right to practice medicine, and the power to decide what other health care professionals should be allowed to do, were physician prerogatives. The exclusivity of the franchise has ended. The new legislation increases the ability of the provinces to manage the health care system, to provide new options for care delivery through professions not on fee-for-service and to promote new partnerships and teams for the delivery of cost-effective care.

Physicians routinely use the argument that expanding the roles of other professionals will be a threat to the public, but the quality of physician decisions has now been sufficiently examined to suggest that many other professionals will do at least as well. All independent health care professionals (including physicians) will, as described in other paragraphs, be subject to evaluation by outsiders, and all will be obliged to routinely seek and accept patient choices.

Physicians will remain more powerful than any other health care profession, but they will, in the future to a greater extent than is now the case, share their former leadership position with nurse practitioners, midwives, physiotherapists, specialist clinical nurses, other nurses, chiropodists and podiatrists, nontraditional therapists, social workers and others.

The professional autonomy of physicians providing care in hospitals, including their opportunity for use of professional discretion, has been steadily decreasing and this decrease is continuing. Canadian hospital law is coming close to American law in the degree to which hospitals are being held responsible for the actions of physicians on staff. As the hospital becomes more liable for physician decisions it also becomes more anxious that those decisions be appropriate. It has been postulated that hospitals may become the major *"mechanism for the control of the medical profession in the 1990s and beyond"*. (Rozovsky, L.E. and F.A. Rozovsky, "Taking Control: Doctors versus Everybody", Physicians Management Manual, Feb 1992, p71-73)

MANAGERS OUTSIDE THE PUBLIC SERVICE

Managers and planners outside the public service, especially those in the private nonprofit sector, are the largest pool of skilled health care executives and planners. Their roles include advising trustees and governments and implementing programs which reflect the directions chosen by higher level policy makers.

These private nonprofit sector leaders are largely responsible for the skill with which health care dollars are spent and are most eligible for criticism when those dollars are poorly spent. They are the leaders, decision makers, evaluators and watch dogs on whom the community, the community boards and the government must rely for optimal service with the resources which are available. These persons have often not provided leadership commensurate with their position and their presumed skill, especially collectively. This in no way diminishes the responsible and intellectual way in which many individuals have promoted and implemented innovative approaches to many challenges including living with cut-backs.

THE ROLES OF MUNICIPAL GOVERNMENTS IN HEALTH CARE

The responsibilities and authority of local and regional governments are as defined by a provincial legislature. Local government rights and functions are not enshrined in the constitution.

Public health services in major cities in western Canada have historically been a department within the city government, and this pattern remained even after services outside of major centres became a responsibility of the provincial governments. In Ontario in recent years in a few major urban centres the public health function has been moved from an appointed Public Health Unit board to a regional government.

In the decades after the first world war both rural and urban local governments in western Canada played major roles in the development of municipal doctor services and of municipal hospitals, and in a few municipalities the hospitals remain under municipal management. Municipalities have commonly, in those provinces in which hospital construction costs are not fully provincially funded, contributed money towards hospital capital costs.

Prior to the appearance of more standardized and provincially funded ambulance services municipalities were often involved in maintaining these services. Municipalities and regions are often assured representation on health planning and management boards and councils. Municipalities in some provinces fund a few minor health services to persons requiring social assistance.

Functions assigned to municipal governments should not be greater than can be competently and reasonably cost-effectively performed with the population and economic base of the municipality. The boundaries of the municipality(ies) should reasonably approximate a service area for services being considered, for example, it may be more reasonable to place a function in a regional government than in each of the internal municipalities (where internal municipalities exist). Social services are in some provinces already locally managed, and creation of separate special purpose bodies to manage regional health care facilities and programs is not as defensible as placing the management of these programs within municipal government (when the geographic base of the municipal government is appropriate).

THE RESEARCHERS

Persons performing significant nonclinical health care research number in the tens rather than the hundreds. The impact of the few has been great, but the army is too small. Unless public policy decisions expand this group Canada will not move quickly to improve professional decisions, public policies and the quality of our spending.

THE INTERNATIONAL FORCES

International forces affect Canadian health care directly and indirectly. Indirect influence comes primarily from the manner in which international financial and industrial forces affect national, provincial and personal wealth. Direct effects can also occur, as when international pressure promoted extension of drug patent protection to 20 years.

The manner and speed with which health care in the United States is altered will have an effect on Canada. The United States has an even greater oversupply of physicians than Canada, and if the United States system evolves in a fashion which reduces expenditures on physicians services the United States will be less attractive to Canadian physicians and some physicians south of the border may wish to come to Canada.

Information from many countries will be important to us, especially information regarding the relative usefulness of a broad spectrum of health care. Hopefully research and experience from the broader global village will not only tell us what decisions should be made, but how to replace inappropriate care with appropriate care.

WHAT EACH OF THE PLAYERS SHOULD DO FOR THE OTHERS

Health care is a very interactive system. Defensive isolationism combined with blaming everyone else for all problems was counterproductive when money was abundant. Now it is suicidal and certainly not in the public's interest. Every player now has responsibilities to other players, and every player has the right to expect certain support and action from other players.

Publicly funded agencies have the right to expect knowledge of next years budget from government well before the fiscal year begins. They should expect policies to be developed cooperatively. Public servants should have a reasonable understanding of the workings of relevant programs in the field. Public servants should also be willing either to involve affected parties in the development of solutions for problems in the field or be willing to leave the field to find tested or innovative solutions, and without unreasonable public policy obstructions.

The field is entitled to adequate time to prepare a response when field advice is sought, to assistance with the development and use of the skills needed to reduce expenditures and spend more cost-effectively, and to payment and evaluation arrangements which are understood, fair, simple, defensible and not conducive to manipulation. Both users and providers are entitled to know of, and to understand, the criteria used as the basis for decisions regarding priorities, eligibility, funding and refusal of funding. When ministries state that there is inappropriate spending the ministry should either have a plan for reduced spending or should be prepared to work with the field to develop such a plan.

Communities and agencies will be better partners in health care if they have access to all data that is available to the government and to useful data produced by other health care providers. Communities and regions can better deliver the culturally sensitive services asked for if provinces permit a reasonable degree of regional and community difference within equitable area funding.

Publicly funded agencies have little or no right to expect governments to provide financial relief in the face of unexpected expense including energy costs, gasoline prices, taxes, pay equity programs and workers compensation costs. Governments should not exempt anyone from the requirement that activities be shown to be cost-effective, should not provide additional funds when budgets are exceeded, should not expect to be asked to solve problems which can be solved through agency or regional thought and action, and should not usually be expected to protect an agency from public criticism. Health care providers, whether institutional or individual, should not expect governments to be any more generous with them than with the many other publicly funded services also important to health.

Governments in turn have a right to expect a number of things from the field. It is reasonable to expect conformity to public policy (respect for the law), that public interest will come before parochial interest and that every agency will plan to live within its allotted funds and then do so. It is reasonable for governments to expect that activities performed by every program will be selected on the basis of contributions to the health of the community, that existing programs will be cut back if activities not currently being funded are seen to be more important to the health of the community, and that activities shown to be of no value will not be funded with public money.

The government should receive no requests for more money unless the requests are supported by (a) evidence of the cost-effectiveness of the activities to be financed, (b) evidence that all other agency activities are already cost-effective and (c) an indication of which services should be reduced to pay for the new activities. New programs within agencies should be financed from available funds when the new programs bring greater public benefit than activities currently being carried out.

Governments are entitled to the assistance of planners, policy makers and administrators in the field in the creation and improvement of public policy. The health care field has many more planners and many more administrators than do ministries of health, plus almost all of the care providers and many important policy makers, and this reservoir of skills in the field makes it imperative that the field not wait passively for the government to promote or mandate desired improvements.

The same principle applies to the creation of the generally supportive environments which are essential to healthy future populations. Leaders in the fields of education, housing, agriculture, and industrial development are essential to the sustainable commercial, industrial and social developments which will protect the health of future generations. (Third International Conference on Health Promotion: Supportive Environments for Health, WHO, Sundsvall, Sweden, 1991)

Governments should be able to feel that the field has a reasonably good understanding of the workings and constraints of government. Governments have a right to expect reasonably competent and sensitive administrative and clinical decision making and a minimum use of media blackmail. There should be acceptance that there is as much public interest in politicians and the public service as there is in the field.

Ministries and Ministers should be able to rely on the field to assist with, and participate in, programs aimed at greater value-for-money, and improved community health should be accepted by everyone as the only valid measure of value. The production of intermediate outputs (days of care, number of X-rays) is not proof of value. Ministries should expect the agencies in the field to routinely use operating funds to examine and improve agency operations.

Users should expect government to be equitable in the spending of public funds. (This can have negative as well as positive effects on individual users.) In the presence of financial constraint equity requires that almost all persons face imperfect access and imperfect services. All anyone can ask for is that their hazards be similar to those faced by others who also wish to receive health care at public expense.

SUMMARY

Power is dispersed. Governments have the constitutional and legislative upper hand, but it is a hand which can only be played well when providers and consumers are involved and generally supportive.

The roles of the players have changed dramatically over the last three decades, and the changes are not over yet.

Chapter 6

Centralization and Decentralization

INTRODUCTION

The established terminology of organization includes autonomy (independence), centralization, networks, systems, decentralization, integration, coordination, authority, hierarchy, and structure, and new terms are constantly being coined. It is difficult to know the extent to which everyone will need to become acquainted with seamless delivery systems and value-added partnerships, or with the differences between devolution, unbundling, decentralization and a number of other terms. Hopefully newly coined terms, and new definitions for old terms, will not survive if they are merely new make-up for old faces or are terminological rigidities which confuse more than clarify.

Organizational issues in health care which merit special attention in the next decade include the selection and creation of new regional structures, the restructuring of community based services, the evolution of systems which support user control and which are user friendly, whether to centralize or decentralize, the formalization of the second tier of health care and the creation of structures which will lead to an improvement in the strategic planning abilities of health departments. This chapter looks only at issues associated with centralization and decentralization, opposites which permeate many aspects of health care.

Decentralization can consist of merely moving bureaucratic agents of a central authority to geographically decentralized offices. This form of decentralization will be given minimal attention.

Current patterns of centralization and decentralization are often more the product of history than of planning. The administration of most psychiatric hospitals is still centralized in provincial ministries of health because provinces long ago assumed responsibility for jails and asylums. The administration of most nonprofit general hospitals remains decentralized at the community or institutional level because the early hospitals came into being as community projects. Community services such as Meals on Wheels, Wheels to Meals, senior citizen centres, group homes, self-help groups and many other programs under voluntary, religious or profit sponsorship emerged in the absence of any overall plan, and they still usually operate outside of regional plans.

Organizational options for total health care systems extend from a completely decentralized system (of which there are few examples) to highly centralized systems such as those in Sweden and Britain before both of them reorganized. Canada is a mix of centralization and decentralization and this will continue for the foreseeable future.

The model which is a mixture of centralization and decentralization offers endless variations. There are few fixed rules and there are examples of almost everything. Policy makers are free to examine and vary the extent to which they centralize, or decentralize, various functions and health care sectors. For most dental care, for example, there is decentralization of capital financing, operational financing, strategic planning, operational planning, evaluation and administration. For general hospitals there is a mix of centralization (operational financing, standard setting and data systems) and decentralization (administration), with many other responsibilities being shared among provinces, regions, programs and institutions.

Centralization has for several decades been the dominant tendency in institutions as well as in provinces, although the trend has weakened in recent years. Hospitals centralized health records, personnel functions, nursing administration and purchasing, to mention only a few. The reasons for the centralization within hospitals were the same as those which led to centralization within provincial and regional systems, in particular the need for critical mass, efficiency, standardization, better data and financial control. In recent years there has been some movement to decentralization of budget control in some hospitals (as with global budgets for departments and programs), and the reasons for this decentralization are also the same as the reasons for decentralization in larger systems. It is seen as an opportunity for participative decision making and for those who spend the money to show they can spend it best.

INTEGRATION, COORDINATION AND INDEPENDENCE

There can be independence, integration or coordination of sectors (public health, long term care) and of programs and institutions. Integration or coordination can be provincial, regional, multiinstitutional or at the point of delivery. Integration is a centralizing phenomenon, whereas coordination is often a prerequisite to decentralization and to continued independence.

The independence of health care sectors is greatest when each has its own budgetary envelope, its own bureaucracy within the ministry and its own network of separate sources of care, as with mental health, general hospitals and public health in most provinces. When this degree of sectoral independence exists there may be resistance to cooperation with other sectors. Organizational boundaries can become barriers to optimal service and spending.

Within a sector there can be an emphasis on integration, as in county or provincial public health organizations or in multihospital boards. There can also be an emphasis on independence, as with private practitioners, many hospitals and most long term care institutions.

Integration of health care is most complete when a single agency is made responsible for a broad range of services, as in a Health Maintenance Organization (the United States), a Regional/District Health Authority or Board (Britain) or some of the rural district health boards in Alberta and Manitoba. These integrated agencies may be responsible for all or most of long term care, emergency care, public health, mental health, acute treatment hospitals, home care and ambulatory care. These umbrella agencies, with their responsibility for many services and often for total populations, can most fully reallocate resources among sectors. This reallocation is much more difficult when each sector has its own budget and the sectors are not organizationally linked.

There can be organizational integration without integration at the service delivery level. A hospital outpatient department and emergency department within the same hospital may provide overlapping services and be operationally completely separate. In community health centres, on the other hand, a melding of the delivery of care can occur through the use of multi-disciplinary teams. Integration at the service delivery level is helpful to users. It carries the connotation of *one stop shopping*. Health and social service centres, by any name, are, in this sense, user friendly.

Quebec has accomplished more province-wide integration of care than the other provinces. In 1971 the Castonguay-Nepveu Report proposed regionalized health services for Quebec in which all health care sectors would be merged. Health services were to be organized and delivered in association with social services. It was recommended that regional Councils be established to plan, implement and oversee a network of institutions including general hospitals, long term care institutions, psychiatric hospitals and community health centres. This new network was to replace the parish based system which was, by the end of the 1960s, on the verge of collapse.

Castonguay became Minister of Health about the time of release of his report, and as part of the *quiet revolution* in Quebec many of his recommendations were implemented. Quebec became the most innovative and experimental of the provinces, especially in its integration of social services with physical health, mental health and public health services. Only private practice physicians were able to resist the integrative push. (Quebec also led the way in reducing the number of medical students, in capping total expenditures on physician services, in capping payments to individual physicians, in varying physician fees on the basis of location of practice, in allocating significant operational powers to some regional councils and in assuring patients full access to their medical records.)

The Quebec reorganization produced one example of coordination/integration which was not foreseen by the government. This was the development by the fee-for-service physicians of a large number of polyclinics. These polyclinics appeared in response to the proposal that the CLSCs (the Quebec version of a community health and social services centre) would become the locale for delivery of much of the provinces primary care. The polyclinics helped prevent the CLSCs from becoming major sources of primary care. In the process, they also improved community access to walk-in and after hours care by merging some of the operations of formerly separate physicians offices.

Integration of the planning, administration and delivery of health services and social services is an attractive option but can only be carried so far. All or portions of education, law enforcement, health care, welfare, day care and other personal services can be seen as social services. All are important to health status, but full organizational integration is not feasible. The establishment of coordinating mechanisms is at least as important as the administrative integration of some services.

Integration or greater coordination at the delivery level can reduce duplication of services and of record keeping, reduce costs and make health care more understandable to users. Comparison of the activities carried out by community health nurses in the Saskatoon Public Health Unit and the activities of family physicians established that the nurses and physicians routinely carry out the same measurements, screening tests and examinations at the two, four, six and twelve month well-baby visits. Closer working relationships could eliminate this duplication. (Hemmelgarn B.R., L. Edouard, B.F. Habbick and J. Feather, "Duplication of Well-Baby Services", CJPH, May-June 1992, 217-20) Another study identified major differences between the patient assessments done by hospital discharge planners and the assessments done by community nurses who provided follow-up care. Some of the discrepancies appeared to arise from a failure of the hospital staff to involve the patient in the development of a discharge plan, but some was probably the result of inadequate communication between the workers. (Townsend E.I., N.C. Edwards and C. Nadon, "The Hospital Liaison Process: Identifying Risk Factors in Postnatal Multiparas", CJPH May-June 1992 203-7) Greater coordination at the community level in Ontario is being studied in a multiparty exercise which is developing a Community Health Framework.

The Victoria Health Project in Victoria B.C. was a voluntary exercise in cooperation between acute treatment hospitals and community based long term care agencies. This cooperation eventually led to a transfer of a million dollars to community long term care agencies from the hospital base budget, and Ministry funds for 60 new institutional beds were redirected to expansions of community care.

To promote increased hospital/community cooperation the British Columbia Ministry of Health in 1989/90 set aside 0.5% of the provincial envelope for hospitals and made these funds available for joint hospital/community projects which improved community service and reduced hospital utilization. In later years the funding of this program was increased to 0.75%. Applications for these funds exceeded the amounts allotted. No new money was needed; provincial reallocation of the provincial hospital funds provided the incentive for joint action.

Another variation on the theme of coordination or cooperation is the linking of larger and more managerially sophisticated agencies or institutions with those less managerially able. The larger unit has specialized skills plus the employee mass necessary to offer the employees of the smaller unit better benefits and better career opportunities. (This type of assistance can only work if the larger unit sees its mandate as service to a community beyond its walls.)

Central planning does not need to lead to loss of administrative independence. Ontario has brought private radiology, laboratory, prosthetic and physiotherapy facilities under public planning through the *Independent Health Facilities Act* (1991), but facility ownership and administration remain as they were. On the other hand, several provinces have centralized most home support services under the provincial bureaucracy and, in the process, reduced or eliminated local administrative control.

Many independent community based services are made successful by the contributions of volunteers and by an ability to generate at least some of their operational funds through their own fund raising. Forced integration may lead to loss of volunteers and local fund raising. A solution which preserves the availability of volunteers and local fund raising while also reducing the consumer confusion and the inefficiencies which can accompany complete agency independence is desirable. A single point-of-entry agency can provide some of the desired balance. Users can gain access to services only through assessment by the point-of-entry agency, but the delivery of service can remain with independent agencies. The single point-of-entry agency represents integration but only of selected functions. Coordination techniques can also allow preservation of agency independence.

Less program insularity should reduce gaps in service, reduce undesirable duplication of service, more effectively find underserved cases, simplify transfer of cases and information between agencies, improve the quality of data-bases and support the development of regional networks.

Coordination at the regional level can increase or reduce costs, may or may not increase the percentage of available money that is used for actual delivery of care, and may or may not improve cost-effectiveness. Regional bed monitoring arrangements, for example, increase administrative costs but may improve bed utilization enough to justify the additional costs.

REGIONAL ORGANIZATION

When decentralization to a region occurs the region may be small or large. It can include one, more than one, or any part of, a province, county, or metropolitan area. This section primarily discusses regions which are parts of a province.

There will be no distinction made between *region* and *district*, although some provinces consider a district to be smaller than a region. The ingredients are the same; a defined geographic area and some authority (board, committee, council, or office) which is responsible for all or some health care functions.

Most of the developed world has for decades been experimenting with regional and district approaches to health care planning, delivery and financing. The recent British reorganization created or strengthened the district and regional organizations, as did the reorganization in Sweden. In 1986 New South Wales in Australia was reported to be moving towards regional health service boards with responsibility for a full range of services. (Dixon,M., "Creating a New Partnership", Vancouver, September 1986)

There are many regional options, but there is no proven relationship between the various options and either cost control or the quality of spending. What is certain is that regional organizations affect where power resides and who may be responsible for control of costs and the quality of spending.

Recent major reports in Saskatchewan, Alberta, Nova Scotia and British Columbia have recommended regional health care boards. Only Quebec and New Brunswick have fully introduced relatively independent multifunctional regional bodies, but all provinces have some examples of regional approaches to some components of health care, especially public health services and health care planning. Saskatchewan appears to be on its way to area health boards, with Alberta also poised to move quickly. The regional concept is consistent with the belief that decisions can be better, and better represent local priorities, if they are made as close as is reasonable to the populations concerned while also being made by agencies with an adequate population base and broad functional responsibilities.

If health care planning and/or administrative functions are to be placed at the regional level they can be made the responsibility of a health services department within a regional government or be assigned to a separate health services council or board. The municipal government option appears to be most suitable if it is saleable and an appropriate regional government exists. The feeling that health care is too special to be merged with the usual municipal functions is still strong in many communities, however, and a separate health services board may be the only acceptable option even when an appropriate regional government exists.

Regional boards or councils can be composed entirely of consumer representatives, entirely of provider representatives or any mix of the two. Members of a regional body can be selected by ballot (as with regional governments, or a regional hospital board elected at the annual meeting of a hospital association), by the minister or other government official (as with District Health Councils in Ontario), by municipal governments (legislation can state that all or some of the members of a board are to be chosen by one or more municipal governments), by users of the regionalized service (as with a regional laundry or purchasing agency) or by other designated groups. Legislation or regulations may state that workers groups, business groups, or ethnic groups, for example, are to choose one or more representatives to sit on the regional body.

A regional body may report to its electorate, to the minister of health, to the deputy minister of health, to the members of a health care association or to no-one.

REGIONAL FUNCTIONS/RESPONSIBILITIES

Although there is a general and sometimes romantic attachment to local control, there are many planning, delivery and evaluation functions which require centralization to units with a population of a million or more. Persons who favor decentralization should be careful not to decentralize to a geographic, population or economic base which cannot perform the tasks being allocated.

Provinces have tended to retain control over financing (the provincial base best avoids regional disparities within publicly financed programs), setting standards, the range of insured services, definitions of beneficiaries, the use of user fees, coverage out-of-province and out-of-country, data to be collected, degree of involvement of the for-profit sector, and consumer rights. There appears to be potential for greater regional involvement and discretion in some of these policy areas.

A regional body may be entirely advisory (Ontario District Health Councils) or have executive powers (the board of a Public Health Unit). Executive powers must be either delegated by a body with the powers to delegate (usually a provincial legislature) or acquired through incorporation.

A regional agency can be responsible only for services within the boundaries of the region, or it may be responsible for a prescribed range of health care, wherever that care is provided, for a defined regional population. The Comprehensive Health Organization in Ontario and the District Health Authority (DHA) in Britain (as created by the recent revisions to the British National Health Service) illustrate the concept of a local authority with a budget which must pay not only for services provided locally to local residents but for some or all care provided in other locations to those residents.

A regional body may be responsible for a broad or narrow range of health services or a broad or narrow range of policy, planning or administrative functions. Agencies with a narrow band of responsibilities are common. Examples include a regional mental health services planning board, a regional agency responsible only for administration of a single-point-of-entry service for long term care and the hospital districts created in Saskatchewan and British Columbia for more equitable distribution of the costs of constructing hospitals. Ontario in 1993 initiated moves towards regional control of children's mental health services (six counties only) and long term care. Each region will have two new regional organizations and boards. These multiple regional agencies with responsibility for only one type of health care will lead to manipulation and confusion at the boundaries of the sectors. The confusion will increase if regional boards are also created for emergency services, adult mental health services, womens services, hospital services, health promotion and more. The isolated regional board with narrow responsibilities is not a good model.

Creation of a regional body with executive responsibilities for administration of health care can move responsibility for cost control and allocation of resources, and for choosing priorities, to the regional level. The province can reduce its cost control problems by downloading the task to the regional body.

Regional cooperation can save money. Hospital group purchasing, for example, has been the norm for decades and has lowered many prices. Other purchasing models might contribute additional savings. The pharmacies of Ontario are served by pharmacy wholesalers who handle both the medical and nonmedical supplies sold by pharmacies. Wholesalers receive orders from pharmacies daily and also deliver daily, with one day turn-around. This arrangement allows the pharmacies to avoid dealing with a large number of suppliers, to order in small quantities if that is desired and to carry much smaller inventories of drugs and other supplies than would be possible with a less efficient distribution system. A similar system for equipment and supplies for health care institutions and offices might lower unit costs and inventory costs, and the Ontario Ministry of Health is currently exploring this option.

REGIONAL FUNDING AND BUDGETS

Regional bodies may have taxing authority (as is the case with local governments and with school boards in some provinces), may be fully funded by outside sources such as a provincial and/or municipal government (as in Quebec), may operate with revenues derived from services provided (as with a regional laundry), or may be funded by some combination of these and other devices and sources.

Provincial funding of a regional agency may be by global budget, per capita payments, a line by line budget, conditional or unconditional grants, a cost-sharing formula or some combination of the above. Allocations to a region may vary with demography, wealth and/or other social and economic indicators.

Regional Health Boards with taxation authority have been proposed by several provincial Commissions. The idea may have its roots in the feeling that health care is central to health and therefore must have access to whatever funds are deemed necessary. It is not a good idea. Local taxpayers already have too many separate governments sending out tax notices.

Regional agencies should have access to, or be provided with, funding consistent with the responsibilities assigned. The budgets assigned to Ontario District Health Councils at the time of their creation 20 years ago were barely adequate for Councils with no experience and limited expectations. The budget formulae have not changed despite increases in functions and ability. A District Health Council serving 500,000 to 1,000,000 people has a base budget of about $500,000. A large hospital may have more planning staff than the Council which is expected to monitor and advise with respect to a broad spectrum of regional sources of health care. Quebec regional councils have 5-15 times the operating budget of their Ontario counterparts.

Whenever regional budgets are created provinces have the dilemma of how much the priorities and resource allocations of one region should be able to differ from those in other regions. The jurisdictional hierarchy is clear (the regions are creations of the provinces) but if there is to be local control then it must be expected that there will be regional differences.

Transfer of some degree of financial control from the province to a region may result in regional income differences for providers, with the variations depending on the supply of providers in the region and on priorities established by the region. Physician incomes may, if global regional budgets include payments to physicians, be lower in regions with a generous supply of physicians (just as they will be lower if the Ministry through central policy establishes regional ceilings on physician payments).

A regional authority with a global regional budget might spend beyond its budget. This should be anticipated and the consequences described. Will deficits be negotiated with the province or be a local responsibility, just as is now the case with hospitals? Certainly the province will, if regional budgets are implemented, need to guard against regional overspending at provincial expense. This protection should be no serious problem. Provinces have lots of experience with controlling overexpenditures by hospitals, municipalities, school boards and others.

Regional agencies should, as with the Ministry and other major spenders, learn to operate with the funds allocated. They should ask the Ministry of Health for additional funds only for activities related to a provincially significant activity, such as prevention programs which may have provincial value, or when the regional funding is thought to be less than a fair share of the provincial pie.

A region with a global budget could, from its budget, allocate global budgets to individual hospitals or other agencies, just as is now done by each province. This is the preferred option. The degree of resource use discretion within the global budgets of programs and institutions would be as defined by the regional body, probably within provincial guidelines.

Expenditures for specific services such as physician payments or payments for drugs could be within or outside the regional budget. If these services which can be received at many different locations are to be covered by the regional budgets the data systems will need to record user address.

Regional global budgets should lead to provincial resource allocation which is more regionally fair. Examination of health care expenditures in the regions of Ontario in 1991 showed major discrepancies in per capita spending on health care. For example, the amount spent per capita on community based long term care services varied among regions by up to 350%. (Partnerships in Long Term Care — A Policy Framework, Ontario Ministry of Health, 1993). These expenditure variations could not be justified by sociodemographic or other regional characteristics. The variances represented the effects of squeaking wheels, politics, inadequate data systems and inadequate provincial planners.

When regional inequities exist and regional budgets are introduced the province has two options. It can increase regional equity through a transfer of funds from areas with high per capita expenditures to those with lower per capita expenditures, or it may gradually reduce inequities by assigning new funds, when they become available, to the less funded regions.

In the Ontario long term care reorganization of 1993 a long term care funding envelope is to be granted to each region. The region will allocate funds first to mandatory programs identified by the province and then to nonmandatory programs chosen by itself. The regional budgets will be composed of current expenditures by facilities and programs in the regions. Equity will be accomplished over time. With respect to the Ontario regional budgets for children's mental health services in six counties, the funding equity will be accomplished by an immediate redistribution of current provincial expenditures.

Global budgets brought hospitals greater policy and spending discretion. Regional budgets will bring similar opportunities to regions. Regional budgets were endorsed by the Premiers Council of Ontario in 1990-91. The Council recommended that *"key elements of health and social services be integrated into a local structure and funded by a regional service envelope"*. If the province requires regions to provide certain kinds of health care and conform to specified rules, and to suffer penalties if provincial standards are not met, then the situation will be similar to that produced for the provinces by the federal *Canada Health Act*.

There could be opportunities for regions to supplement the money provided by the province. Provincial transfers to the regions could represent less than 100% of the public expenditures on health care for the residents of the region. If voluntary regional contributions to health care costs are allowed then there are likely to be regional variations in the degree of universal public access to health care and/or in the quality of that care. Wealthy regions, and regions which assign a high priority to public funding of health care, will have a higher level of publicly financed health care than poorer regions or regions who give health care a lower priority. If there are to be regional contributions to health care funding the formula for provincial contributions to regional budgets could be similar to that used in the original federal-provincial hospital and medicare cost sharing agreements. Provincial contributions would be greatest to the regions least able to raise local funds. This principle already applies to some provincial funding of municipalities and school boards.

When regional agencies with regional global budgets are responsible for populations rather than programs the agency becomes responsible for some or all health care received by regional residents from providers outside the region. In this situation the agency must be provided with, or must develop, devices by which it can limit expenditures on services provided outside the region as well as inside. If tools for control of expenditures by outside facilities or providers are not developed the regions can face major and unpredictable externally generated costs. This situation is equivalent to that faced by early capitation funded community health centres (CHC) in Ontario who were told that capitation payments from the Ministry would be reduced to the extent that rostered persons received outside care which could have been provided by the CHC. This *charge-back* process would have made the CHCs financially nonviable.

Health Maintenance Organizations in the United States and District Health Authorities in Britain do not have unlimited responsibility for elective care obtained from unapproved locations or providers. Elective care which is not approved need not be paid for from the regional or HMO budget. The constraints are acceptable to the Health Maintenance Organization members because everyone knows the terms of the contract between the HMO and its members. Limited access to publicly financed care outside of their region but within their own province would, however, be a new experience for Canadians.

Districts or regions could be allowed to tender for care. In both Sweden and Britain district health authorities are allowed to buy both internal and external services from the lowest cost locations. (The Swedish Institute, October 1991)

CENTRAL CONTROL AFTER DECENTRALIZATION

Regions can be given a considerable degree of local discretion or be constrained by detailed provincial regulations. (The province may refer to the regulations as guidelines, but if the guidelines are mandatory the title is inappropriate.) Provincial regulations can spell out in unreasonable detail what regional or local services must be provided, who must be served and the standards which must be met. If these constraints are combined with reduced funding then the regional authority has few if any opportunities to pursue local priorities. When responsibility for serving a community or region is transferred to a community or regional board the province should give the boards enough discretion to allow local priorities to be partly honored. Without this flexibility one of the important advantages of decentralization is lost. (Health System Decentralization, Concepts, Issues and Country Experience, WHO, 1990)

Some provincial direction is inevitable and desirable. Agencies are likely to have to continue to serve a defined clientele and provide a defined spectrum of services within at least a vaguely prescribed set of guidelines and perhaps within a proscribed set of priorities, and these directives are likely to remain in place whether funding is reduced or increased. Hospitals and programs may not, for example, have the option of discontinuing a service such as an emergency or obstetrical department. In the presence of a regional agency with significant operational or planning authority the region would replace the province as the source of some or all directives and guidelines within which institutions and programs would operate.

ARGUMENTS IN SUPPORT OF REGIONAL BUDGETS

There are many arguments which support regional agencies and budgets. Decisions can be made closer to home. Planning and operational variations can more closely reflect local priorities. Regional or community leaders and populations will have a greater incentive to confront the trade-offs which are now unavoidable. There may, over time, be reduced expectations that the province will, when pressured enough, provide more money. Both individuals and groups may become more aware of the impossibility of funding all of the many activities which are seen as desirable.

Many examples illustrate the kinds of local choices which could be made within regional budgets. In 1992 and 1993 Cornwall, Ontario, experienced a series of very difficult scandals involving the sexual abuse of a large number of children. The community decided it should have a sexual abuse therapy centre, and $100,000 in donations was collected. The community hoped that provincial funds would be available to complete the funding of the project. When the provincial funding was not available the project died. If there had been a regional budget the community would have had the option of reducing expenditures on hospitals, physicians, optometry, ambulances or home care so that the sexual abuse centre could be funded.

In 1993 an advocacy group in Ottawa continued to vociferously demand replacement of the existing ambulance staff with paramedics able to perform defibrillation and other advanced life saving measures. With a global regional budget the region could have, if they had so wished, reallocated the needed funds from other local services and facilities, whereas in the absence of local control the approach was the classical one of blaming the provincial ministry. The necessary funds could have easily been voluntarily provided by programs and institutions in the region, but without a regional agency to carry out the reallocations they did not occur. The money needed to upgrade ambulance staff was about 0.1% of health care costs in the region.

In 1993, also in Ottawa, the children's hospital received almost $4 million of additional funds. Without a regional budget the region and its residents did not have the opportunity to debate the most appropriate allocation of the $4 million, an opportunity which they should have had.

In 1989 the Alberta Ministry of health refused to provide additional funding to the Holy Cross hospital in Calgary for an expansion of their clinic for eating disorders. The hospital and the political opposition placed the blame for the inadequacies of the clinic on the provincial government despite the ownership by the hospital of a global budget which it could have reallocated to serve the clinic if that had been its wish. The reallocation would have been even better discussed at the regional level. Everyone is willing to blame someone else, but global budgets bring responsibility to those who control the global fund.

Regional budgets might make it easier to involve special population groups and total populations in discussions of how to make better use of health care dollars and how to produce better balance in the distribution of public funds to the many public policy areas which are important to health.

DISADVANTAGES AND PROBLEMS

There are many disadvantages and problems associated with moving from a provincial to a regional emphasis. All options are flawed. With regional agencies and budgets, there will be a regional wish to have control of functions which cannot be reasonably carried out with the regional population base and the regional resources available. Provinces will have difficulty avoiding creation of provincially funded but locally dominated boards who will enthusiastically blackmail or embarrass the provincial government rather than perform the policy selection and administrative responsibilities given.

There is also the possibility of merely creating new and dysfunctional bureaucracies. Protection lies primarily in good planning, a clear understanding of the roles of the region and a transfer of power from agencies to the region as well as from the province to the region.

In the 1970s British Columbia created Community Resource Boards who were to advise the government on health and social service priorities and spending. The Boards were partly appointed and partly elected. They were largely a failure in practice although sound in principle. Expectations of both the province and the communities were too high and process was not well enough thought out.

In all discussions of regional budgets and the decentralization of various functions there must be acceptance of the smallness of many Canadian provinces. For provinces with a population of a million or less it is necessary that many functions remain with the province. Some functions can be decentralized, but for many purposes the province must be the region. In 1993 the four provinces in the Atlantic region recognized this problem of size and joined together in one administrative region for selected health care activities.

When considering disadvantages, the big question is, *disadvantages compared to what?* If the comparison is with perfection there are too many disadvantages to bother doing anything, but if the comparison is with the status quo then the regional option is attractive.

SUMMARY

The issues associated with centralization and decentralization will never be fully resolved. There are often no choices which will please even half of the people.

Many questions will be asked by those who must choose between centralization and decentralization.

- What are the objectives, and how important is each objective?
- What functions are involved?
- What is the smallest unit which can adequately and at reasonable cost perform the function being assigned? Does the decentralized unit under consideration have the necessary population base, financial capacity, skilled personnel and/or the number of cases? (Exceptions may be desirable on the basis of geographic isolation or cultural sensitivity.)
- What effects will the alternatives have on consumer control? Consumer control and agency sensitivity may not increase with decentralization if powers are decentralized to a nonelected, nonaccountable and insulated body.
- What effects will the alternatives have on provincial equity? Delegation of policy functions to decentralized bodies, each with the ability to exercise discretion, will inevitably lead to regional differences. If these differences are unacceptable to a province, as may be the case with levels of taxation or with many kinds of discrimination, then central control must remain to the degree necessary to avoid or reduce inequities.
- Will decentralization be politically hazardous or politically advantageous? Decentralized boards/councils with executive responsibilities and public money to spend can blame the central government for everything. On the other hand, the ministry can make the decentralized body responsible for providing services with reduced resources. The rationing decisions are transferred to the decentralized centre of power.
- Which option makes it easiest for consumers to find the required services?
- Who will be the winners and losers? How great will their losses and gains be, and can the resistance of the losers be overcome?
- If decentralization is to occur, to what type of body or agency will the decentralized functions be assigned?

- If central funds are being transferred to a regional or local agency, are cost control devices in place, or at least available, to protect against overexpenditure?

Regional, district and/or community agencies should have increased responsibility for setting area priorities, allocating tax generated health care funds and coordinating or integrating health care services.

Chapter 7

Other Organizational Options

INTRODUCTION

The previous chapter looked at the organizational options associated with centralization and decentralization. This chapter looks at policy options associated with other aspects of the organization of total health systems or of specific health service sectors.

PROVINCIAL INDEPENDENCE VERSUS
NATIONAL STANDARDIZATION OR COOPERATION

Health care is affected by the extent to which provinces choose to be isolationist versus cooperative with other provinces and with Ottawa. Should provinces each go their own way or should they seek national consensus and action with respect to such matters as the principles in the *Canada Health Act*, the identification of health goals, technology assessment (including machines, supplies and drugs), educational and training standards, licensing standards, clinical practice guidelines, data collection, terminology and services to residents of other provinces?

Some of the areas in which collaboration could occur are highly technical, such as the evaluation of technology and drugs and the standardization of data. Collaboration in these areas can be of mutual benefit without reducing the autonomy of any province. Others such as education have greater cultural and provincial significance.

Some policies are of importance to Canadians who wish to move freely within Canada. Collaboration on policies regarding education, training and licensing, for example, is not essential but is sensible and is important to those affected. Collaboration should occur so long as there is no major threat to provincial goals. Such a threat could occur, for example, if physician licensing practices in one province threatened attempts by another province to control doctor supply. When an all province consensus cannot be reached, as was the case in 1992 when all provinces but Quebec and Newfoundland agreed that new physicians would need additional years of post graduate training to be licensed, a partial consensus may be better than none.

Before the appearance of national hospital and medical care insurance each province financed and regulated health care as much or as little as it wished. Federal cost sharing led to standardization with respect to hospital and physician policies and practices, but did not affect other services. Services unaffected by the Canada Health Act have now been given a higher priority in the provincial health care networks, and provincial differences have become more noticeable. There are differences with respect to user fees, coverage for health care outside Canada, access to abortion, the organization of ambulance services, the populations covered by public drug and dental programs and the availability and quality of community mental health programs.

It is probable that provincial differences in hospital and medical care services will increase quickly if standardization is no longer required by federal policy. Provincial differences may increase with respect to such policy areas as the roles of the private for-profit sector, the approval and regulation of a second tier of health care, the nature of provincial health goals and the extent to which specific services are insured only in specified situations.

Despite the probability of new differences in provincial health care policy there may also be new areas of provincial cooperation. The Ministers and Deputy Ministers of Health have recently worked together effectively to control the costs of health care. In 1992 the provinces agreed to a 10% reduction in medical school enrolment, and in 1993 a 7% reduction occurred. There have also been joint policy statements on drug prices and on public education programs aimed at soliciting consumer assistance with cost control and better spending. A greater role for the Canadian Blood Agency has been approved.

Several provinces currently evaluate drugs and related products which have already been evaluated by the federal government. These provincial evaluations determine the extent to which the products will be insured in the provincial programs. These many evaluations are at least partially duplicative. The provinces and Ottawa should seek nonduplicative processes of initial and on-going evaluation which would not bind any province to the same policies or list of insured items, but which would provide a commonly available pool of high quality information. Cooperation with other countries may also be helpful. A European Medicines Evaluation Agency has recently been established in London, England. It will evaluate drugs for the entire EEC. There will be major savings for drug companies who will deal with only one agency, and drugs will come on the market more quickly. (BMJ, 12 Feb, 1994, p. 308)

THE ORGANIZATION OF HEALTH CARE INSURANCE

Major policy options pertaining to the organization of health care insurance include how to assure universal access, how many insurance carriers there should be, whether to approve private health insurance for hospital and physician services (a completion of the second tier of privately funded health care), who should operate the second tier of insurance if there is to be one, and the integration of medicare programs and the health care financed by Workers Compensation Boards.

Options to achieve universal access to health care insurance

Canadians have, through elections and opinion surveys, indicated their wish for universal access to insurance coverage of at least physician and hospital care. The policy options are to provide universal coverage through a single public program, a single private program, many public programs, many private programs or some mix of public and private programs. The private programs may be profit or nonprofit.

In 1964 the Hall Commission, largely on the basis of success in Saskatchewan, recommended medical care coverage of all Canadians by a single public program, and this is the current model in all provinces and territories. In most provinces the hospital and medical care coverage is combined in one insurance program, and this program usually also covers other services such as optometry and chiropractic care. In some provinces there are additional public programs which provide access to drugs, ambulance services, long term care, home care, assistive devices and other health care.

At the time universal medicare was introduced the physician associations recommended an option in which everyone unable to afford the costs of medical care insurance would have their private insurance premiums paid by the government. Other persons would be responsible for their insurance premiums. Governments can, if this model is chosen, legislate premium levels to assure access for those who will consume a lot of health care. This model can, if only one insurance carrier is used, bring the advantages of a single carrier. This model is privately operated but partially publicly financed. There are options with respect to who would receive full or partial public assistance with premiums, the extent to which there would be standardization of premiums across the population, who would monitor and control the appropriateness of spending, and which services would be within the guaranteed coverage.

British Columbia uses a mixed public/private model for drug insurance. The achievement of universal access through a mix of public and private insurance carriers has both advantages and disadvantages. In the British Columbia model there can be any number of profit and/or nonprofit private carriers but there is also a public program which provides coverage for everyone who is not covered by a private program.

To government the substantive advantage of the mixed model is that it can markedly reduce public expenditures. The disadvantages are that the public system must be less attractive than the private coverage or few people will opt for private coverage, data integration may be more difficult, there will be some confusion at the interface of the public and private programs as beneficiaries move from one sector to the other, and total administration expenditures will be higher than with a single public program.

This mixed insurance model should not be confused with a two tier system in which everyone is covered by a publicly managed universal program but beneficiaries are able, if they so wish and can afford it, to add a second tier of private coverage. In the mixed model of universal coverage used in British Columbia only a portion of the population is covered by the public plan.

There are variations on this mixed management theme. In Germany the upper income portion of the population is not covered by the quasi-public *sickness programs* which insure the remainder of the population.

Arrangements such as in the United States where there are both public and private insurance programs do not qualify for discussion in this section. Universality is not an objective.

How many insurance carriers?

The single payer principle has been an inherent part of Canadian hospital and physician services insurance for over 35 and 25 years respectively, and it is often cited as one of the reasons for more successful cost control in Canada than in the United States.

The single payer model is cheaper, simpler and better. It reduces administrative costs, is simpler for the users and the providers, increases the ability of the payer to control prices, lowers the opportunities for manipulative billing practices, increases the quality of the data bases and allows more complete monitoring and correction of patterns of care. The single payer model largely eliminates variations in access due to differing regional abilities to pay, makes it easier to deliver care on equal terms and conditions throughout the population, increases the possibility of altering worker roles to either improve quality or decrease costs, and reduces or eliminates the need to withhold insurance coverage from high risk populations.

The existence of a number of competing health care insurance carriers (the multiple payer model of the United States) brings no identifiable advantages to society as a whole. Competition between multiple carriers definitely brings higher prices and does not improve quality. Competing health care insurance carriers spend large amounts on administration and marketing merely to determine who will have the privilege of delivering the consumers money to the providers. The system is made more complex and expensive without social benefit.

Multiple carriers can, in the short term, be helpful to groups within populations who can, by virtue of their good health, be offered health insurance at low annual premiums. If healthy low risk populations pay for only their own care then their insurance premiums can be relatively low, although it is likely that these same persons will, through taxes and industry manipulations of premiums, pay for much of the care provided to the high risk groups unable to afford to insure themselves. The low risk persons and populations will also, when multiple private carriers sell insurance, find that their coverage will end or be reduced if their state of health declines. Only a universal single carrier can assure reasonable access to care regardless of level of need, and administrative costs are reduced by 60-90%.

In some provinces the single payer model applies to not only hospitals and physicians but also to all or most of public health services, home care, long term care, prescription drugs, ambulance services, children's dental care, chiropractic services, chiropody and optometry.

One tier versus two tier health care insurance

Prior to universal medicare it was taken for granted that those who couldn't afford health care got less of it. The introduction of universal public coverage of hospital and physician services created the myth that wealth would no longer affect the amount of health care a person received. This myth led to the belief that Canada had a one tier health care system.

The terms *one tier* and *two tier* are not clearly defined, but one interpretation is that in a one tier system all necessary services are provided through a universal public insurance program. In the one tier system people cannot obtain insured services except from the public system. Providers are not allowed to receive payment from anyone but the public plan for the delivery of insured services to a beneficiary of the public plan. The public program is therefore a legally protected monopsony.

In a one tier system private health care insurance can be bought only to cover services which are not covered by the public insurance plan. Beneficiaries cannot (when in their home province) personally buy health care which is covered by the public plan. In a two tier system all beneficiaries have the option of either using the care offered by the public universal plan or buying care from private health care sources, either for cash or through the use of private insurance. The two tier option exists in Britain, where over 10% of the population now carry private insurance. To a large extent Canada has a one tier system for hospital and physicians services, although there is to a small extent a second tier even with respect to these components of health care.

Canadians tend to believe that they have universal access to health care, but Britain comes much closer to universal access than does Canada. The British National Health Service insures a much broader range of health care than is insured under medicare in Canada.

In Canada there is a respectable level of nationally guaranteed equity of access only for hospital and physician services. With respect to home care, dental care, alternative therapies, mental health services, immunization, nonhospital pharmaceuticals and long term care, a Canadian with money to spend has always, and in all provinces, been able to receive a more complete range of services than someone without money to spend. In 1991, 70% of drug expenditures in Canada were in the private sector, and this percentage will be higher in the future as provinces reduce expenditures on outpatient drug programs.

In order to privately and legally buy physician's services which are covered by the provincial insurance plan a Canadian must cross any border, either international or interprovincial. To privately buy inpatient hospital care a Canadian must leave Canada. A Canadian with money to spend has always been able, when he or she so desired, to buy physician and hospital care from the Mayo Clinic or anywhere else outside Canada, but that person could not privately buy those same services at home.

In more recent years the queue jumping has begun to be possible within Canada. If a beneficiary of a provincial medicare plan wishes a cataract removal without a wait and is prepared to pay a $1300-1500 facility fee and, for the residents of Saskatchewan, physician's fees, he or she can go to the Gimble Clinic in Calgary. (A second private ophthalmology clinic in Calgary is currently being planned.) A private MRI facility also opened in Calgary in 1993, and an increasing array of similar examples will appear. The second tier of physician and hospital care is gradually becoming more visible at home.

Some provinces are beginning to restrict payments for care provided in another province. In 1993 Saskatchewan stopped paying any part of the cost of services provided to Saskatchewan residents by the Gimble cataract clinic in Calgary. Other provinces still pay the physician fees but not the facility fee. Quebec will not reimburse residents for the full cost of elective care received out of province if that care was also considered to be available (within a reasonable distance) in Quebec and if the out of province costs were higher than they would have been in Quebec.

Allowing physician and hospital services to be bought at home at private expense is seen by some as the beginning of a two tier system. This interpretation is nonsense. The two tiers are already here.

The *Ontario Independent Health Facilities Act* (IHFA, 1990) was partly a device to eliminate charges to patients by outpatient health care facilities which were providing services which had previously been available only in public hospitals and which had, therefore, formerly been fully insured. The IHFA eliminated elements of a private health care system which was operating alongside the public system. It eradicated some of the emerging elements of a second tier of institutional services, but financial, intellectual, legal, public and provider pressure will soon force enlargement of the second tier.

In Britain the presence of a second level of coverage has not threatened the universal programs any more than did the trips by Premier Bourassa to the United States for treatment of his malignant melanoma. Use of private funds is, in fact, a protection for the public system. Spending outside of the public system reduces pressures within the system. The appearance of a private health care network will not reduce tax revenues so long as expenditures on privately purchased health care which is also available within the public system are not tax deductible. Expenditures on private education are not tax deductible and the same rules could apply to private health care expenditures.

Disadvantages of a two tier system

The most often described disadvantage of a two tier health care system is that access to some health care varies with ability to pay. Low income populations have less access, or no access, to services outside of the publicly financed first tier. This disadvantage is serious if publicly financed health care does not offer a good basic level of good quality protection.

When two tiers exist the publicly financed first tier can, if the public so wishes or allows, offer services which are difficult to find or are of low quality when found. (This is the case in many third world countries but is not limited to poor countries.) On the other hand, the public health care system in Canada will, if the public so wishes, offer good access to good quality care.

The presence of a private health care network will encourage physicians who reach their public program income ceilings to seek additional income within the private system. This can produce a conflict of interest. Physicians may find it to be in their best interest to intentionally make the public services (the first tier) unattractive so that people able to pay will move to the private network. This appears to be the case in Israel. The experience of Israel suggests that when physician income from public sources does not satisfy income expectations physicians find ways of expanding income from private care. (Barer M.L., A. Gafni and J. Lomas, "Accommodating Rapid Growth in Physician Supply", International Journal of Health Services, Vol 19, No 1, p95-115, 1989).

Britain, on the other hand, has avoided the conflict of interest by limiting the opportunity for general practitioner income from work outside of the public system. The key difference is that Israel, as is the case in Canada, provides all physicians with access to public income; Britain does not. Limits on access to billing numbers, combined with reasonable physician incomes from service within the public program, should minimize manipulation in Canada.

In a two tier system the maintenance of a complete data set (of all health care) is more difficult. In Canada the best data-bases are in the fields of hospital and physician services, which come closest to having only one tier. Data-bases describing services provided mostly in the private sector, including nonwestern practitioners, dental care and drug use outside of publicly funded programs, are not nearly so complete.

Consumer protection may also be more difficult to provide when health care is bought in the private sector, although consumer protection in health care should be no more of a problem than in other social and commercial fields. When worrying about quality in a privately funded health care network it is wise to remember the extent to which evidence shows imperfections in the current publicly financed system.

The percent of total national expenditures on health care which are spent in the private sector will probably rise if a two tier system is legitimized, but this percentage has been rising for the last decade and will continue to rise even if there is a continuation of the myth that a one tier system exists.

Until a significant part of the public accepts the inability of the universal plan to provide endless service, and accepts the idea of a two tier system, change is politically risky. The Alberta government in 1987 announced that private insurers would be allowed to operate alongside provincial health care insurance, but within 2 weeks the proposal was withdrawn. The time was not yet politically right (but it soon will be). The 1991 Report of the Premier's Commission on Health Care for Albertans recommended the approval of sale of private health care insurance covering services insured under the universal provincial plan. The recommendation was rejected by the province. The necessary level of public acceptance is, however, almost here.

Disadvantages of a one tier system

A one tier system is intolerably expensive. It relies on public financing for all health care. This has been shown to be a threat to balanced public spending on the various social services which are of importance to health. The threat is greatest when physician payment is by fee-for-service and when there are no limits on the number of physicians who can bill the public plan. In a one tier system it has been assumed that all physicians who wish to will be able to work within the public system, but if billing numbers are limited this assumption cannot be correct.

A physician who is refused a billing number is equivalent to a physician who has voluntarily opted out of medicare. Patients must pay their own bills and there is no reimbursement from government. The patients also cannot, under existing provincial laws, buy private insurance to cover these costs because the law prevents private insurance companies from offering coverage of services insured by the provincial medicare and hospital insurance plans. A home care nurse or a chiropractor who cannot find work in the public system can provide services which are privately insured, but patients who seek physicians services at home outside the public system are discriminated against. Patients, providers and the public system are all losers, and the losses stem from the existence of elements of a one tier system and its associated legislation. The one tier arrangement offends the rights of both physicians and patients.

A one tier system forces Canadians to go abroad to buy services which they could buy less expensively, and at greater national, provincial and personal advantage, at home. Even with high levels of public spending in a one tier system there will still be individuals who will wish to buy more health care than the publicly funded system can or will provide, and so shopping abroad is inevitable.

In summary, a one tier health care system is not a reasonable objective. With a one tier system individuals find it difficult to spend disposable income at home on legal health care services, individuals lose the right to buy their way into a Canadian private health care network when the waiting time in the public system is longer than they choose to accept, Canadian money flows out of the country to buy services which can be produced at lower cost in Canada, the myth of the central importance of health services to health status is perpetuated and public control of health care expenditures is made more difficult.

At the moment there is a good chance that a comprehensive, high quality and publicly financed first tier of health care can be maintained with the present levels of public funding or perhaps with somewhat lower levels. Private spending on additional health care is not, and will not be, a threat to a good publicly financed health care system if the public does not want it to be. The presence of a privately funded educational option has not threatened our Canadian publicly financed school system, and the same can apply in health care.

Publicly funded hospital and medical care insurance plans are becoming increasingly unwilling or unable to provide all of the care people would like to have. Provincial governments should reconsider their prohibition of private insurance for hospital and physician care. Pretending that Canada has a one tier health care system is preventing a rational examination of how a two tiered system can be made to work best for everyone. The important questions are how good the first tier will be and who will be in charge of the second tier.

Choices for operation of the second tier

If residents are given the option of privately buying insurance which covers the same services as are covered by the universal public health care insurance programs then provincial governments have options regarding how this second level of insurance coverage will be administered.

The second tier of health care, the tier which is not funded with public funds, can be managed by a public agency (or agencies), a private agency (or agencies) or a mix of public and private agencies. The private agencies can be profit or nonprofit.

If managed by a private agency there can be varying degrees of public regulation. In Australia the second tier is in private hands but the private insurance companies must charge the same premiums to everyone. (Medical Post, Jan 26, 1993) In Sweden the fees charged by the private providers are regulated to be in line with the fees paid in the public system (Swedish Information Service, 1991). These and other options are available to Canada.

If the second tier of insurance is sold by the for-profit sector Canada will see the development of a new perspective in health care. Demography will not just be of interest because it affects the kind of services people will need, it will be of interest because health care can be marketed quite differently to different age groups, ethnic groups and income groups.

Governments can, if they wish, be the carriers of the second level of insurance as well as the basic universal plan. This second level public insurance would be self sustaining and not as concerned about cost control as the universal plan, but it could easily work with the universal plan to monitor trends, identify hazardous or inappropriate care, standardize and integrate data-bases and protect users in other ways.

As publicly funded programs become more conscious of the need for careful selection of what health care should be paid for, how much of it should be paid for, and under what circumstances, there will be an additional reason for users to wish to have supplemental insurance. The restrictions on care which the public program sees as wisdom may seem, to the user, to be too restrictive. Users are not always impressed with advice as to what health care they should seek or receive. It can be assumed with safety that many persons who are told by the public plan that a particular operation, pill or investigation is not indicated will, despite this opinion, still wish to have that operation, pill or investigation, and they will wish to have that health care covered by insurance of some kind.

RELATIONSHIPS BETWEEN MEDICARE PROGRAMS AND WORKERS COMPENSATION BOARDS (WCB)

Provincial medical and hospital insurance programs do not pay for services which are the responsibility of Workers Compensation Boards.

Workers Compensation Boards are fully financed by employer contributions, rather than government taxation, but Medicare and WCBs have a common clientele and a common set of health care providers. Policy determines the degree of integration of the functions of the two agencies.

In the early years of medicare there were no policy or operational relationships between the provincial medicare plans and the Workers Compensation Boards. In some provinces there is now major operational cooperation between, or integration of, the two agencies.

A number of provinces have fully standardized the payments made to physicians by workers compensation agencies and by the provincial medicare plan. They use a common fee schedule. This standardization is sensible. It is fair to physicians, especially if additional payment is made for completion of the required compensation forms, but the standardization was resisted by physicians and other providers who lost the premiums often paid by compensation agencies. The standardization is of no consequence to employees or taxpayers, but is slightly helpful to employers who pay the medical bills.

The processing of the claims of the two programs can be integrated. Claims processing in provincial medicare programs tends to be highly automated with low per unit administration costs. Addition of the much smaller number of workers compensation health care claims adds very little to the total claims handling costs, has little if any effect on most providers and no effect on users. There are strong reasons for the use by workers compensation agencies of the claims handling capabilities of the provincial medicare plans.

Integration of claims processing is not only efficient. It also helps identify physician billings which are either implicitly or explicitly improper. These billings are difficult to detect if the accounts submitted to the two payment agencies are processed separately. Integration will also be helpful to utilization review programs such as those which monitor the use of prescription drugs or the delivery of other care.

Complete integration of the provincial plan and the health care component of the workers compensation program would involve the removal of health care from compensation agency operations and responsibilities. Care for injury and illness arising from employment would be delivered and billed in the same way as care for illness and injury originating from any other cause. This integration would be another step in the move from fragmented health insurance coverage to a global one in which all illness and injury is looked after within a single system. There would be only one system for providing services and paying providers.

This final stage of integration is unlikely unless governments are assured of recovery from employers of the costs of work related health care. Devices for this recovery are available. The costs of health care arising from work related injuries and illnesses might be charged back to employers via the WCB. WCB incentives to encourage employers to make their workplaces more safe need not change. Full health care integration might encourage correction of current anomalies which lead to selected workers and employers being exempted from workers compensation programs. These exemptions, which vary by province, may apply to medical and law offices, funeral parlours, golf courses, professional athletes, hair salons, farm workers and self employed populations.

Medicare agencies and WCBs both collect data on the care provided, including to whom, by whom, where, when, for what diagnosis or diagnoses, and at what cost. The compensation agencies also collect information on the origin, nature and probable sequelae of the work related injury or illness. Integration of data-bases and data handling would not appear to be difficult.

GATEKEEPER OPTIONS

A *gatekeeper* in health care controls access to some element of that care. Physicians are the most easily identified gatekeepers, but users, user agents, health care professionals other than physicians, and administrative personnel also perform this function. Physicians currently are the gatekeepers to hospital care, most investigations and most prescription drugs. Family physicians are major gatekeepers with respect to access to specialist services, although many specialists see patients without referral and specialists also refer to other specialists. The case manager (usually a nurse) in a home care program is the gatekeeper regarding access to home care, a geriatrician controls access to a geriatric assessment program and a social worker usually controls entry into addiction rehabilitation programs. In those provinces with single points of entry to long term care the single point-of-entry agency is the gatekeeper for a broad range of long term care services and facilities. The actual assessor is usually a nurse.

Case managers are gatekeepers and resource brokers. They represent many interests and are accountable to several masters, including the user to whom resources will be assigned or from whom they will be withheld, the other users who also wish the resources, the providers who will deliver the care and the agency and taxpayers who provide the money. Case managers have been described as one good way to constantly review both cost and quality. (Robinson, et al., "Balancing quality of care and cost-effectiveness through case management", Anna-J, April 1992)

The case managers who are best known in Canada may be the nurses who develop and approve patient care plans for patients in Home Care. These case managers control the volume and type of resources that will be delivered to a patient. Through periodic case reviews they decide whether the care plan should change and they monitor the extent to which the care delivered was consistent with the care plan originally proposed. They decide when care should be discontinued.

Case managers are also used in hospitals. Nurses playing this role at the Toronto Hospital have reduced length of stay, reduced costs and improved outcomes for selected categories of patients. These case managers coordinate care, identify risks and participate in discharge planning. They function much the same as clinical specialist nurses who teach and advise with respect to a particular type of patient, but the assignment of the title of case manager may signify an expansion of role. This expansion of role, if it becomes widespread, will increase the potential for nurse/physician conflict while also increasing the opportunities for greater interdisciplinary support and cooperation.

Case managers are not all nurses. For decades the care of patients arriving at the Mayo Clinic has been coordinated by a designated internist who stays in constant touch with the patient regardless of the nature of the patient's problem. This agent makes sure that the patients schedule, which can include many specialist consultations per day, is followed and is understood by the patient, and that the concerns and questions of the patient and family are addressed.

General practitioners in Britain have, since the introduction of the National Health Service, controlled elective referrals to the hospital based specialist services. Recently the *fund-holding* general practitioners have become responsible for buying health care for their patients at the lowest possible cost. Their role as gatekeeper has expanded.

Second opinion programs use a second person, usually a physician, as a form of gatekeeper. Services will not be delivered unless supported by the second opinion.

A gatekeeper can be an organization as well as an individual. In Ontario in 1991 a Provincial Cardiac Care Registry and Referral Network became operational. The functions of this Registry include application of standardized provincial criteria for coronary artery by-pass surgery. Using province-wide patient data the Registry assures patient access on the basis of clinical priorities and also assures more complete and equitable use of available resources. The Registry largely eliminated earlier problems of delayed access to cardiovascular surgical units. This type of provincially initiated and funded solution to a clinical problem is likely to be a prototype. The solution prevented patients from being on long waiting lists for selected surgeons or in selected locations when other surgeons and other locations were much less busy. The solution established a gatekeeper who made certain that persons in the queue should be there, and who assisted persons to find the resources needed at the time they were needed.

In the United States the role of gatekeeper for elective care has at times been assumed by third party payers. Insurance companies often seek evidence that care is required before payment is approved, a process known as preadmission certification. Office staff have become the defenders of the payers purse and the gatekeepers of care.

PROVINCIAL OR NATIONAL HEALTH COUNCILS

Provincial and national advisory health councils are a relatively minor organizational option. Most provinces at some time in their history have had such a broadly mandated council, but they have now mostly disappeared. Nova Scotia is an exception. It has a newly formed Provincial Health Council which in 1993 released its first report. Provincial Health Councils have not been found to have any special ability to bring forward sensible recommendations nor do they have any special ability to speak on behalf of anyone but themselves. Some Provincial Health Councils disappeared because they consistently recommended actions which were not affordable or not consistent with government policy. Ministries and Cabinets are more representative of the public than an appointed Board or Council.

The general rejection of the broadly based advisory provincial health council has not applied to sectoral advisory Councils. These sectoral or problem specific advisory Councils have been useful and continue to be widely used. They have in various provinces been created to advise with respect to mental health, emergency health services, services to the physically disabled, suicide prevention and other issues and services.

ALTERNATIVES TO PRIVATE PRACTITIONERS AND FEE-FOR-SERVICE

Most provinces have either promoted, encouraged or at least tolerated health care delivery arrangements involving physicians who do not bill on fee-for-service. Community health centres (by many names) are the most common model.

The objectives of community health centres (CHC) and the expectations of the provinces are not always clear. Are the CHCs meant to reduce costs, place an important social service under the control of the community, decrease the power of the medical profession, provide services to populations who are poorly served by fee-for-service practitioners, reduce the use of fee-for-service, increase attention to primary prevention and health promotion, increase the innovative use of non-physicians, expand user control over their personal health care decisions, deliver a higher quality of care, integrate health services with other social services, mobilize the community to fight social injustice, or some combination of these and other objectives?

There is great confusion and variation with respect to the extent to which priority should be given to service delivery versus community development or community animation. Quebec has in the 1990s opted clearly and decisively in favor of service delivery, a complete reversal of the primary orientation of many centres in Quebec in the 1970s. The Ontario centres have no standard orientation.

Provincial policies regarding CHCs have covered the full spectrum. Governments may support the model but only when communities provide the initiative (as in Ontario in the 1980s and 1990s), actively promote a province wide network (as in Quebec with CLSCs), actively promote the model but primarily in isolated communities which have trouble with continuity of medical coverage (as in B.C. in the 1970s) give no support because of objections from organized medicine (as in Saskatchewan after the signing of the Saskatoon agreement which ended the doctors strike of 1962), or oppose them (as in Ontario when Dr. Potter was the Minister of Health in the early 1970s).

CHCs usually have a community board (although in Quebec most board members were until recently not representatives of the community), salaried physicians, some integration of health and social services, a global budget and a commitment to prevention and health promotion. Supporters of Community Health Centres have for decades been touting them as the wave of the future and as a source of savings and high quality care. With the exception of Quebec, however, no Canadian province has made CHCs an integral and universal part of its health services network. Community Health Centres still are looking for a defined role in most provinces.

Users, staff and communities like CHCs. There is considerable evidence that they are less expensive than fee-for-service outlets, but not much recent evaluation. They offer consumer and community control over an important human service, local level integration of health and social services, greater use of nonphysicians in the delivery of care and greater opportunities for integration of ambulatory care into regional planning. These reasons are in themselves ample reasons for CHC expansion regardless of the possibility that they may not always be more cost-effective than other delivery options.

Experience suggests that without a regional or provincial plan, and without a strategically identified role for CHCs within that plan, the individual CHCs which grew from the efforts of committed community supporters rapidly settle into a state of funded contentedness from which balanced and integrated systems are unlikely to grow. CHCs (in provinces other than Quebec) usually operate with little reference to other CHCs. After Quebec, Manitoba has the most CHCs, with at least fifteen in operation (ten in Winnipeg), but with no provincial network. After twenty years of existence in Ontario, and with about forty CHCs operating, they serve only about two percent of the population and have not developed into anything resembling a cooperative community service with plans for growth.

Health Service Organizations (HSOs), which exist only in Ontario, are funded by a capitation payment for each patient on their roster. A rostered patient is one who has indicated that the HSO will be their primary source of a defined range of health care. When persons who are on the rosters of an HSO obtain care from professionals unrelated to the HSO, and when the services are equivalent to those for which the agency receives a capitation payment, some of the external costs are charged against the HSO. HSOs, which are physician, hospital or university operated, were all originally fee-for-service practices. Payment was switched to capitation at physician request. There are more than seventy HSOs in place in Ontario, but expansion of the program was frozen in 1993. In 1993 the physicians in Nipawin, Saskatchewan began a capitation experiment.

Comprehensive Health Organizations (CHO) in Ontario and Les Organisations de soins intégrés de santé (OSIS) in Quebec are other capitation alternatives. With leadership from the Ontario Ministry of Health, planning for CHOs proceeded vigorously in 1990 and 1991. Progress slowed considerably in 1992 and 1993.

The CHO is in some ways similar to the rural multi-service boards in Manitoba in the sense that both have an inclusive budget from which to fund a network of local services. They differ in the range and location of services for which they are responsible. A CHO is funded to provide or buy services for a defined population, whereas a health board in Manitoba or elsewhere is responsible only for the operation of a number of sources of care in its own community or region. The CHO is responsible for a population; the rural board is responsible for a series of institutions and programs.

The future of the CHO model appears uncertain. Both CHOs and OSIS are Canadian mutants of the Health Maintenance Organizations (HMOs) of the United States, but differences between the two countries may make regional budgets a better option for Canada.

WALK-IN CLINICS

Most provinces now have *walk-in clinics*. They are an entrepreneurial model in which an owner/manager (who may or may not be a physician) employs physicians on a shared income basis. These clinics are often in shopping centres. They are usually staffed by physicians who assign a percentage of their fee-for-service billings to the clinic. The physicians providing care may be residents earning extra money, new physicians seeking additional income while establishing a practice, physicians who wish to avoid the investment associated with opening an office, or physicians with other full-time jobs who are moon-lighting.

Walk-in clinics do not pretend to provide on-going care to patients. They have been accused of duplicating services better provided by a personal family physician. Provinces and permanently established physicians have sought to control their proliferation.

There will be no payoff from extensive analysis of these clinics unless useful techniques for their control can be found. Control will be easier when there is limited physician access to billing numbers.

The impact of walk-in clinics on costs and on other health care sources is not well documented. They have been credited with, or blamed for, the 10% drop in emergency room utilization which occurred in the late 1980s in Toronto hospitals. They represent a smaller financial threat in provinces with caps on total payments for physicians services than in provinces without such caps.

THE ROLE OF HEALTH CARE COOPERATIVES

The Canadian cooperative movement promotes health care cooperatives (Apland, L.E., Restructuring Canada's Health Services System, 1992, p365-76) but it is not easy to see the difference between a health care cooperative and a community health centre. Perhaps there is none.

The cooperative movement believes that their health centre model will promote collaboration between community based economic development and community organized social services including health services. This coordination of economic and social development sounds desirable, but collaboration should be able to occur whether or not a community sponsored health centre conforms to traditional cooperative organizational characteristics.

ORGANIZATION AT THE MINISTRY LEVEL

Alternatives which have been tried by one or more governments include placing all health care responsibilities in one ministry, placing insurance functions in one ministry and other provincial health care responsibilities in another, and placing all health and social services in one ministry. Choice of organization is not so important as the quality of senior personnel. Interministerial and intraministerial cooperation and coordination are needed no matter what ministries exist.

Within Ministries of Health there are endless vertical and horizontal alignment options, and optional degrees of emphasis on matrix or program based organization charts. Once again, organizational form is not as important as corporate mood, intent and competence.

Options also exist for performance of strategic planning functions. It probably makes very little difference whether the Ministry establishes a separate strategic planning unit or disperses this function to all operating units. The main requirement is that someone competently perform the strategic functions. It is equally unimportant whether all major insurance programs (hospitals, physicians and perhaps drugs) are placed under one assistant deputy minister (ADM) or whether each program is given its own ADM. The important requirement is for competence at the top.

INSTITUTIONAL VS COMMUNITY CARE

The choice between institutional and community care may not be primarily an organizational issue but it has significant organizational implications. Some services are inherently institutional while others are necessarily delivered in the community, but often either location can be appropriate. When choice exists, policy can opt for delivery in the community, from institutions, or both.

Palliative care, respite care, services to most of the long term psychiatrically disabled, addiction rehabilitation, care of minor emergencies, abortions, many surgical procedures, uncomplicated obstetrics, early post natal care, care of the severely developmentally handicapped, care of chronically disabled individuals on respirators, and most long term care usually associated with institutionalization are among the examples of health care which can be delivered either in the community or in an institution.

Many seriously psychiatrically disabled, developmentally handicapped, brain damaged or severely physically disabled can with appropriate support successfully and happily live in the community. Other persons who benefit from stable, safe and uncomplicated environments, who often suffer from multiple handicaps and who have a markedly limited capacity to visualize and take advantage of their environment, are probably best served, and perhaps at lower cost, in large facilities able to offer a broad range of in-house social and specialty opportunities. The line between those for whom the institutional environment is best and those who will benefit from community placement is unclear. The level of cognition, the existence of family, the ability and willingness of the family to be involved in care, and the wishes of the client (when these wishes can be known) will affect choice.

Choices will be more rational and defensible if a number of guidelines and principles are kept in mind:

- Neither institutional nor noninstitutional care should be seen as inherently good or bad. Each can be either.
- Choices should be made primarily on the basis of relative cost-effectiveness and community/user preference, not professional or bureaucratic preference or historical patterns.
- Preferences cannot be generalized. Different patient characteristics require different choices.
- Policies and systems should allow patients to move easily from community to institution and vice versa as needed. For many households a mix of community and institutional care will be best. Coordination will be needed in the field and between bureaucracies.
- Care in the community will at times be tolerable to the disabled and their household caregivers only if the support systems are flexible. Respite care, for example, should if possible be tailored to fit the needs of each household.
- Patient and family preferences should be routinely identified and should dominate resource allocation and patient placement, with the proviso that user and family choices should not be allowed to lead to major additional public cost.
- Inadequate institutional care should not be compared to good community care and vice versa.
- There will be significant regional and population differences in preferences regarding institutional versus community care. If equitable provincial funding is offered, local and individual discretion could be allowed.
- The wheel does not need to be reinvented. There is now a large literature on the options and many operating examples of almost everything.

Objectives may determine success. Saskatchewan pioneered community care of the psychiatrically disabled and confirmed its success. Their aim was a higher quality of life for the users. There was no search for savings. Ontario closed psychiatric institutions in the 1970s to save money and succeeded by moving patients to residential ghettos or to sidewalks. To the users there was little success.

The undesirable effects of deinstitutionalization can be due to a failure to put adequate levels of community services in place before patient discharge. This failure may be intentional (the transfer may have been supported as a way to save money and new services would defeat the purpose) or may arise from inadequate strategic and operational planning skills, possibly associated with inadequate interministerial communication. Patients may move from a health department program to a social service program in another department, and therefore joint planning is needed.

A perception that all long term institutionalization is inherently bad, and that all long term psychiatrically disabled, developmentally handicapped, physically disabled or cognitively impaired persons are better off in group homes or other community based services than in institutions, will lead to social and financial failures. This proposition, which has powerful proponents, has never been defensible in either financial or outcome terms. (Wattie, B., "The Deinstitutionalization Debate", Perceptions, Nov/Dec 1982)

Deciding whether to promote (or mandate) institutional versus community care should not be an act of faith. Choices ought to be made on the basis of principles and of evidence, with user preference being important if the cost-effectiveness of options is similar or if user funds are used to cover additional costs associated with a more expensive option. In evaluating the options the possibility of undesirable outcomes because of care in the community should be given no more or less consideration than the possibility of undesirable outcomes because care is given in an institution, and in the documentation of outcomes the good and bad side of the options should be measured against a broad range of objective and subjective indicators.

Short term care, as with long term care, can also often be delivered in either institutions or the community, as with post surgical recovery and recovery from paediatric illness. The important criteria are, as with long term care, cost-effectiveness, protection of public funds and patient choice. Usually the making of the choices is easier in short term care than in LTC.

Whether minor emergency care should be provided primarily by hospital emergency departments or by nonhospital facilities is not yet decided. If almost all hospitals are to operate an emergency department (as is now the case) then they should serve patients with minor problems or unit costs will climb. If, on the other hand, there is only one 24 hour emergency service for each million or half million urban population, and if there are fewer rural 24 hour departments than now exist, then it is reasonable to assure communities of access to additional locations where minor emergencies can receive attention 16-18 hours per day. These locations could be in hospitals or elsewhere. The objective is a regional network which adequately, and at reasonable cost, responds to physical, psychiatric and psychosocial emergencies.

Quebec in 1990 announced that the CLSCs would become minor emergency centres. The proposed change of function will, to be clinically and financially successful, require an expansion of the diagnostic and treatment capabilities of the CLSCs and the closure of many hospital emergency departments.

SUMMARY

Organizational choices can promote or inhibit good planning, good management and good spending. The organizational choices are not important in themselves, but they are means to an end or ends. They are not as important as is often thought.

The nonprofit and single payer patterns which now dominate should be continued for universal publicly financed programs. The desirability of a two tier health care system should be accepted. Health care should be delivered through a variety of delivery and payment models. Mixed public-private insurance should be carefully considered as an option which can preserve universality and lower public costs. There should be full integration of health care funded by the province and health care funded by Workers Compensation Boards.

Whether a separate network of women's health centres is needed is unclear. There is certainly a need for more user friendly, more female sensitive and more female controlled health care.

Chapter 8

Planning and Evaluation

INTRODUCTION

Policy options do not include whether or not to plan; everyone wishes to plan. There are options, however, with respect to the goals to be served, how to plan, who should do the planning, who will pay for it, how long to spend doing it, which factors to take into consideration, what information should be seen as important, what indicators, criteria, measures and standards to use, how to choose the criteria, indicators, measures and standards, who will be in charge of, and who will participate in, the various processes and what relationships and organizational structures will provide interaction between planners, consumers, providers and agencies.

The links between evaluation and planning are strong and therefore both planning and evaluation options are reviewed in this chapter.

BASIC CHOICES: THE BIG PICTURE

In this world of new competition for public dollars, governments, in particular their Ministries of Health, have several general options within which they can plan. These options lead to quite different futures.

Option 1. The open-ended 1970s

The open-ended option would perpetuate the myth that health care is central to health status. Planning within this erroneous theorem would lead to continued demands for endless health care at endless public cost. The pressure in the political pressure cooker would rise until the heat would force financial bail-outs for the sources of health care, especially hospitals and doctors. There would be infusion of new money into health care at whatever rate the taxpayers could stand. This option would emphasize *"more and more powerful interventions, guided by better and better science"* (Evans R.G., and Stoddart G.L., Producing Health: Consuming Health Care, CHEPA, WP 90-6), but with too few improvements in health status to merit the cost. There would be perpetuation of the myth of a one tier health care system and of the emotional rejection of user fees for hospital and physician services.

This option can in fantasy be supported. It can be claimed, but not proven, that the hospitals and others who deliver health care are the best place to put public dollars. It can, but not wisely, be assumed that health care providers will allocate resources wisely.

Option 2. Top-down cost control: the option of the 1980s

In the top-down cost control option the government quite arbitrarily decides how much to spend on health care. Spending ceilings are selected partly in response to new evidence but primarily on the basis of the capabilities of the treasury. Because there is, and will be, no magical formula to assist the government to know how much to spend on health care, all it will do is prescribe expenditure ceilings and protect them. The ceilings will be protected through the use of many regulatory techniques such as reductions in insured services, increases in user payments and restrictions on the number of providers.

This option will protect the taxpayer as taxpayer but will not protect him or her as a health care consumer.

Option 3. Better spending without cost control

If this option is chosen the government will assume that a serious and well funded effort to improve spending will bring health care costs under control while also bringing more health per dollar spent. Government might also assume that if dollars are being spent more carefully and productively it would be wrong to limit the supply of them. Within this option there would be little emphasis on the use of regulatory cost control devices.

This rationale led to the creation of Professional Standards Review Organizations (PSROs) (later changed to Peer Review Organizations [PROs]) in the United States 20 years ago and to an emphasis on prospective payment mechanisms. There is also a similarity to the situation in the 1960s when it was assumed that in time health care costs would settle down as unmet needs were taken care of by unlimited access to health care.

This option would see great attention to improved professional decision making and reduced provision of inappropriate health care, but the total spending on health care would be allowed to continue to rise if there was additional useful health care to be bought. This option would bring better use of health care dollars but costs would continue to rise. The financial risks are high.

Option 4. Better spending plus rigid cost control

In this option there would be a major emphasis on better spending of health care dollars in combination with continued regulatory top-down cost control through caps and global budgets. Continuation of the tight cost control would be likely to be more tolerable to all parties and would be more likely to be able to be maintained in the long term because of the associated emphasis on better spending.

Cost control would be joined by evaluation, accountability and improved professional decision making. Services provided would become more consistent with the wisdom of the day. Access to cost-effective services could in the short term be maintained with current levels of spending. At the least, access to necessary health care would be better maintained than would be the case if noncost-effective services continued to be provided. The process for improved spending would rely heavily on widespread participation of users and providers. Consumers would hopefully become more supportive of continued limits on public spending on health care.

Ceilings on spending are a necessary complement to better spending. The ceilings provide incentives for users and providers to spend more judiciously, protect the public purse while better spending is being implemented, and protect the public purse in case the improved decision making does not lower costs. Without rigid expenditure controls the managers and planners of the system would probably not have found, or at least would not have implemented, the majority of the devices which have allowed providers to maintain service levels with fewer resources. Without tight ceilings on spending the field will clamour for bail-outs rather than assign their energies to improved spending.

Option 5. The addition of Healthy Public Policy

This option would combine better health care spending and cost control with aggressive promotion of Healthy Public Policy. Health Impact Analysis would become a routine part of policy analysis.

This option accepts the idea of all government spending being for health. The question of how much should be spent on health care remains, and must be dealt with, but it is dealt with in a larger context in which all spending is *health* spending. Acceptance that health care is not one of the top determinants of health status promotes control of health care spending; this in turn allows a more balanced distribution of public funds to all social sectors.

The Healthy Public Policy concept acknowledges the need for all government ministries and programs to see protection and elevation of health status as a part of their mandate. It also accepts the idea that the primary prevention of illness and injury is a responsibility of all departments/ministries including the Department/Ministry of Health. This option will expose the competition between health care spending and spending on other social services, and it will expose the lack of a clear boundary for what is called health care.

The finding and funding of foster homes in Ontario is an example of the inequities which will become more noticed. In 1992 30-40% of children in Metro Toronto requiring foster home placement had to be sent up to 150 miles away because foster homes could not be found in Toronto. This situation attracted almost no attention, whereas the need to send some cancer and cardiovascular surgical patients out of Toronto for care produced headlines. The disruption to the children of leaving their schools and friends was almost surely greater than the disruption caused by travel to receive relatively short term cancer or cardiovascular therapy. When *health* becomes the top priority *health care* will not always receive special status and attention.

Until the principles of Healthy Public Policy are in place the glamor and cost of health care may lead to inadequate protection of other areas of social policy.

Option 6. Let's pretend.

In this last option there would be a pretence of support for better spending (as in options 3 and 4) and for Healthy Public Policy (as in Option 5) but no allocation of resources to the task. This is in reality options 1 and 2. It is the option of smoke and mirrors, of intentional or unintentional deception. It is the scenario in which Ministers and Deputy Ministers of Health speak regularly about the wish for better spending of public dollars but establish no mechanisms to bring it about.

GOALS

Goals can be frivolous or substantive. They can be taken seriously or be ignored. They can be window dressing or the basis for development of strategic plans from which actions will flow.

The identification of provincial and federal goals for health and for health care has not to date been a controversial process. Goals usually have had almost unanimous if not unanimous support. The lack of controversy around goals which are often quite futuristic is encouraging, although acceptance is unlikely to be so universal when the general directions are converted into programs.

Agreement with respect to general goals is only the first step. General goals do not identify the appropriate balance between prevention and treatment or between ideological options such as public and private insurance. They do not help much when dealing with the mundane issues of organization and delivery.

One reason for lack of controversy in the presentation of health care goals has been a willingness to present a list which contains internal incompatibilities. When this is done the list becomes acceptable to everyone. The British Columbia Royal Commission on Health Care and Costs, for example, recommended provincial endorsement of the five principles in the Canada Health Act and also recommended that the system must be reformed within existing levels of funding. Universal application of the principles in the Canada Health Act would require full first dollar public funding for drugs, dentistry and all other health care. This is impossible within present funding.

Goals can be sincerely offered by a Minister and ignored in resource allocation. In Ontario during the 1980s there was a stated special interest in improving mental health services, but in the period 1979-80 to 1989-90 the proportion of the budget of the Ministry of Health which was actually spent on mental health services is said to have declined from 7.7% to 4.6%. (Lurie, S. and J. Trainor, Canada's Mental Health, March 1992, p12)

Health goals versus health care goals

Through their *health* goals governments express their hopes regarding the length and quality of life of their residents. All policies of all departments and programs, including departments of health and their health care programs, will affect the extent to which the government will accomplish the established health goals.

Health care goals describe what a province wishes to accomplish through publicly funded health care. These *health care* goals, to the extent they are accomplished, will, in combination with the outcomes from the policies and programs in other departments, allow the province to meet its *health* goals.

National versus provincial health goals

Some sources strongly support national health goals. The Canadian Public Health Association (CPHA) has argued that *"Canada needs to establish an overall strategy for health"* and that *"national health goals should be broad in nature and related to the remediation of structural social inequalities"*. (Caring About Health, Sept, 1992) These sentiments represent a point of view which is shared by many, but they ignore the right of provinces to go their own way. They also can be seen to be inconsistent with the strong support of the CPHA for local and regional empowerment, a concept which can be applied to provinces as well as other regions.

All levels of government have areas of jurisdiction which are of significance to health. If each government (especially the provincial and federal governments) accepts the proposition that its first responsibility is the preservation and improvement of the health of its people then each will develop goals and work to achieve them. But it will be no tragedy if goals differ. The general directions are seldom likely to be totally contradictory, but if provinces wish to go different directions then that is their right. Worrying too much about the refinement and standardization of goals could consume energies better directed towards attaining goals which are consistent with the capabilities and philosophies of individual governments.

Standardization of goals probably is unattainable when, through the democratic process, different jurisdictions produce governments with different philosophies.

Federal health goals and health care goals

The federal government is, in the constitution, given jurisdiction over many policy areas including interprovincial trade, interprovincial and coastal waters, unemployment insurance, interprovincial transportation, national defence, banking, the money supply and national issues in agriculture, fisheries, and environmental protection. Federal policies in all of these areas could promote accomplishment of federal health goals.

The federal government has committed itself to the Ottawa Charter on Health Promotion (as approved by the first World Health Organization conference on Health Promotion in 1986), to the United Nations Charter of Childrens Rights, to the environmental concepts of the Bruntland Commission and of the environmental summit in Brazil in 1992, and to many other similar international and domestic statements. These commitments are important to health, and all are reflections of national health goals.

Health goals should be expressed in terms of health status and they should in some general way clarify targets. Statements evolved from goals, usually called objectives, will express the targets in more precise terms. The Ottawa Charter on Health Promotion produced a framework which included specific strategies (fostering public participation, strengthening community health services and coordinating healthy public policy) directed towards increasing equity, emphasizing prevention and supporting self-help, mutual aid and healthy environments. (Achieving Health For All, Ottawa, 1986)

Besides writing *health goals* the federal government should write *health care* goals with respect to those limited populations for which it has constitutional responsibility for health care.

Provincial health goals

The Canadian constitution gives provinces jurisdiction over health care, education, social services, employers and employees associated with industry or commerce operating entirely in one province, intraprovincial highways and traffic and determination of the roles of local government. Provinces are also responsible for most law enforcement and for the administration of justice. Provincial governments are major players in health and the dominant players in health care.

The defining of provincial health goals was a growth industry in the 1980s. Quebec preceded most of the field with its report in 1984. Ontario in 1987 produced the Evans Report, the Spasoff Report and the Podborsky Report, and other provinces have produced similar documents.

Provincial health goals or objectives tend to have been selected after examination of the causes of premature death and of the hazards to health status. Hazards targeted for action may be selected on the basis of their frequency (prevalence), the severity of their consequences to the health status of the population (their impact on mental, psychosocial or physical health), the financial impacts of the hazard and the potential for producing change. (There is no payoff in targeting a hazard which cannot be overcome at tolerable cost.)

Goals are by definition quite general but even broad statements can reflect major shifts in direction, as illustrated by the five goals chosen by the Ontario Premiers Council on Health Strategy in 1989. The goals chosen were:

1. Shift the emphasis to prevention and health promotion.
2. Foster strong and supportive families and communities.
3. Ensure a safe, high quality physical environment.
4. Increase the number of years of good health for the citizens of Ontario by reducing illness, disability and premature death.
5. Provide accessible, affordable and appropriate health services for all.

These goals had been presented in support of an associated vision. The vision was:

"We see an Ontario in which people live longer in good health, and disease and disability are progressively reduced. We see people empowered to realize their full health potential through a safe, nonviolent environment, adequate income, housing, food, education and a valued role to play in family, work and the community. We see people having equitable access to affordable and appropriate health care regardless of geography, income, age, gender or cultural background. Finally, we see everyone working together to achieve better health for all."

One of the striking features of this vision and the associated goals is the extent to which the goals cannot be accomplished through health care. They require the attention of all the departments and policies of all levels of government, and attainment will be more likely if there is active support from the private sector.

The Ontario documents setting out health goals were followed, in a document titled *From Vision to Action*, by presentation of the key elements of a strategic plan for health care.

Provincial health goals, and objectives in support of those goals, can be expressed in more concrete terms than were used by Ontario. The objectives described by Quebec in 1984 were:

• reduce the number of children born with serious defects
• promote the emotional and social development of children five years of age and under

- reduce traffic accident fatalities, especially of the young
- reduce the number of unwanted pregnancies
- reduce the incidence and severity of mental health problems in 15-24 year old persons
- reduce occupationally related physical and mental health problems
- reduce the incidence, severity and impact of joint diseases
- reduce the incidence and impact of cancer
- promote autonomy of the elderly

Provincial health care goals

With respect to health care each province is, in constitutional terms, a country. Each country is free to develop health care systems as it sees fit; each Canadian province has the same right. The selection of health goals and health care goals is part of that right.

Provincial health care goals and priorities have, in the past and to a lesser extent to-day, often been more evident in what was done than in what was said. Priorities and policies were indicated by actions rather than explicitly expressed goals or objectives. Until 20-30 years ago (depending on the province), for example, the psychiatrically disabled were intentionally given the least attention possible, but this intention was not explicitly stated in policy.

Provinces have now (whether stated or not) accepted the health care objectives of limits on spending, de-emphasis of acute care, de-emphasis of institutional care, protection of quality of life as well as length of life, more prevention and health promotion and greater user control. (Brunet, J., S. Dillard, Y. Brunelle and M. Blanchet, 1985.)

In 1990 the Quebec report *Une Réforme Axée Sur le Citoyen* set out the following health care goals.
- greater accountability
- greater efficiency
- greater consumer control
- increased personal and regional equity
- greater emphasis on outcomes as a measure of success
- emphasis on prevention and health promotion
- provincial affordability

Actions recommended in support of these goals included:
- new functions and importance for CLSCs as intake points
- an accreditation process for physicians (this was later abandoned)
- closure of Community Health Departments in hospitals
- fewer chronic care patients in acute care beds
- an additional 7000 residential extended care spaces

What can be seen as health care objectives for Ontario were spelled out in the Framework Agreement between the Ontario Medical Association and the Ministry of Health in 1991.
- to maintain the principles of medicare, including universality and accessibility;
- to ensure a stable, constructive and long-term relationship between the Government and the Ontario Medical Association;
- to enhance the quality and effectiveness of medical care;
- to co-operate in more effective management of physician services to achieve more value for health care spending in Ontario;
- to co-operate with other health care providers on a range of broader health care management issues to achieve more value for health care spending by Ontario and to improve the quality of care;
- to ensure fair and equitable compensation for physicians;

- to contribute to the achievement of an appropriate number, mix and distribution of physicians based on Ontario's needs.

In this agreement there is a greater emphasis on better spending than is present in many other statements.

Other provinces have produced similar documents such as Quality Health for Manitobans: The Action Plan (1992) and A Saskatchewan Vision for Health (1992).

ISSUES IN PLANNING: AND APPROACHES TO THE ISSUES

What planning is not

Planning is not the collection of data. Planning, even poor planning, is barely begun when everything has been described. Inventories, census data, balance sheets, health surveys and productivity records are merely inputs into the planning process. They are part of the background. Epidemiologists have been known to believe that if enough data is collected not only will decisions flow automatically from those data, but the decisions will be good. If only things were that simple.

What planning is

Planning is a dynamic process, a thinking exercise, which involves, among other steps, the identification of alternative goals, choosing a goal (or more than one), the identification of alternative processes through which the goal(s) might be accomplished, and then choosing the preferred implementation process or processes.

The planning process has a number of generic steps and characteristics but is not a recipe. The steps and characteristics change significantly as the milieu and the issues change. The milieu includes the stability in the organization. Policy development and planning are quite different when an organization is undergoing major changes in direction, as is now often the case in health care in Canada. (Bartunek, J. and L.M. Reis, "The interplay of organization development and organizational transformation", in Research in Organizational Change and Development, Vol 2, JAI Press, 1988, pp 97-134)

The terminology and process of planning

The terminology is, as usual, less important than the concepts and processes. Rigid or personalized interpretations of terms can lead to unproductive dispute.

During the first stage in planning someone decides what to do, and at a later stage someone decides how to get it done. The first is usually called strategic planning; the second is usually called operational planning. The first determines the activities to which resources will (and will not) be assigned; the second determines the manner in which the resources will be used.

That looks pretty straight-forward, and it is in theory, but the process is cyclical and invites confusion if terminology is thought to be important. Those who like everything to be neat and academically presentable quickly disagree over which activities fit in which category and who is entitled to say they are strategic planners.

Consider an example. Governments (politicians) decide they wish to fund universal health insurance. This certainly is a strategic planning decision. If it was reached through a careful analysis of options (a policy analysis) then it was a good strategic planning process and it should have ended with a wise decision.

Is that the end of strategic planning? It may be to the politicians, but not to the next level of decision makers. Someone must now deal with how to fund the program, who will administer it, exactly what services are covered and how providers will be paid. The public servants or committees or others who must answer these questions will certainly think they are deciding what to do, and therefore they are strategic planners. But they also are deciding how to get something done, so they are operational planners.

Let us assume that the second round of policy analyses leads to a decision to include the services of faith healers in the universal plan and to authorize user fees for these services. Now a new set of committees or public servants will continue the policy development process. They will examine the various types of user fees that might be used and decide what kind would be most appropriate. The higher level decision makers may think that all of the strategic planning decisions have been made, but the new decision makers know they are trying to decide what to do and therefore they too are strategic planners.

The conclusion should be that the extent to which selected persons are identified as strategic planners versus some other kind of planner is not very important. The process is what matters, and for everyone the process is the same. Know what is wanted, examine the alternatives to get it, and choose one. Then, within that preferred option, examine the next set of options and choose one, and then continue ad infinitum (or so it seems). Don't fuss about whether you are allocatively efficient or whether someone else thinks you are strategically important or unimportant, or what your title is. Just use the right process and it will lead to a better decision than if a less defensible process had been used.

It is self evident that some policy makers and planners make more global decisions than others. For the rest of this discussion the term strategic planning will apply to the activities of senior policy makers (however you care to define senior).

Strategic planning decisions are likely to be best, and acceptance highest, if everyone knows the constraints which are firm, for example, that total expenditures are capped, that equity will be sought, that choices will be made on the basis of objective evidence when it is available, that users, providers and payers will routinely be part of the decision making process, and that no-one is going to get everything they want.

Who does the planning and where

Who controls the planning, and where it is done, varies with the extent to which senior power brokers prefer technocratic versus democratic decision making, prefer open versus closed processes and prefer consumer, government or provider control.

Shared control over planning is attractive. Consumers, through opinion polls, community development processes and other participation exercises can indicate what they would like to emphasize. They might, for example, indicate support for user fees and regional budgets. Policy makers and planners can then devise systems which acknowledge user preferences while also recognizing technocratic and political preferences.

Strategic planning in health care tends to be a provincial responsibility, with varying degrees of regional participation. Provincial policy makers and planners tend to decide what is to be done. They may or may not be involved in deciding how it will be done. The strategic thinking is usually done within the ministry, although the Ontario Ministry of Health for many years assigned this function to an outside agency, the Ontario Council of Health. When this Council was abandoned it left a large Ministry without a corps of strategic planners, a deficiency from which it has not yet recovered.

Strategic planning decisions are, in Canada, usually made by representatives of the public rather than by representatives of providers, a characteristic consistent with the consumer era and with a system in which there is a great deal of public funding.

Area-wide (regional) planning

Area-wide planning was one of the first tools endorsed by governments for improved spending and cost restraint. Area-wide planning may be centrally or regionally initiated and controlled, but the provinces are now the dominant players. For smaller provinces the province is dominant because regions or districts within the province are able to be responsible for only limited types of planning. Larger provinces can, if they wish, have regional planning agencies with significant responsibilities for strategic and operational planning.

Area-wide planning has to date tended to emphasize eliminating undesirable duplication, increasing coordination and taking advantage of economies of scale. These objectives have, in the hospital sector, led to the closure of many pediatric and obstetrical wards, to regional shared services such as laundry and purchasing, and to the concentration of specialized services such as dialysis in only selected institutions. The main objectives have been the lowering of unit costs and the elevation of technical quality. In the future these objectives will be joined by the objective of improving the extent to which the services provided are clinically appropriate and are consistent with community priorities.

Comprehensive area-wide plans for emergency care, mental health services and ambulatory care are still in the future for most regions. Far too many 24 hour emergency departments still operate, integrated mental health service networks have been described well but seldom implemented, and ambulatory care is still delivered through individualistic and noncommunicating offices and clinics.

Regional planning will become more essential as funding continues to shrink and regional budgets become more common.

The quality of decision making in planning

Strategic planning in health care tends to be weak because not much of the planning is rooted in an assessment of public benefit per dollar spent. It is difficult to evaluate policy alternatives well and choose the preferred one when the alternatives cannot be evaluated in terms of their relative cost-effectiveness. The problem is accentuated if strategic planning skills are in short supply.

At the macro policy level intuition and ideology will for the foreseeable future, in most circumstances, be more important determinants of policy than will hard evidence. Higher level policy decisions will often continue to be made through largely unscientific processes because there is much less evidence to guide these policy makers than there is to help health care professionals dealing with only one patient. Health Impact Analysis (HIA) should routinely be performed, but it will be a decade or two before the process will be refined to the point where the analyses of most policies will be dominated by sound objective data. This does not mean that HIA should be abandoned, or that these analytical skills should not be refined. It does mean that many of the emphases and directions in health care, such as the expansion of community based services, should be recognized as representing a guess or a hunch with only very primitive supporting objective evidence. This uncertainty will continue for some time.

Health care professionals dealing with individual patients produce *care plans*, which quite accurately indicates that planning is being done. These planning decisions are increasingly dominated by objective findings and hard data, especially for physical health problems.

Strengthening strategic planning

Some provincial ministries of health do not contain a corps of competent and creative strategic planners. These persons are a prerequisite to the preparation of policy options for presentation to a minister or cabinet. These persons may or may not be responsible for the analysis of operational alternatives through which ministerial or cabinet objectives might be met.

Strategic thinkers are particularly important for new ministers of health. New ministers may be well briefed on what is going on in the ministry, and even what is firmly in the pipeline, but they would benefit from briefings regarding the options which may be worth exploring. This strategic thinking function is most likely to be acceptable if the actors are philosophically in tune with the minister, but competence and experience are even more essential.

The process of strategic thinking will be strengthened if there is, throughout Ministries of Health, encouragement of controversial and intellectual discussion on many fronts. Bright and motivated individuals can contribute to and improve the brain storming which leads to better planning, implementation and management, but they are likely to contribute only if milieu and mechanisms so allow.

Planning is strengthened when it is centered in units which contain a *critical mass* of individuals. The critical mass principle applies whether one is designing a health care system for to-morrow or planning for the care of paraplegics or any other patient group. It also applies to the planning of information systems, ambulance services, special operating rooms, and mental health programs. Single individuals can plan, but plans will be better if many heads contribute.

Saskatchewan was the innovative planner for 20 years (1945-1965), which could suggest that perhaps 1 million is the best size for a planning region. But Quebec has been the innovative province for the last 20 years; perhaps 6 million is best. On the other hand, the hospitals of Hamilton have for decades produced far more than their share of leadership and creativity, and in the field of long term care the Welland-Niagara region was out front for decades. Very recently the city of Victoria and region, and the Foothills Hospital in Calgary, have been leaders in specific areas. It seems likely that geographic size and population base are less important than the presence of a nucleus of thinking leaders with courage, skill and the public interest at heart.

Strategic planning is strengthened if it has the appropriate emphases. Several desirable trends have appeared in the past decade. These include a move from ideal to affordable, from assumed usefulness to proven usefulness, from professional judgment to use of evidence, from optimal for the individual to optimal for the population, and from health care to health.

Strategic thinkers and planners need to have a good appreciation of opportunity costs. In each province the policy makers should be aware of what could be done with 1% or 2% of the provincial health care budget. In Ontario they would find that the 2% would finance another several thousand public housing units, a massive increase in the number of subsidized day care spaces, a ten fold increase in the community support services available for battered women and their children or another hundred kilometres of divided highway with its much lower rate of injuries and deaths. These kinds of comparisons allow more realistic evaluation of the merits of continuing that last 1-2% of spending on health care.

The same opportunity for examination of trade-offs exists within health care. Examination of opportunity costs was not a high priority when new demands were routinely met with new money, but reallocations are now the name of the game. All those involved in planning in Ontario need to know, for example, the opportunity costs associated with maintaining ceilings on annual physician earnings at the level of $400,000 and $450,000 rather than $350,000 and $400,000. Similarly, how much money could be allocated to other health care if expenditures on drugs or ambulances or home care were reduced by 1% or 5% or 10%?

Resource planning vs demand planning vs needs planning vs outcomes based planning

Resource planning (the planning of inputs) dominated in the 1960s. There was a desired ratio for all sorts of resources, such as one Public Health Nurse for every 5000 people and five acute treatment hospital beds per 1000 population. Demand planning comes from the same era. An estimation of future utilization of health care was converted into resource requirements.

The next phase was needs planning with measurement of needs and unmet needs. It was assumed that if the needs were known the system could be planned to meet them. The appearance of needs planning was refreshing in the sense that the users became central to planning, but it was erroneously thought that if needs were known the appropriate services would be able to be put in place. It was also naively expected that all needs should be addressed. Needs studies, usually local and usually poorly done, became the norm.

Unfortunately planners usually did not know what mix of workers and programs could best respond to various needs. As a consequence, even when needs were well measured response was not necessarily adequate. Knowing the volume of alcoholics, child abuse, arthritis, low back pain or schizophrenia did not lead (and still does not lead) to a predictable network of services. There was, and still is, little agreement regarding the best way to respond to the various needs, and when there was consensus there was a good chance the consensus was wrong.

Needs planning strengthened the possibility that resources would be assigned to meet needs which could not be met, or would be assigned even when the costs of meeting the needs were unreasonable. Some needs cannot be affected by the provision of health care, and in these situations no services should be delivered at public expense. This is not to suggest that palliative services or support services should not be funded; these services meet important needs and bring important outcomes. When there can be no change in outcomes, however, or only minor changes which are very costly, there usually should be no attempt to accomplish change at public expense.

The preferred planning approach is now planning which places emphasis on impact per dollar spent. This could be called outcomes planning, although the title and its precise definition are not important. If planning seeks to maximize impact per dollar spent then resources will be allocated to wherever they make the greatest difference. Resources will not be allocated to where the needs are greatest or the noise the loudest unless that allocation is the most cost-effective.

The outcomes planning option is just emerging. The necessary skills and information are primitive, but with effort both will improve. If outcomes planning becomes dominant primary emphasis will be given to deciding what should be done. Improvement of efficiency will come next. Both macro and micro decisions will improve.

The key planning questions have changed over time. Early planners asked *how many resources do we have?* and *how many resources do we need?*. An interest in efficiency then led to *how are our resources being used?*. With the arrival of needs planning the question became *what are the problems of the community and how big are they?*. In the future the key question will be *what resource allocations will bring the greatest benefit per dollar spent?*.

The experience of the needs based planning phase remains important. Data about needs are still important as part of a situation analysis or environmental scan, but they should not be seen as anything but one of the forms of information to be used in resource allocation and program development.

The process of policy selection

Policy choices are influenced by impact, cost, advice, the feasibility of implementation, policies already in place and the degree of political acceptability. Political acceptability will be influenced by media coverage, opinion surveys, the date of the next election and the power of those who will approve or disapprove. Advice may be sought from public servants, advocacy groups, consumer groups, relevant professionals and other experts in the field. Whether sought or not, advice will be received from vested interests.

A number of screening questions will assist in selection of strategic policy.
- Can this issue be avoided?
- How completely is the problem already being met?
- Is this issue high on the priority list of anyone, e.g. the government, the public, the minister of health, health care sectors?
- Has a commitment been given to act on this issue?
- Is the issue financially significant in terms of either costs or savings?
- How many people will be affected, and how significant will the effects be?
- What will be the effects of no action?

- What is the relative cost-effectiveness of the alternatives?
- Will there be a need for new legislation?
- Has action on this issue already begun? If so, is it at the stage of study, policy development, public consultation, preparation of legislation or regulations, or operational planning?
- Is development and implementation realistic with available resources?
- Who are the major players?
- Has this problem been dealt with elsewhere?
- Is it culturally and ethically acceptable?
- Should this be in the public sector?

Common planning mistakes

Most mistakes are mistakes of process. Others relate to data. Mistakes in process include a failure to follow the problem solving process, the examination of too many minor factors, a failure to identify veto factors and a failure to meet deadlines which cannot be moved. Decisions based in values are not mistakes.

Usually only a small number of determinants are important to the question of deciding what to do or how to do it. These key factors should be identified early and other factors can then be ignored or given very little attention. If there are factors which are absolute prerequisites to success then these prerequisites must be known to exist. If there are factors which, if present, make success impossible, then these must be known to be absent.

Deadlines and windows of opportunity cannot be missed. The steps in planning are always somewhat the same, but the steps must at times be compressed or accelerated to accommodate the realities of a dynamic milieu. Planners cannot always be governed by the standards and niceties of textbook planning.

Some mistakes pertain to information. It is unacceptable to not have a reasonable awareness of what others have done. Often too much time is spent collecting information which is not useful at all, or information which goes beyond the degree of perfection which is necessary. Exact measurement of case-loads, for example, is not necessary if new programs will serve only part of the estimated case-load. There is an unjustified belief that diagnostic data are important. Diagnosis is a poor predictor of health care needs or usefulness. Data on disabilities, handicaps, hazards, symptoms and probable outcomes are more necessary for the planning of health care services than are diagnostic data.

The role of arbitrary decisions in planning

Preoccupation with process, democracy and rationality can lead to a failure to notice the frequency with which decisions are made, and sometimes properly so, without a lengthy process and without much objectivity or democracy. For example, a person with the required authority may quite arbitrarily (or in a fashion which is seen to be arbitrary) implement user fees or improve access to abortion, or may oppose free medical care for the poor. If a single value is completely dominant the policy selection process may be simple. If there is, in the minds of those who will make the final decision, no perceived possibility of other choices then prolonged evaluation of options may be a poor way to spend time and money.

Proactive vs reactive planning

Reactive planning responds to events. It may seek, and need, a quick fix. It may reflect panic more than thought. It can lead to instant bed closures, arbitrary and even retroactive reductions in global budgets, across the board budget reductions and the transferring of costs to someone else (as with user fees or removing services from the list of insured services). The reactive response is usually not totally unplanned, but the only alternatives considered are those which respond to events.

Proactive planning anticipates future events or it plans desirable events. It will use many of the same tools and decisions as a reactive response, but it is characterized by prior consultation, prior analysis of alternatives, ample warning of impending changes and a greater likelihood of achieving expected outcomes.

A province can develop long range plans and work towards them or fight fires when heat makes inaction impossible. Saskatchewan was the epitomy of proactivity from 1945 to 1965. The credit is usually given to Tommy Douglas the visionary and political leader, but it should at least equally be given to Tommy Douglas the administrator and personnel motivator. He knew how to find and attract creative and competent thinkers and then give them enough freedom to make things happen.

Proactive leadership throughout the full spectrum of health policy has, since the early 1970s, been seen in Quebec. Few provinces have attempted to bring together such a mix of theorists, regional planners, public servants, academics, user groups, providers and others who can contribute to creative proactivity. Many political leaders have shown a good grasp of what they would like to do but few have had the team to make things happen. Without dedicated and competent staff Ministers can do very little. Their time in office will be characterized by more reactivity than proactivity.

Governments have far too often left it to others to determine the track along which health care will evolve. For the past 15 years in Ontario, for example, Community Health Centres have been endorsed as a legitimate and desirable model, but they are put in place only when a community provides the leadership and energy. There are few provincial guidelines or policies which encourage regional CHC networks or assure cooperation between CHCs in the same area. This reactive planning model remains in place despite an expressed provincial wish for growth in the number of CHCs.

The current frantic search for greater cost control is also reactive. The problems of inappropriate care and rapidly increasing expenditures have been evident for years, but vigorous response was delayed until provincial austerity made reaction unavoidable.

In 1991 a Task Force of the Hospital Council of Metropolitan Toronto studied emergency health services in 30 hospitals. They said, in part:

> *"Despite warning signs for many years of impending fiscal constraints and the resulting impact on bed availability, many of the hospitals appear to have refused to fully acknowledge this reality and have little, if any, bed management, utilization review, quality assurance and discharge planning ... in place"*

Reactive planning is not limited to governments.

Increasing control over private sector planning in health care

Some limitations on private sector planning in health care have existed since the appearance of the earliest public health and hospital legislation. Limitations expanded with the universal provincial health insurance legislation which eliminated the sale of private insurance covering the provincially insured hospital and physician services.

In 1990 the *Independent Health Facilities Act* (IHFA) in Ontario expanded public control over private sector health care. This *Act* brought a broad range of private profit and nonprofit diagnostic facilities (including radiology, ultrasound, pulmonary function studies and nuclear medicine) and therapeutic ambulatory care facilities (including those which provide laser therapy, abortions, surgery and in-vitro fertilization) under public regulation. This Act makes it possible to plan public and private outlets as a single system, a great improvement over the former situation in which public outlets (often operated by hospitals) could not plan sensibly because there was no way of knowing when private facilities might open, expand or close.

The legislation was considered necessary partly to improve the quality of public planning and partly because there has in the last decade or two been a major move of medical care procedures from hospitals to community based facilities. Another factor was the appearance of charges to patients for services which were insured if provided in hospitals but were either uninsured or only partially insured when offered in a nonhospital facility.

In Ontario, approximately 1400 private diagnostic facilities and 25 treatment facilities are now licensed and evaluated. New or expanded facilities will be licensed only when their operation is consistent with regional health plans. The quality assurance function (creating standards and monitoring quality) has been assigned to the Ontario College of Physicians and Surgeons.

The licensed facilities are usually funded by a global budget rather than on fee-for-service. This method of funding allowed a number of technical fees to be removed from the fee schedule.

The *Independent Health Facilities Act* provides a mechanism for managing the growth of private facilities which provide insured services, for funding overhead costs in private outpatient facilities so that there is no charge to provincially insured patients for insured services, for elimination of one set of fee-for-service payments, for the implementation of a mandated quality assurance process and for the establishment of facilities operated by health care professionals other than physicians. (MacMillan, R. and M. Barnes, "The Independent Health Facilities Act", in Restructuring Canada's Health Services System, U of T Press, 1992)

This legislation may be the most encompassing of its kind, at least in North America. British Columbia has been licensing laboratories for 20 years and Saskatchewan passed the *Medical Laboratory Licensing Act* in 1989, but the licenses are primarily to assure quality control in the laboratories operated in physician's offices.

The *Independent Health Facilities Act* does not affect private facilities which offer services which are not insured by the provincial plan. These facilities, such as the Prostate Centres in Windsor and Mississauga, are unlicensed and can do pretty well as they please and charge what they please.

OPTIONS FOR HEALTH CARE EVALUATION

Evaluation is the process of making a judgment about the adequacy of something. The evaluation can be entirely intuitive, it can be completely based on an analysis of objective evidence, or it can be based on any mix of evidence, values and gut feelings.

Evaluation can be designed to produce conclusions which will be accepted by most or all interested parties, or it can be manipulated to assure that conclusions will reflect preestablished preferences. In the multiparty environment of Canadian health care it is desirable that the evaluation process be seen by all parties to be fair, and the first option is therefore preferable.

In general, evaluation of health care can be concerned with measurement of whether the right thing is being done (the strategic phase) or whether the thing is being done in the right way (the operational phase). The right way includes the right sequence, the right place, the right time, the right person or persons and the lowest possible cost.

The evolution of evaluation

The historical tendency was to look almost exclusively at the care of one individual during one episode of care, or at one particular activity within one episode of care. This interest in individual care has now been joined by an interest in the care of populations and the activities of groups of providers.

Until recently, evaluation of health care almost exclusively meant evaluation of the clinical judgment or performance of one professional by her or his peers. Professionals, especially physicians, believed that evaluation of health care was entirely their domain. Both the process and the era have changed, but physicians and their associations have not fully noted the change. The Ontario College of Physicians and Surgeons recently stated *"—it seems self-evident that doctors should be responsible for deciding what constitutes good care, —"*. (College of Physicians and Surgeons of Ontario Members Dialogue, April 1990) One can only hope that in the period since 1990 the College has come to realize that *good care* is defined in terms of both costs and outcomes, that costs are not the world of physicians, that estimating the relative value of outcomes is not the domain of health care professionals and that statistical information can be examined by all interested parties. Statistically based evaluations of activities or patterns of activity, and of outcomes, are now more important than subjective peer review of individual acts or decisions.

Evaluation of health care practices has in the past often concentrated on the outliers. This approach (the *bad apple theory*) assumed that physicians or other providers whose clinical practices were inappropriate would look statistically different from their colleagues. This perception is mentioned only so it may be dismissed. Inappropriate care must be identified by a much more decision specific analysis. Unusual practice patterns are worthy of study, but their examination is not as important as evaluation of the individual every day patient care decisions of all professionals.

Factors important in evaluation of health care programs, policies and activities now include efficiency, effectiveness, relative cost-effectiveness, user and professional acceptability, accessibility, equity, accountability, cultural sensitivity, protection of patients rights, respect for patient priorities, technical accuracy, provincial affordability, political tolerability, operational practicality, legality and compatibility with existing legislation. (All factors are not relevant to every situation.)

In 1990/91 the Ontario Premiers Council on Health Strategy (now replaced by the Premiers Council on Health, Well-being and Social Justice) evaluated policy options using a few basic criteria including the number of persons who might benefit, the magnitude of impact of the policy on health, the strength of the evidence proving the impact, the degree of public support for the policy, the congruence between the policy and the values of the government and the feasibility of implementing the policy. The use of this set of criteria and measures was a big step forward from the time when physician opinion, overall cost and political acceptability were the dominant considerations.

Some health care reports refer to cost almost apologetically, as if the cost and the quality of health care were unrelated. This is not the case. A wasted dollar, or a poorly spent dollar, is a dollar which cannot be spent on necessary care, and failure to spend each dollar wisely means fewer services for someone.

Evaluation protocols still often give inordinate attention to minutiae. There may be more pages and effort given to technical adequacy (calibration of equipment, accreditation requirements, fire safety) or to work measurement than to whether the services being delivered reflect the wisdom of the day and whether health status changes achieved are enough to warrant the public expenditures involved.

In general, evaluation in health care has moved fully or partially from evaluation of individual care to evaluation of population health status changes, from individual researchers and small evaluation projects to multicentred, multicountry and longitudinal randomized clinical or other trials, from retrospective to prospective review, from examination of inputs to examination of process and impact/outcomes, from technical criteria to a combination of technical, economic, cultural and behavioral criteria, and from professional domination to shared responsibility.

Who might be responsible for evaluation

The evaluation of care can be left to the professionals, assigned to a public bureaucracy, assigned to an independent agency or be considered to be a multiparty responsibility in which payers, consumers and providers participate. The historical pattern was not to use outsiders to evaluate professional decisions but the current trend is towards evaluation of everyone and everything by everyone.

The evaluation of high cost technology, for example, can be the responsibility of technocrats, consumer groups, or a combination. In all scenarios technocratic advice would be available and probably used, but in the last two options the decisions would be made with due regard for the values and priorities of consumers.

Evaluation can also be left to courts, inquests and academic researchers. All are undesirable as major players. Courts and inquests often evaluate far too critically and often recommend changes which are impractical and not cost-effective. Academics from many faculties (health sciences, public policy, political science, administration, ethics, and social sciences) can usefully support the activities and enquiries of the major players, but they also should not dominate.

Evaluation can use locally generated measures and standards or use standardized tools and processes. In the 1970s and 80s there was support for the idea that every hospital, every medical society and every evaluation agency should produce its own clinical practice guidelines. This process was said to be necessary for the guidelines to be acceptable to the providers. This process is completely the reverse of the process used in medical schools and other training programs in which the experts tell the students what should be done.

When evidence clearly establishes the desirability of certain processes and activities there is seldom a valid reason for significant degrees of local discretion. Exceptions may arise from a need for local adaptation to lack of resources and local culture, but these exceptions will be uncommon. Guidelines or protocols with broad support among providers, users and payers should very seldom be open to revision to suit local belief or the interests of local providers. The acceptance of universal guidelines, along with a universal monitoring of events, will improve the likelihood that resources will be used for cost-effective care. (Brook, R.H., JAMA Dec 1, 1989, p3027-30)

Evaluation can be performed locally or systemically. The local or regional level might be best suited for evaluation of user satisfaction, with larger units being best able to compare the performance of the local or regional unit to that of other similar units.

Retrospective, concurrent or prospective evaluation

Retrospective analyses have established the inappropriateness of many health care decisions, but retrospective analyses often do not lead to changes in what is done.

Evaluation at the time a service is being delivered, or a decision is being made, allows correction if correction is indicated. This type of evaluation is possible when a pharmacist receives a prescription to be filled and that pharmacist has immediate access to a drug profile of the patient. The pharmacist is able to assess the hazards of the drug(s) in light of the drug profile and suggest revisions in the prescription if revisions appear indicated. Similar evaluations of other elements of care can be carried out by any provider with immediate access to the necessary information. For example, a physician or other provider can test his or her tentative decisions against computer based diagnostic or therapeutic advice.

Prospective evaluation is a misnomer in the sense that one cannot evaluate decisions not yet made, but the term is used when preestablished standards are applied to decisions after they are made. The Prospective Medical Audit was proposed by the Canadian Council on Health Facilities Accreditation 15 years ago. This audit was never widely implemented, but it consisted of the process described. The actual evaluation was retrospective; decisions made were compared to preestablished standards.

Ongoing evaluation is part of the currently popular Total Quality Management (TQM) and Continuous Quality Improvement (CQI) processes.

The difficulties of health care evaluation increase as comparisons become more complex. A health care service can be compared to other similar health care services, as when there is comparison of two beta blockers, or comparison of the costs and outcomes of two different approaches to gall bladder removal. In slightly more complex examples, one can compare surgical treatment of gall bladder disease to the medical treatment of the same disease, or compare beta blockers to some other drug group with similar clinical purposes. These comparisons are fairly commonly done, although the majority of health care has not, as yet, been well evaluated even at this level.

A health care activity can also be compared to other health care activities with different outcomes. In this comparison the cost-effectiveness (the social benefit per dollar spent) of one health care sector or type of care, such as home care, would be compared to that of a different sector or type of care, such as institutional care or preventive services. This comparison requires the selection and acceptance of a set of indicators and measures which allow evaluation of diverse health care activities with diverse outcomes. The required evaluation tools are evolving. Comparisons often will be criticized and difficult to defend, but the need for these comparisons is sufficiently acute to warrant continued effort. Evaluation tools will eventually be developed which will allow reasonably acceptable comparisons of quite different outcomes.

The comparison base is broadened even further if health care is compared to other social services. This comparison is a prerequisite to the implementation of the Healthy Public Policy concept. It requires estimation of the effects on health status of policies in very different social policy fields. The necessary skills are only in their infancy.

The common practice of comparing an activity or outcome to a norm is an acceptable process only if the norm is based on scientifically validated findings. Norms based in conjecture or professional preference can be faulty and they also have a second hazard. The target may not be realistic. Performance in this case may be compared to perfection rather than to an attainable cost-effective goal.

The role of data-base integration

Evaluation can be assisted by the integration of data-bases. Large Area Networks (LANs) now make such integration possible.

Integration of information from radiology and from surgery, for example, allows comparison of radiological and postsurgical diagnoses. This comparison allows evaluation of the usefulness of radiological investigation. A matching of laboratory and blood transfusion records allows examination of the relationship between haemoglobin levels and other factors and the use of blood transfusions. This relationship will help evaluate the wisdom with which blood transfusions are used. Integration of the records of several physicians would allow comparison of prereferral and postreferral diagnoses.

Obstacles to more complex analyses may be technical, although the technical impediments should now be manageable. The more significant obstacles may be financial (the analyses may be costly), legal, ethical or attitudinal. The concept of cost being a major determinant of whether health care should be provided, and of which services should be chosen, is still seriously questioned by many providers and users, and many desirable analyses will be resisted.

Micro level evaluation

Evaluation of health care at the micro level means evaluation of the decisions made by a health care professional as he/she cares for a patient. The evaluation examines the appropriateness of each individual decision. The providers frequently have considerable discretion as to what they do, and they often make inappropriate decisions.

If there is to be significant improvement in the quality of clinical decisions the changes should usually be implemented with the support of providers and consumers, and provider and consumer support will be most likely to be offered if both the providers and users are involved in the selection and planning of the changes. Improvement will occur when the appropriate decision is known, when the inappropriate decision is identifiable before it is implemented, and when there is a mechanism for replacement of the inappropriate with the appropriate decision.

Micro level evaluation deserves special attention because macro level evaluation is much more difficult. Many attempts have been made to decide whether a hospital is or is not a good one. Accreditation tries to do this and fails. Economists have tried to create models to evaluate the cost-benefit, cost-effectiveness or cost-utility of significant policies, but have found the task difficult. It has been equally difficult to decide who is a *good* physician or nurse or administrator. Assessment of the appropriateness of policy, or the quality of an institution, program, or professional, is unlikely to be the best place to put emphasis at this time. Macro level evaluation should not be ignored, but alteration of the decisions made by one health care professional when caring for one patient offers more promise for early improvement.

Emphasis on evaluation and improvement of micro resource allocation decisions is favored because in many situations evidence is available to indicate the preferred decision and because many trials and experiences have shown that decisions at this level can be improved. Evaluation at the micro level offers the best hope for involvement of large numbers of providers and consumers in a program for better spending.

Government roles in evaluation

Waste is now the greatest single threat to access to publicly funded useful health care. Governments will increasingly monitor, and ask for changes in, professional decisions. Governments should not perform this monitoring function alone but they should wish to participate in it and they have every right to do so.

Hospitals and professionals have led the way in evaluation of professional decisions, but governments, with their rapidly improving data-bases and their concerns over cost and benefit, are now becoming major players. Provinces such as Saskatchewan, who have excellent drug use data, have already demonstrated the potential of these data. Some of their studies of drug use led to significant alterations in the prescribing practices of some physicians.

Many Ministries of Health promptly replace a hospital board with a government appointed administrator if the board is unwilling or unable to operate within financial guidelines. British Columbia has stated that the grounds for replacement of the board by a public administrator will now include failure to adequately protect quality of care, which now includes quality of spending. This objective will require greater government involvement in the evaluation of the adequacy with which money is spent.

Health Impact Analysis (HIA)

Health Impact Analysis is an evaluation process which is central to both macro and micro decisions. It is the process by which there is estimation of the impact on health of a policy or of a decision. Governments, communities and individuals cannot make healthy choices unless the healthy and the unhealthy choices have been identified.

The Healthy Public Policy concept cannot be operationalized unless there has been evaluation of the effect on population health status of a broad range of public policies. Healthy lifestyles cannot be promoted unless there has been estimation of the effects of different lifestyle choices, and the Healthy Communities projects are as likely to be wrong as right in what they recommend unless there has been estimation of the usefulness of various community and municipal actions.

The impact of smoking was evaluated and personal and public policy choices changed. The effects on health of spraying for the spruce budworm were evaluated and no policy change was found to be necessary. Transportation agencies have for decades evaluated the risks associated with level railroad crossings and have replaced these with an overpass or underpass when the impact of the level crossing on health and on transportation was too negative. Decades ago iodine was added to salt because iodine had been shown to eliminate the most common form of goitre. In all of these examples an estimation of health impact assisted in the introduction of healthy policies.

Cost-effectiveness health care research can be seen as a form of Health Impact Analysis, or Health Impact Analysis can be seen as a form of applied cost-effectiveness research.

Accreditation programs

Seventy-five years ago surgical leaders created a hospital accreditation program. This program looked at the environment in which care was being provided and at selected aspects of hospital activity. It contributed greatly to the confidence the public had in its hospitals and was, in its day, an important program. The emphases which guided the early accreditation programs are, however, no longer adequate. The environment has changed and accreditation programs have not adapted adequately to the new milieu.

Governments have several policy options available as they consider what to do about the inadequacies of the agencies which accredit hospitals, long term care institutions, public health units and community health centres. The accreditation processes involve significant agency fees and much larger agency expenditures in the form of the staff time associated with preparing for an accreditation survey.

One government option would be to oppose expenditures on accreditation. This would have negligible if any effect on the quality of the agencies involved or on the populations to whom they deliver care, but it would probably destroy a desirable concept.

Another option would be to work with user groups, other governments and the organizations involved to alter the process, criteria and measures used in the accreditation process. This is the preferred option. The aim would be to identify the features of an agency which are now most central to good community service and devise an accreditation review which examined those features. There could be attention to the degree of congruence between what is done and what is known to be best, to administrative efficiency, to the use of cost-effectiveness as a determinant of resource allocation, to the extent to which an agency contributes to regional planning and regional delivery networks, to the adequacy with which consumer priorities are identified, to the degree to which what is done reflects user priorities, and to the processes used to assure the delivery of services which respond to community needs and values.

If the accreditation processes cannot become contemporary then public funds should not be spent on them.

Evaluation of new versus existing programs and professionals

Governments have the choice of evaluating only selected programs and professionals, of evaluating all of them, or of evaluating none of them.

Physicians, through their associations, have frequently asked for rigorous evaluation of new health care delivery forms, such as Community Health Centres, before the new models are encouraged. In a 1993 presentation to a parliamentary committee on alternative therapies, Quebec physicians said alternative therapies should be scientifically evaluated before given official recognition. There have not been equally vigorous demands that new therapies proposed by mainstream physicians be scientifically evaluated before they are put into use, or that well established but unevaluated traditional practice habits be vigorously evaluated.

Evaluation of new health care professionals, or of new health care delivery forms, should not be any more vigorous than evaluation of existing professionals or established patterns of delivery. The evaluation of new models and professions should not be considered final until the newcomers have matured and stabilized.

Technology assessment

Technology assessment includes the assessment of high-tech and expensive equipment and medical devices, but it also includes the assessment of pharmaceuticals, laboratory procedures and all other technical aids to health care.

The evaluation of drugs improved soon after the thalidomide tragedy almost 30 years ago. Legislation requiring assessment of machines and devices appeared a decade later (1976) in the United States, and Canada followed.

In 1992 there were still many devices on the United States market which had not been assessed. These included items such as drainage tubes for ears, a variety of joint implants, snakebite kits, cranial electrotherapy stimulators, dental bone implants and a stair-climbing wheelchair. Others, such as silicone breast implants and the Bjork-Shiley heart valve, had by 1992 been assessed and been found to be unsatisfactory. They were on the market for years before assessment established their hazards. In Canada until recently the only devices which were evaluated before being put on the market were those which were placed permanently in the body.

Interest in technology assessment has grown rapidly in the last half decade. This expanded interest in technology assessment is the product of several factors including:

- Technology is often in general use before it is evaluated.
- Technology is often found to be much less valuable than is claimed by its producers.
- Increases in health care costs have been most marked, and most difficult to control, in the tertiary level hospitals, and these are the locations in which expensive technology tends to be aggregated.
- There is a great demand, especially by physicians and hospitals but also by other providers, for access to the latest new and expensive technology, and an appropriate response to these demands is difficult when the technology has not been adequately evaluated.
- Expensive technology may be used when less expensive tools produce equally satisfactory outcomes.
- There is a mistaken belief that technology assessment will markedly reduce health care costs. (Romanow R., Hospital Trustee, July/August, 1985, and the McMaster Study Group)

The interest in technology assessment may be partly a product of a false hope that the control of health care costs will be simple. Assessment of expensive technology may be emphasized by those who wish to avoid having to deal with the much more difficult problem of inappropriate professional decisions, some of which involve misuse of technology.

Policy issues associated with technology assessment include how much emphasis should be given to it, who should do the assessment, who should pay for it, what criteria should be used and who should be responsible for monitoring after initial approval. Factors to be taken into consideration when provinces are assessing technology include relative cost-effectiveness, social acceptability, whether its use should be an insured service, what limits on location or access should apply if insured, what supply is reasonable and whether inappropriate use will be able to be controlled.

Both national and provincial governments have increased their technology assessment ability. In 1989 the federal health department established the Canadian Coordinating Office for Health Technology Assessment. Quebec had earlier established a Council for Technology Assessment in Health Care, and British Columbia has its own Office of Health Technology Assessment.

Payment for assessment is not an issue when the technology is a new drug. The costs are borne by the manufacturer who will market the drug if it is approved. However, this principle often does not apply to the manufacturers of operating room equipment, a new mechanical bed or arm, or a myriad of other new nonpharmaceutical technologies.

Criteria used in technology assessment can emphasize intermediate products or can emphasize outcomes. In the field of imaging, for example, CAT scans and magnetic imaging (MRI) produce better pictures than an X-ray or ultrasound, but if the better picture does not improve patient outcomes then the better picture is not worth much, if anything. Technology can lead to wasteful and even dangerous practices when evaluation looks at intermediate products rather than at effect on outcomes.

Technology assessment is an integral part of health care evaluation, but it will, in itself, produce only modest reductions in cost. Technology which is useless, excessively hazardous or not cost-effective should be identified and not used, but the identification and prevention of inappropriate use of useful technology is more important. Technology assessment which is not supported by monitoring and improvement of professional decisions will bring little overall improvement in the quality of spending or of health care. One hazard inherent in the current technology assessment programs is the possibility that this assessment is seen to be the same as, and therefore can substitute for, the assessment of the clinical decisions through which technology is used.

Improved post-marketing drug surveillance is one form of technology assessment which will probably become prominent in the near future. It is clear that the long term and the rare effects of new drugs, and other new technologies, cannot be identified in the clinical trials conducted before initial approval, and it is clear also that there is currently no adequate program in place to detect the rare effects described above. Hopefully an increased attention to post-marketing surveillance will not be at the expense of efforts to improve the manner in which approved technologies are used.

SUMMARY

Planning objectives, and the amount of health care provided (the volume of resources consumed), should not be determined by needs. Objectives should emphasize the best outcomes at the lowest cost, recognizing that reassurance, comfort and a sense of personal worth are among the worthwhile outcomes. The expenditure of large sums of public money on what are accepted as very limited extensions of life, for example, is justified only when there is a realistic expectation that new therapies will arrive during that brief extension of life.

The planning of networks must precede institutional and program planning. This practice is firmly in place in some locations and sectors but needs more universal implementation.

Planning of a publicly funded health care network should encompass all elements of the network, including those which are privately owned but providing insured services. Systems cannot be fully efficient if walk-in clinics, private diagnostic clinics, agencies providing home visits, and other service outlets offering insured services can operate as they please. Only those providers who are operating completely without public funding should be allowed to operate largely outside of the public planning process.

It is the responsibility of planners and policy makers to develop opportunities for Canadians to privately purchase, in Canada, all forms of health care. Planning and policy development should assure sufficient regulation of privately funded health care to assure an adequate health care database and protection of vulnerable users.

Drugs, and their use, have been evaluated more than other health care components. The use of, and decisions of, physicians and hospitals have also received a significant amount of attention. The components of health care most targeted for expansion in the 1990s (community health services, mental health services, long term care, health promotion) are less well evaluated.

Chapter 9

Financial Issues and Options

INTRODUCTION

Financial issues and options regarding public spending on health care pertain to how much to spend, the rate of growth of spending, how to control costs, which health care spending, if any, will be open-ended, who will be responsible for control of spending, how funds will be distributed to providers, and how the money will be raised.

No-one knows exactly how much per capita, or what percentage of the Gross National Product (GNP), Gross Provincial Product (GPP) or any other measure of economic activity, should be spent on health care. It is clear, however, that spending over 7-8% of GNP is not supported by an examination of the health status and health care spending of other nations. These health status indicators are, in the United States, not as good as in Britain or Japan, but the United States per capita spending on health care is twice that of the other countries. It may be impossible to know exactly how much should be spent on health care, but it is easy to defend the proposition that Canada and the United States are spending too much.

This chapter introduces general questions associated with cost control. Chapter 10 looks at cost control techniques. When considering cost control options the first choice should, theoretically, be cost control versus no cost control, but endless spending on health care is not an option for Canada. Only the United States remains even modestly divided on the question of whether the private market can be allowed to decide the volume of public spending on health care, and even there the advocates of a dominant role for government in cost control appear to be winning.

Spending only as much as one can afford, or as much as seems reasonable for the benefits bought, is part of every day life. The supply of money is the most common instrument of cost control. Concern regarding debt is next. When an individual, household, agency or department runs out of money each tends (voluntarily or involuntarily) to stop spending. Only an accident of history gave Canadian health care an interval in which there were almost no ceilings on public spending, and that interval has now ended. Health care now must adapt to the ceilings and caps and fixed budgets which characterize other publicly funded social sectors.

Choices made long ago reduced the cost control problems of Canada to-day. If, 30 years ago, Canada had not decided to use the single payer model it would now be in the same position as the United States. The United States opted for regulation of a market driven health care system, but despite many statutes and many regulatory agencies the profit driven providers and their allies have won. United States health care costs are out of control; Canadian costs are merely too high.

The literature on cost control is massive and confusing. Reduced expenditures have been said to be possible through regionalization, rationalization, scientific management, greater use of less expensive personnel, less government intervention, more government intervention, more attention to what the experts say, less attention to what the experts say, fewer active treatment beds, fewer chronic patients in acute care beds, fewer chronic care beds, fewer physicians, less fee-for-service, use of user fees, more incentives for better use of health care, more emphasis on prevention, a more humane and less expensive process of dying, control of user abuse, greater value-for-money, more involvement of physicians in administration, more education of the public, utilization management, privatization and more emphasis on community care. Many of these choices are explored in this and other chapters.

WHERE FINANCIAL DECISIONS ARE MADE

Financial decisions are made by those who establish health care policy, by those who plan and administer health care, and by those who deliver and consume it. (Figure 9.1) All players therefore can contribute to cost control or impede it.

Central financing has made cabinets the central players in cost control. For example, in 1993, the Alberta government announced there would be a $900 million reduction in public spending on health care, a reduction of about 20%. No other player in Alberta could have seriously proposed such a reduction in public spending on health care.

Financing of hospitals and of physician services was decentralized before the introduction of universal health insurance. Centralization occurred partly because only senior governments could finance a universal system, partly because central financing allowed use of a single insurance carrier with its associated low administrative costs, and partly because equality of access is unlikely with decentralized financing.

Macro level financial decisions are made by legislatures, cabinets, Ministers, boards of health care facilities and programs and the senior administrators and planners throughout the system. These macro decisions usually affect many persons and are usually regulatory. Macro level cost control is possible in Canada primarily because there is centralized financing and planning of health care. Macro level control may limit the public resources available for health care or portions of it, may require that certain decisions be made or may prevent certain decisions from being implemented.

Micro level cost control, cost control which is applied at the point of delivery of care, is implemented through the decisions of health care providers and consumers. Micro decisions tend to affect only one part of the care of one person. The micro decisions are made daily in offices, hospitals, other institutions, homes, schools, workplaces and all other places at which individual health care delivery decisions are made. These micro decisions can be affected by the policies of governments and boards, but are more directly influenced by the habits and priorities of providers and users. The micro level decisions are particularly important for better spending (cost-effectiveness), but they are also important for cost control.

DETERMINANTS OF HEALTH CARE SPENDING

It was once thought that the amount spent on health care should be determined by the providers, mostly the physicians. This led to open-ended spending. It is now clear that the amount of public money which will be spent on health care is determined only by the amount the funders are willing or able to provide. Each program or sector spends everything it can get. Reallocations within global allottments are essential for greatest social benefit per dollar spent, but total spending is only indirectly affected by better spending.

The techniques which lower the cost of a service or of caring for one person during one episode of illness are therefore not cost control devices for governments unless spending on the care or services is open-ended. When there is no cap on expenditures the avoidance of any service, or the low-

Figure 9.1

THE LOCATIONS AND DEGREE OF CONTROL OF PUBLIC SPENDING

Type of Decision	The decision makers			
	Pract'r and pt	Inst and Program	Regions	Govt
Strategic resource allocation (macro)	Minor	Moderate	Major*	Major
Operating efficiency	Moderate	Major	Minor	Minor
Individual care (micro level allocation)	Major	Moderate	Moderate	Moderate

*This assumes the presence of a dominant regional planning agency.

ering of the cost of any service, can lower total expenditures, but large scale open-endedness is rapidly disappearing.

SHOULD HEALTH CARE COSTS BE CONTROLLED; AND HOW TIGHTLY?

Governments can, if they so choose, limit public spending on health care. Publicly funded programs will then be tailored to fit the amount of money available. Governments can, as an option, decide which services they will pay for, and what populations will have access to those services, and then provide enough money to provide the described services to the eligible population. This second approach is open-ended. It is spending in response to demand. Benefits and beneficiaries are defined but the costs are not. When physicians and hospitals were considered to be the key determinants of health status, and when the money could be found, spending on physicians and hospitals was routinely open-ended. All provinces have now decided they cannot afford the open-ended approach.

The rate of growth of public spending on health care can be tied to economic growth, to some other variable, or be arbitrarily chosen. Unless the growth is tied to an economic indicator health care costs are likely, during times of economic stagnation or shrinkage, to quickly consume a greater proportion of national and provincial wealth. This happened during the recession of 1979-83, when the percentage of GNP spent on health care rose quickly from 7% to over 8%, and it happened again in the recession of 1990-93 when the figure grew quickly to over 10%.

The current level of understanding of the cost-effectiveness of social spending on health care versus education versus the environments or other publicly financed activities is too weak to allow the most appropriate health care spending level to be accurately determined. Resource allocations to social sectors must of necessity be on the basis of guesses, public wishes, historical patterns, political pressures and economic realities.

There are strong arguments to support limiting increases in public expenditures on health care to less than, and certainly not more than, the growth in GNP, or the rate of change in provincial revenue. Other factors are now accepted as being more important to health than is health care, health care is already very generously funded, one quarter or more of the health care currently being provided is considered to be inappropriate for public financing and other countries which spend less on health care have people who are more healthy than Canadians.

A defence of cost control was given in the final report of the Canadian Medical Association Task Force on the Allocation of Health Care Resources in 1986, when it addressed the question of whether the health care system is underfunded. The Task Force said that additional spending on health care could only be justified if there was convincing evidence that spending more money would indeed provide a measurable improvement in health, and evidence that this improvement would be greater than that which could be achieved by spending the money in some other way. Such evidence is not available.

The proponents of underfunding are quiet, but primarily because the public purse is empty. If it wasn't, there would still be many who would wish to see health care spending increase. These increases would not be desirable even if funds were available; the opportunity costs are too high. (Culyer, A.J., Health Care Expenditures in Canada: Myth or Reality — Past and Future, Canadian Tax Foundation, 1988 Chapter 5) There are many services, such as social support for abused families and disturbed adolescents, which are important to health and which are inadequately publicly funded. It is in this atmosphere that the control of health care costs must be considered.

The end of open-ended spending altered the vocabulary of health care. *Capping*, *partial capping*, *ceilings*, *global budgets* and *envelopes*, terms which are conceptually similar and operationally often identical, became dominant. All are devices for, among other things, making expenditures predictable to the payer. By any name they are merely a fixed amount of money to be spent in a fixed period of time, usually by identified providers and for a specified set of activities or services.

A cap, ceiling, globe or envelope is a maximum beyond which payments or expenditures will not be allowed to go. When demand exceeds the cap, the cap wins. A cap may be complete or partial. A partial cap can be exceeded, but once the cap is exceeded the rules change. The price per unit of service may go down, some of the payments already made may be recovered by the paying agency, or payments in some other cost centre may go down.

Some of the terms associated with cost control have become quite firmly identified with specific components of health care. Cabinets cap the budget of the Ministry of Health, but it isn't called a cap or a global budget; it is just a budget or an envelope or an allocation. Sections of ministries are also funded through envelopes, which can be similar to global budgets or may resemble, or be, line-by-line budgets. Hospitals receive a global budget. Hospitals put a ceiling or cap on the allowable expenditures of each of their departments but this ceiling or cap is usually referred to as merely the budget of the department.

When is a budget not a global budget? It is usually called a global budget only if the department (or the hospital or other agency) has a reasonable degree of control over how to spend its allocation. If the amounts which can be spent on specific activities (staff, travel, supplies) can only be changed with the approval of a senior level of management or some outside authority then the budget is a line-by-line budget.

Putting a cap on selected components of health care such as physician services has met with considerable resistance, but it should not have. Putting limits on the total payments to physicians, or on any other formerly open-ended service, is only worthy of notice because these expenditures were open-ended for so long that the change seemed revolutionary. These services which formerly enjoyed special status have found it difficult to tailor their activities to fit the amount of money available, but this adjustment is one that is routinely expected from most of the world.

When school boards or police commissions or highway departments can't find the money for another teacher or policeman or divided highway, the new person is not hired or the next task is left undone. Health care is now in that position. Some sources of health care, such as public health programs, have always experienced macro level cost control. Sources of health care such as hospitals, physicians, drug programs and laboratory programs became accustomed to open-ended spending before they were faced with spending ceilings, but these sectors are now adapting to the constraints which have always been faced by most other publicly financed programs.

Capping as used in Canada has conceptual similarities to the prospective payment arrangements which are common in the United States, but they also are different. Both capping and prospective payment set limits on what will be paid (or spent), but in the United States the fixed payment puts a cap on what will be paid to a provider (a hospital, Health Maintenance Organization or physician) for a service or series of services. (This is similar to the composite fees in a physician fee schedule.) Canada has opted for the capping of spending by programs and sectors. Comparison of the degree of cost control which is possible through capping at the level of individual services versus global capping of sectors and programs suggests the global capping approach is more successful. Capping is discussed more thoroughly in Chapter 10.

SOURCES OF PUBLIC FUNDING

Financial policy choices do not pertain only to spending. They also determine how the money is raised. The options for public financing of health care are general revenue, premiums, earmarked (funded) taxes and miscellaneous sources such as income from public lotteries. General revenue is the source of funds for most Canadian social programs including most publicly financed health care.

The option of a fully earmarked (funded) special health care tax is not used by any province although some provinces have increased taxes or introduced new taxes to offset increased spending on health care. The income from these taxes is not earmarked for health care; it goes into general revenue. Placing all government income in general revenue is the preferred approach. It allows better money management.

Premiums which provide only part of the costs of a public insurance program are merely a tax. They are expensive to collect and are considered by some to be regressive because they do not vary with ability to pay. Almost all provinces prefer more efficient forms of general taxation. By 1991 only British Columbia and Alberta were still collecting health insurance premiums. British Columbia premiums were $840 per year for a family not on social assistance, and half that for a single person. The Alberta premiums were $624 and $312 respectively. In Alberta the premium was treated like a tax, and payments to hospitals and physicians for services rendered were made whether or not the premiums were paid. In British Columbia payments were not made to physicians for services provided to persons who had not paid their premiums.

Special personal income taxes can lead to recovery of 100% of health care expenditures made on behalf of high income persons. This claw-back is only indirectly a health care funding mechanism. It is merely a form of taxation in which the level of taxation can reach 100%. It is sometimes considered to be a user fee, but user fees are usually paid to the provider rather than to the department of revenue.

In some provinces gambling income (lotteries and casinos) is all or partially assigned to health care, and in all provinces charitable donations are a source of health care revenue.

OPTIONS FOR PAYMENTS TO HEALTH CARE INSTITUTIONS AND PROGRAMS

Provincial payments to health care agencies and institutions can be through a per diem payment, a line-by-line budget, a global budget, multiple global budgets, a block grant, capitation, payment per case (prospective payment), payment per activity (fee-for-service), incentive payments and some combination of these. Funding by any method can be lowered through use of penalties.

After the introduction of universal hospital insurance hospitals were initially paid either on a per diem basis (a fixed fee for every day a patient was in hospital) or on the basis of a line-by-line negotiated budget. Use of a per diem rate provided both hospitals and physicians with an incentive to admit often and discharge late. (Until 1993 Germany paid its hospitals a per diem and struggled with long lengths of stay and frequent readmissions.) The line-by-line budget discouraged good management and proved difficult to control. Hospital costs grew quickly with both the per diem payment and the line-by-line budget and both were abandoned. Per diem payments are still used for some institutional long term care, and line-by-line budgets are still used for some community health services and some provincially operated institutions and programs.

For hospitals the global budget became the instrument of choice. In the early years of global budgets double digit growth in hospital costs continued, primarily because provinces were prepared to pick up deficits. The hospitals quickly learned how to exploit any opening which might lead to increases in the global base or the recovery of a deficit. Provinces gradually funded fewer operations outside of the global budget and reduced the possibility of deficit recovery. These changes contributed significantly to the current degree of control of hospital costs.

It is customary for the global budget base to be adjusted each year. The adjustment may be negotiated or arbitrary, and may be an increase or a decrease. Adjustments may be designed to improve equity among hospitals, encourage high quality management or reflect inflation, new utilization patterns, new operating costs or other factors. New operating costs could include costs associated with new government programs such as gender equity, increased Workers Compensation rates or energy cost increases. Changes in utilization could arise from the implementation of new or expanded programs, unanticipated changes in demand (as with an epidemic) or new technologies. Alberta and Ontario have developed global base adjustment formulas which encourage lower costs per case.

Budgeting for a deficit may be allowed or not allowed. Budgeting for a deficit invites greater pressure on the Ministry for more money at the end of the year, and is best not allowed.

The global budget of a program or institution may or may not include all cost centres. Specified hospital operations such as dialysis, cardiac surgery and total parenteral nutrition may be excluded from the global base. Cost centres which are outside of the global base may be financed through a separate global budget or a line-by-line budget or any other chosen arrangement.

There are strong arguments in favor of a single encompassing global budget with no negotiation of deficits or unexpected costs. To leave major cost centres outside of the global base invites manipulation, and a willingness to discuss new revenue for unexpected costs invites discussion of an endless array of such costs. The use of nonionic dye in radiology provides an example. In this example hospitals faced significant new costs in the operation of the radiology department, an expenditure area fully within the global budget. The new injectable dyes were ten times as expensive as the ones in use, and they were said to be much safer. The issue was whether the Ministry should provide additional funds for the new dye.

Different provinces took quite different positions on the issue. Some Ministries picked up all of the new costs. In these provinces the new dye became the only one used. When the province did not pick up the new costs the hospitals tended to use the new dye in selected circumstances. The development of a rational mix of ionic and nonionic dye was delayed when the Ministry provided the money. Some ministries unnecessarily became involved in what should have been an internal hospital resource allocation problem. Subsequent clinical trials have found that the more expensive dye is, at best, only slightly safer.

Expensive anesthetic agents present a similar set of options. Patients recover much more quickly after use of the new and expensive agents. Hospitals should be left to decide whether, and when, to use the more expensive anesthetics. Some hospitals have chosen to use them only when the patients are going home immediately, a rational choice which might not have been made if governments had offered to provide extra money so that the more expensive anesthetics could be routinely used.

PROSPECTIVE PAYMENT SYSTEMS (PPS): PAYMENTS PER CASE

Preestablished payments for described episodes of care (the PPS method) have been used by the United States federal government for over 10 years. The payments are based on Disease Related Groups (DRG) as originally developed by Yale University and modified since then. Hospitals receive a lump sum for an entire hospital stay.

Introduction of this method of payment obliged hospitals to care for a patient for not more than the lump sum paid or lose money on that patient. In response to the capping of payments for each case the hospitals shortened lengths of stay, reduced the volume of investigative tests and reduced the use of expensive drugs. Studies have indicated that the greatest source of significant savings was elimination of the one to four days of hospital stay at the end of ordinary high volume cases. (Physician Manager, May 1991, p. 9-12)

The lump sum payments to hospitals are predetermined based on patient age, diagnoses and surgical procedures. As the mechanism has matured there has been increasing adaptation of the payment to reflect severity of illness. In general terms the assigned fee reflects the average regional cost of caring for the relevant type of patient, although payments also reflect public policy decisions. Governments have at times arbitrarily reduced payments.

This payment mechanism provides hospitals with an incentive to admit unnecessarily, to select patients on the basis of whether or not they will be profitable, and to provide less care than is desirable. In response to these threats the United States established Peer Review Organizations to monitor care. Most of these agencies are operated by medical societies. Surveillance is also provided by a federal Prospective Payment Assessment Commission and by the Department of Health and Human Services.

In Canada the DRGs have been adapted, renamed Case Mix Groups (CMG) and further refined by application of weightings for severity of care. They have not yet been used as the exclusive basis for payments to Canadian hospitals, but have been examined to determine how they might be applied. If CMGs are used as a basis of payment there are arguments in favor of combining the physician and hospital fee so that the total service is within the fee and the physician shares in both decisions and risk.

Estimation of what the income of a Canadian hospital would have been if payments had been based on CMG fees gives some indication of the efficiency of the hospital. In a presentation to the fourth Canadian Conference on Economics in 1990, Lee Soderstrom expressed the belief that a Canadian Prospective Payment System is possible.

The Prospective Payment Systems (PPS) used extensively in the United States may be possible in Canada but they do not appear to be desirable. Global budgets are simpler and more difficult to manipulate. Costs per case should be known but primarily as an aid to communities, hospitals, providers and governments who wish to evaluate the quality of hospital management. They also could be the basis for rewards or penalties. The absence of profit incentives in Canada reduces the need for the complex regulatory and review processes which characterize PPS in the United States.

NONGOVERNMENTAL INCOME

Hospitals receive income from sources other than the provincial hospital insurance plan of their home province. These other sources include revenue from commercial ventures (joint ventures, flower shops), charitable agencies including foundations, charges for uninsured services (TV, telephone, semi-private and private rooms), Workers Compensation Boards, hospital insurance plans of other provinces, lotteries ($322 million or 71% of lottery profits went to hospitals in Ontario in 1991-92) and nonresident patients who personally pay for their care or have it paid for through private insurance. Provincial policy determines the extent to which the income from these outside services reduces the Ministry allocation to the hospital.

Provinces differ considerably in their approach to this revenue. Ontario has, since 1982, allowed hospitals to keep it all. Prior to 1982, 75% of most of this revenue was charged against the provincial allocation. Most provinces reduce the global base by at least part of these revenues.

One possible source of hospital income has received too little attention. Health care for Americans could be a growth industry in Canada. Canada can provide high quality health care less expensively than can the United States. Our medical fees are lower, our hospital costs per case are lower and our dollar is worth less than an American dollar. Hospitals have wanted to market their services to Americans but governments have tended to either discourage or openly ban such marketing. With hundreds of hospital beds now closed in Canada the opposition to attracting American users should stop. The excess hospital space might become a source of foreign dollars and of Canadian employment.

Many Americans have their health care provided as an employee benefit, and large corporations should find lower cost Canadian care attractive. In 1993 hospitals in Britain signed a contract with major United States buyers of health care to perform open heart surgery on United States residents. Even after payment of the transportation costs (patient and spouse) and hotel costs for a spouse the total cost is significantly lower in Britain than the cost of similar services in the United States. Canada can almost surely compete with Europe. Selling health care to Americans, plus greater efforts to keep Canadians home for their health care, would offset some of the expenditures by Canadians in the United States.

Providing health care to foreigners has always been the pattern in prestigious institutions such as The Hospital For Sick Children. This foreign access has not interfered with access by Canadians, or at least has not been seen to interfere. Governments should encourage the sale of health care to Americans by Canadian nonprofit hospitals, and should encourage expansion of private sector health care which would be sold to foreign residents as well as to Canadians. In 1993 the Toronto Hospital and the Hospital for Sick Children teamed up to market *"brain surgery, cancer treatment and other medical services"* to Americans. (Ontario Medical Review, April 1993)

OTHER FUNDING OPTIONS

There are no examples of hospitals being funded by capitation, and examples are unlikely to appear.

Block grants are commonly used by governments to assist community based agencies. They provide financial support without a commitment to close surveillance or expanded funding.

The power to tax could be granted to a regional health board but it appears to be inappropriate for a hospital or other health care facility or program. Municipalities can, if they wish, allocate tax dollars to health care.

User fees can be a source of provider income. Provinces can allow or direct health care institutions, programs and individual providers to charge users for any part of the cost of any service, but so long as the *Canada Health Act* remains in force a province may be penalized if users are charged for hospital or physician care. The *Canada Health Act* does not penalize provinces when hospitals bill medicare beneficiaries for semi-private and private rooms, for services which are not considered to be necessary patient care (rental of television sets, gourmet meals, telephones), when the patient has been medically discharged but remains in hospital, for charges for room and board when a patient is defined as a chronic care patient or for supplies and drugs associated with outpatient services. The extent to which users must pay for these services varies from province to province and also among hospitals within a province.

CAPITAL EXPENDITURES

Policy options relate primarily to the source of the funds, the level of total capital spending and the percentage of total costs which will be met by the province. Capital expenditures, most of which relate to hospitals, represent 3 to 4% of total health care costs. Hospitals believe that the current levels of replacement and renewal of hospitals are far too low, but there is no evidence to show that increased capital spending would improve community health status. Recent capital projects have tended to emphasize expansion of outpatient services and of improvements which will lead to greater hospital efficiency. The hospital bed supply per 1000 population continues to shrink.

Provincial support for capital projects ranges from 100% of all approved projects to some established percentage. Where provincial funding is less than 100% the balance is raised from the public, from operating hospital budgets or from municipal or regional governments. Provinces tend to provide depreciation allowances in global budgets only for equipment.

OPTIONS REGARDING WHO WILL FACE FINANCIAL RISK

In open-ended payment arrangements financial risk is borne entirely by the payer, whether the payer is a patient, a government or a private insurance company.

When incomes are capped (whatever the cap is called) financial risks are assumed by the providers, as when payments to hospitals or other providers are limited to a preestablished price for care associated with a particular case (the Prospective Payment option). When payment is by capitation the total cost of care to all capitated persons must not exceed the income from all capitation fees or the agency is not financially viable. When a global budget is exceeded and no-one will assist with the deficit, the agency is liable for the expenditure over-run.

Financial risks are also assumed by providers when there is a ceiling on total sectoral payments and expenditures beyond the ceiling will be recovered by the government. This recovery, or *clawback*, has now occurred in a number of provinces with respect to payments to physicians and other fee-for-service professionals. Providers are even more at risk if they are responsible for over-runs in generated costs, as with physician responsibility for drug costs beyond a ceiling (as in Germany and Britain, and, in a modified way, in New Brunswick).

The use of ceilings (caps) on the costs of services in a sector using fee-for-service has one advantage to the provider. A greater degree of professional freedom can be preserved without financial risk to the payer. The providers are at financial risk if the volume of activities rises but they may remain more able to deliver services as they please.

Financial risk could be used as an incentive for appropriate use of services. User charges could be used in situations in which the patient has control of the decisions, and provider charges or penalties could be used in situations in which the provider is the decision maker.

OPTIONS FOR STAYING WITHIN BUDGET

Techniques to allow a government or an agency to stay within their budget range from the crude to the sophisticated. Crude options are of the burn and slash variety, including across the board cuts in funding to all departments and programs, the cancellation of spending on such things as travel, continuing education, subscriptions and the use of consultants, and the suspension of new admissions when budget overruns are imminent. Both governments and agencies can stay within budget by reducing service volumes. Almost anybody can spend less by producing less.

Another set of options can lower the costs per case or per unit of service. Actions include reductions in administrative costs, reductions in the prices of what is bought, shortened lengths of stay, improved productivity and transfer of functions to less expensive staff. The potential for additional savings through greater productivity from caregiving staff is now minimal, but there are thoughtful options which reduce activity and throughput with little or no reduction in community benefit. There may be an increased threshold for entry to care, a requirement that care plans be justified or fewer decisions which are fully or partially inappropriate.

JOINT VENTURES

Health care groups and institutions in the United States are partners in many joint ventures, many of which fail. In Canada the Ontario Business Oriented New Development (BOND) program (1982) invited hospitals to seek new sources of revenue and keep the profits, and many hospitals developed *main streets*, sold gourmet foods or ventured into real estate. Some increased their revenues, others did not. St. Michaels Hospital in Toronto ended up sixty million dollars in debt due to aggressive but unwise financial management.

The financial managers in health care are not necessarily acquainted with the hazards of free market challenges. It is preferable that whatever skills are available be used to spend available health care dollars in the ways which bring maximum community benefit. The system is still generously funded and should primarily concentrate on using its funds well rather than on competing in entrepreneurial markets in the hope of expanding revenue.

USER ROLES IN DECIDING WHAT TO BUY

Provincial policies can determine the roles of consumers, providers and payers in choosing the services which will be delivered.

Legislation, medical directives and court decisions have clearly established the right of users to refuse care. The users have a veto, but they seldom have much control over what services are offered to them. Policies could increase the control of users over the selection of the health care services which will be provided at public expense. This would be consistent with the current trend towards increased consumer control. Consumer control is weakened when someone else controls how money is spent. Consumer control is strengthened when purchasing power is fully or partially in their hands.

There are precedents in other social policy fields for full or partial user control over publicly provided funds. Canadians in need of assistance with expenses of daily living (food and accommodation) are given money (welfare or a pension) with which to meet these needs. Sometimes the funds can be spent in whatever way the recipient wishes, as with a welfare cheque or an old age pension. On other occasions the funds can only be used for specified purposes, as with a housing allowance. The size of the housing allowance is determined by policy or by a professional and the money can only be used for accommodation costs. The United States food stamp program also gives the user purchasing power but, once again, only for the purchase of specific items.

The need for health care could be evaluated and the consumer then given money or credit with which to buy health care. There could be many or few limits on what the user could buy. The consumer could be free to purchase services from the provider(s) of their choice, and within user rather than provider priorities. This approach has been used. In British Columbia, public funds are transferred to families with severely disabled children after assessment of the needs of the family and client. The family decides how to use the funds to best serve the disabled child.

The payer and/or professional gatekeepers could retain control of some funds while giving the user control over the remainder. Case managers would establish the level of public expenditure and would monitor care. The generosity of the transfer payment would reflect provincial or agency wealth and philosophy. The user allotment could be reduced to reflect costs such as emergency care which would unavoidably continue to be the responsibility of the public program even if the user had no funds left.

To the extent the user is given control over funds he/she would, within limits set by the payer, choose which care to purchase. The user, or his or her agent, might, for example, prefer to use the funds to support voluntary caregivers rather than buy professional care. Funders would be likely to proscribe safeguards to prevent the voluntary caregivers from using these arrangements to the disadvantage of the patient, but it is unclear whether patient advantage is most threatened by professional caregivers or by household caregivers.

If the money were actually given to the user a marketplace would be created. Institutions or community programs would provide care only if the user chose to buy services from them. This process appears to be especially appropriate for persons with chronic disabilities and illnesses. It would be welcomed by persons who wish to have greater control over their lives, and would be rejected by persons who prefer to leave responsibility with others.

Care decisions can also rest with the payer. This is inherent in the *managed care* process in which a provider prospectively asks the payer for approval of care. If payer approval is not forthcoming the care will not be delivered at the expense of that third party.

TRANSFER OF FUNDS WHEN THE SITE OF CARE IS CHANGED

The relatively fixed budgets of programs and institutions usually change very slowly in response to changes in utilization patterns. If some of the care given by a hospital or other program is moved to another institution or program the budgets of the two programs may not change. One program must give additional care with no new money, and one program gets the same amount of money despite loss of an expense. When the amounts are small and not predictable it may be best to ignore the apparent injustice, but some changes in patterns of care have led to large transfers of costs.

In the past when the site of care changed the agency with the money kept it and the Ministry usually provided new money to the agency with the new costs, but these add-on costs are no longer tolerable. In to-day's financial climate, the money should move when the care moves. If the money is not free to move then the desirable redistribution of care may not occur. The inflexible and separate funding of institutional and noninstitutional physician services in Germany, for example, made it almost impossible to move inpatient care to outpatient and community care.

Early discharge programs can shorten the hospitalization of an uncomplicated obstetrics case to 24 hours or less. This reduces hospital costs per case and is safer for the mother and baby, but it places new demands on community services. Office surgery, community based geriatric assessment, outpatient addiction rehabilitation programs or community care for heavy care chronic patients (mentally or physically disabled) can represent a similar transfer of costs from an institution to a community agency. In all cases, institutional costs go down. In most cases some community agency is obliged to provide service.

The Public Health Unit in Ottawa, as part of its response to new priorities, cancelled its support for an early obstetrical discharge program. This program should have been continued but with hospital money. The hospital was the beneficiary in terms of costs per case.

The problems associated with changes in location of care might be reduced by a different form of global budget. If all costs related to surgery were funded from a global budget the transfer of surgery from a hospital to an office would not lead to increased expenditures on surgery. It was once assumed that expansions in outpatient and office surgery would lead to less inpatient surgery, but this has been shown not to be the case. Inpatient surgical volumes may continue to rise as outpatient surgery also increases. A Manitoba report recommended closing surgical beds to assure limits on growth of inpatient surgery as outpatient and office volumes of surgery increased. (Shapiro, E., Manitoba Health Care Studies and their Policy Implications, Centre for Health Policy Evaluation, 1991)

New examples of cost transfers appear regularly. A new drug (Proscar) which shrinks enlarged prostate glands was approved in 1993. If the drug is successful the volume of prostatic surgery will fall but there will be a rise in outpatient drug costs. It is unlikely that the drug costs will be charged against the hospital system.

A voluntary intersectoral transfer of funds at the regional level occurred in Victoria B.C. in the Victoria Project. This experiment led to hospitals voluntarily transferring a million dollars of their global base to community services. Experience had shown that community agencies could produce more long term care per dollar spent than could the institutions. Experimentation with palliative care, postnatal care, much of paediatric hospital care and other health care might produce similar findings, but desirable system changes may not occur unless funds are able to move with the patients.

In 1992/93 three long stay patients in The Hospital for Sick Children (HSC) were transferred to a chronic care facility and the funds to support the children were moved with them. They had been in HSC for an average of five years and funding the transfer was considered preferable to their continued use of HSC beds. (HSC Annual Report, 1992/93)

Agencies currently funded to provide a service could, in some cases, be obliged to fund that service when it is provided elsewhere. For example, clozipine, a new and expensive drug to which some severe schizophrenics respond, allows discharge of some previously untreatable schizophrenics, but after discharge the costs of the drug and associated laboratory tests may not be the responsibility of the hospital. Hospital occupancy goes down but the hospital budget does not. Community care costs or user costs go up. In this situation some or all of the costs of the community care could reasonably be a charge against the hospital budget. (Newer less expensive drugs for schizophrenia may reduce the magnitude of the problem produced by clozipine.)

Hospitals are the beneficiaries when hepatitis B and influenza immunizations reduce admissions. Should hospital funds (either at the level of the provincial hospitals envelope or from the budget of individual hospitals), be used to finance a hepatitis B and influenza immunization program? Despite the decreased hospital utilization which follows both hepatitis B and influenza vaccination very few hospitals administer these vaccines to high risk patients who are hospitalized.

TRANSFERS WITHIN GOVERNMENT

Cost transfers can occur within governments as well as between governments and providers and users.

In 1977 children's mental health services in Ontario were transferred from the Ministry of Health to the Ministry of Social Services. This transfer moved these mental health services into a department without the visible appeal of the Ministry of Health, and as a consequence the costs of these services did not, over the years, grow at the rate of the costs of other health care services. The move gave the impression of a reduced rate of growth of health care expenditures but the only spending that went down was on children's mental health services. Whether children in need of mental health services were damaged or not by the reduced funding of their services is not known. When psychiatric institutions in Alberta were transferred to the Department of Health from Social Services the reverse occurred, institutional budgets increased immediately. The ease and degree of cost control varies with the Ministry involved.

TRANSFER OF RESPONSIBILITY FOR COST CONTROL

When governments place limits on the funds they make available to providers (whether institutional or personal) the responsibility for cost control may be transferred. Hospital global budgets, for example, cap transfers to hospitals and at the same time make the hospitals responsible for allocation of scarce funds. In the same way, regional budgets transfer responsibility for cost control from the province to the region. Regional bodies become responsible for allocating available funds to the many health care sectors and for being certain that programs and sectors live within their allocations.

The eight regional Health Boards created in New Brunswick in 1993 have been assigned physician quotas. If the quota is exceeded the region must find the additional physician payments from within its budget as well as face provincial penalties for exceeding its quota.

In British Columbia it was proposed (but not implemented) that new billing numbers would only be granted to physicians who had been granted hospital privileges. This regulation would have transferred to the hospital boards and their medical staffs some of the responsibility for control of physician costs. The ability of a new physician to provide insured services, and produce provincial costs, would depend not only on the final decision of the hospital but on the speed with which a decision was reached.

In British Columbia payments to radiologists for Magnetic Resonance Imaging (MRI) interpretations were capped at $150,000 per hospital per year (for the three hospitals which had an MRI). This capping of provincial responsibility transferred cost control to the hospital. If payments to radiologists for MRI interpretations exceeded $150,000 the excess would come out of the hospital global budget.

In Britain, by 1993, over one quarter of all general practitioners had been assigned a budget for the purchase of selected services for their patients. If the costs of the prescriptions written by the practitioner, of elective surgery and of selected other services exceed the assigned budget the excess is charged back to the practitioner. This arrangement not only transfers responsibility for cost control to individual providers, it penalizes the providers who do not exercise cost control. Some health care budgets in Germany operate the same way.

PUBLIC INVOLVEMENT IN PROFESSIONAL INSURANCE

Several provinces now pay all or a portion of the malpractice premiums of physicians. If provincial funding of physician insurance premiums is continued it will be reasonable for other independent professionals with a direct patient-provider relationship and who are paid from the public purse to ask for similar assistance. In Ontario in 1992-93 this reimbursement cost close to $100 million, or about $4,500 per physician.

Governments have options regarding the form of professional insurance that will be used. The main choice is between the current Canadian model and the no-fault insurance in place in Sweden since 1975. (Bergstrom, H., "Pressures behind the Swedish Health Reforms", Swedish Information Service, July 1992) In Canada legal costs now regularly exceed awards to patients for injury. The Swedish experience suggests that with no-fault insurance the legal costs are much lower, patient awards can be maintained or improved and maximum attention can be diverted to reducing patient risk.

A province could also, if it wished, operate a physicians insurance company. Quebec has discussed this option.

PREFERENTIAL TREATMENT FOR
HOME BASED PRODUCTS, INVESTORS AND PROVIDERS

This is not really a health care decision. It should be made by Ministries responsible for economic development.

Purchasing and pricing policies can favor drug manufacturers based in Canada or in a particular province. Quebec gives preference to pharmaceutical products manufactured in Quebec, up to a price differential of 10%.

Payment arrangements can favor small pharmacies. Small pharmacies tend to be locally owned and may serve communities where prescription volumes are low.

SUMMARY

Health care spending growth should be kept at less than the rate of inflation and less than the rate of growth of provincial revenues. There should in most provinces be a reduction in the percent of provincial spending which goes to health care.

Chapter 10

The Control of Costs

INTRODUCTION

Forces and techniques which can be used to control health care expenditures are strung across a broad spectrum from very direct and immediate to very indirect.

The major tools for direct control of costs are capping, competition, price setting, reduced coverage, supply management, substitution, improved administration and controlled access. These policies with a direct effect on costs tend to be implemented by regulation. Regulations are rapid in their effects and are the most reliable if dollars must be saved. They are imposed from above, often without much warning. They are not always well accepted by the providers and consumers of care, and manipulative responses are common.

The diversity of cost control locations and players provides many options for cost control. Governments in Canada have to date given greatest attention to macro level cost control techniques. Hospitals, especially teaching hospitals, have the most experience with micro level cost control. In the United States, control of micro level decisions is routine in agencies funded on capitation or by fixed payment per episode of care (Prospective Payment Systems). Many locations, players and techniques are needed for effective and tolerable cost control, but this chapter will look mostly at the macro and regulatory techniques used by governments.

CAPPING

Capping of public expenditures is everywhere in health care. Expenditure caps can be applied to one individual user for one type of service, (as is done in the provinces which place a ceiling on the amount that will be paid in one year for chiropractic services to any one beneficiary), to all providers of one type (for example, to all physicians), to one type of service in one setting, to individual providers, to a program or institution, to all programs and institutions within a region, to all services within one sector, to a government department or to a portion of a government department. Caps are also routinely applied to one service, or to a set of services, provided to one individual. The cap is, in this case, called a fee.

Ministries are routinely capped. Their cap can be exceeded only if the cabinet approves supplementary estimates. In the early years of publicly financed health insurance these supplementary funds were almost routinely requested and obtained, but in the 1990s the Ministries of Health are expected to live within their initial allotment. Ministry capping means that open-ended public spending on one type of health care leads to fewer public dollars for other types of health care.

Ministry capping has heightened the need for Ministry control of all of its cost centres. Global budgets have helped. Global budgeting combined with a refusal by provinces to cover deficits provided the provinces with a reasonable level of predictability of hospital costs. Global budgets also returned management control to the individual hospitals, with the hospitals having the ability (within provincial guidelines and constraints) to make trade-offs within their global budget. Agencies became responsible for deficits while also being able to carry a surplus forward to the next fiscal year. This eliminated the rush to spend money at the end of the year so that it would not be lost.

Global budgets were welcomed by both hospitals and Ministries of Health. They gave local managers, providers and Boards the ability to use resources more efficiently and they increased ministry ability to predict and control costs. Global budgets decentralized decision making from a Ministry to an agency or region, which was and is consistent with societal values. They allowed individual institutions, programs and regional boards to adapt to local differences.

When money for health care was plentiful global budgets were seen by the hospitals as a totally positive change, but the pleasure of internal control has now been joined by the stresses of deciding which departments, services, physicians and patients are to feel the effects of cut-backs. As provincial spending has become more and more constrained the global budgets of hospitals and other providers have not grown at anywhere near the rate considered necessary by the spenders. Global budgets are now much more of a cost control mechanism than was originally envisioned.

Regional budgets, although still in their infancy, offer a chance for governments to control costs through regional rather than institutional global budgets. Regional budgets offer more opportunities for multiservice cooperation than exist when each institution and program receives a separate budget from the Ministry. Each institution and program now tends to protect its budget and it is not easy for money to move when patients and costs move. With a global regional budget money could move within a region as it does now within a Ministry.

Ontario in 1993 prepared for regional budgets for long term care (Ministry of Health) and for children's mental health services (Ministry of Community and Social Services). This fragmentation of the regional budget will result in excessive bureaucracy and confusion at the sectoral borders. The fragmentation is a product of the insularity of sectors, the absence of an overall provincial plan for health care and the shortage of strategic planners.

Decentralization of responsibility for cost control will motivate many agencies, professionals and boards to actively work with their province to improve spending. The process has worked reasonably well in institutions who have decentralized some parts of spending responsibility to in-house departments or other cost centres, and the same results should occur with decentralization to regions.

Besides sectoral capping, capping of components within sectors is also necessary. In the ambulatory care sector, for example, if payments to physicians and laboratories are not tightly controlled their growth could leave little or no money for other community health care activities and agencies.

The capping of service volumes

The capping of service volumes can be used to control expenditures. Services will not be paid for beyond the approved volumes. For example, the Alberta government caps, at 2400 per year, the number of lens implants for which payments will be made to the Gimble Clinic in Calgary. This policy transfers rationing decisions from the Ministry to a private for-profit clinic, which is not desirable.

Hospitals can also be faced with, or impose, such ceilings. The Calgary Foothills Hospital in 1990/91 had used up its funds for lens implants by January and stopped this surgery until April 1. (Medical Post, Feb 5/91)

Rationale for system, sectoral, regional and program capping

There are many arguments in support of the concept of spending caps. First, they work, and they work at all levels.

Tight financial control of hospital costs was at one time thought to be impossible, but hospitals have shown they will, when it is unavoidable, spend as directed and continue to provide acceptable volumes of care. Administrators and providers can learn to spend less without significant public complaint and without significant, if any, hazard to users. As the quality of professional decisions improves, the difficulties with constraint will be even more manageable.

Health care was very generously funded for two decades. It is now desirable that funds be more equitably distributed to programs which respond to, or prevent, such problems as family violence, emotionally disturbed children, unemployment and environmental preservation. Global, sectoral, regional and local capping of health care spending will make it more likely that funds can be reallocated to less well served populations and problems.

Capping may not only control costs. It may also encourage better spending. Once users and providers accept the idea of a limited supply of money (and that acceptance is becoming more complete each year) efforts may be directed to the evaluation of trade-offs and opportunity cost and away from a search for ways to squeeze more money out of the system. Ceilings should provide everyone with an incentive for identification and reduction of undesirable spending. Emphasis may change from *how can we can get more money* to *how can we spend our money better*. The demand for improved professional decision making will at times decrease professional discretion and freedom and will, at times, produce conflict, but it will also improve social benefit per dollar spent.

With global capping the providers know that better spending will not reduce the global budget. The benefits of better spending stay within the relevant cost centre, and review of all expenditures within the Zero Base Budgeting process is encouraged. If each expenditure and program is examined on the basis of its impact on health status and its priority in the community then new ideas, new needs and poorly served populations may have a better chance to compete on a level playing field with established programs and with populations already served. When new money was available hospitals and other agencies used new programs as a device to attract new money. Now these new programs may be allowed to compete, on the basis of merit, for funding from the global budgets.

Global capping is also desirable because there is no attractive alternative. The United States has tried to control costs through new payment arrangements (Preferred Provider Organizations, Prospective Payment Mechanisms), new external surveillance mechanisms (Professional Standards Review Organizations and Peer Review Organizations, and managed care) and an extension of capitation payment (Health Maintenance Organizations). Despite these efforts health care costs in the United States rose very rapidly in the 1980s. (Newcomer, K., "Health Insurance out of Reach", in The Crisis in Health Care, Jossey Bass Publishers, 1990). The United States is teaching us that putting a lid on total expenditures is essential to cost control.

Capping brings its own set of problems, but these problems are manageable and are less threatening than the problems of open-ended spending.

Putting steadily lower caps on health care costs is an exercise rooted in courage. It is the act of telling almost everyone to forget what they formerly believed and accept new truths, but despite the difficulties rigid ceilings, and lower ceilings, should almost completely replace open-ended funding. Within sectors, institutions, programs or regions there may be service areas which cannot be totally capped, but spending overruns in isolated cost centres must be funded by transfers from other parts of a larger and related global allotment.

Arguments against capping

Arguments against the capping of spending on health care revolve almost exclusively around the inevitable reduction in availability of publicly funded health care. Fewer health care services will be able to be delivered. Unless providers and users are able to identify, and discontinue, the inappropriate health care that is currently being delivered then some of the health care that will not be available at public expense will be care which is appropriate and useful. If capping is combined with better spending, however, health will be minimally affected, if at all.

There will be disagreement as to which care should not be financed. Providers and users will, at times, wish to deliver, and to receive, care which the province, region or program believes should not be publicly financed. Capping will increase conflict between payers and managers on one side and users and providers on the other.

With continued capping of public expenditures there will be increased pressure to allow establishment of a private health care system alongside the public system. If private funding of physician and hospital services is allowed then the two tier system which already exists (but which many people choose not to see) will be legitimized.

Capping is almost surely objectionable to some planners, administrators, health care professionals and users because it requires development of new skills and the improvement of old ones, and change can be painful. Capping should also increase user and payer interest in the quality of professional decision making, and this will be objectionable to some professionals.

CONTROLLING GENERATED COSTS

Capping works less well when the volume of activity is controlled by someone who is not affected by the cap. Capping the costs of a drug or laboratory program may not change the number of prescriptions written or the number of laboratory tests ordered. The physicians generate the prescriptions or the orders for laboratory tests and the physicians may not be affected by the cap on laboratory or pharmacy costs. Single sector capping may, therefore, not be an adequate technique for the control of generated costs.

The mechanisms used to date in Canada to control generated costs include a reduction in the spectrum of insured services, the introduction of user fees and/or the lowering of prices paid. These devices reduce costs but may not improve spending, they may transfer costs to other agencies or to users and they may, when managerial skills are inadequate, not prevent spending beyond the ceiling.

New techniques for the control of generated costs have appeared in the last two decades, but not in Canada. An inclusive capitation fee, as is used in Health Maintenance Organizations in the United States, links generated costs to provider profits. Use of a fixed payment per case (Prospective Payment) makes the hospital or other insurer the loser if total costs exceed the fixed payment. In Britain the latest National Health Service reform has (to date) designated about 25% of all general practitioners as *fundholders*. These fundholders are given a fixed budget from which the physician must buy a broad range of services including drugs and elective surgery. Overspending on outside services reduces physician income. All of these techniques have been shown to alter the volume of generated costs. In Germany there is a regional ceiling on expenditures on drugs, medical and surgical supplies and medical aids, and if the ceilings are exceeded the excess is taken from the global fund for physician payment. (Altenstetter, C., "Making Global Budgets Work", International Health Policy Forum, Washington, D.C., Nov. 1993.)

The policy of establishing ceilings on generated costs and charging overruns to the prescribers brings cost control but may not protect outcomes. The policy assumes that physicians will prescribe optimally, and although this will sometimes be true it often will not be. A utilization improvement program aimed at both users and prescribers should accompany ceilings on expenditures.

At one time it was thought that global budgets for hospitals would not work because hospital costs are mostly the product of physician decisions. This problem has been overcome, but the system is still learning how to protect community health status while spending less. Cost reduction has usually been an exercise in lowering unit costs or lowering the volume of service. In the long term these approaches should be combined with greater attention to the elimination of services of limited or no value. (See Chapters 15 to 18)

COST CONTROL THROUGH PRICE SETTING

Provinces may, if they wish, set the prices of goods and services which are constitutionally within provincial jurisdiction. Provinces have the authority to determine the price of health care, subject only to the limits of the Charter of Rights and Freedoms and to federal jurisdiction over health care to selected populations. This authority to set prices can apply to an office visit, a prescription or an appendectomy, just as it can also apply to the price of a ton of gravel or a trip on a subway.

Setting prices sometimes works very well, at least when seen through the eyes of government. The provincial monopsony, combined with constitutional powers, has allowed provinces to freeze or lower fees to practitioners, pharmacists and private laboratories, to set prices for care in profit and nonprofit nursing homes and to reduce or to freeze drug prices.

Provinces have the authority to pay different prices for the same services provided by different workers and to make different payments to identical workers in different locations. A province can legislate a higher fee for a physical examination done by a physician than by a nurse practitioner (or vice versa), even when the examinations are of equal quality. It can pay higher fees to rural physicians than to urban physicians, and it can pay more (or less) to established physicians than to new registrants. Income or payment differentials tend, when they are a product of public policy, to be directed towards the objectives of worker redistribution, worker substitution or the discouragement or encouragement of entry of new workers into the work force.

Provinces and other payers can, at their discretion, establish the maximum payment which they will make for an item or service but leave it for the buyer and seller to decide whether there is to be payment beyond the amount available from the province. This approach is used in some assistive devices programs. The province will pay not more than a fixed amount for a wheel chair, but the user may buy a more expensive model if he or she wishes. This approach is illustrated by any payment arrangement in which the user fee is not regulated by the province, as with chiropractic services in Ontario.

THE USE OF COMPETITION TO LOWER COST

Tendering is one way to introduce competition. Tendering can be national, provincial, regional or by individual institution or program. It is a price setting process which normally results in supplies or services being bought from the lowest bidder. It is ineffective if there is only one supplier, as with drugs under patent protection.

In health care the tendering process has, at times, been altered. Suppliers compete to see whose price is lowest, but there may be little if any assurance that the lowest bidder is the one who sells the goods or services. In many hospital group purchasing arrangements there is no requirement that the hospitals in the plan purchase from the lowest bidder, and after the bidding is over the other suppliers usually lower their prices to match the price of the lowest bidder. The same situation applies in the Ontario drug program with respect to multi-source drugs. Each supplier quotes a price, and the lowest price is the only one paid regardless of which product is used, but there is no requirement that pharmacies buy from the manufacturer who quoted the lowest price. Other drug suppliers routinely sell to pharmacies at the lowest quoted price.

In Saskatchewan multi-source drugs insured in the provincial plan are bought through provincial tendering, and the product of the winner becomes the dominant drug used. Approximately 500 products are bought this way. It seems likely that tendering produces the lowest prices if the low bidder is assured of at least a defined portion of publicly financed sales, if not all sales.

Who will be allowed to compete?

Provincial policy determines whether private nonprofit agencies, in particular hospitals, are allowed to compete for the opportunity to provide health care. If nonprofit agencies are allowed to compete with private for-profit providers, policy will determine the terms and conditions. Hospitals have advantages in terms of taxes and the way in which capital costs are met and these advantages need to be acknowledged if profit based bidders are to compete on a level playing field.

Hospitals should be allowed to compete with for-profit agencies for the provision of laboratory and other services. Hospital operating costs are increased by the need to maintain laboratory stand-by capability, and it would be of advantage to the hospital, the province and the taxpayer if the hospitals were allowed to compete for the right to provide, and be paid for, laboratory services for patients other than those in hospital. (In Ontario a hospital which performs laboratory work on specimens from outpatients must finance these services from the global budget. This assures the use of fee-for-service private laboratories for most outpatient laboratory work.)

Useless competition

Competition is wanted because it brings lower costs for an equivalent product, or the same cost for a higher quality product. Competition among sources of care which all charge the same price and provide the same product is not an example of a free market, even when the competing sources are privately owned. Private ownership is, in itself, not proof of the presence of useful competition.

Private laboratories on fee-for-service, for example, bring none of the advantages of market based competition. In the five provinces with private laboratories there is competition only with respect to which laboratory can attract specimens. Prices do not change and the quality of all laboratories is regularly monitored. In this situation competition does not benefit the consumer or the payer.

The current practice of paying private laboratories by fixed fee-for-service is expensive. The fees in the fee schedule are set to adequately compensate a low volume laboratory. There are major economies of scale in laboratory services, and high volume laboratories can, therefore, perform tests at a much lower cost than can low volume laboratories. There were 174 private laboratories operating in Ontario in 1990. Many of the small volume laboratories would go out of business if price competition was introduced, but total expenditures on outpatient laboratory services would fall. They will fall the most if hospitals are allowed to compete.

Some provinces who wish to license new publicly funded long term care beds invite competing proposals from agencies or investors. The winner of the competition knows that the new beds will be immediately occupied by persons eligible for public support. In Ontario the for-profit operators complain loudly about the inadequacy of the public per diem payment, but competition for licenses is vigorous and the selling price of the licenses (when being transferred to another owner) is healthy. Private owners like guaranteed and noncompetitive pricing.

When should tendering be used in health care?

Tendering, or price competition of some other form, is simple and easily defended when there is more than one provider of technical goods or services for which specifications can be clearly written and quality effectively measured. Examples include laboratory services, imaging services (radiology, ultrasound, CAT), drug dispensing, medical and surgical supplies, oxygen, nutritional supplements, pharmacy services to long term care institutions and home care, and multiple source drugs.

Competition is particularly attractive when costs go down and quality goes up as volume increases, as with laboratory services. Quality specifications for laboratory services are easy to write, and quality testing programs are already in place. Tendering could be used much more to lower prices of components of Canadian health care than is now the case, and quality will not go down if the services being bought can be adequately described and measured.

When considering competition in health care it may be useful to look at the way competition is used in other public sectors. The highways department, for example, decides which bridges should be built and then has the bridges built by those who submit the lowest acceptable tender. Current health care arrangements are often analogous to a situation in which the bridge builders decide how many bridges should be built, and what type of bridge. In the past in health care the builders also would have decided the price.

The providers of health care could be asked to compete for the right to perform services such as surgical procedures or ultrasound examinations which have been identified by someone else as necessary. This competition is inherent in the United States health reform proposals, and is part of the health services reform in Britain.

Tendering (contracting out) can lower costs, and often does lower costs, by paying workers lower wages. If the benefits of competition are desired, but not at the expense of workers, a tender can specify a minimum rate of pay for those who will be employed.

Competition for the right to deliver services which are difficult to define and difficult to evaluate, such as long term care, may lower costs but may also bring social unease in the face of conflict of interest. The need for profit can be seen as a cause of inadequate quality. The quality of care delivered may be seen as inadequate regardless of the funding or payment method used, but when profit is part of the picture the concern over quality can become more acute and ideological. Tendering is usually inappropriate when precise specifications cannot be written and quality is difficult to measure.

When considering the use of competition as a means of cost control the failures and successes of the United States system should be kept in mind. Competition between providers lowered costs per case, but it also lead to undesirable duplications of service and excessive administration costs. It also did not reduce delivery of inappropriate care and it did not stop a rapid escalation of total costs.

Tendering for the delivery of personal health care would disrupt, although not necessarily destroy, the opportunity for users to choose their providers. The loss of choice is especially noticeable if the tendering unit is small, as when the unit has only one pediatrician or surgeon. If the tendering unit is large, as in United States Health Maintenance Organizations and the District Health Authorities in Britain, then the user can have choice.

To restate, competition for components of health care should be sought when specifications can be written and quality adequately monitored, and hospitals should be allowed to tender in competition with private nonhospital bidders so long as there is recognition of the advantages available to the hospitals. Tendering for health care for which precise specifications cannot be written, and for which quality measurement is difficult, should be approached much more cautiously than for other types of care.

Competition to lower the price of a broad spectrum of health care

Tendering can be used to get the lowest price for a laboratory service or a pound of laundry, but it can also be used to establish the lowest possible price for a full range of health care for a population. This level of competition is not currently in use in Canada, but it exists in other countries.

In the 1970s the Health Maintenance Organizations (HMO) in the United States (which were direct descendants of the Kaiser-Permanente Group Health Foundations and a variety of Cooperatives) became a national force. Capitation had been shown to be less expensive, and better, than indemnity insurance paying providers on fee-for-service, and American big business endorsed the concept.

The capitated HMOs deliver integrated physical and mental health services, and often dental and other health care. The HMOs compete in an open market for the opportunity to provide a broad spectrum of care for a fixed price. The capitation payment usually does not cover unapproved elective services received from providers outside of the agency.

The competitively established HMO capitation payment is quite different from capitation models in which the capitation fees are fixed, as in Britain (general practitioner services only) and in Ontario Health Service Organizations (HSO). A British general practitioner competes with other general practitioners for patients to enrol in his or her roster, but the capitation payments from the National Health Service are the same for all general practitioners.

In the Clinton health care reforms in the United States all carriers will be obliged to offer an identical package of services, plus supplementary benefits if they wish. Competition will be at the level of price and quality (as perceived by the users or by an employer). (Iglehart, J.K., "Managed competition: Options for controlling costs", NEJM April 22, 1993) Details will not be clear until the Senate and the House of Representatives approve a reform package.

The British National Health Service is introducing open competition. District Health Authorities and the fundholding GPs will contract with whoever will provide care at the lowest cost. Time will tell whether these changes can bring the advantages of lower prices while avoiding the administrative inefficiencies which plague health care in the United States. Competition equivalent to that in Britain and the United States will, in Canada, not become a viable cost control alternative until government eliminates the current right of a patient to receive care from any provider of choice and from as many providers as are chosen.

Canadian provinces are in many respects similar to a Health Maintenance Organization in the United States. Instead of trying to establish a series of HMO like organizations within the province it would be better for each province to examine the processes used in the United States, Britain, Germany and elsewhere to control costs and improve spending and then implement as many of them as are useful and acceptable in the Canadian context.

While recommending that provinces look to HMOs for lessons in cost control it is necessary to note that HMO premiums have been growing at 15-20% per year, although on a lower base than costs in other delivery arrangements. (Coddington, C.C., et al., The Crisis in Health Care, Jossey Bass Publishers, 1990, Ch 5) Competition in health care, as used in the United states, has not been a great success.

THE RANGE OF INSURED SERVICES AND INSURED PERSONS

Cost control by the federal and provincial governments has always been primarily through limits on the range of services available at public cost plus limits on the number of persons allowed access to publicly funded services.

Preventive public health services and institutional mental health services were the first health care services to be publicly funded. Physician and hospital care for indigents was added in most provinces in the 1930s and 1940s. Universal hospital and physician services insurance came next. Each addition expanded either the range of insured services, the percent of the population covered, or both.

Through the 1970s and 1980s all provinces expanded their list of publicly funded services, and often without federal financial support. Long term care, optometry, chiropractics, assistive devices, ambulance services, health promotion, prescription drugs and home care became publicly funded although with differing degrees of generosity and universality in different provinces. To a much lesser extent public funding was extended to dentistry, nonprescription drugs, acupuncture, outpatient physiotherapy, chiropody/podiatry and a variety of other forms of health care. Midwifery was added in 1994 in Ontario.

Whether a service became insured had little to do with whether it had been proven to be useful. The main criterion was whether the service was acceptable to, or provided by, physicians practising western style medicine, with public and political priorities being a second important force.

No province has added a significant range of nonwestern therapies to their range of benefits. When acupuncture was finally recognized as having therapeutic value it was legalized in most if not all provinces, but it was not insured in most provinces. Nontraditional health care (homeopathy, reflexology) is offered in some Community Health Centres but is not usually listed as an insured service. (Sandy Hill Community Health Centre Annual Report 1991-92, Ottawa)

Provinces have all limited the range of services available at public cost. At least three provinces (Newfoundland, Nova Scotia and New Brunswick) have no coverage of chiropractic services. (The Porter Report) Only Manitoba, Saskatchewan and British Columbia introduced universal drug insurance. Provincial differences exist with respect to abortion, in-vitro fertilization, outpatient physiotherapy, laboratory services in private laboratories and a variety of immunization programs. In most cases cost has been the factor which has prevented a province from insuring a more full range of health care.

In recent years several provinces have, in the interest of controlling government costs, stopped paying for health care services previously covered, or have tried to stop. Alberta in 1987 removed tubal ligation, vasectomy, the insertion of intrauterine contraceptive devices and eye exams (refractions) for persons 18-65 years from the list of insured procedures. The delisting of many of these services was seen as an attack on women and all decisions were reversed in 1988. In 1993 Alberta delisted penile prostheses (gender equity was restored).

Manitoba and Alberta have recently cancelled public support for their in-vitro fertilization programs. In some provinces it was never an insured service. It is now insured only in limited circumstances in Ontario. Ontario in 1992 stopped paying for hair electrolysis after it had become a virtual industry in the hands of a few high income dermatologists with large numbers of employed electrolysis technicians. From 1988 to 1992 Ontario removed over 2000 items from its list of items insured under the provincial drug plan. (This brought the Ontario benefits in line with other provinces) In 1991 Ontario sharply reduced its coverage of health care outside Canada, a move which again brought Ontario's level of coverage closer to that of other provinces. In 1993 the North West Territories deleted annual physical examinations from its list of insured services.

Removal of items from the list of insured services does not appear to have been based on universal or clearly established criteria. It also has been an all or nothing choice, and these are not the only options.

When delisting is being considered, the attractive options are to fully delist services proven to be ineffective or undesirable (which is fairly easy and of minor importance) and to partially delist services which are only cost-effective when used in selected circumstances (which is quite difficult but is very important). (Reduced access is discussed in a later section.)

The option of reducing the number of persons who are covered by publicly funded programs is being increasingly used. Saskatchewan, for example, markedly amended its universal drug program in 1993. It now offers basic protection to only seniors and persons on public assistance. Quebec in 1992 stopped paying for some eyeglass examinations for persons 18-40 years of age, and reduced the cut-off age in the children's dental plan from 13 years to 10 years. Ontario in 1994 deinsured about a dozen services, but these services, in total, represented only about 0.1% of total provincial health care expenditures.

Removal of a service from the list of insured services is one way to accelerate abandonment of services found to be of no value. This occurred when a number of insurance programs in the United States deinsured Intermittent Positive Pressure Breathing (IPPB) because it had been discredited by a large randomized clinical trial in 1983. Delisting led to a rapid decrease in use of IPPB.

Cancellation of a noncost-effective service does not necessarily reduce costs. Providers and users will, if they can, find a substitute service which is insured, but whether or not substitution occurs the use of the delisted service will drop. (Soumarai, et. al., "Withdrawing Payments for Unscientific Drug Therapy", JAMA, 1990, 263:831)

Because many health care services have not been adequately evaluated there are some attractive policy options which cannot yet be fully implemented. It would, as an example, be unreasonable to stop paying for services whose value has not been proven. This would completely end payment of most of the care for many conditions.

Public coverage may be available only as a last resort. New Brunswick requires that individuals with coverage by both public and private health care insurance must use their private insurance. This reduction in access to publicly financed services transfers costs to employers, as does the policy that services covered by WCB are not provincially insured.

PAYMENT FOR SERVICES OUT-OF-PROVINCE AND OUT-OF-COUNTRY

By national agreement all provinces insure their residents for physician and hospital services received in another province if those services are insured in the home province. All provinces but Quebec reimburse their residents, or make payments to the providers in another province, at the rate paid in the province in which the service was received.

Quebec will not pay, or reimburse, more than the rates paid in Quebec, with one exception. Out-of-province rates will be paid if the service is not available in the region in which the Quebec resident lives and it is reasonable to seek care out-of-province. This allows residents of western Quebec to obtain some services in Ottawa with the Ontario providers being paid at Ontario rates. A 1993-94 investigation into inappropriate ownership of insurance cards suggested that many Quebec residents were avoiding the possibility of limited coverage for Ontario services by maintaining medicare registration in both Ontario and Quebec.

Saskatchewan slightly reduced its compliance with the national portability agreement when it stopped paying for any part of the care provided by the Gimble Eye Centre in Calgary to Saskatchewan residents. Saskatchewan formerly paid the physicians fee (as is done by other provinces), but the Minister stated that if a person could afford the fee of over $1000 for the facility (a cost not reimbursed by any province) then that person could also afford the physician fee(s).

Payment (or reimbursement) for out-of-country care can be limited to situations in which prior approval was given, and can be limited to emergency care. There can be full reimbursement of incurred cost or reimbursement only to an amount equivalent to what would have been paid for the same services if received at home. This reimbursement may be only a small percentage of the foreign costs incurred.

Most provinces offer coverage for elective out-of-country care if the care is approved in advance, and approval is likely if the service is not available in the province or adjacent provinces. The place at which an out-of-country service is insured may also be provincially determined. There may be locations at which the province has preestablished the price. Reimbursement for approved care is usually at 100% of cost. Payment may be directly to the provider by the province. Services covered (with prior approval) can include organ transplants, alcohol rehabilitation, rehabilitation of head injured patients, and special pediatric psychiatry services.

In the present financial squeeze, and with our foreign balance of nontrading dollars already massively unfavorable, it would be reasonable to offer no public support for out-of-country care unless there is prior approval, and approval could reasonably be denied if the services are available in adjacent provinces. Canadian services are less expensive.

COST CONTROL THROUGH REDUCED ACCESS

Public expenditures, especially on open-ended programs, can be reduced by putting limits on the frequency with which, or the conditions under which, specified services can be received at public expense. Expenditures on tests for eye glasses, for example, go down if access is limited to one routine examination per year, and the costs go down even further if there is coverage of only one routine examination every two or three or more years. Experience in the United States with a low income population showed a 30% drop in the number of prescriptions filled if there was a limit of three insured prescriptions a month. (CPSO Chartbook, 1989). Alberta will pay for a test for Prostate Specific Antigen (PSA), but only in specified hospitals and only when the patient meets specified criteria. Ontario pays for this test only when it is used to monitor established prostatic cancer.

Limits can also be placed on the locations and/or practitioners who are authorized to provide care. These limitations are imposed to improve use and/or to reduce cost. Very expensive drugs, for example, such as those for thalassemia or organ transplant patients, can legally be sold by any drugstore and prescribed by any physician, but governments can (and sometimes do), pay for such drugs only when they are prescribed or dispensed through specified clinics, practitioners or pharmacies.

In Germany the *Sickness Funds* (the privately funded but publicly regulated insurance programs) pay for preventive check-ups but only for designated examinations at designated times in life. (Family Practice, Nov 2, 1991, p. 4) The German choices regarding approved examinations are similar to the advice given by the Task Force on Periodic Health Examinations since 1978 and ignored by most Canadian public insurance programs.

Limits on volume and location can be designed to assure reasonable rather than 100% accessibility, chevrolet rather than cadillac service. They can be a mechanism for equity. The available funds are able to serve more people.

In deciding what level of public protection against health care costs is defensible it is reasonable to look at other public policy areas which also are important to health. Police services are adequate but not endless, publicly financed education is of good quality but does not provide all services which might be useful to each child, and roads are of good quality but are not always divided or clear of ice when it would be safer if they were. Most programs which are important to health are not endlessly financed at public expense. The same must apply to health care and limits on access are one device for reduction of cost with minimal loss of adequacy. Limits on utilization and access are, and will continue to be, one of the trade-offs which often will be made in the interest of equity and optimal social benefit per dollar available.

Limits on access to publicly financed health care are usually severely criticized by physicians and their associations. The objections are often expressed in silly ways, for example, claims that bureaucrats will decide whether you need your appendix out.

The concept of limits on what physicians are allowed to do, and of limits on what insurance companies should pay for, has long been endorsed by physicians. In the days before Medicare, when physician administered medical care insurance programs were dominant in Canada, these programs reserved the right to declare the practice patterns of some physicians to be abnormal and to not pay for all or some services. For decades physicians, through their hospital medical staff organizations, have helped control hospital costs by placing limits on the freedom of medical staff members through such devices as mandatory stop orders and limited ability to order selected drugs and investigations. Governments should endorse widespread use of the actions and devices pioneered by physicians to control costs and increase quality.

The cooperative participation of physicians in the development of new provincial policies will improve these policies. Both providers and users can be better served. Fortunately many physicians appreciate the rationale for the changes which are occurring, and appreciate the need for cooperative involvement.

COST CONTROL THROUGH SUPPLY MANAGEMENT

The supply of facilities, equipment and personnel can affect costs. More doctors can mean more billings, and fewer long term care beds mean lower long term care institutional costs. Limits on the supply of workers, equipment or space may reduce the number of persons who will be able to receive care, whether that care is admission to a home care program or access to radiotherapy. Limits on points of access are not the same as a financial cap, but some of the effects are the same.

Supply management can control supply within the public system or it can also control supply in the private sector. In long term care, for example, government may limit the number of beds which will be publicly funded but may allow unlimited growth of similar beds in the private market. Governments can limit the total public and private supply of CAT scans or can ignore total supply and merely limit the number of places at which a CAT scan can be provided at public cost.

The supply of very high cost technology items, such as imaging devices [CAT, MRI, PET) and lithotripters, has frequently been targeted in the search for cost control and better spending. If, however, a global hospital budget includes the operating costs of the expensive equipment, and if the province will not cover hospital deficits, then the operating and capital cost of the new equipment is a greater threat to the ability of the hospitals to serve their communities than it is to provincial coffers. Control of the costs associated with sophisticated technology in hospitals was more important to provinces when global budgets were less well controlled.

New technology is often introduced with the hope that it will lower health care costs for selected types of patients. Instead, costs often rise. Reasons for the higher costs include failure to reduce use of the older services, underestimation of the costs of the new technology and expansion of the number of patients who now are thought to be likely to benefit from care or investigation.

It is difficult to know how much high tech equipment Canadian hospitals would have bought if governments had not sharply limited such purchases. Canadian hospitals do not have the financial incentives which led to major oversupply and overuse of high tech equipment in the United States (where hospitals make money out of their expensive equipment), but our hospitals do have a history of wanting the latest whether it is proven or not or needed or not.

There appears to be at least one unfortunate by-product of the current governmental preoccupation with the distribution of high tech equipment. This preoccupation may be delaying attention to the use of low tech health care. Improvement in the everyday use of high volume but low cost items is financially more important than better use of a small number of expensive items.

Limits on the supply of necessary items can be a product of societal actions, or inaction, as well as of public policy. Solid organ transplantation programs, including heart, kidney, liver, lung and heart-lung programs, are constrained by the lack of availability of organs. The shortage of kidneys is financially as well as functionally unfortunate; kidney transplants are the best and most cost-effective treatment for end-stage renal disease. The cost-effectiveness of other solid organ transplants is less certain or is unproven.

To bury a healthy kidney which could have been retrieved is to deny someone a better life and continue to spend on dialysis. A successful kidney transplant leads to savings of at least $15,000 per year. There are more than 5,000 persons on dialysis in Canada and the number of transplants has been falling rather than rising. Policies to increase the availability of kidneys, and perhaps other organs, should be studied more vigorously.

There is now a reasonable degree of public control of physician supply. It will be many years before the physician supply stops growing more quickly than our population, but at least the rate of increase in the physician population has begun to slow. These supply management policies are important to long term control of the costs of health care.

In the absence of firm caps on public spending on physician services, increases in physician supply increase public expenditures on health care. The number of services provided per patient and per population unit increases steadily as physician supply increases. (Barer, M., A. Gafni and J. Lomas, "Accommodating rapid growth in Physician Supply: Lessons from Israel, Warnings for Canada", International Journal of Health Services, Vol 19, No. 4, p. 17.)

Public policy has reduced the acute treatment hospital bed supply per 1000 population by 30-50% in the past two decades. Supply fell from 6 to 7 beds per 1000 to 3 to 4 beds per 1000 in some parts of some provinces. In 1992 Ontario announced a target of 850 days of hospital care per thousand population per year, a big drop from the 1400 to 1700 which were at one time the norm across Canada. The lower figure is still above the experience of the United States and Britain. In 1994 Alberta announced an intention to reduce hospital beds by as much as 50% in three years.

A reduction in bed supply does not necessarily mean a reduction in hospital costs. In the United States the supply of hospital beds fell steadily in the 1980s but expenditures on hospital care grew at two and one half times the rate of growth of the Consumer Price Index. Despite these data, control of the supply of hospital beds will continue to be part of Canadian cost control.

Reductions in hospital bed supply occur naturally if fee-for-service is replaced by capitation. Hospital use goes down 15-40%. No total reduction in regional bed use occurs, however, if some physicians are on capitation but a significant portion of the physician population is on fee-for-service. The beds not used by the capitation physicians are utilized by the fee-for-service physicians, as has been the case in Sault Ste Marie for decades.

An oversupply of physicians, equipment and institutional beds is less of a financial threat to provinces when sectoral public expenditures on health care are capped. So long as there are ceilings on total allowable expenditures on hospitals and physicians, the supply of hospital beds might seem to be of no interest to government. In reality, bed reductions are necessary to improve utilization patterns and to reduce pressures on government for more funds.

COST CONTROL THROUGH INCENTIVES AND DISINCENTIVES

When hospital deficits were quite routinely picked up by government there was an incentive to spend. When deficits became the responsibility of the institution there was an incentive to stay within budget. Refusal to assist with deficits has provided a successful cost control incentive.

Practitioners paid on fee-for-service have an incentive to maintain volume. This incentive complicates North American efforts to reduce costs and alter practitioner habits. Practitioners on salary or sessional payments, on the other hand, do not have any financial incentive to be productive and waiting lists may grow while resources are underused, as was the case in Sweden. Capping of individual and total physician expenditures has reduced physician incentives to expand volume when payment is by fee-for-service.

In 1990 Alberta introduced a Hospital Performance Index to evaluate hospital efficiency. A hospital is bonused or penalized on the basis of its ability to lower the cost of individual services and improve community service. (Calgary hospitals were early winners and the University Hospital in Edmonton was a loser.) The rewards or losses are limited to a maximum of 1% of the operating budget. This program does not reward hospitals for performing only necessary health care; it rewards them for being efficient and for acting in ways which are consistent with its goals and objectives.

The BOND program in Ontario was a program of incentives for hospitals, but not of incentives to either be more efficient or more cost-effective. It encouraged hospitals to seek additional income through business ventures, presumably to reduce the need for public funding. The BOND program was an unwise decision which merely diverted board and administration attention away from their primary task of wisely spending available money on the delivery of health care which best serves the community.

Legislation which threatens hospitals with management by a government appointed trustee if they do not operate within budget, or close to it, provides incentives for greater hospital attention to cost control.

The random reporting to patients of bills submitted to medicare programs discourages fraudulent billing. Experience in Saskatchewan in 1962/63 indicated that the billing patterns of some physicians change noticeably when it is known that verification with users might occur.

The provision of statements to all users showing annual health care expenditures on their behalf has been discussed and endorsed in principle as an incentive for honest billing and user awareness, but administrative costs and impracticality have prevented their use. The same applies to suggestions that users should sign physician accounts before these accounts are submitted to the provincial plan. Even if these programs were implemented, there is no evidence to suggest that they would alter utilization patterns any more than is accomplished by the random and less expensive surveillance now in place.

There appear to be very few examples of controlling costs through tangible incentives to users. One United States Health Maintenance Organization pays mothers $75 to stay in hospital for two days or less after delivery.

User disincentives are common. User fees of all kinds are a disincentive for some users. User fees which vary with the cost of the service provide the most constant user incentive to keep costs down. Culturally insensitive services also provide a user disincentive.

THE IMPACT OF SUBSTITUTION OF LOWER COST WORKERS OR SERVICES

In theory it would seem that providing services in less expensive places or with the use of less expensive personnel should reduce provincial spending on health care, but in the past this has often not been the case.

Transferring long stay patients from acute care beds to long stay beds is often proposed as a cost saving measure, but unless expenditures on acute care beds go down total health care costs increase. Transferring services from physicians to nurses or other health care workers leads to new and additional costs unless total expenditures on physicians services go down at least as much as the costs of other services increase. The same rationale applies to the replacement of inpatient surgery with outpatient surgery, or the replacement of institutional care for the chronically ill with community based care.

Transfer of duties from physicians to nonphysicians was not attractive to governments so long as physician incomes were not controllable. Savings from the use of less expensive workers could not occur when physicians were able to maintain incomes by finding new services to provide. Governments have now, however, learned that there are several effective devices for controlling total expenditures on physicians services, most notably capitation or, when fee-for-service is the method of payment, a combination of capping and limits on billing numbers. The costs associated with the use of the substitute workers can now, if a government so wishes, be removed from the global allotment for physician services.

Competition between professionals will increase as midwives, physiotherapists, nurse practitioners and others are granted new professional powers including the right to see patients without physician referral, prescribe drugs, refer patients to specialists and order laboratory and other investigations. Price competition may increase as governments encourage provision of care by the least expensive professional.

On occasion governments may wish to promote the appearance of new kinds of health care workers so that competition is increased. This option could lead to the training of nurse dermatologists to care for high volume problems currently cared for by dermatologists, or of surgical technicians qualified to perform less complex surgical procedures. These two examples are realistic. They will be financially tolerable and clinically excellent, and will be financially attractive so long as expenditures on the new workers are taken from the global budget of the existing providers.

The care of the dying should include more high touch and less high tech. An acceptance by Canadians of the fact that dying is what living leads to might alter expenditures during the last days of life. A slight delay in the inevitable should not be bought with public funds. Those funds should be reserved for improvement of the quality of life or for protection of life of persons whose death is not imminent.

IMPROVED ADMINISTRATION

Improved management can reduce expenditures throughout the health services network. Improved efficiency is a product of good management, and good management can also contribute to improved clinical decision making. It can produce substantial savings. (Sheps, S.B., G. Anderson and K. Cardiff, "Utilization Management: A Literature Review for Canadian Health Care Administrators", Health Management Forum, Spring 1991). In 1989-90 the University of Alberta Hospitals in Edmonton lowered the cost per hip replacement by over 20%. This was accomplished by the development and implementation of guidelines governing all phases of care. These guidelines were supported by all staff and did not lower quality of care. (D Schurman, "Health Care Crisis— TQM as a potential Solution", Healthcare Management Forum Winter 1992)

Managers can create barriers to cost-reducing innovations as well as be the initiators of these innovations. Barriers include top down management which fails to harness the interest and creativity of all staff, fails to create devices through which all employees can contribute to greater efficiency, is unwilling to spend operating money exploring new ideas and creating the forums in which the ideas can be identified, and fails to produce and then disseminate the information which all partners must have if they are to most intelligently assist with better spending. Managers can, on the other hand, reward efficiency and cost-effectiveness, encourage involvement of all staff in the search for greater efficiency and better decisions, encourage cross-departmental efforts and provide consistent support and example during the search for better spending. (Richardson, P.R., "Lean, Keen and Healthy: Proven Methods to reduce costs in Health Care," Working Paper 90-16, July 1990, School of Business, Queen's University)

One barrier to innovation is the fear that change will encourage layoffs. Honesty and fairness will reduce but not eliminate the fear. Spending cuts will, if salaries and wages are unchanged, lead to lay-offs whether or not money is spent more wisely. When funding is reduced lower personal incomes are often the only device which can fully preserve employment levels.

Ontario, Quebec and New Brunswick, and presumably other provinces, know there is abuse of the provincial health systems by ineligible persons such as residents of another country. The number of health care cards in circulation has for many years been known to exceed the population of the provinces. Persons who wish to receive free benefits either use someone else's card or fraudulently have a card produced in their own name.

Quebec has proposed a card with the picture, signature and, eventually, medical history of the beneficiary as one device to reduce fraud. A photo health card is also proposed in Ontario beginning in 1994. Lack of earlier development of devices to reduce fraudulent use of the system speaks unfavorably of the interest and competence of the managers of these programs.

The administrative costs of universal insurance plans are low, but some expenditures can be still lower. Expensive patient reimbursement arrangements could be avoided and provider accounts should all be by electronic billing. Most provinces charge the provider a fee for every paper claim submitted.

In some health care services, (hospital emergency departments, ambulance systems, bed availability information networks, hospital laboratory departments) major stand-by costs are incurred. Costs can be lowered by reducing the level of stand-by capability or by greater cooperation and rationalization of the network. Reduced stand-by capability brings risks, but if these risks are acceptable then costs go down. With network rationalization costs can go down with no loss of community protection. In early 1994 four large Toronto hospitals announced an interest in greater cooperation with respect to laboratory, pharmacy, dietary, security and other services. In 1994 the replacement of five downtown Montreal hospitals by one new 1000 bed institution was also announced. Consolidation will reduce administrative costs.

COST CONTROL APPROACHES WHICH DON'T WORK

Asking patients to visit emergency departments less often, or not to use walk-in clinics, does not work. Need is as seen by the user and, when services are both *free* and convenient, people will use them even when the perceived need is quite small. (Despite the fact that advertising campaigns which conflict with user interests are not effective there is considerable evidence that public education programs which help the public to consider alternatives, such as self diagnosis or care, do work. User perception of need can be changed.)

Removing a drug or service from the insured list may also not lead to reductions in cost. There may be an offsetting use of something which is still insured, and the substitute may be even more expensive. If, for example, over-the-counter analgesics (pain-killers) are not insured, but prescription analgesics are, then physicians may offer, and patients may ask for, prescription rather than nonprescription analgesics. The prescription drugs will be more expensive. Similarly, when home-maker services are only insured if a professional service is also delivered there may be unnecessary nurse visits merely to assure coverage of needed homemaker services.

Even promotion of lower cost alternatives may lead to increases rather than decreases in the total cost of health care. In the 1980s Dr. Bob Evans of the University of British Columbia studied surgical patterns in British Columbia to see what effect bed closures were having on surgical volumes. Everyone knew outpatient and office surgical volumes were increasing, but the actual volumes, and the changes within hospitals, were not known. Dr. Evans discovered that the total volume of surgery had continued to rise despite the closure of many surgical beds. Not only had the outpatient and office surgical volumes increased, but the inpatient surgical volumes had not fallen. Surgeons had in the process of adapting to the decreased bed supply started to come closer to the hospital lengths of stay of the United States, where surgical patients have tended to stay in hospital fewer days than in Canada.

There are many interactions between costs in different sectors of health care. Shorter hospital lengths of stay can reduce institutional costs per case by transferring costs to users or to community programs. Total health care costs may rise. A shorter hospital length of stay may result in more surgery being performed. The extra surgery will lead to more bills to Medicare, which will increase total costs unless collective payments for physician services are tightly capped. The additional cases will also increase use of outpatient drugs and laboratory programs, which will increase total costs if these programs still have open-ended budgets.

The promotion of alternatives to FFS may, when the objective is cost reduction, also be disappointing.

RESPONSES BY MINISTRIES OF HEALTH TO COST CONSTRAINT

When Cabinets give Ministries of Health less money the agencies and programs funded by the Ministries get less money. These agencies and programs are left with the problem of how, with fewer resources, to deliver services which satisfy the public and the government. There has as yet been no province led, organized, province-wide, integrated and participative program in which government works with the providers and communities who must get along with less. Chapters 15 to 18 look at this deficiency.

Cost control has not always been supported by public servants. The lack of support is not necessarily rebellion or sabotage. It is more likely to be an inability to do that which has been asked for. When, for decades or for all of ones career, increased spending has been the norm, when growth has been automatic, when high standards routinely have been given higher priority than control of spending (regardless of whether there was proof that the higher standards improved outcomes), when there is little if any experience with the concepts of trade-offs and opportunity cost, and when every user or provider complaint has in the past been thought worthy of response, it is difficult to suddenly change direction and begin to effectively deal with shrinkage and cost-effectiveness.

160

In 1990 a subcommittee of the National Advisory Committee on Immunization met to consider two polio cases which had occurred in 1989. (Canada Weekly Diseases Report, April 13, 1991) They carefully reviewed the two cases about which they were already fully knowledgeable. The example is a minor one, but it illustrates the willingness of technical experts to have a little get together at public expense unless someone is watching the till. A conference call would have been adequate, but there are mind-sets which oppose cost-effectiveness or just don't think of it.

Ministry officials have, in some provinces, found it difficult to be of help to political leaders who wish to spend less and spend smarter. They have also been of little help to health care providers to whom fewer resources were being given, and on occasion have not even known how to pass on the message that there is no more money or to act themselves as if there is no more money. They have been slow at times to revise or abandon earlier commitments which have become too expensive.

Within some Ministries of Health the inadequacy of the implementation of cost control and better spending has been partly due to a failure to implement a process to prepare staff for the new paradigm. Ministers and Deputy Ministers appear not to have noticed that speeches about the need for restraint and the value to health of services other than health care, whether made to the public or to staff, seldom, in themselves, lead to change. Pronouncements need to be accompanied by a planned, staffed and funded exercise of information, discussion and skill development. The exercise needs top level support and repetition so that those who are on the front line (in both the ministries and the field) are better able to serve objectives which are easy to express but difficult to attain.

Some ministry actions are inconsistent with financial realities. In 1992 and again in 1993 Ontario assessed all residents in long term care institutions and promised to fund additional care whenever the assessments indicated the need for more care, despite a ministry-wide restriction on spending. Alberta had done the same thing many years earlier but had warned the institutions that the objective was equitable funding rather than a new infusion of funds. By 1993 Ontario had committed over $300 million to an upgrading of the quality of institutional care, money that did not serve one additional person and which was committed in years of unprecedented financial constraint. The agreement by some Ministries of Health in the 1980s to pick up all additional costs associated with the use of new and expensive nonionic contrast media in X-ray departments was also an example of noncost-effective policy which public servants should have avoided.

Limited access to abortions is also contrary to cost control, although other factors are at play in this example. It is much more expensive to provide care during a pregnancy carried to completion than to pay for its termination.

Ideology can increase costs. The Ontario decision to encourage use of FFS for-profit laboratories for outpatient specimens has almost surely increased costs, as did its commitment to gender equity.

The decisions of one level of government can be damaging to the cost control efforts of other governments. Federal Bill C-91, which retroactively extended drug patent protection to 20 years and placed other restrictions on the appearance of generic drugs, will cost the provinces and other payers hundreds of millions of dollars before the end of the century.

New programs established without consideration of how they should be monitored, and of how they will affect other programs, can unexpectedly increase costs. In Ontario in the middle 1980s the government decided to expand addiction assessment and referral capabilities, and Assessment and Referral Units were established in many centres. Within a few years, thousands of Ontario residents were being sent to addiction recovery centres in the United States because the case-finding mechanisms were operating in the absence of treatment capacity. There was no evidence that recovery rates after treatment in the United States were better or even as good as were attainable in Ontario, or that the referral could be justified in terms of likelihood of recovery, but professionals had been given the task of finding addicts (usually to alcohol) and referring them somewhere, and they did exactly that.

It may have been assumed that the professional assessors had the skill to refer for treatment only persons for whom the treatment was likely to be cost-effective. Another possibility, and this is more likely, is that no-one considered the possibility that assessors who were not empowered to treat, and who were told to refer, would not look at the big picture and would become advocates for addicts to the extent that tens of millions of dollars would be spent providing a month or more of rest and relaxation for individuals who often had failed previous rehabilitation trials, had little likelihood of recovery and on occasion were intoxicated on the way home on the bus. The failure to monitor professional decisions (in association with what appears to have been a rather faulty policy analysis process) led to a lot of public money being wasted, and wasted outside Canada.

The federal government was slow to implement AIDS testing of all who apply for resident status. Such testing is consistent with the long established practice of requiring investigations, such as a chest X-ray and a general medical examination, to ascertain whether an applicant has health problems considered incompatible with acceptance as a new Canadian. The sensitivity over AIDS testing was a triumph of irrationality and led to a public policy inconsistent with cost control.

IMPLICATIONS OF GOVERNMENT IMPOSED COST CONTROL

Who are the winners and losers as government expenditures on health care are controlled? Who may be at risk as spending on health care goes down?

Users are at risk if cut-backs result in failure to deliver useful care, but they are not at risk if better spending habits can lead to delivery of the same amount of useful care as was delivered before.

It would be reasonable for users and their families to expect reduced access to health care as spending is constrained, and they might reasonably expect this reduced access to be a hazard to their health. There are, however, few if any data which suggest that cut-backs, to the extent they have been implemented in Canada, increase user risk or produce poorer outcomes. Cost constraints have definitely led to shorter hospital lengths of stay, and one must now be more sick, more at risk or more disabled to merit admission to hospital or a long term care institution than was the case 15 years ago. These altered criteria can bring economic costs due to days off work to care for a sick child or other family member, but is there a threat to health status? Apparently not. Spending less time in hospital may actually reduce hazard and improve outcomes (hospitals are unhealthy places, and the less time one spends in them the better - up to a point). To the extent that any individual has had urgent hospital care delayed the blame usually must rest with physicians who control hospital admissions, not with governments who have reduced spending.

Direct expenditures by users are increasing in all provinces, with the biggest losers being those who completely lose coverage and are unable to afford needed but deinsured services. Increases in user payments reduce access to drugs for lower income populations, but the effects of this reduced access are not known. There will be persons whose health will be damaged or threatened by failure to fill a needed prescription, but the health of others will be improved when drug consumption is reduced.

Those who make their living delivering health care are obviously at risk. Their jobs may disappear or their incomes fall. Cost constraint in hospitals has meant unemployment for a significant number of administrative and clinical personnel. The gross incomes of many physicians have fallen. Private laboratories, pharmacists, chiropractors and optometrists have all had fees frozen or rolled back in one or more provinces.

Institutional managers and boards are at risk of at least greater stress if they are given less money and told to accomplish the same as before.

Besides the direct impact of cost constraint on the users, providers and payers, there also are effects on the relationships of various providers. A reduced supply of public dollars heightens competition between different provider groups (one medical specialty vs another, or physicians vs chiropractors), different health care sectors (public health vs hospitals) or different cost centres in an institution (administration costs vs care costs). If there can be no growth in the system, or shrinkage in it, then anyone who becomes better funded or even preserves former levels of funding does so at the expense of someone else.

Who benefits from the constraints on health care expenditures? Almost everyone. Taxes may be lower and national and provincial deficits may be lower. When a smaller portion of available provincial funds is consumed by health care there is more money for education, roads, security, income maintenance, job creation and all of those other activities which also are important to health. Increasing scrutiny of spending on health care will almost surely, in time, increase the cost-effectiveness of that spending, which in turn may mean that there will be no loss of access to cost-effective health care. The same outcomes for less dollars is a good deal for everyone.

EXPERIENCES IN OTHER COUNTRIES MAY NOT BE USEFUL

Britain introduced a requirement that all elderly must be seen at least once each year at home by their family physician, and all other adults must be seen at least every three years (not necessarily at home). The objective was, presumably, to avoid the underservicing which has been said to occur with payment by capitation. Being seen once a year, or once every three years, was presumably thought to be a preventive activity which would improve community health status. These new services may cost the National Health Service nothing. The patients are already on the physicians roster and monthly capitation payments are being made, but there is no proof that these compulsory visits will serve any useful purpose.

A requirement for regular physician visits would be inappropriate in Canada. These visits would be inconsistent with the current move towards greater personal responsibility for health and greater user control over health care. They would use an expensive health care worker to do things which can be equally well done by less expensive workers. They would be contrary to the proposition that routine physical examinations are a waste of time. (The current recommendation is that healthy adult males under 40 need only a blood pressure check every few years, and this can be done in a shopping centre or at home. After age 40 an annual rectal examination is added to the blood pressure check, but full routine physical examinations are still not indicated. Healthy adult females should have their blood pressure checked and have a PAP smear at established intervals, and both of these can be done by a nurse.)

COST CONTROL DEVICES NOT USED BY GOVERNMENTS

Not all of the cost control devices which are available are compatible with the philosophies and objectives of Canadian governments or the Canadian public. These devices are, therefore, rarely used by government but continue to be used by, and be appropriate for, the private for-profit insurance sector.

Public insurance has dominated Canadian health care for so long that many Canadians do not remember the rules of private insurers. As Canada adapts to financial constraints it will be useful to remember the features of private insurance which were part of the reason for introduction of public insurance. The effects of cost constraint in public insurance programs may offend some of the basic principles of Medicare, but the changes become more palatable when compared with the undesirable features of private health care insurance.

Our public insurance system continues to be dedicated to protecting populations and individuals from most of the costs of health care. Profit based insurance must be dedicated first of all to making a profit. They must therefore protect themselves against groups, individuals or situations which represent excessive financial risk. They may refuse to continue to insure persons or populations whose costs are likely to be excessive or have been excessive.

The financial safety of payers is increased by the use of annual ceilings on expenditures per person or per episode of illness or injury. For example, there are now many drugs which cost $5,000 to $25,000 per person per year, and almost all private drug insurance companies (both profit and nonprofit) have therefore placed ceilings on expenditures which will be made on behalf of any one beneficiary in one year. If a beneficiary needs a truly expensive drug the insurance protection quickly disappears. The ceiling is $2000 per patient in Blue Cross Ontario. In 1992 Green Shield was the only drug insurance company (out of over 100 in the Ontario market) offering drug coverage which did not have a ceiling on expenditures per person per year. (Green Shield and Blue Cross are large nonprofit drug insurance carriers.) This use of ceilings on annual drug costs is inequitable considering that similar ceilings do not apply to physician and hospital services. (The ceilings on drug costs may be partly a tool through which provinces are pressured into paying for very expensive drugs.)

Individuals seeking individual coverage with private insurers may face rejection because of the likelihood of high costs. There may also be an exclusion of costs arising from preexisting conditions. Even worse, private insurance must be regularly renewed, and at the time of renewal the new coverage may exclude costs associated with chronic conditions which developed in the previous coverage period. The insuring of groups rather than individuals, such as all of the employees of a firm, provides protection from some of the hazards mentioned, but high risk groups such as the elderly or the chronically disabled find it difficult to obtain protection in the private insurance system. High risk persons may even be undesirable as employees because they threaten the costs of employer financed group health insurance.

Public insurance brought the concepts of noncancellability, no diagnostic exclusions, universality and no limits on the amount of care that could be received. These open-ended concepts are financially demanding. Governments writing policy in the presence of financial constraints may be forced to compromise some principles, but they will hopefully resist the simple and user unfriendly approaches used by private insurance carriers. There are better ways to spend less.

SUMMARY

Health care spending can be controlled and it should be. Responsibility for cost control is steadily being decentralized, and it should be. Regulatory macro level controls by governments will continue to be crucial to cost control.

Experience indicates that caps (ceilings) imposed by a single payer are a prerequisite to the control of expenditures on health care. Many other devices affect the impact of the ceilings (the global caps), but it is the ceilings which make health care costs predictable at the provincial level.

Cost control is not nearly so intellectual a process as is that of improved spending. Cost control can be performed without economic models and without expert advice. An accountant with an abacus can do it, as can a cabinet in a moment of panic.

Fortunately the situation is not totally bleak. Decisions do not have to be random or fully intuitive. There is good, although seldom conclusive, general evidence to support tighter controls on some parts of the health care network than on others. On the basis of this general evidence, regulatory control of health care costs should concentrate on expenditures on institutions, drugs and fee-for-service practitioners.

Alterations in the size of the population covered and in the range of insured services are dominant cost control options and all Canadian governments have shown a willingness to implement these forms of rationing. These devices are not as desirable or equitable as other devices such as limited access to services and limited public financial responsibility for care.

Additional public costs should usually not be incurred so that provider or user preferences can be satisfied. Public responsibilities should end at the cost of acceptable levels of care in the most inexpensive setting or format. This principle will often lead to restrictions on the services available at public expense and on the locations at which those services can be received. Worker substitution should be much more aggressively pursued.

Comparison of the benefits of different spending patterns will allow users and providers to implement desirable trade-offs within global allocations. The comparisons which will be made will require use of evaluative frameworks in which cost, outcomes, political reality and community priorities will dominate. Those seeking resources will know that maintenance of funding depends on proof of outcomes and/or public support.

Resources should be reallocated to prevention when prevention is more cost-effective than therapy. All social expenditures should be treated as a single fund.

The number of facilities and professionals funded by government should be only as many as are required to deliver as much care as can be afforded. Governments have no obligation to fund any particular worker or program. Patients should, to the extent reasonable, be directed to locations with excess capacity. Existing capacity should be efficiently used before more capacity is added.

Ministries of Health and the programs they fund should accomplish cost constraint without transferring costs to other provincial departments or other levels of government.

Chapter 11

Physician Services

INTRODUCTION

Physicians represent 0.2% of the population, but their decisions determine the way in which 6 to 8% of GNP and 20 to 25% of provincial budgets are spent. Government interest in what physicians do, and in the decisions they make, is inevitable.

Across Canada there is increasing societal influence over physician services, fees and incomes. Users and governments are becoming health care decision makers, and physicians lives are being affected.

Physicians are uncertain about their future. Positions of economic and professional privilege which were thought to be permanent are threatened. It is in this context that the policy options and choices which affect physicians must be examined.

Public policies of significance to physicians include those which determine:
- whether there will be limits on incomes
- the level at which total expenditures on physician services will be capped
- the kinds of expenditures which will be charged against the global fund from which physicians are paid
- the levels at which fee-for-service (FFS) payments to individual physicians will be capped
- the kinds of income which will be taken into consideration when determining whether individual income ceilings have been reached
- the extent to which generated costs will affect physician incomes
- the extent to which payment methods other than FFS will be encouraged or allowed
- the extent to which physicians will be able to control or influence the evolution of new roles and powers for other health care workers
- which services will be insured, and where
- the conditions under which a physician will or will not be issued a billing number
- who will control physician fees
- the conditions under which payments will not be made for specific insured services
- the extent to which regulations will require or prevent selected professional decisions, in other words, the extent to which physician discretion will be limited
- whether there will be direct payments by patients to physicians (user fees), and, if so, under what circumstances and in what amounts
- whether payments will vary with location
- the rules which will govern a physician who is unable to obtain a billing number, or who does not wish to have one
- the terms and conditions under which a physician will be granted hospital privileges

Many factors affect the decisions of physicians and the cost of those decisions. Some factors affect the cost of one individual service, whereas other factors affect the cost of all physician services. Some factors affect public expenditures on physician services, other factors affect expenditures in the private sector, and other factors act everywhere. Some factors are cultural, others political, others economic. The factors include the supply of physicians, the method of physician payment, the method of payment for the services which physicians order, the organization of health care, the degree to which individual and collective physician costs are capped, the extent to which physician activities are monitored, the family physician/specialist mix, the utilization habits and the perceptions of users, the information available, the health of the population, the demographic characteristics of the population, the manner in which care is delivered and the medical/health care culture. These factors are discussed either in this chapter or in other chapters, primarily chapters 2, 4, 9 and 10.

POLICY AND PROFESSIONAL FREEDOM

Individual professional freedom is measured by the extent to which an individual professional is free to exercise clinical discretion, choose his/her method of payment and choose her/his practice place and style. Collective professional freedom is measured by the extent to which the profession has responsibility for evaluation and discipline of its members and the setting of fees.

Individual discretion is limited when the decisions of a government, an institution or a professional body reduce clinical, location, payment or other choices. Freedom is decreased when choices are eliminated or are made mandatory. Collective professional freedom is reduced when any outside agency (government, hospital, employer or private payer) makes decisions in areas which physicians consider to be their domain.

Examination of physician decisions is not new, and care patterns change when scrutiny increases. In the 1950s and 60s tonsillectomies and appendectomies were bread and butter procedures in many medical practices. The volumes of these procedures decreased markedly and quickly when tissue committees in hospitals began to notice and question the number of normal appendices being removed and when tonsillectomies were identified as an area for scrutiny. Other examples are given in Appendix 1. In the 1990s similar attention is appropriate for all services for which standards are available, evidence of abuse exists and change appears possible.

Many limits on the discretion of individual physicians have been shown to improve quality and often lower cost, and users and payers are interested in both quality and cost. Evidence indicates that many desirable limits on physician discretion are not likely to be put in place unless consumers and their representatives provide the initiative, and initiatives by users and payers are therefore inevitable.

Regulations which interfere with the professional freedom of physicians were pioneered by physicians and are implemented daily in hospitals on the recommendations of the medical staff. There are complex and widespread hospital regulations governing when referrals must be made, which antibiotic can or cannot be used and which laboratory or other investigations are expected, demanded or not allowed. In the United States the same types of regulations also exist in many ambulatory care settings. Physician participation in evaluation of applicants for hospital privileges has, on occasion, been used to reduce competition for existing medical staff.

Physicians who object to external regulation would be well advised to note the extent to which physicians themselves established the need for regulation and the usefulness of it. They should also be aware of the extent to which physician decisions have been shown to be inadequate. External regulation is now unavoidable, and physicians should work closely with public agencies and consumer groups who would like the advice of physicians as new regulations and processes are developed. Processes which involve everyone and which use all tools available will produce the greatest number of win-win situations.

Professional freedom can be enhanced by policy. Public policy has produced professionally controlled licensing and monitoring bodies and has in several provinces provided the opportunity for professional incorporation.

THE PAYMENT OF PHYSICIANS

The methods of payment are fee-for-service (FFS), salary, capitation, sessional payment, incentive payments or a combination of two or more of these. Sources of payment include governments, other third party payers and users. Canadian physicians generate income through all of these methods and from all of these sources. Evaluation of physician payment options should include consideration of such factors as legality, potential for cost control, potential for promotion of improved clinical decision making, acceptability to the public, political tolerability, physician support, effects on geographical distribution of physicians, effects on other health care costs and cost of administration.

Private practitioners, including physicians, chiropractors, optometrists, pharmacists (for the professional component of a prescription) and dentists, are usually or often paid on FFS. FFS is also, in some provinces, a common method of payment for private laboratory services, hospital outpatient laboratory and X-ray services, private ambulances, private physiotherapy services and prosthetic and orthotic services. A fee may apply to a single service, a part of a service, an episode of care or a fixed period of time such as one hour or 15 minutes. Payment for an episode of care is embodied in composite surgical or obstetrical fees. Complex rules are written governing when care is within, or outside of, a composite fee.

Fee-for-service is payment by piece work. Piece work is traditionally a form of payment which is used to exploit workers. It is favored by employers in situations in which the payment per item of work can be lowered to subsistence rates. Physician experience has shown that the piece work model is very desirable when workers have a monopoly and can set their own fees. Physicians now have lost much of their control over prices and, in the opinion of some of them, are becoming exploited workers. Public opinion is likely to support that view when physician net incomes approach those of other professionals.

Professionals, including physicians, are usually salaried in community health centres, public health programs, universities, pharmaceutical companies and provincial psychiatric hospitals. A few physicians are salaried in emergency and radiology departments and in long term care institutions. Some physicians on salary are employed by other physicians. Many physicians are paid on a sessional basis for work performed in clinics, federal hospitals, occupational health programs and workers' compensation facilities.

Payment by capitation is a lump sum paid per month or year to an agency or an individual provider for provision of a specified range of services, as needed, to a rostered user. A general practitioner in Britain receives a monthly fee for each person on his or her roster, as do Health Service Organizations in Ontario. Physicians working in agencies who contract to provide care for a capitation fee usually are paid by salary, with or without a profit sharing arrangement.

A capitation fee is similar to but different from a premium paid to an insurance carrier. The similarity is that in each case the user is assured of access to a designated range of health care services for a fixed payment. The difference is that with capitation the agency or individual provider receives the lump sum. There is no middle man. The provider becomes directly interested in the costs of care and in those devices which will reduce the needs and demands of the users.

Payers and providers interested in capitation should consider the size of the payments, the services which are to be provided, whether the entire payment is to be in the form of capitation payments or whether there will be a basic stipend plus the capitation payments, whether the capitation payments are to be affected by generated costs, whether there are to be incentives or disincentives associated with specific health status or health care goals, and whether and how payments will be affected when the services covered by the agreement are obtained from outside sources.

In Ontario the capitation payments to the Health Service Organizations are roughly the average costs (per month or year) of care delivered by FFS physicians to persons of similar age and sex. Additional payments are made when utilization of hospitals is below average. Negotiations in 1993 led to reductions in capitation payments, reduced bonus payments for low hospital use and increased liability for care received outside of the HSO by rostered patients.

The earlier rather pathological attachment of medical societies to FFS has become muted. There has been an increasing acceptance of other forms of payment. One is now less likely to hear that salaried physicians will have less interest in their patients. (Nurses and school teachers, and many physicians, are paid on salary and their interest in those they serve has never been shown to be less than the interest shown by FFS physicians in their patients.) As physician incomes from FFS become more constrained there will almost surely be an increasing willingness by physicians to look at any method of payment which produces a reasonable and secure income.

In 1992 the College of Family Physicians of Canada (CFPC) recommended a mixed payment arrangement which would be less volume driven than the current FFS method but which would require provision of a basic amount of service if income was to be maintained. They recommended that there should be reduced compensation for services beyond reasonable volumes, and little or no payment for volumes of service beyond that considered to be the most one person could reasonably provide with maintenance of quality.

The option of part salary and part FFS should be attractive to physicians who like to spend more time with their patients or who have many patients who require a great deal of time. FFS tends to produce low compensation for physicians who care for complicated patients such as those with AIDS, or who provide the counselling and support sought by many patients. A mixed form of payment also might encourage location in underdoctored areas and mitigate the current situation in which the physicians who concentrate on the performance of procedures are the ones with the highest incomes.

The mixed payment option would increase the incomes of some physicians. At least some of the physicians who select a payment method other than FFS make the change in the interest of higher incomes. Ontario promoted capitation payments through Health Service Organizations in 1990-1992 and was surprised when costs rose, but the increases were predictable. Few people will change their method of payment if the change brings a lower income.

Long term care institutions in Quebec may, at their discretion, pay their physicians on salary or by FFS. About half have medical staff who are on salary. (Champagne, F., CHEPA conference, June 1990) Physicians on salary write 30% fewer prescriptions than those on FFS and spend considerably more time with patients.

Capitation experience in Canada and in the United States has proven that a full range of high quality medical services can be delivered with 50-70% of the number of physicians per thousand population that now are licensed in most of Canada. In light of this experience all jurisdictions should aggressively control physician supply while taking steps to reduce the delivery of inappropriate care and the number of physicians working within the publicly financed system.

Even with the present physician numbers it will not be possible to fully employ all Canadian physicians in the public system if the delivery of care is rationalized. Controlling supply will decrease the dislocation of the lives of the excess physicians. The surplus physicians may not increase the cost of Medicare, but that will not be much consolation for those facing an uncertain income.

Physicians who like FFS, and it has some advantages, must aggressively cooperate in actions to control its disadvantages. If the problem of inappropriate service is not addressed, and if fee schedule revisions which promote equity and public priorities are not supported, then representatives of the public may justifiably act without physician involvement to either increase regulatory control of FFS or introduce other payment options. Cooperative protection of the public interest may preserve a greater degree of flexibility in how physicians are paid.

Fee-for-service has been blamed for most of the ills of health care and is surely responsible for some of them. The fee-for-service payment method promotes high volume care and discourages termination of some inappropriate care. Unfortunately every other method of payment would also have brought problems.

EFFECT OF METHOD OF PAYMENT ON COSTS AND DELIVERY OF CARE

The method of payment of providers has been shown to be important in determining how much health care is delivered, what kind is delivered and how much it costs. The Kaiser programs in the United States first demonstrated that payment by capitation rather than fee-for-service leads to a 30% or more drop in hospital and pharmaceutical use, to greater use of other health care professionals, to at least a one third reduction in the number of physicians needed per thousand population, and to increased emphasis on prevention and patient education. When payment is by FFS discretionary procedures represent about 50% of total procedures performed, whereas with capitation they represent about 30%. (The Porter Report, p. 33)

Fee-for-service discourages patient follow-up through other than additional office visits. The phone is an efficient way to follow-up many patients, but short office visits are more economically sensible. Electronic communication via a FAX or electronic bulletin board will increasingly become an excellent way to ask questions of patients or deliver information to them, but these substitutes for office visits will also not be attractive when FFS is the method of payment.

Fee-for-service discourages minor consultations. Even if a problem is very simple and could be dealt with in a very short time and with only a very brief comment on a chart, there are fee schedule requirements which demand that certain records be kept and certain actions taken if a consultation fee is to be defensible. When a more complete examination is performed and the required records are kept the service has a higher value.

Physician FFS billing volumes have increased rapidly. The increased billing volume, which can also be called increased utilization, increases the cost of physician services even when increases in individual fees are relatively well controlled. Table 11.1 indicates the extent to which specialty groups in Ontario increased average individual utilization and increased collective utilization over the six years reported. Growth in physician supply within the specialty categories can be estimated through use of the two columns.

General surgeons were the only group whose numbers decreased, and their utilization increases were modest compared to other physician types. Cardiovascular/Thoracic Surgeons doubled in numbers but increased their utilization per physician the least of all groups. Diagnostic radiologists did the best job of increasing both their individual and collective billings.

Working longer days could account for some utilization growth, but it is reasonable to assume that physicians were, in 1984/85, working as hard as they could (most have for many years reported very long work weeks). They probably were not working any more hours in 1990/91 than in 1984/85. Improved efficiency measured by more services per hour of the same type and quality would also allow increased utilization, but a 10-40% improvement in physician efficiency in their offices and in the hospital seems unlikely in the six years reported. It seems likely, therefore, that utilization increases were due to a combination of factors including greater efficiency, changes in the fee schedule and changes in the way work is reported.

The consensus in North America is that doctors on FFS provide too many services. Sweden and Britain, on the other hand, have worried that doctors paid by salary, session or capitation do too

Table 11.1

CHANGES IN UTILIZATION PER PHYSICIAN, AND IN UTILIZATION BY SPECIALTY, IN PERCENT, ONTARIO, 1984/85 TO 1990/91		
	Per physician	All physicians
General Practice	7.0	35.6
General Surgery	10.5	9.4
Internal Medicine	23.4	65.7
Obstetrics and Gynecology	21.1	33.8
Pediatrics	11.6	33.5
Orthopedic Surgery	13.6	41.6
Otolaryngology	20.8	34.1
Urology	24.8	43.5
Diagnostic Radiology	42.7	81.9
Anesthesia	11.6	38.7
Neurology	9.8	43.3
Psychiatry	10.8	45.0
Ophthalmology	31.4	56.7
Dermatology	32.4	62.3
Pathology	11.9	76.1
Neurosurgery	17.0	34.0
Plastic Surgery	10.7	40.8
Cardiovascular/Thoracic Surgery	7.6	112.6
Physical Medicine	31.3	90.4
Therapeutic Radiology	11.2	58.0
All Physicians	13.5	43.8
Specialists Only	17.0	48.1

*Ontario Medical Association Reports to Council, June 1-2, 1992

little and/or refer too often. (Bergstrom, H., "Pressures Behind the Swedish Health Reforms", Swedish Information Service, No. 12, July 1992) Over-referral may occur when solo or small groups of general practitioners are on capitation or salary, but there is no incentive to over-referral when referrals are inside a service delivery unit. Internal referrals occur when the delivery unit contains both family physicians and specialists, as in the Sault St Marie Health Centre, the Saskatoon Community Clinic and American Health Maintenance Organizations.

Fee-for-service has been associated with open-ended costs, but payers are now learning how to limit expenditures even when FFS is the method of payment. The introduction of caps on total physician payments and on individual incomes is reducing the importance of method of payment as a determinant of physician costs, and limits on billing numbers will increase control even farther.

Altering physician payment mechanisms alters practice patterns but does not automatically improve clinical decisions. For these decisions to improve there must be credible and defensible information supporting change, credible and preferably powerful supporters of the change and an identified process through which the changes will occur. (The first two exist; this book is an effort to accelerate the arrival of the third.) Regardless of the method of payment, physician's habits, and those of other health care professionals, may not reflect what is known to be best. Habit and culture can be stronger determinants of professional performance than information, good intentions and method of payment.

The preferred payment arrangements for physicians are those which minimize incentives to over-service or underservice, preserve incomes of physicians who practice holistic medicine, encourage physicians to work closely with other health care professionals, encourage the development of delivery arrangements which emphasize full use of the special skills of all types of health care workers, produce predictable public expenditures, are acceptable to at least a reasonable percentage of providers, reduce the incidence of inappropriate decisions, encourage health promotion and disease prevention, encourage a strong primary health care network and establish the primary health care network as the gatekeeper for most specialized care.

EFFORTS TO REDUCE USE OF FEE-FOR-SERVICE

Alternate payment mechanisms have been promoted in several provinces in several different ways but with limited success. The percent of the population cared for by non FFS ambulatory care outlets is still under 5% in all provinces except Quebec and Manitoba. Attempts to tie funding of new hospitals and new equipment in Ontario to non-FFS payment arrangements have been largely unsuccessful due to vigorous resistance from medical associations. Fee-for-service has been replaced by global budgets for the technical component of many outpatient diagnostic and therapeutic services in private facilities in Ontario. In several provinces university teaching units providing education, research and service are now on some form of block funding (global budgets) and do not bill on FFS.

THE NATURE AND CONTROL OF FEE SCHEDULES

Fees can be controlled by government by virtue of a combination of single payer power and constitutional power.

Governments have, since the introduction of provincial medical care insurance, gradually increased their control over fees for physician services. Initially the provincial programs paid some specified percentage (such as 85%) of the fees in the fee schedules of the provincial medical associations. Later, provinces produced their own fee schedules and paid 100% of its fees. (Other paying agencies also have their own fee schedules, including Workers Compensation Boards, for-profit insurance companies, and the Department of Veterans Affairs.)

Creation of a government fee schedule was an attempt by government to control expenditures on physicians services. Governments thought that if the fee for each service was controlled then the cost of physicians services would be controlled, but governments have learned that costs continue to rise even if the fees do not.

Despite controls on fee increases the payments to physicians in the 1980s still increased at several times the rate of inflation. Governments did not control growth in the physician population, physicians remained in *de facto* control of additions to, and interpretations of, the fee schedules (in all provinces but Quebec), physicians controlled the volume and mix of services rendered, there was minimal monitoring of either the volume or mix of services rendered, and physicians controlled the manner in which accounts were submitted.

Fee schedules often give billing and service options to physicians. Sometimes additional work (needed or not) allows higher billings. Sometimes changes in service description can increase income without increasing the volume of work.

In 1978 the accounts submitted to the Saskatchewan medicare program by family physicians for office visits produced approximately the same number of minor, intermediate and major office visits. In 1988 the total number of accounts from family physicians for all types of office visits was almost unchanged, but minor office visits had dropped almost to zero. (Table 11.2) In one decade either people stopped going to family physicians with minor complaints or family physicians began to bill minor office visits as intermediate visits. (Intermediate visits have almost twice the fee of a minor office visit.) The number of major office visits was unchanged; it is probable that medicare program limits on major visits (complete examinations) made it difficult to convert intermediate examinations into complete examinations. Several provinces have abandoned the designation of visits as minor or intermediate.

The experience of several provinces indicates that there is a need to use cost control devices other than the control of fees. In British Columbia from 1979-1983 total physician payments rose 18.5% per year despite controls on the growth of fees. In 1983 the province began to limit the issuing of billing numbers and also negotiated a partial ceiling on physician payments. In the years 1983-1988 the annual increase in total payments to physicians was only 5%. (Barer, M., R. Evans and N. Haazen, Restructuring Canada's Health Services System, 1992, p. 13-17)

In Alberta the government allowed no fee increases in 1984, 1985 and 1987, but expenditures per Alberta resident for physicians services went up 12.8%, 6.3% and 8.2% respectively in those years. In those years physician population grew at 4.6% per year. (Plain, R., Restructuring Canada's Health Services System, 1992, p. 24)

Manipulations of billings consist primarily of artificially creating a basis for a higher fee (upcoding), breaking a service down into several components which have a greater value than a single composite charge (fragmenting, exploding or unbundling) or choosing a diagnosis which legitimizes additional charges. All of these may be completely legal and able to be supported by material in patient files, but the costs will be higher and there will be no increase in benefit to the user. It may, for example, be advantageous to be certain that the diagnosis given on a follow-up visit is not the same as was used at the time of the initial visit, or it may be advantageous to be certain that the initial visit or consultation before surgery is sufficiently separated from the surgery to allow separate billings for the visit(s) and the surgery.

A quick look at a provincial fee schedule used by physicians to submit accounts will confirm the opportunities for creative billing. In Ontario in 1991 there were 27 pages of interpretive comments followed by 167 pages of individual fees. Over 60% of the pages were for surgical services. The 27 pages of interpretive comment define such things as the circumstances in which services provided at the same visit can be billed separately, as with an office visit fee and a urinalysis fee, and the frequency with which a particular service can be billed.

The writing and amendment of fee schedules is a game based in dollars and egos accompanied by a touch of reality. Every specialty regularly petitions the provincial medical association for fee variations in response to some new diagnostic or therapeutic approach or feature. Requests for fee schedule changes seldom ask for a simplification or a reduction in a fee.

Table 11.2

BILLINGS FOR OFFICE VISITS IN SASKATCHEWAN 1978 AND 1988
NUMBER OF SERVICES PER 1000 MEDICARE BENEFICIARIES*

	1978	1988	% change
Complete examinations	364	376	+3
Intermediate visits (partial assessments)	1597	3857	+142
Minor office visits (minor assessments)	1272	150	−88

*Annual Reports of Saskatchewan Medical Care Insurance program

The use of a relative value fee schedule in which all services are assigned a point value (an approach strongly championed in some provinces) might increase equity between physician groups but would have little if any effect on cost. In the presence of a relative value fee schedule physician energy would be transferred to attempts to change the number of points assigned to the services provided, and the wish to increase the number of items individually listed would not change.

The increasing complexity of fee schedules is the product of increasing specialization, the emergence of new procedures, the competition between physician groups and physician efforts to maintain or increase incomes. The process is in most provinces carried out entirely by the provincial medical associations without payers or consumers being partners in the process. The fee schedules quite expectedly represent the interests of the physicians rather than a balance of the interests of all affected parties. The medical associations are marketing boards without consumer representatives.

Fee schedules influence patterns of practice. These patterns of practice affect public service and the way physician services fit within a regional or provincial health services delivery plan. The design and content of fee schedules are therefore of interest to all who plan and receive health care.

Provinces can concentrate on capping total expenditures on physicians services and leave the distribution of the available dollars in the hands of the physicians. They may instead, however, decide to cap costs and also influence the way in which physician dollars are distributed between family physicians and specialists, or among specialties, and they may wish to participate in, or dictate, changes in payments for specific services.

CAPPING TOTAL PAYMENTS TO PHYSICIANS

Capping total payments to physicians has allowed the provinces to take financial control of these expenditures. It is not the only device available for control of physician costs, but it is the most effective when physicians are paid by FFS.

Quebec was, in 1976/77, the first province to experiment with capping. Expenditures on physician services have, since then, gradually been capped in additional provinces, with British Columbia being second in 1986. (Lomas, J., C. Fooks, J. Rice and R. Labelle, "Simultaneous control of Price and Quantity of Physician Services", McMaster CHEPA Working Paper 10, 1989). By 1988 four provinces had placed partial caps on total physician payments by use of a formula in which some of the cost of additional utilization would be charged against the physicians. If costs rose beyond the established ceiling the government was partially protected. By 1993 all provinces were controlling total expenditures in some way. (Feeley J., "A Review of Negotiated Economic Agreements in other Canadian Jurisdictions", Ontario Medical Review, Feb 1993)

In one pattern, by way of an example, the first 1-2% increase in the cost of physicians services is absorbed by the government. The impact of the next 1-2% increase in cost is shared by government and the physicians, and additional increases are fully charged against the physicians and recovered in some way. This rate of increase in total payment to physicians may be uncommon in the future, especially the near future. Roll-backs are now more common than increases.

As a variation on the theme of a fixed cap, overexpenditures in one year can lead to fee changes next year. This approach does not limit expenditures in one year but next years fees are reduced by a percentage designed to restore expenditures to some predetermined base. This does not recover the overpayment made in any year but reduces the likelihood of overexpenditures in subsequent years. One disadvantage of this approach is that it favors the high volume physician. It rewards the physician who is good at increasing utilization, whereas it decreases the income of responsible high quality physicians who choose not to decrease the time they spend with each patient.

In the 1980s West Germany held its growth in health care spending very close to the growth in national income. This was surely helped by the steady growth in national income, but also was partly a product of the policy of linking physician fee changes to the volume of services billed.

Volume increases led to fee decreases. In the 1990s fee decreases were joined by recovery of over-runs. (Iglehart, J., "Germany's Health Care System," Health Affairs, Winter 1992, 503-508).

Putting a cap or partial cap on total payments by the provincial medicare plan to all physicians does not mean billings will stay within the cap. It does mean that when billings exceed the cap, or may exceed the cap, payments to physicians are reduced or recovered so that total expenditures do not exceed the cap. A percentage of all payments may also routinely be withheld in expectation of billings in excess of the ceiling, with adjustments as required at the end of the accounting period. This last option is the Quebec formula.

When total billings exceed the cap a claw-back occurs. The claw-back formula can target the highest billers by increasing the amount of claw-back as billings increase and/or by lowering individual income ceilings. The claw-back can also be applied equally to all physicians regardless of their billing volumes, or it can be a uniform percentage of total billings. A claw-back formula could also target physicians who generate high health care costs relative to other physicians treating similar patients, or could target specialties or physicians whose billings increase excessively over billings in the year before.

In Quebec the family physicians and the specialists have separate global funds. It may also be reasonable to have global ceilings for specific specialties or groups of related specialists.

SELECTING AND AMENDING A GLOBAL CEILING

The formulas for establishing ceilings for total expenditures on physician services may be simple or complex, and provinces use different factors when establishing their ceiling. Factors considered may include inflation, population growth, unexpected demands for health care, scientific improvements in health care or an increase in physician numbers. Adjustment can be retrospective or prospective. Governments also may use no defined formula or process. They may arbitrarily establish a new ceiling.

In 1993 Ontario informed all public sectors that there would be a 5% decrease in spending. Physicians, as one of those sectors, saw their global cap shrink from $4.1 billion to $3.9 billion. This cap will not grow in 1994 or 1995. The reduction in total physician payments in 1993 was, because of other associated changes, less damaging to physicians than were the reductions which were imposed on other occupational sectors, but the change did demonstrate the capacity of a provincial government to lower the ceiling. Similar reductions were imposed in Saskatchewan and Alberta.

In 1988 a court ruled in Saskatchewan that governments must continue to make payments to physicians even if a preestablished ceiling is reached. This ruling should not be considered to be of importance. There are many devices by which governments can legally either reduce initial payments (as in Quebec), reduce next years payment or accomplish desired claw-backs.

The process of selecting or amending the cap on total physician payments is complicated by the fact that other concurrent changes may affect physician incomes and could be taken into consideration. If a province shortens the list of insured services then the cap could, and should, go down. The provinces are buying less and should not spend the same amount on less care. When services are deinsured physician incomes may or may not fall. All or some of the deinsured services will continue to be bought in the private market and will produce income for physicians. The global ceiling on physician payments should also be lowered when other costs are transferred out of the public program, as with increased use of user fees, the rejection of claims for services which are the responsibility of other third party payers (such as services to refugees or other populations), legislation which transfers costs to other parties, and other related changes which increase opportunities for preservation of physician net incomes.

THE EFFECTS OF CAPPING

A cap on total payments to all physicians gives physicians who bill conservatively an incentive to attempt to reduce the delivery of excessive care by other physicians. If the total volume of services continues to grow when total payments to physicians are capped then payment per unit of care will to go down. This can penalize the careful physician providing necessary care much more than it penalizes the volume driven physician who increases throughput as income per service goes down. Payments to physicians will be most fair to careful and skillful practitioners if the profession works with government and users to constrain practitioners whose practice patterns emphasize volume.

With incomes capped the practice patterns of physicians may change. Unattractive services or clientele may be abandoned first, or physicians may alter services in ways which they feel will be most embarrassing to governments. Capping requires increased Ministry monitoring of delivery patterns.

With the capping of total expenditures on physician's services, fee schedule proliferations and creative billing are no longer as significant a financial threat to provinces as they once were, and they may even be no financial threat at all. If total payments to physicians are fully capped, and this is rapidly becoming the norm, then changes in fees, and in the ways in which services are described, can increase the incomes of one group of physicians only at the expense of other groups of physicians. Internal power struggles will increase.

WHAT MIGHT BE INCLUDED IN THE COLLECTIVE CAP

The global fund from which all physician payments are made could, in its most restrictive form, be used only for payments to FFS physicians. Within this option an increase in the funding of physicians through alternatives to FFS might increase the incomes of FFS physicians, and it would increase costs to the province.

The global fund could also finance all payments to all physicians for clinical services. In this option the fund would pay for clinical services provided by physicians being paid by salary, capitation and sessional fees as well as FFS. The global fund could also cover office and other costs associated with services provided by physicians not on FFS. Within this option a transfer of functions from physicians to midwives or other professionals would increase total government spending and would make it less likely that the transfers would occur, but increased payment of physicians through methods other than FFS would not increase total cost.

A third option is to establish a global fund, or perhaps more than one global fund, for payments to a variety of workers who provide services traditionally provided by physicians. Physicians, midwives, optometrists, nurse practitioners, chiropodists, mental health counsellors, specialist clinical nurses and others would be paid from the same global fund. A variation on this option would be to annually estimate the extent to which functions have been transferred to or from physicians and remove or add funds to various global budgets. Creating a broadly inclusive global pool or pools within which professionals compete is an attractive option.

A fourth option would be to produce global funds which would finance both payments to professionals and some or all costs generated by the decisions of the professionals. For example, outpatient prescriptions and laboratory tests could be funded from a pool from which physicians would also be paid. This is the arrangement now in place in Britain for those general practitioners who are *fundholders*, and in Germany for all nonhospital physicians. This option could be combined with any of the earlier options.

As another variation, the provincial global fund from which physicians and/or other professionals are paid could be the source of payment for similar services provided to Canadians both at home and outside the country. Inclusion of out-of-country expenditures would provide physicians and others with an incentive to discourage trans-border shopping for provincially funded health care.

CAPPING AND BINDING ARBITRATION

Binding arbitration has been used in Manitoba. Early settlements were expensive for the government. Arbitrators looked at traditional income relationships and economic indicators, and they ruled on fee increases rather than on income increases.

In the absence of a cap on total payments to physicians, binding arbitration led to significant income victories for physicians. These are not likely to be repeated. Provincial authority is sufficiently encompassing to make it possible for a province to accomplish, over time, whatever it wishes if its procedures are proper and its lawyers competent. In the current Canadian economic climate provincial governments are unlikely to let binding arbitration interfere with the need to control health care expenditures.

If settlements are considered by governments to be too expensive there are other mechanisms available to government to bring expenditures back to the desired level. Placing limits on the number of physicians who can bill the provincial plan is an example.

The constitutional dominance of provincial governments does not mean that physicians are without protection. No government can abuse any worker group beyond a level acceptable to the population or the constitution, and most governments would rather reach agreements with workers than impose settlements. It is to the advantage of all parties to seek solutions in which some of the objectives of each are met, and physicians, as with others in similar circumstances, will usually be best served by a search for semi-acceptable solutions.

CAPPING INCOMES OF INDIVIDUAL PHYSICIANS

Capping of total payments to all physicians is separate from the question of whether, or how, the incomes of individual physicians are curtailed. Many provinces now have complete or partial caps on both individual incomes and aggregate physician payments. Placing a cap on individual incomes affects only the expensive physicians. In Quebec the caps on individual incomes were introduced with the encouragement of family physicians who saw them as a way to preserve equity after a global cap on total physician payments was in place. (Lomas, J., C. Fooks, et al., CHEPA Working Paper Series #10, McMaster, 1989) The caps protect, rather than have a negative effect on, the incomes of most physicians.

Capping public payments to individual physicians was first used in Newfoundland. Pediatricians had an annual ceiling on their billings to the short-lived childrens medicare program 30 years ago. Some pediatricians exceeded their full year quota long before the year ended and practiced in Nova Scotia or elsewhere for the remainder of the year.

After billings exceed the individual ceilings payment is at some portion of the regular fee. The reductions may be in 2 or more steps and payment eventually may be as little as 25% of the full fee. In 1991 Ontario negotiated a ceiling of $400,000 for payment at 100% of the fee schedule (all types of physicians), 67% of the usual fee between $400,000 and $450,000 and 33% thereafter. These ceilings affected about 7% of physicians. It would seem reasonable for income caps to affect at least a quarter of all physicians, and it would also appear to be reasonable for caps to be different for different types of physicians.

WHAT MIGHT BE INCLUDED IN THE CAP OF INDIVIDUAL PHYSICIANS

In its simplest form only payments from the provincial medicare plan are included in the cap on individual income. Other income could, however, also be taken into consideration, including income from sessional or other work for public health units, from hospitals for administrative duties, from Workers Compensation Boards, from services to persons covered under federal programs (such as war veterans, RCMP and aboriginal peoples) and from the medicare programs of other provinces. The 1990 Quebec Report *Une réforme axée sur le citoyen* recommended, among many health care reforms, that physician ceilings should include income from all public and quasi-public sources.

In the future it is likely there will be provincial collaboration in calculation of physician incomes. In the absence of this collaboration some physicians will provide services within more than one province so that income will fall under different provincial caps.

Physicians are concerned about simultaneous control by government of fees, individual incomes and total payments to all physicians, especially if the global ceiling does not increase with increases in physician supply. If physician numbers increase more rapidly than population, and if the total payments to physicians cannot grow faster than population growth (and payments could grow at less than the rate of population growth), then average gross physician incomes from public sources will go down.

THE LIMITING OF BILLING NUMBERS

To be paid by an insurance plan a physician must have a billing number. Until a few years ago all provinces automatically issued a billing number to all physicians licensed in the province if the physician wished one. This is changing. Canadian provinces have not yet decided how many physicians should be given a billing number, but the first small limits have been put in place.

Many countries limit the number of physicians who are paid by the public insurance system. Such limits have been part of the British National Health Service (NHS) since its inception almost 50 years ago. The limits led to the emigration of large numbers of British physicians who were surplus to the requirements of the National Health Service. Many of these physicians came to Canada. The limits also assured an equitable geographic distribution of physicians and ensured a low cost health system.

In Europe many tens of thousands of physicians are unemployed or significantly underemployed because there is no room for them in the state plan. These numbers will grow rapidly in the face of European medical school enrolments which grossly exceed the numbers needed to replace retiring physicians and accommodate population growth. (European Health Services Handbook, European Healthcare Management Association, 1992)

In British Columbia from 1983-1985 the issuance of billing numbers was restricted but without a statutory basis. In 1985 legislation was passed establishing regional quotas for billing numbers. Physician supply was left unregulated but the supply of billing numbers was restricted. This legislation was ruled unconstitutional in 1988, but eminent jurists have stated that provinces have the constitutional authority to make payments to only a limited number of physicians.

Physician associations have until recently opposed limits on billing numbers, but the capping of total expenditures has changed the milieu. Physicians already in practice see limits on billing numbers as a source of protection given the increasing physician population and a shrinking and controlled total fund available for physician payments. In early 1993 the Nova Scotia Medical Society asked the province to place limits on billing numbers. In 1993 Alberta physicians asked the province to limit billing numbers but it refused. In 1993 Ontario began to withhold billing numbers from graduates of Canadian medical schools outside of Ontario. If these physicians wish to practice in Ontario they are offered non FFS contracts in an underdoctored area. New Brunswick has established regional physician quotas. A 1994 five year physician/government agreement in Manitoba limits the number of doctors who can practice.

Once billing numbers are put in place in several provinces all provinces will either quickly follow suit or be inundated with new registrants. The limits on billing numbers are no longer as crucial to cost control as was the case before provincial ceilings on total payments to all physicians were found to be possible, but, with both physicians and governments in favor, limits on billing numbers will become universal.

Restrictions on the supply of Medicare billing numbers will lower costs. Fewer patients will be seen as insured patients because there will be fewer physicians able to provide insured services.

Limits on billing numbers will make it easier to move funds from physician payments to the payment of other providers, when indicated. The required funds can be found by reducing the number of physician billing numbers or reducing the global cap on payments to physicians.

Restrictions on billing numbers will result in some physicians being unable to submit bills to their provincial insurance program. This will for some physicians mean unemployment or underemployment. There have been no licensed Canadian physicians on welfare since the 1930s, but Canada will, as has Europe, accept the proposition that unemployed or underemployed physicians are as unavoidable (and as unfortunate) as unemployed teachers, steelworkers, nurses or scientists. Limiting the number of physicians able to bill the provincial medical care plan is consistent with the limits placed by governments on the numbers of police, school teachers, nurses, air traffic controllers and others who are on public payrolls. If billing numbers are restricted then a physician without a billing number will be in a position equivalent to a teacher who can't find a job. That physician will also be equivalent to an opted out physician whose patients cannot claim reimbursement.

The limiting of billing numbers in the presence of current provincial medicare statutes may place physicians without a billing number in an untenable position. Physiotherapists, social workers, security workers, school teachers and nurses who cannot find a job within a publicly financed program can provide services which are privately insured. Provinces should be certain that their legislation gives physicians the same opportunities.

Limiting physician supply and physician billing numbers can be supported by noting current provincial differences in physician supply. There is a 15% difference between the Ontario and the Alberta supply of physicians per 100,000 population but each of these provinces is proud of, and content with, their health care. If all Canadian provinces reduced the supply of billing numbers to a level comparable to the current physician supply in the Atlantic provinces, or even in the prairie provinces, there could still be universal access while expenditures on physician services would fall considerably. Expenditures in Ontario and British Columbia would fall the most.

Policies will be needed to govern situations in which the existing supply of billing numbers already exceeds a provincial or regional quota. Physicians who already have billing numbers could continue to bill but within regional expenditure ceilings by specialty. Some types of physicians could be identified as not eligible for billing numbers, for example, those over 65, those with annual billings below some established figure, physicians employed full-time in a publicly funded position (such as in a community health centre) or physicians in training as residents and interns.

There will be a need for policies regarding replacement within the billing pool when a physician is temporarily not practising, or is temporarily practising part-time, as with maternity leave, educational absence, illness, or extended holidays.

Limits on billing numbers will soon apply to chiropractors, optometrists and other fee-for-service practitioners as well as to physicians, especially in those provinces who pay the full costs of these services.

PRESERVING A UNIVERSAL AND COMPREHENSIVE PROGRAM
WHILE CONTROLLING PHYSICIAN COSTS

Preserving universal access to a comprehensive range of publicly financed physician services while controlling physician costs is possible through either limitations on the number of physicians whose income is largely or entirely from the provincial plan and/or by lowering average physician incomes from the public plan. Lowering average physician incomes can, in the short term, be a successful cost control device which has minimal effect on community service. Universality and cost control are also accomplished by use of capitation (as with family physicians in Britain), by establishing a fixed number of positions (as with specialists in Britain) or by limiting billing numbers. All options assure control of expenditures for physician services while preserving universality and making it easier to geographically distribute physicians equitably.

Public expenditures could be lowered further, while preserving universality, by allowing private insurance to play a larger role. This combination is used in British Columbia to assure universal protection against major drug costs.

FEE-FOR-SERVICE BILLING OPTIONS

Early in the life of medicare in Canada many different billing options were offered to physicians by different provinces. Policy options are available regarding who may or must do the billing, who receives the payment and how many forms of billing may be used by one physician.

Physicians on FFS can be obliged to bill only the provincial plan for all insured services provided to insured persons. The physician can also have the choice of opting out of the plan for all patients, in which case no bills will be submitted to the provincial plan. Patients may or may not be able to claim full or partial reimbursement for their payments to opted out physicians. The preferred option is no reimbursement.

Physicians can also be allowed to bill for each service in whatever pattern they choose. They may bill the plan or the patient. If this option is chosen and extra-billing is allowed some physicians will bill the plan for those patients who are unlikely or unable to pay and will ask other patients for a payment greater than that which is available from the provincial plan. The plan would then reimburse patients an amount equal to that which would have been paid if the account had been submitted to the plan by the physician. This arrangement is optimal for physicians, but is unattractive to everyone else and is no longer in place in any province.

Provincial assistance to patients with respect to medical bills which are the responsibility of the patient can be made on receipt of a bill or of a receipt. Physicians are much more protected if reimbursement is made only when the bill has been paid, but patients short of cash would like to get their money first. If funds are sent to patients on the basis of a submitted bill rather than a receipt, then some of the money will never get to the physician. Provinces can also allow patients to instruct the provincial plan to assign their reimbursement to the physician. These options are irrelevant when there is no reimbursement for services received in one's home province (which currently is universally the case). All opted-in physicians in all provinces must bill the province for insured services provided to insured residents, and must accept the provincial payment as payment in full.

If a physician opts out of the provincial plan the province may, if it chooses, regulate the fees which the opted out physician is allowed to charge. The fees may also be left to patient-physician negotiation. If the fees which opted-out physicians are allowed to charge a patient are set by the province, and if the fees are close to those which would have been received from the plan if direct billing had been used, then very few physicians will opt out of the plan. If there is no reimbursement to patients for services received from opted out physicians then, once again, almost no physicians will opt out.

Policy options are available regarding the name in which an account is billed and the person or agency to whom payments will be made. It is routine to require that the physician who actually provided the service, or who was responsible for it, be identified. The account can usually be submitted by a clinic or other employer, and payment can usually be assigned by the provider to an employer.

Providers eligible to bill the provincial plan should continue to be obliged to either (a) opt fully out of the system, with no reimbursement to patients for payments made, or (b) agree to bill the provincial plan for all insured services provided to beneficiaries of the plan. The provincial payment should either be payment in full or should be reduced to reflect any user fees approved by the province.

USE OF INCENTIVES AND DISINCENTIVES

Incentives and disincentives can alter volumes of care, types of care, location of care and volumes of generated costs. Incentives and disincentives are usually financial, as with physicians and clinics on capitation in Ontario who are rewarded for lower levels of hospital use. In the restructuring of Quebec health services in 1991-93 physicians were given additional incentives to have an affiliation with a CLSC (community health center).

Britain uses financial incentives to increase general practitioner attention to immunization and Pap smears. The physician is paid a bonus (beyond capitation payments) if 70% of the relevant population are immunized, with another bonus if a 90% level of protection is reached. For PAP smears the levels are 60% and 80%. This use of personal physicians to accomplish national prevention goals is not easily applied in Canada with physicians on fee-for-service and patient access to all physicians, but all options for use of payment as an instrument of public policy are worth exploration.

Disincentives can be associated with generated costs. Physicians in the United States may, when income per patient for hospital care is fixed, lose hospital privileges or face lower incomes if their costs per patient are greater than those of colleagues caring for similar patients. These penalties provide a powerful incentive to learn to order fewer expensive drugs and fewer investigative procedures. Similar disincentives to high generated costs exist in Britain and Germany.

Fee schedules can provide incentives or disincentives for selected billing patterns. Reduced fees for house calls, for example, lower the volume of house calls; higher fees do the reverse. Changes in payments for services outside regular working hours have the same effect.

If regional health care budgets are introduced, and if payments to physicians are made from the regional budget, physician payments for identical services may be different in different regions. The level of payment may vary with the number of billing numbers approved by the region and with the priority given to physician services by a particular region. Income discrepancies will alter physician choices.

In the 1970s Quebec, in a relatively unsuccessful attempt to encourage physicians to practice in underdoctored areas, introduced variable fees based on place of practice. New Brunswick did the same in the early 1990s. The Ontario Medical Association in 1993 explored lower fees for new registrants, presumably in an attempt to make Ontario less attractive as a place to establish a practice.

HOSPITAL IMPACT ANALYSES

Hospitals in all provinces have control over the granting of hospital privileges. Hospital boards have historically accepted the recommendations of the medical staff (usually the Medical Advisory Committee). Some provinces now require that hospitals assess the economic impact of a new addition to the medical staff. New physicians on staff can bring unexpected new costs in the form of requests for special equipment or staff, and it is preferable that the required funds be known to be available before an application for medical staff membership is approved.

The prospective evaluation of the impact of a new physician is a good idea. Continual monitoring of the impact of each individual physician on hospital costs is an equally good idea. Identification of physicians whose utilization patterns are significantly more expensive than other physicians caring for the same types of patients would allow an institutional response when indicated. This *economic credentialling* is common in the United States.

With the increasing regionalization of medical staffs, as in Kingston, Saskatoon and Regina, the hospital impact analysis will be replaced by a regional impact analysis.

THE RAND FORMULA

Provincial medical associations have either been fully acknowledged in law as the bargaining agent for physicians or are treated as the bargaining agent.

Legislation has in many provinces made it mandatory that all physicians pay medical association membership fees. Policy determines the categories of physicians who must pay these fees. In Ontario the legislation is very encompassing. The Rand Formula usually limits mandatory payment of dues to persons actually working for a particular employer or actually providing a type of service. In Ontario, however, the law demands that all licensed physicians be members of the Ontario Medical Association (OMA) regardless of whether or not physicians are delivering any clinical services, subject to an exemption by the OMA. The criteria for exemption have not been established. The physician may be fully retired or fully employed in a nonclinical position but still be required to pay the OMA fees if she/he maintains membership in the Ontario College of Physicians and Surgeons.

THE WEAPONS OF PHYSICIANS; AND HOW THE PROVINCES MIGHT RESPOND

Physicians wishing to defend their interests can go on strike, finance media campaigns, attempt to find public support through direct physician appeals to patients, seek binding arbitration, refuse to submit bills to the provincial plan, be administratively uncooperative, work constructively with other parties, find innovative ways to bill patients as well as provincial medicare plans, or a combination of these.

Withdrawal of services is the most confrontational weapon. Several lessons can be learned from strikes in the past. Governments will not allow inadequate maintenance of basic emergency services, and physicians lose public support if these services are not maintained. Failure to continue with such services as cancer treatment may bring anger against both physicians and government. There is now a public realization that in the short term there is little if any public hazard associated with reduced access to nonemergency physician services. Regardless of the other issues involved there are usually financial elements in the dispute, and physicians who are seen to be striking for higher incomes tend to receive little public support.

Work stoppages can be promoted by, and made more successful by, inept government tactics. The doctor's strike in Saskatchewan (1962) was strengthened by the Medicare starting date of July 1. A significant number of physicians who were ambivalent about the new public insurance plan went on holidays rather than continue to work and offend colleagues. In addition, the government was tactically insensitive in its failure to remove a clause in the legislation which suggested government intrusion into professional decision making. This clause offended many otherwise neutral physicians. Ontario (1987) repeated the mistake. The Ontario statute made extra-billing a criminal offence. This was seen by many physicians as unnecessarily harsh when a variety of administrative penalties would have been just as effective.

A two day doctors strike in Manitoba in 1990 preserved professional access to binding arbitration. The strike was strategically aligned with a provincial election.

There will be a steadily increasing array of other health care professionals able to legally provide primary care to patients without referral from a physician, and who can order investigations and prescription drugs. The position of these professionals may be enhanced by future physician withdrawals of service, and physician strikes may accelerate the granting of new professional powers to physician competitors.

Physicians may cite waiting lists and waiting times as proof that health care is inadequately funded and that the health of those waiting is threatened. This claim is probably not widely believed. The proper response to waiting lists is an improved use of resources. The supposed shortage of cardiovascular surgical capacity in Ontario evaporated with the appearance of standardized provincial criteria for by-pass surgery plus a bed registry to assure quick service when the need was urgent. Waiting lists, and undesirable waiting times, should not be ignored, but they are best used to promote improved administrative and clinical decision making rather than to embarrass government. Physicians who make semihysterical speeches about a patient who waited six weeks for brain surgery (or equivalent) should remember that it is physicians who determine the sequence of admission of patients to hospital and delays will eventually bring more discredit to physicians than to government.

Refusal to bill the provincial plan has been threatened when agreements with the province have expired or provincial legislation is unacceptable. There are many hazards in this tactic, but it could be difficult for the province if physician solidarity is high. The hazards lie primarily in the constitutional ability of the province to legislate payment arrangements and in the anger of patients when they are personally billed.

In 1992, in the midst of a prolonged contract dispute in British Columbia between physicians and governments in which the issue of a global ceiling on physician payments was central, about 100 physicians stopped billing the provincial plan and started billing their patients. A Decima survey during the dispute found a small majority of British Columbians opposed a ceiling on physician payments. (Forty-five percent supported a ceiling.) The dispute ended with a ceiling on expenditures in place.

Several provincial medical associations (British Columbia, Ontario, New Brunswick) have responded to cut-backs with expensive advertising campaigns designed to convince the public that cut-backs are a threat to patient health. Whatever success these campaigns had in earlier years, they now must contend with a public which has accepted the shortage of public money and accepted the need to reduce spending on all public services including health care. It would be useful for physicians and their associations to recognize the urgency of the financial agenda of government, recognize the power of the evidence of inappropriate professional decisions and seek win-win situations in which physicians may retain slightly more income or professional turf than may otherwise be the case.

As provincial payments have fallen some physicians have begun to charge patients a flat fee per year for uninsured services or for continued service in the future (a sort of American Express membership fee). The uninsured services being paid for in advance include telephone advice, prescription renewals and filling out forms. In 1994 Ontario used legislation to prohibit the charging of these *block fees*.

Physician performance has at times been admirable. In Sweden when physicians were asked what measures should be taken to improve health, they gave highest priority to measures to defeat unemployment. (Swedish Government, The Swedish Health Services in the 1990s - Unemployment and Health, as quoted in `Nurturing Health, A Framework of the Determinants of Health', Premiers Council on Health Strategy, Ontario, 1991)

PHYSICIAN ACCEPTANCE OF CONSUMERISM

The right of consumers to information is now legally protected, and the need to respect user wishes is equally protected. Physicians have choices while a user is making a choice from among the preventive, treatment or investigative options available, and physicians have another set of options available after the user choice has been made.

While the patient is evaluating the clinical options the physician may choose to say nothing, may provide balanced information on the options and state no preference unless asked for it, may provide information on the options and express a preference whether or not asked for it, may give information on the options but present the information in such a way that the preference of the physician is made attractive, may assure the patient of support regardless of her/his choice, or may advise the patient he/she will have to go elsewhere for care if they choose an unacceptable option.

After the user has made a choice the physician can now work with the user to implement the choice (which is the preferred option), can indicate disagreement but implement the choice as well

184

as possible, can indicate disagreement and be unwilling to implement the choice, can actively attempt to alter the decision made or can actively seek to obstruct implementation of the user's decision. The last option is medically unethical, and some other options may be.

CONFLICTS OF INTEREST IN MEDICINE

Conflicts of interest arising from financial ties between physicians and drug, optical or equipment companies, or laboratories, are uncommon, are unethical and can lead to disciplinary action by the provincial College of Physicians and Surgeons. Other conflicts are more common.

Conflict between loyalty to an individual patient and the need to distribute public resources equitably and cost-effectively has received considerable attention. This conflict is real and is difficult, but it may be more tolerable if recognized as similar to the conflicts faced by many other professionals inside and outside of health care. Professional engineers, air traffic controllers, meat inspectors, day care workers, police officers, social workers and loggers all routinely must deal with the incompatibility of demands from employers, environmental protection agencies, budgets, the public (who are being served or who are at risk) and other interested parties.

The conflicts inherent in the practice of medicine also appear to be no greater than those faced by persons such as parents, in particular mothers, who must reconcile parental roles with the wish, and/or need, to be at work. For young female physicians the conflicts between patient advocacy and taxpayer protection must be handled while also dealing with the challenges of a demanding profession and of motherhood. (Walters, B. and I. McNeill, The Annotated Bibliography of Women in Medicine, Ontario Medical Association, 1993)

There will at times also be conflicts between the desire to protect the confidentiality of patient information and the need to provide information for payers or for evaluation of provider and user performance.

THE MORALE OF PHYSICIANS

Canadian physicians are not as optimistic as they once were. They feel abused, and half of them believe life would be better in the United States. The main sources of unhappiness are the perceptions of too much government intrusion and too little funding. The great majority, however, still are satisfied with their choice of work, would do it again and would recommend it to their children. (Ontario Medical Association survey, 1993)

Few of the changes in the future will be likely to reduce physician dissatisfaction, especially if satisfaction is closely tied to income. For those physicians who accept a higher community health status as a personal reward, and whose incomes are already relatively low because of the practice habits they have personally selected, the future holds real promise. These physicians will approve of policies and practices which reduce inappropriate health care decisions and lower the incomes of production oriented physicians.

Physician morale depends partly on how physicians choose to see the situation. They have less public esteem than was once the case but more than most professions. Their average incomes are falling and will continue to fall but will continue to be higher than the incomes of almost everyone else. There will be increasing external control of professional decisions but no more controls than apply to most other professions, especially those whose incomes are primarily from the public purse. There will be a possibility of unemployment but not as great a risk as in many other professions.

A survey reported in the New England Journal of Medicine (April 8, 1993) compared physician perceptions in Canada, Germany and the United States. Only United States physicians reported difficulty with access to hospital care, and United States physicians expressed the greatest concerns regarding external review of clinical decisions. Canadian physicians expressed the most concern regarding access to high tech equipment. Canadian and United States physicians shared concerns about the demands made by patients, and German physicians said they wished they could spend more time with patients.

A 1993 survey by the Quebec federation of family physicians found that the 800 physicians on salary were happier with their work than were physicians on fee-for-service.

SUMMARY

In general, it is necessary that expenditures on physician services be controlled and monitored. Payment emphasis should change from fee-for-service to payment-for-health. Implementation of this change will lead to an increasing number of physicians who will not be employed in the publicly financed health care system, and the practices and decisions of most physicians will change.

The incomes and job satisfaction of physicians are threatened. They share this threat with miners and loggers whose incomes and personal lives have been altered by technological and social change, with farmers whose lives have been disrupted by international trade wars, with manufacturing sector workers whose jobs have moved south, with armed forces personnel who have felt the impact of the end of the cold war and with middle managers throughout health care who have lost their jobs as a result of downsizing. As with everyone else, physicians cannot expect to be untouched by new information, new paradigms, rising public debt and opportunities for service delivery by less expensive personnel.

Experience in a number of provinces and countries indicates that both the short and long term control of physician costs will be best accomplished through simultaneous use of a number of tools including collective and individual income ceilings, limits on increases in physician supply, limits on the number of billing numbers, limits on fee increases and a restructuring of the fee schedule.

Use of a combination of devices will allow control of both price and quantity of services. Quebec in 1977 revised the fee schedule, reduced the number of billable items and introduced individual billing caps for family physicians. There was an immediate 5% decline in physician billings. (Lomas, J., C. Fooks, et al., McMaster University, WP #10, 1989)

Ceilings on physician incomes should include income from all public sources, including other provinces and salaried work in a CHC, as well as all income from Workers Compensation Boards. There should be provincial and regional limits on the number of practitioners able to bill the public medicare plan on FFS.

Provinces should intervene in fee schedule design so that it becomes an instrument of public policy. Pricing of services should help assure provider profiles which reflect appropriate care in the most appropriate place and time and by the most appropriate professional. Fees for physician services should not exceed the costs of providing the same services through use of other qualified personnel. When other health care workers provide services formerly provided by physicians the costs associated with the new workers should be removed from the global physician envelope.

The control of expenditures on physician services is somewhat different in a large province than in a small one. Small provinces face the hazard of a sudden influx of physicians if larger provinces begin to limit the number of physicians who will be issued a billing number. Ontario licenses 1000 new physicians each year. If half of these were denied a billing number in Ontario they would, to a large extent, quickly settle in any province without limits on billing numbers. Even 300 new full-time physicians would mean a 20% increase in Nova Scotia or Newfoundland.

The changes underway in health care have disturbed the traditions, workplaces and personal lives of physicians, and the disturbances will continue. The volume of services performed by physicians at public cost will go down. Total payments for physicians services will go down. Individual average physician gross incomes from public sources will fall. Too many physician services are inappropriate for the situations in which they are delivered, and users and payers will seek improvement.

Canadian physicians have, to date, seldom been monitored in terms of the costs they generate, nor have physician incomes been affected when the costs which they generate are higher than average. It is likely that public payers will, in the future, become more interested in the extent to which physicians order drugs and investigations, and in the frequency with which physicians refer patients for consultation.

Chapter 12

The Role of Consumers

INTRODUCTION

This chapter discusses the influence of ordinary Canadians on the planning and delivery of health care.

Terminology is a problem. Should individuals be referred to as citizens, consumers, users, clients, patients, lay-persons, taxpayers, or something else? *Patient* is passive and users often are not. *Lay-person* carries too many inferences of incompetence. *User* and *client* infer involvement at the moment, and they are good terms. *Taxpayer* is limited to the payer function and will be used but only when funding is being discussed. *Citizen* and *consumer* are broad and useful. When The Centre for Health Economics and Policy Analysis in Hamilton had a 1991 conference on the roles of the public in health care they opted for the term citizen. We have opted for greatest use of *consumer* and *user*, but also have used other terms.

Other terminology is equally thorny. Do consumers *participate*, or do they *get involved*? Is *consultation* the same as *participation*? When a lot of people act together should they be referred to as *the general public*, the *population*, the *community* or something else? Once again we will use many terms and hope that terminological imprecision will not obscure ideas and concepts.

There will be discussion of the currently popular objectives of community mobilization and community empowerment, although these terms are seldom used. There will be discussion of the process known as Community Development.

Individual consumers play many roles in health care. Sometimes they receive care. Sometimes they make decisions regarding care. At other times they are the advocates or agents of individual users or of groups of users. They can be a source of funds and can be evaluators of health care. Individuals can also, although not very effectively, provide advice on policy. It is only as members of boards, committees, and other groups, or as the representative of many individuals, that one individual can contribute significantly and directly to the macro decisions which govern health care.

Consumers affect what is bought, who it is bought from, and how much of it is bought. They affect the wisdom with which money is spent. This chapter examines the policies and processes which affect the ease with which consumers play their many roles.

PUBLIC EXPECTATIONS AND PERCEPTIONS

The public are a funny bunch. They often don't seem to know their mind from minute to minute.

A 1988 study by Dr. Gail Siler-Wells identified five paradoxes, to which two others have been added. These ambiguities within public perceptions and wishes routinely make it impossible for governments to please everyone and sometimes make it difficult to please anyone.

1. The desire for complete access for *me* but not for *we*; consumer vs taxpayer.
2. The wish for unlimited high quality publicly funded health care but concern about pressures on the public purse; entitlement vs capacity to pay.
3. A wish for high quality publicly funded health care even when the problem was produced by user choice, but concern about abuse of health care.
4. A wish for personal control over choices in health care at a time when there is steadily increasing centralization in government of health care planning and priority setting.
5. The wish for a more efficient and effective health care system but resistance to many of the changes associated with greater efficiency and effectiveness.
6. A willingness (almost an eagerness) to spend disposable income in the United States (where prices are lower because taxes are lower because taxes finance fewer public services) while at the same time wishing Canadian governments to provide free and endless health care, generous unemployment insurance, old age pensions, high quality education and an adequate range of other public services.
7. A public wish for responsive governments but public demands which cannot be fulfilled. The public is much like a dying patient who cannot be saved, and who knows he cannot be saved, but who is angry because those in power are not preserving her/his life.

The public is struggling with how to react to the cut-backs in spending on health care. It is supporting an increase in services which assist persons to remain independent in their own homes and communities. It is supporting greater attention to the state of our minds as well as our bodies. It is adamantly opposed to the market driven health care system in the United States. It believes health care dollars could be spent better. A survey in 1990 by the Canada Health Monitor showed that the majority of respondents felt that many people in hospital could be looked after at home (63%), many people use health services they don't need (74%) and doctors often prescribe unnecessary medicine for patients (64%).

An Ontario Hospital Association survey in 1990 found public opposition to continued reductions in hospital services but high levels of satisfaction with the supply as it existed, a supply much lower than a few years earlier and a supply in which ward closures and other restrictions on access were routine. A major reduction in hospital bed supply was accomplished without significant public outcry or notice, and therefore presumably with tacit public approval. Ambiguities abound.

REASONS FOR CONSUMER INVOLVEMENT

Governments have not traditionally given a high priority to public participation, although efforts are increasing. Why should participation be promoted? The most fundamental reason is that consumers have a right to be involved. The money being spent is their money, and the health that is affected is their health.

Consumers also need to be involved because their perceptions and priorities differ from those of providers and bureaucrats. If providers and bureaucrats advocated the same priorities and trade-offs as do users, and if they saw problems in the same way as problems are seen by users, then the delivery and outcomes of health care would be the same no matter who was in charge, but the differences between the users and the providers and bureaucrats are often profound. When discharged psychiatric patients speak of *support* they tend to mean friends and companions; when professionals speak of *support* they mean programs (housing, day care, monitoring, counselling).

Professionals cannot decide what will help a user feel independent, and cannot know the importance to a patient of isolation, pain, loss of mobility or loss of bladder control. Professionals may medicalize events which are natural, such as childbirth and menopause. They may overrespond to events which are of little importance to patients, such as impaired mobility, and may ignore factors of great importance to patients, such as visits from friends and family. Programs for the elderly may, if dominated by the priorities of professionals, emphasize elements of physical health. If dominated by the elderly the emphasis will much more often be on psychosocial health. Clients may tolerate or prefer patterns of living and activity which are no threat to anyone but are not acceptable to providers and therefore are the basis for care plans which the providers mandate and users, to the extent possible, reject.

When decisions are based on values, consumers must be able to be in charge if they wish to be. Consumers are, for example, the only ones who can decide what outcomes are most preferred. Consumers are also the only ones who can say what risks they are prepared to take, and which risks are most unacceptable.

Accountability and responsiveness are part of the consumer era. Financial audits, which make certain that funds are spent on approved activities, have now been (or should have been) joined by social audits which make certain that expenditures reflect consumer and community values and priorities. Social audits (which are seldom called audits but which serve this function) need the wisdom and the perspective of consumers and communities, not of experts.

Consumer involvement is particularly important in this age of cut-backs. Reduced spending on health care may mean that some users will not have access to all of the care which might be of benefit. Certainly there will be users who would like to receive care which will not be paid for with public funds. When populations or persons cannot be completely served it is desirable that priorities be set by, or at least directly influenced by, communities and individual users. Consumer involvement is especially essential when considering value laden policies such as the extent to which patient cooperation should be a condition for receipt of publicly financed care.

Consumer involvement is important to governments. Involvement increases understanding, and increased public understanding of the logic which supports reduced public expenditures on health care will make it easier for governments to sustain the global capping and other cost constraint measures which are now necessary.

FACTORS WHICH SUPPORT OR IMPEDE CONSUMER/COMMUNITY INFLUENCE

Governments can invite communities and consumers to be involved in health care planning and delivery, but the invitation can be ignored. The invitation is more likely to be accepted if it has strong and sincere support at the top, if communities and individuals consider this support to be sincere, if resources are made available to support the process, if the information available to government is given willingly and completely to communities and other participants, if there is a well described long term plan for continued involvement and if there are community leaders who are anxious to contribute to solutions rather than complain about the problems. Fortunately there are, in most communities, many individuals who will welcome a chance to be involved and be responsible. These individuals need to be found and supported.

Resources can be a prerequisite to consumer and community involvement. There should be provincial, regional, community and program budgets for activities which support participation.

A supportive corporate culture will assist groups and individuals to influence health care policies. When such a corporate culture exists users will be a respected, expected and regular part of policy development and of health care delivery decisions. User opinions will not be a frill, something to be brought out on occasion and with flags waving. User opinions and preferences will be built into the fabric of agencies and the priorities of leaders. They will then become as commonplace and as welcomed as wearing a seat belt or being immunized.

The required corporate culture requires special skills and attitudes in the bureaucracies with whom the public will interact. Attitudes are often supportive (although often not) but the skills are seldom adequate. Good intentions are not enough. Bureaucrats at all levels need an understanding of public participation processes and principles.

One impediment to greater consumer and community participation is the feeling of communities and individuals that they have no power and can have no effect on what happens. This mood is part of the public cynicism regarding all governments and all leaders. Anything which reduces these negative attitudes will increase the likelihood of successful public participation. Successes of participation should be noted. In Ontario three new free standing birthing clinics and the legitimization of midwifery are a tribute to public preferences and organized comment.

Community involvement should be promoted with a clear understanding of the groups and individuals who will either overtly or covertly oppose it. Some health care professionals and other leaders will not wish to see their own influence reduced. Some administrators and board members will not wish to have to respond to another outside force, and for some the opposition will be based in a fear of an unknown or an unwillingness to learn new skills. A community participation process increases the need for competent and decisive bureaucracies. Identification of opponents, along with sensitive but sturdy responses to the opposition, may be prerequisites to sustained and successful community involvement.

Caregivers and consumers may oppose the participation process if it is funded with dollars currently being spent on the delivery of health care, and since there is unlikely to be any other source of funds this resistance may be strong. Others will object to the many hours of new and perhaps unpaid work that usually accompany community participation. There will also at times be objections to the delays in decision making which can accompany the participation of a broader mix of players.

Community involvement which can be sustained and be seen as worth the trouble is unlikely unless the objectives of the process are clear, and objectives can differ. To a government the main objective of the participative process may be validation of an already selected policy, whereas communities and individuals may wish to participate in the selection of policy.

The expectations of the participants must be realistic. Communities need to be told, and need to accept, the right of government to remain in charge of many decisions. The agenda of the consultation, including the limits on that agenda, should be spelled out. The problems being addressed should be identified, and there should be an attempt to separate local from broader issues.

Public consultations on health care which ask for advice on what to do without specifying the financial limits within which action will take place border on the dishonest. If trade-offs are inherent in change then participants should be asked to comment on trade-offs much more than on the vast array of additional services they would like to have.

Associated with the need for an honest agenda and for an appreciation of the limits of the process is the need for willingness to compromise. Players will be happier and more useful to policy development if they concentrate first on finding areas of agreement rather than on trying to find consensus in areas of serious disagreement. Agreement may lead to action, and any bit of success encourages a continuation of the process.

Consumer interest in macro and micro health care decisions may rise if they can see a payoff from being involved. The payoff can be in improved access, greater protection, money saved, lower taxes or increased satisfaction.

INFORMATION AND SKILLS NEEDED FOR INFLUENCE ON POLICY

If consumers and communities are to participate in selection of priorities and programs they need information similar to that which is required by health care planners. The level of detail may be different, but the strengths, weaknesses and implications of policy options should be sufficiently understood to allow informed advice or decision making.

Consumers and communities may wish to be aware of what keeps them well or makes them sick, of the extent to which injury and illness can be prevented and how, of the extent to which health care can or cannot respond to various needs, of the extent to which various needs appear to be met by current programs, of how their situation compares to that of other communities and groups, of the amount of public money being spent on different categories of services and users and of the impact of spending money in different ways. Communities need to be given reasons for government actions. They have a right to know the options which were available and why the chosen option was considered to be best.

Information will be more useful to communities if it is expressed in ways which make it directly relevant to the community and to the problems and situations of the persons who are participating. Deaths per 100,000 population per year may be less helpful than a summary of the local causes of death in the past 5 years. Blue Cross Atlantic has prepared material for employers and employees describing the rationale for conversion from a traditional benefit structure to managed care. This type of information would be of benefit to all Canadians as they try to understand the changes which are occurring.

Communities and residents are usually not health care technocrats, and they need not be. Their appreciation of the options and issues can be completely adequate for useful participation without the verbiage and detail dispensed by many technocrats and especially by academics. Any wish to make communities into technocrats will fail, and information overload will only confuse. Information should be offered in many forms and places, but not in the forms and volumes thought by technocrats to be necessary. Consumers will ask for more information if they want it.

If communities are to be influential in policy development they must have some sense of their sources of power and of the environment in which decisions are made. They may need a better understanding of the extra-parliamentary process. They may need to know something about building alliances, for in numbers there is power. They may need to understand how government works. They may need experience with the art of compromise and with the dynamics of committees. Health and Welfare Canada (now Health Canada) has produced a *Community Action Pack* to assist agencies and community groups with the many problems and tasks associated with community action.

Communities may need to better understand the processes through which decisions are made and how to affect those processes. But often they will already know enough. High levels of sophistication are not a prerequisite to an understanding of most issues, and the extra-parliamentary process is not new. Continuity, universality and top level support could be new.

Community leaders with patience, energy and an ability to take abuse will often be in short supply, but the supply will improve as participation replaces confrontation.

INFORMATION NEEDED BY INDIVIDUALS

Individuals need information both to participate in health care decisions and to protect their individual health status. The concept of informed consent is now well refined. For example, the Canadian Medical Protective Association (CMPA) has set out the obligations of physicians to inform patients.

"The patient should be told the diagnosis and should be advised if more than one diagnosis is being entertained. The patient must be given an adequate explanation of the nature of the proposed management (investigation or treatment) and of its anticipated effect. There must be plain explanation of any associated risks which the patient could reasonably be expected to consider significant or material. Remote risks, which do not ordinarily have to be disclosed, should be discussed with the patient if they are serious, such as paralysis or death. The patient should also be advised of any alternate forms of treatment and of the consequences of refusing treatment. The doctor should give the patient the opportunity to ask questions and these questions should be answered in a forthright manner with as much detail as is required for the particular patient's understanding. The informa-

tion communicated by the doctor must be such as will allow the patient to reach an informed decision." (CMPA Information letter, Fall, 1989)

It has been estimated that users have enough knowledge to allow them to make an informed choice in one quarter of all health care situations. Most of these choices pertain to chronic care. (Pauly, M.V., "Is Medical Care Different? Old Questions, New Answers", Journal of Health Politics, Policy and Law, 13, No. 2, (1988) 227-38).

Consumers need information to assist them with their lifestyle choices as well as their health care choices, and lifestyle information is becoming a bit overwhelming. An eight year study of 80,000 women, and a shorter study of 45,000 men, showed a sharp reduction in cardiovascular risk when Vitamin E was taken daily. Use of beta-carotene, another antioxidant vitamin, appears to give similar results. Many large studies have shown that modest alcohol consumption lowers risks from cardiac disease, with wine being better than liquor or beer and white wine being better than red wine. Many studies have shown that lowering the percent of calories derived from fat, especially animal fat, lowers cardiac risk, and that if fat represents less than 15% of calories then the risk of atherosclerosis is almost zero. Smoking is clearly the greatest hazard. It would appear that if everyone took Vitamin E, drank white wine, didn't smoke and ate less fat then the cardiovascular surgical units would go out of business. If fibre is added to the diet then colon cancer becomes less common. Changes in exercise and diet, especially early in life, reduce the risk of osteoporosis, as does oestrogen after menopause. The list of proven or suspected healthy lifestyle choices is growing rapidly. How the general public will react to this jungle of information is not known, but it does invite new public policy initiatives.

Some of the relationships between lifestyle choices and the use of health care are poorly understood, and these uncertain relationships bring more challenge for the public. There is a strong possibility, for example, that the incidence of breast cancer and of the symptoms of menopause would be markedly reduced if North American diets were more similar to Japanese diets. The change would appear to be mostly a reduction in fat. (Japanese women suffer almost no menopausal symptoms and have a very low incidence of breast cancer. The incidence of both of these health problems in Japanese women converts to North American patterns if the Japanese women move to North America.)

The choices made by individuals are dominant in determining the number of persons who enter the health care network with strokes, many cancers, and coronary artery disease. Less abuse of tobacco and alcohol, safer driving habits, healthy diets, physical exercise, stress coping skills, healthy interpersonal relationships, the support of other individuals who are in need, and other activities and decisions which are at least partly under personal control alter the mix of practitioners and services which will be needed.

The impact of providing individual users with information regarding the cost of their health care is not known. Some Ontario hospitals are currently testing the provision to selected patients of a statement of the cost of hospital care. Alberta tried such a program in the 1980s, but the program was expensive, its usefulness was unproven and it was dropped. Users could also be provided with information regarding the performance of providers. Massachusetts and New York have legislation which obliges hospitals to provide obstetrical patients with caesarian section rates and other obstetrical rates. (Young, D., "Maternity Information Act passes in New York", Birth, Vol. 16, no. 4, 1989)

Information should be presented to all age groups. Children are already taught in school and in their communities about the health risks they face and the role they can play in staying healthy. There should probably be greater attention to the relative importance of various health problems, such as cavities in teeth, lacerations, headaches, depression, and control of infectious diseases, and more discussion of the priority setting routinely faced by families, communities and governments.

There is considerable discussion about cultural sensitivity in health care, but information is often not available in the language of the user. Providing services in many languages can be expensive, but providing printed information should be manageable. Materials produced in other countries for their domestic populations should be reviewed for amendment to fit the Canadian milieu.

THE TOOLS FOR COMMUNITY INVOLVEMENT IN MACRO DECISIONS

The tools for community involvement are primarily those of the extra-parliamentary process.

Participation techniques vary with the number of persons involved and with the nature of the groups and individuals involved. Techniques, costs and schedules suitable for the participation of even two or three percent of a population (which is a high participation rate) are very different from those which are most appropriate when the users or communities are represented by a small group of identified leaders such as a committee or council. Similarly, processes may need to be changed in the face of illiteracy, language barriers and cultural differences.

Community involvement can be initiated by a central authority or by the community itself. Direct participation techniques initiated by a government, profession, political party, corporation or agency include public opinion polls/surveys (by telephone, door-to-door or other) and public hearings (public consultations), although governments have also sponsored Community Development (by various names).

Elections have been proven not to be good devices for public comment on single issues. Referendums and plebiscites could provide this comment but are not a dominant part of Canadian practice. Public representatives on Commissions, Councils, and Boards have, as with elections, not been shown to provide the public with a chance to comment on a variety of diverse issues, although they do bring a degree of public representation.

Public participation need not be avoided when the subject matter is highly technical. Public representatives can evaluate drugs, medical devices, professional decisions and individual professionals, and they can advise on complex policy issues.

In 1990 Oregon began a health insurance experiment in which health services were ranked by a Health Services Commission with the assistance of an extensive public participation process. The state Medicaid program then paid for services on the basis of the rankings of the Commission and the availability of program funds. The plan, which was sponsored by Senator John Kitzhaber, M.D., allocated funds on the basis of public priorities and impact on collective health status rather than professional power and choice. The choices made appear to spend the available money more wisely than when the decisions were left with the professionals.

Public participation can be built on the Community Development model of nondirective support for groups seeking consensus so that they may have influence. The introduction of this model should no longer need the persistence and passion of the pioneers who showed it could work. The milieu is more welcoming now, but the process is unlikely to be successful unless there is stable funding.

Public consultations (public hearings) are currently very much in style. They usually consist of a travelling team which visits communities and hears from interested parties. The topics may be very broad, from views on constitutional reform to reform of the health care system. Topics can also be quite narrow, such as the location of landfill sites or a restructuring of children's mental health services.

Public hearings assure response from those with an axe to grind. The views heard may be mostly those of strongly biased individuals. Other devices can be used to assure contact with a broader cross section of public opinion, including surveys and interaction with audiences which more closely reflect the total population.

Public consultations are useful, but there is a tendency to see them as the end of a process when they may be merely the beginning. A long series of public consultations in Ontario led to general

Ministerial decisions regarding the restructuring of long term care. The ministry then proceeded to internally develop a complicated set of arrangements and guidelines to implement the new system. It would have been better if the initial consultation process had been followed by ongoing consultation with the regional and local groups and agencies who would eventually be responsible for the operation of the new decentralized system.

General consultations can help governments with top level macro decisions. Second and third level consultations are likely to be with a different set of players, such as specific populations, specific agencies, specific experts, specific local governments or a mix of many of these. The questions are different as the process proceeds, but the usefulness and appropriateness of external advice for central policy writers does not decrease.

THE TOOLS OF INDIVIDUAL INVOLVEMENT IN MICRO DECISIONS

The most personalized device for delivery of information to users is a provider who is prepared to take the time to supply information, but in the long run it will often be more cost-effective to assure user access to written, video-taped and/or computer stored information. Tapes, videos, booklets and software have now been produced on many diseases, problems, drugs and surgical options. Some of the videos are interactive and therefore are especially useful when choices must be made. Graphic and interactive devices can describe to patients the outcomes and risks which are associated with various treatment, investigative, preventive or rehabilitative options. For many years the United States Foundation for Informed Medical Decision Making has been producing these interactive videos for use by patients. A nonprofit group in Winnipeg has produced tapes for use by persons with cancer and other diagnoses. The tapes are chatty and particularly designed for persons when alone and depressed, as in the night.

Libraries will increasingly be the source of user information. Thirty years ago libraries did not provide information on health care and on legal matters. Now these sections are large and heavily used. User information will also be available in pharmacies, health centres, hospitals, the offices of a variety of health care practitioners and other sources of health care. Some of the promising devices for information dissemination are high tech. Computer networks such as Internet will allow everyone with a personal computer to immediately access information on health care policies and practices. Interactive TV may soon do the same.

Public information can alter health care utilization through altered user choices. For example, user education can reduce demand for care associated with acute upper respiratory infections (URI) by 30-40%. (JAMA 1983, pages 1986-1989 and 2952-2956; J of Amb Care Man, 1986, Vol 9, no. 4). Similarly, prostate surgery rates in the Denver Kaiser-Permanente Group, and in the Puget Sound Group Health, fell 44% and 60% respectively after introduction of routine viewing by users of a prostate video describing the treatment options available and the risks and benefits of the options. (Wall Street Journal, Feb 25, 1992) Another study produced similar findings, with the most marked changes in surgical patterns occurring in males over 85. (Jack Wennberg, Conference at the University of Calgary, 1990) A current project in Ontario is attempting to reduce public use of health care for colds and the flu, and many jurisdictions have tested programs aimed at better use of drugs by seniors.

Information can be delivered individually, as with videos or pamphlets, or through mass media techniques such as a theatrical presentation called *Side Effects* which examined the abuse of women by the pharmaceutical industry. Individual advice can also be supplied through information hotlines such as the Kids Help Line in Toronto which answers 1200 calls a day.

Programs which focus on emotional well-being and how to improve it could be usefully sponsored by governments, regional agencies and health care institutions and programs. Information which will help people lead long and healthy lives can be delivered (as it often is) in schools,

196

libraries, workplaces and throughout communities as well as through one-on-one encounters in health care providers offices.

Information can be provided to patients waiting for health care. The Ontario Medical Association has produced a video on emergency care which will be run in hospital emergency waiting rooms. It explains the workings of the department with the aims of reducing user frustration and improving the use of emergency services.

Technology can help bridge patient-provider communication barriers due to language, culture and literacy. Twenty percent of Canadians can read and understand only simple sentences. One survey suggests over 35% of adults are functionally illiterate. Figures are higher for the elderly. (CPHA Digest, Autumn 1992)

User control and user's rights now require that providers honor user wishes, but the wishes of users cannot always be known. This has led to the evolution of documents which make user preferences known to health care providers when the user is temporarily or permanently unable to directly participate. Whether in the form of living wills, advance directives or the legal establishment of a surrogate decision maker, all of these offer hope that the wishes of users will be known and respected in the event of a prolonged state of intellectual incapacity. Tube feedings, assisted breathing and infection control for permanently vegetative persons will be less likely to occur. Death will be understood to sometimes have occurred long before medical interventions are stopped.

Dr. D.W. Malloy of the Geriatric Research Group at McMaster University has estimated that perhaps 5% of all health care expenditures could be avoided if the mentally competent elderly and their families could be actively involved in preparation of Health Care Directives which would come into use when dementia or other factors made it difficult to decide what level of care was appropriate and wanted. (The Porter Report p. 43)

The delivery of information by professionals to consumers is sometimes poorly done. It has been reported that over one-half of physician instructions to elderly patients regarding drugs are forgotten immediately. (Stewart and Caranosos, "Medical Compliance in the Elderly", Medical Clinics of North America, 73:1551-1553, 1989) This suggests that the delivery of information necessary for informed decision making must be done carefully and certainly slowly, and perhaps through different processes than are currently used.

Providing information to patients takes time, and for a physician on fee-for-service time is money. For a physician on capitation the time spent with patients brings long term benefits; the patients will be seen less.

Policy could strengthen user control over health care decisions and also increase user responsibility for them. When physicians promote the use of brand name drugs rather than generic equivalents the users signature could be required on the prescription indicating they concurred with the use of the more expensive drug. When access to expensive drugs or therapies is available at public expense only when less expensive therapies have failed the users signature could be required confirming the failure of the less expensive therapy.

THE CONSEQUENCES OF INVITING CONSUMER/COMMUNITY INVOLVEMENT

One consequence of public involvement may be public disagreement with what is recommended by the experts and the professionals, or rejection by the public of policy directions considered unavoidable by government. New garbage disposal sites and new user fees are hard to sell. Public involvement may confirm all solutions as unacceptable.

This kind of rejection should accelerate rather than slow the process of public involvement. Objections will be raised whether or not there is a formal program of public participation, and additional participation may alter public perceptions and find friends as often as foes.

Another consequence of consumer power is, or will be, a wish by the sellers of health care to influence consumers as well as, or rather than, providers. When consumers buy private insurance the many competing companies advertise directly to the consumer. Nonprescription drugs have always been directly advertised to the consumer, and now that consumers are being asked to make health care decisions there is direct advertising of prescription drugs. Advertisements aimed at consumers have recommended the use of drugs to avoid having a cholecystectomy. Medical Associations acknowledge the power of users when they sponsor advertisements asking the public to object to cuts in health care spending.

Consumer involvement can bring greater awareness of consumer errors and perhaps correction of them. Ten percent of children reporting to an emergency department in Boston were found to have antibiotics in their urine although the parents denied administering them. (Interscience Conference on Antimicrobial Agents and Chemotherapy, Atlanta, Georgia, 1990) This inappropriate drug use might be reduced by greater user involvement and better access to information.

Regular consumer and community involvement may improve the quality of public advice. Better participation processes may make public influence more routine and more rational than the mass hysteria which now sometimes dominates.

Any discussion of consumer involvement should acknowledge the frailties of the process. It is often characterized by manipulation, unrealistic expectations, dominance by the self-selected few and pockets of energy surrounded by a sea of disinterest. Whatever its weaknesses, it contributes to the vigor and quality of democracy and it embodies the spirit of the consumer age.

THE CONFLICTS BETWEEN INDIVIDUALS AND GROUPS

The wishes of individuals as users of health care may conflict with the objectives sought by groups. When receiving health care the wish is for optimal safety, maximum service, a high degree of cultural acceptability, care which reflects the latest knowledge and an outcome which reflects individual values and priorities. Participants in policy development may wish equity before perfection, priorities which reflect community rather than individual values, cost-effectiveness, a reasonable attention to acceptability and care which reflects the latest knowledge. The two lists have more differences than similarities.

Individuals and groups may also differ regarding the extent to which the health care utilization records of individuals should be examined. In 1993, Manitoba established a *Patient Utilization Review Committee*. The Committee has reviewed the unusual utilization records of about 100 persons. One patient had made 247 visits to 71 different physicians in the course of a year while some of the individuals had been seen by only one physician. The Committee discussed the utilization with the concerned physicians and patients. British Columbia has a similar committee.

LIMITS ON CONSUMER CONTROL

Consumers cannot always be in charge. Providers, payers and other users also have rights. A consumer can reject any therapeutic or investigational proposal, but cannot always decide what will be done, especially when it will be paid for by taxpayers. Consumers have strong veto powers but they do not have the right to decide how much public money will be spent on them. Consumers also should not, and usually do not, have the authority to order individual providers to do what those providers do not wish to do. Providers should, however, use resources and provide advice in ways which respect user priorities and culture.

In Canada, the consumer often has the opportunity to select the provider who will deliver care, but this opportunity is not fully assured nor should it be. If the provider the user prefers is not appropriate for the services required, or is more expensive than other acceptable providers, then public funds should not be used to fulfil the inappropriate user choice. The consumer may also have only limited ability to select the location in which insured care will be delivered.

Persons in long term care should have the opportunity to make as many lifestyle choices as are compatible with their state of health. They should live with people of their choice, decide which services are of highest priority and, if personal disposable income is available, decide which additional services to buy. Many persons in LTC institutions have their lifestyle choices unnecessarily restricted. There have been many improvements over the paternalistic practices of two decades ago, but people often still share their home (an institutional room) with someone they did not choose and resource use may reflect agency rather than user priorities.

THE ROLES OF SPECIAL POPULATIONS

The population is not homogenous. Women, aboriginals, ethnic groups and populations with particular health problems each may wish to advocate on their own behalf, and each will bring their own issues to the participation table. These unique groups will need tangible and psychological support as they struggle to clarify their priorities and provide policy advice.

WHY UNHEALTHY PERSONAL CHOICES ARE MADE

There is evidence that some, and sometimes many, individuals will avoid hazards if evidence of the benefits are properly presented. On the other hand, many fully informed and rational persons continue with hazardous activities and choices.

There are several reasons for unhealthy personal choices. Sometimes the evidence is not believed, and sometimes those who benefit from the harmful practices, such as the tobacco industry, promote the disbelief. Sometimes people consciously choose the dangerous lifestyles. The benefits of mountain climbing, smoking and working in an unsafe environment may be considered to be greater than the risks. Sometimes the benefits are cultural. It may be a status symbol to practice unsafe sex and with multiple partners.

There may be a poor understanding of how to change. How, for example, does an addict kick the habit? Information alone is usually not enough. There is a need for a wish to change, a willingness to attempt to change, some idea of how to change and, sometimes, assistance with the change. The hazardous behavior may be a learned behavior. Change requires an understanding of how to replace that learned behavior with a new one. There may also be a need for social support, appropriate role models and identified material or personal incentives to change. Without some or all of these the avoidable risks are likely to remain a part of someone's life. (M.M. Murphy, "Resistance to the Promotion of Health", CJPH, Dec, 1982)

Some unhealthy actions pertain to medical care. It has been said that 50% of persons who are given a prescription do not fully follow instructions. (Understanding Canadian Prescription Drugs, Key Porter Books) Failure to comply occurs for all categories of medication and for many different reasons.

THE ROLE OF SELF-HELP GROUPS

The Self-Help Clearinghouse of Metropolitan Toronto lists over 300 self help groups and organizations. Many of these voluntary groups and agencies are informal and operate without public funding. They are characterized by members who share a common problem in their own life or that of a family member. These problems include addiction, chronic disease, a problem such as physical abuse, or a physical or mental handicap. The self-help groups may operate without by-laws, membership fees or a budget, but they contribute immensely to the well-being of persons who face often overwhelming challenges.

The positive impact of self-help groups on quality of life and length of life is well established. Persons with adequate levels of social and emotional support have fewer illnesses, live longer with the illnesses they have and are better equipped to handle the disruptions and hazards which illness brings. Even persons with life threatening illnesses such as cancer have been shown to live longer and have a higher quality of life when supported by knowledgeable and sympathetic persons facing similar problems. International, national and provincial reports have stressed the role of mutual aid and self-help in preserving and restoring the health of individuals. (Achieving Health for All, 1986, HWC; Mental Health for Canadians: Striking a Balance, 1988, HWC)

Self-help groups provide services not available from anyone else and they meet needs which would otherwise usually go unmet. These groups support the concepts of user control and user options. They are excellent vehicles for providing users with the information necessary for informed choice. They may assist in correction of socially unacceptable behavior (Alcoholics Anonymous, child abuser groups), provide long term assistance for households facing chronic illness and disability (Alzheimers or Schizophrenia) or provide emotional support for persons facing serious illness and disability (breast cancer, quadriplegia, ostomies) or a life crisis such as single parenthood or spousal loss.

Some self-help is promoted by national societies. The Arthritis Society is promoting an Arthritis Self-Management Program which, through information and sharing, gives patients a greater understanding of pain control options and greater control over the management of their disease. The program has been offered in Alberta and British Columbia since 1989. It combines the power of positive thinking with the satisfaction of knowing there are things which you, the victim, can do.

Self-help groups are endorsed by medical associations, but many such groups succeed in spite of, rather than with the encouragement of, local physicians.

DIRECT CONSUMER ALTERATION OF HEALTH CARE DECISIONS

"Giving all the health care people need, to those who need it, is a difficult but probably sur-mountable challenge. Giving all the people the health care that they are marketed to want is impos-sible." (Dr. Martin Barkin, Canadian Medical Association Annual Meeting, 1991) Consumers should accept the idea that some of the providers of health care do not have the interests of the user or the taxpayer at heart. Consumers are more likely to alter health care decisions if they appreciate that they are in charge and that they may, if they wish, question the therapy proposed, ask that all alternative health care therapies be fully described, ask for description of the non-medical alterna-tives and choose the option which appears to best fit their values and priorities.

Appropriate drug utilization offers many opportunities for user influence or control. Individuals can question the need for suggested drugs, enquire about the availability of alternative lower cost drugs and of alternative nonpharmaceutical therapies, ask that drugs in long term use be dispensed in large quantities (to reduce dispensing costs), be certain the professional is aware of all other drugs (prescription and nonprescription) which are being used, immediately report anything that may be an unexpected reaction to the drug, use the drug in the manner prescribed and only in that manner, and encourage discontinuance of the drug or reductions in dosage, even as a trial, when this is medically defensible. To do all of these things individuals must have information in an under-standable form, and this may at times require statutory enshrinement of user rights and publicly financed sources of information.

Many consumers have difficulty placing their preferences ahead of those of a physician. A life-time of believing that physicians automatically know what is best is not easily discarded just because there is evidence that professionals are frequently not right and frequently are seeking dif-ferent outcomes than would be chosen by the user.

While encouraging greater user influence over health care, it is important to remember that some persons, and in some circumstances many persons, do not wish to make health care decisions.

Especially in the face of emotionally challenging problems consumers may wish decisions to be made by providers. Public surveys have reported a public wish for more involvement in health care decisions, but most newly diagnosed cancer patients wish decisions to be made by health care professionals. (Degner, L., "Patient Decision Making", Summary Report of the 4th annual Health Policy Conference, McMaster University, 1991, p. 29)

In 1990 an advisory panel on cancer services recommended a greater role for users in the management of cancer, and recommended much more attention by cancer treatment units to the psychosocial, spiritual and economic impacts of cancer. Other advice has emphasized a need for agencies, such as the Cancer Society, to give greater attention to prevention, which would inevitably lead to a greater involvement of populations. Whether these recommendations will have a significant effect on an authoritarian and paternalistic part of health care is as yet uncertain, but funding agencies have in the past few years begun to assign small sums to prevention.

The timidity with which prevention has been approached is unfortunate. Prevention would lower the incidence of cancer whereas the latest generations of chemotherapy and radiotherapy tend not to live up to their advance billings.

THE PUBLIC AS CARE GIVERS

For many persons the most important sources of support and/or recovery are the family, extended family, friends, churches, other community organizations, self-help groups and voluntary advocacy and service organizations.

Because the unpaid caregivers are so essential it is wise to train them and to support them. This is particularly true when chronic illness and disability are involved, for example, Alzheimers, quadriplegia, schizophrenia, diabetes and AIDS. Training can improve care, reduce stress on the voluntary caregivers and reduce long term public costs. (Brodaty, H. and K.E. Peters, "Cost-effectiveness of a training program for dementia care", Int-Psychogeriatr, Spring 1991, 11-22)

Volunteer no-cost care is becoming increasingly competent. It is now common for respirators to be used at home, and home use of defibrillators is expanding. If home use of defibrillators becomes widespread it will at least partially replace the current emphasis on CPR, and probably increase the survival rates of persons who suffer a cardiac arrest outside of hospital. (Similar increases in survival may occur if implantable defibrillators become more common.)

ROLE OF USERS IN UTILIZATION

Utilization is usually under the control of providers but the role of consumers is increasing. Consumers are being asked to make choices.

User habits which are inappropriate include requests for investigations, referrals or treatments which are not indicated, visits motivated by a wish to avoid some form of administrative penalty (often associated with absence from work), requests for services out of usual working hours for a problem which is not new or acute and failure to responsibly contribute to recovery or protection of health. (Woodward, C.A., and G.L. Stoddart, "Is the Canadian Health Care System Suffering from Abuse?", Can Fam Physician, Feb 1990)

Double and triple doctoring at public expense, with the same category of physician and in the same week, does occur. The causes are many, and the cures are untested, although payment arrangements can reduce the phenomenon. The British panel system, with insured primary care available only from the family physician chosen by the patient, and with access to specialist care primarily on referral by that one family physician, is effective. The patient cannot go to a second family physician at the expense of the National Health Service.

Despite the confidentiality issues inherent in searching for and evaluating users with unusual utilization profiles, such reviews should be considered. If the persons involved are not identified it will be impossible to personalize response. Only file identification followed by personal review and discussion will allow payers, providers and users, working together, to decide the extent to which unusual utilization patterns are a product of the system versus the individual.

How should the system respond when there is a personal unwillingness on the part of the patient to prevent or reduce costs? Many persons who are on cholesterol lowering drugs are also smokers. If the individual would stop smoking then their risk of a heart attack would fall much more dramatically than the lowered risk which comes from the use of cholesterol lowering drugs. (Detection and Management of Asymptomatic Hypercholesterolemia, Report of the Ontario Task Force on Use and Provision of Medical Services, 1989) Should the cholesterol lowering drugs be supplied at public cost when user cooperation in control of cardiac risks is low?

Some users clearly abuse services. A survey of prescriptions in New Brunswick paid for by Green Shields (a private nonprofit insurance corporation) found that one in every 30 patients received the same prescription on the same day from two different physicians. A similar study in Ontario confirmed this phenomenon.

CONSUMER ROLES IN ASSESSMENT OF HEALTH CARE

Consumers have an opportunity and a responsibility to assess health care through such agencies as governments, hospital boards, regional planning bodies and CHC boards. Assessment infers accountability, and all health care providers should be accountable to some element of, or some representative of, the public.

Consumers and their representatives should reserve the right to assess any or all elements of health care. This assessment will be most necessary when professional groups are not adequately assessing themselves, but is legitimate in all circumstances. In addition, consumers or their personal agents are the only ones able to comment on the convenience, cultural sensitivity and personal acceptability of health care.

Consumers may wish to dominate in the evaluation of sources of health care. This does not mean that individual consumers will stand in the operating room and decide whether a neurosurgeon is doing a good job, as some providers infer. It does means that consumers will, through governments and other accountable agencies, use appropriate experts and appropriate evidence to evaluate components of health care and individual providers of health care.

Physicians have the best record of assessment of peers, but consumer interest is still appropriate and required. Medical Review Committees may be responsible for the evaluation of the accounts submitted by physicians to the provincial medical insurance plan and for the appropriateness of the medical care purchased by the government, but usually only the accounting/financial evaluation is given serious attention. The Ontario Medical Association has stated that *"because of the difficulty in debating and determining medical necessity, the main purpose of medical review is to ensure adherence to the requirements of the Schedule of Benefits"*. Medical necessity is too important to be ignored, and user/payer initiatives should make sure it is not ignored.

USER FEES IN HEALTH CARE

When should individuals be expected to contribute from their own pocket towards the cost of health care? What criteria should be used when deciding whether to approve or reject user fees? Should ability to pay be a criterion? Should failure to cooperate be a factor?

When consumers must, at the time of service, pay part of the cost of that service, that payment may be called a user fee, coinsurance, a deterrent fee, extra-billing, cost-sharing, co-payment or a utilization fee. Physicians refer to these fees as balance-billing when the fees bring the income per service up to an amount which the physician considers justified. The term *user fee* is usually used only when the user pays only part of the costs, but the largest user fee is incurred when the user pays 100% of the costs.

Premiums imposed by provincial governments to cover part of the costs of a provincial insurance plan are not considered to be user fees. They more closely resemble a poll tax or head tax and should be seen as merely a form of taxation. Addition of all or some health care costs to taxable income, resulting in higher income taxes to the user, or in lower tax rebates, may be seen as a tax or a user fee.

User fee policy options

Theoretically the first policy choice is whether to have user fees in health care or not to have them. These options are theoretical. All provinces require partial user payment for many health care services, and the complete abandonment of user fees is too impractical to consider. The other extreme of applying user fees to all services and all people in all locations is as unlikely as their complete abolition. The significant policy choices relate to when, where, in what form, from whom and with respect to what services.

When politicians, other policy makers or other persons express strong objections to user fees in health care these objections tend to be rooted more in mythology than in what actually goes on in the health care delivery system or in other social systems. User fees are common and accepted, except with respect to physician and hospital services. The emotional objection to consideration of the introduction of user fees in association with physician and hospital services is explainable only as a carryover from the days when physicians and hospitals were considered to be the main protectors of our health. The terms of the federal hospital and medical care insurance acts, terms later incorporated in the *Canada Health Act*, effectively prevent provincial approval of user fees in association with services provided by physicians and hospitals, but the *Canada Health Act* does not prevent provincial use of user fees associated with other publicly funded health care programs.

User fees have, in different provinces at various points in time, been applied to hospitals, long term care, fee-for-service practitioners (including physicians, chiropractors and physiotherapists), home care, ambulances, drugs and assistive devices. Hospital user fees were in place in British Columbia and Alberta from the 1950s to the 1980s, and Saskatchewan had user fees for physician services in the 1960s and 1970s. These fees transferred costs from the province to the users. Most user fees associated with hospital and physician services, to the extent they still existed, disappeared with the enforcement of the terms of the *Canada Health Act* in the late 1980s, but user fees in association with other health care services have continued and are becoming more common.

There is need for a less emotional examination of the question of user fees. Is it rational to exempt, or wish to exempt, all services provided by hospitals and physicians from user fees when users must pay all or part of the cost of other important health care services?

Users of provincial drug plans have in the last few years seen benefits cut and/or co-payments rise as governments sought cost reductions. Figure 12.1 summarizes some of the drug plan changes introduced in the early 1990s. All of these changes transfer costs from the government (the taxpayers) to the specific user. See Chapter 18 for additional discussion of cost control in drug programs.

Users who prefer nontraditional care such as acupuncture, biofeedback, naturopathic care, yoga or other alternative therapies, rather than western medicine, usually must pay the entire costs themselves. There has been a rapid growth in use of these forms of health care, which suggests that consumers are willing to fully pay for services which they believe will be useful.

In some cases increased costs to the consumer have gone almost unnoticed by the press and the public. In 1982 Ontario allowed hospitals to keep all income from private and semi-private rooms and also allowed hospitals to set their own rates for these rooms. Many hospitals doubled their rates, a form of windfall income at the expense of individuals and of employers paying for preferred accommodation. Most insurance covering preferred accommodation is sold by Blue Cross Ontario, a nonprofit insurance company operated by the Ontario Hospital Association. The insurance carrier was unlikely to complain about a doubling of rates when the beneficiaries of the new rates owned the company.

User payments for private and semi-private rooms in acute and chronic hospitals vary greatly from province to province with Ontario having the highest rates. The Ontario rates are particularly excessive in chronic hospitals. It can cost up to $1000 per month to avoid having to share one's home (room) with a stranger.

Policy choices determine who will set the amounts and types of user fees. In Canada these choices are usually made by a private insurance agency or a provincial government. In Sweden local health authorities determine the level of the user fees which apply to most health care services in their region.

Arguments in support of user fees

User fees have been defended for ideological and for economic reasons. One ideological defence is based in the perception that people appreciate things more if they have to pay for them. Programs which offer services at no direct cost are said to destroy the moral fibre of the recipients and damage their ability to be competitive.

User fees can be seen as a tool to promote consumer interest in the appropriate use of health care. This user interest has become more important with the recognition that user decisions are one of the determinants of costs, and that user control over health care decisions will increase.

There is also an ideological defence of user fees which is based in the wish for equity. This defence proposes that there is not, and there will not be in the future, enough public money to provide to everyone all services which would improve health. There will always be more useful health care services to be delivered than there will be public dollars to pay for them. If this is true then either many persons will pay part of the cost of many health services or some persons will pay all of the costs of some necessary health care.

User fees can be defended as the lesser of several evils. When health care dollars cannot fund everything should governments, as an example, remove useful services from the list of insured services, or should they find the money to insure a broader range of services by the introduction of user fees? Suppose a $5 fee for physician office visits would produce enough public savings to fund a

Figure 12.1

PROVINCIAL DRUG PLAN RESPONSES TO COST CONSTRAINT IN THE 1990s		
PROVINCE	**YEAR**	**ACTION**
Nova Scotia	1991	coinsurance introduced; increased in 1992
New Brunswick	1991	delisting of antihistamines and other drugs
	1993	fewer seniors covered
Ontario	1990-92	delisting of approximately 2000 items
	1993	delisting of another 100-200 items
Manitoba	1990-92	coinsurance increased from 20% to 25%
Saskatchewan	1991-92	coinsurance increased from 20% to 25%
	1993	major reductions in population with full coverage by the drug plan
Prince Edward Island	1992	after 30 years of free insulin, oral diabetic agents and urine testing materials, a $5 copayment was introduced.

comprehensive community mental health service, and that without the user fees the network would not be funded. A choice must be made between the benefits of the community mental health services and the benefits associated with having no user fees on physician visits. In the interest of equity it would seem reasonable for public policy to distribute the available funds so that many people will pay small amounts rather than some people pay a lot and others none at all.

User fees can represent a trade-off deemed to be necessary because of national or provincial financial difficulties. New Zealand in the early 1990s introduced charges of $50 per day for up to 10 hospital days per year, and $31 for the first 5 outpatient hospital visits per year. (Medical Post, Nov 5, 1991) These user fees, along with many other devices to lower social expenditures, became necessary when the level of national debt led to an inability to continue to borrow, a situation which is close at hand in some Canadian provinces.

The economic defence of user fees in health care is based on the fact that user fees lower public expenditures in two ways. First, the cost to the government per unit of service goes down because the user is paying part of the cost and, second, the number of units of service delivered goes down because users avoid some health care when there are direct payments to be made. Drug utilization, for example, falls 10-20% with even modest user fees. (Hurley, Research paper for the Lowy Commission, Ontario, 1990) The extent to which there is reduced use of the less important services while retaining the most useful services is unknown, but certainly evidence indicates that when the volume of services goes down the reduction usually affects appropriate as well as inappropriate care.

Provinces transfer costs to many parties in many ways. When the rules are tightened with respect to services provided at the request of third parties the costs rise for users or for someone else. This includes medical examinations for licenses, employment or insurance. When out-of-province benefits are lowered the costs rise for those who use such services. User fees are merely one of many devices used to transfer costs to users.

User fees can also be seen as defensible when a portion of the cost of a service is the result of user choice. Public responsibility could be limited to the cost of the least expensive service.

User fees are about trade-offs, equity and opportunity cost. They are not inherently good or bad, they are merely an option which should be routinely considered.

Arguments against user fees

User fees discourage or prevent access by some persons to desirable health care. They are a regressive form of taxation. They resemble a sales tax in that the costs to the user do not vary with income; the fee seems bigger when income is smaller. The inequity of user fees can be tempered by the size of the payment, by ceilings on total payments, by various tax deductions or credits, by administrative arrangements which reduce the need for cash up-front and by exempting selected low income populations from all or some of the fees, but none of these devices fully eliminate the negative effects of the fees.

User fees are unpopular with users, and they can therefore be politically unattractive. This does not apply only in health care. When municipalities propose garbage collection fees they are usually vigorously opposed even although experience has shown that after the introduction of a fee per bag of garbage the volume of garbage going to the dump goes down significantly. Almost everyone is the winner in the long run, but many people oppose the loss of any free service.

User fees are inherently objectionable to individuals who believe that health care should be free. They are also objectionable to persons who have been receiving care without cost at the time of service and who do not wish to lose this free access.

User fees associated with hospital and physician services are seen as incompatible with the traditions of medicare. They have a special symbolic importance. Their use will be seen by some as another step in the dismantling of Canada's system of publicly financed health care.

Providers can dislike user fees, especially if public payments are reduced by the amount of the user fee. An easily collected guaranteed payment may be replaced by an uncertain payment with serious collection problems. User fees can also make administration of public programs more complex and costly. User fees can reduce the quality of data and can lead to manipulation by both users and providers.

Effects of user fees on utilization

User fees lower total utilization in situations in which the final decision is made by the patient, as with eye-glasses and prescription drugs. The larger the user fees the more utilization falls.

User fees do not reduce utilization of health care in situations in which the system stays full with or without user fees, as with hospital co-payments. When hospital per diem charges were in place in Alberta and British Columbia the available beds remained full although the exact persons in the beds may have changed a bit. When there were user fees for office visits to physicians in Saskatchewan the physicians saw fewer low income persons but the total volume of visits remained relatively unchanged.

There are not good data on the effects on utilization of user fees in home care, ambulance trips and diagnostic procedures, but presumably the usual patterns apply.

Neither public costs nor health care utilization go down when user fees are introduced and the provider or consumer can substitute fully insured services for the services with user fees, or can manipulate services to offset the cost of the user fee. The introduction of user fees in drug plans can cause the cost of the average prescription to rise. Users may, if it is to their advantage (and this depends on the nature of the user fees), try to reduce their costs by asking for larger quantities of drugs per prescription, or they may ask for more expensive drugs because they are fully insured. The lesson in this example is that the habits and events within the health care system change when the rules change. The system adapts in whatever ways are beneficial to the players who have control.

User fees may not prevent increases in utilization. In Ontario, with no user fees on physician services but with substantial and growing user fees on chiropractor services, the use of chiropractic care has continued to rise.

Types of user fees

Policy will determine which type of user fee will be put in place. The options include deductibles, co-payments, ceilings and payments which are required when users and/or providers choose options of low cost-effectiveness.

The user may pay all costs until some preestablished expenditure total is exceeded, for example, 100% of cost to a maximum of $100 per year. The $100 is called a deductible. When the deductible is quite large, such as $2000 per year, the insurance is called catastrophic coverage.

Deductibles have the advantage of avoiding provincial expenditures on behalf of the many persons who use only a few services per year. Deductibles are a problem for major users of health care. They require substantial payments in the first month of the fiscal year, but by the second month or shortly thereafter the deductible will have been exceeded and third party assistance will begin.

The user may pay some part of the cost of every service. This partial payment (co-payment) may apply regardless of how many services are used, for example, a $5 charge for all visits to emergency departments starting with the first visit and continuing indefinitely. If there is a deductible (during which 100% of cost is paid by the user) the co-payment can apply to all services after the deductible ceiling has been reached. This arrangement applies in the provincial drug program of Manitoba. The co-payments may also have a ceiling, for example, after user payments of $300 per year 100% of costs may be covered.

Co-payments which are a percentage of total cost, as with the 25% drug co-payment in Manitoba, give the patient an interest in total cost. A fixed sum per service, such as $3 per prescription or $45 per ambulance trip, gives a patient an interest in the number of services but not the total cost. The co-payment may also be the cost of a particular component of a service, such as the dispensing fee associated with a prescription.

User fees can also operate completely the reverse of the deductible. The user may be required to pay all or a portion of costs beyond (rather than up to) a prescribed maximum. For example, wheelchair costs may be covered to a maximum of $500, expenditures on drugs may be covered to a maximum of the cost of the lowest price equivalent, only a fixed amount will be paid towards a visit (as to a chiropractor in Ontario), or there may be a ceiling on public expenditures per year (as with chiropractor services in Ontario). These expenditure ceilings are common in private drug insurance programs, where ceilings of $2-3,000 per year per person protect the plan against very high drugs costs.

Criteria regarding when to impose user fees

Decisions to impose or not to impose user fees can give consideration to the characteristics of the service, the location of care, the type of provider, the degree of cost variation among equivalent providers, the availability of less expensive alternatives, political acceptability and the income of the user. User fee options can be evaluated in terms of their effects on user equity, their effects on cost, the extent to which they affect outcomes, the extent to which they encourage use of cost-effective services and discourage use of less cost-effective services, the impact they have on user involvement in health care decisions, the administrative problems they bring, their effects on those who must collect them and the extent to which they are unfair to one or more types of providers.

If similar services have different costs but the same outcomes, then users could be responsible for all costs above those of the least expensive option. Persons who preferred an expensive option would be obliged to pay a user fee. Generic drugs are an example, as would be the use of different health care professionals for marriage counselling. If psychiatrists cost $100 per hour and social workers cost $50 per hour, and if marriage or family counselling can be done just as well by a social worker as by a psychiatrist, then a person choosing to obtain counselling from a psychiatrist could reasonably expect the provincial plan to only pay $50 per hour to the psychiatrist. The remainder would be the responsibility of the patient. The same principle could be applied to diet counselling by physicians and dietitians, and to spinal manipulations by chiropractors and physicians.

In the Oregon experiment in health care rationing, services were ranked on the basis of comparative benefit to the entire population being served. The ranking was combined with public values (as determined by a public consultation process and a telephone survey) to determine which services would not be funded. A similar process could be used to assist those who are deciding on the use of user fees. Collective benefit and public values could determine who would pay user fees.

When deciding where to place user fees there is an argument in favor of their use in those situations in which users have choices. If the user can exercise discretion then the user fee becomes more justifiable. If decisions regarding utilization rest with a professional then user fees have little effect on utilization and are less justifiable. User fees will also have minimal if any effect on utilization when the need for the service cannot be ignored, as with significant injuries.

User fees can increase or decrease discrimination among professions. As just described, a $50 per hour user fee for counselling by a psychiatrist discriminates against psychiatrists (and would also affect family physicians), but the rationale for the discrimination is known. At the moment in all provinces social workers and psychologists are discriminated against, and there is no visible supportive rationale. Counselling by physicians is routinely, and without question, covered by medicare, but the services of the social worker or psychologist are usually insured only if she/he is employed on salary by a hospital or some other publicly funded agency. Both physicians and chiropractors treat joint and back problems, but in most provinces there is only partial payment for chiropractor services. This discriminates against persons who prefer to use chiropractic therapies and discriminates against chiropractors.

Administrative issues can be significant in the evaluation of the use of user fees. If hospitals are told to charge users $5 for every emergency room visit, and if the global base of the hospital is reduced accordingly, the exercise is merely a complicated and unreasonable way to reduce the funding of hospitals. Collection costs may exceed hospital revenue. The inappropriateness of the fee is increased if the hospital is instructed to collect it only when the visit was unnecessary. The hospital has an even more hopeless and thankless task. There are already enough problems in the emergency department without trying to convince someone they should pay $5 as a penalty for what is deemed to be an unnecessary visit. Quebec had suggested this type of fee.

Administrative options

The administrative arrangements chosen to implement user fees can reduce or increase the financial problems of the patient. Arrangements which allow the provider to always know how much of the cost is the responsibility of the user are simplest for the user, payer and provider.

Ceilings on user payments, whether the ceiling is on deductibles, co-payments or a combination of the two, are, in the absence of on-line computer systems, administratively complex for providers, users and payers. Patients must accumulate receipts and make a claim for reimbursement when personal expenditures exceed a ceiling. These arrangements require cash up front. They discriminate against persons with small incomes and those who have trouble submitting a request for reimbursement, as with the illiterate, semi-literate, those without a fixed address and those who cannot communicate in an official language.

In the presence of an on-line central data-bank, such as is used in the public drug program in Saskatchewan and New Brunswick (and which is planned in Ontario), or a Smart Card, (which has not passed the experimental stage) health care providers can know whether a ceiling has been reached. If a ceiling has been reached then a user fee may not need to be collected. The provider knows immediately whether the insuring agency will pay, and how much it will pay. In the absence of information regarding whether or not a ceiling has been reached the provider (whether physician, pharmacist or other) must ask the user for payment.

Although reimbursement arrangements tend to be administratively complex they can be less expensive for the insurer. A significant number of patients either lose their receipts, do not bother applying for reimbursement or do not have the skills to apply for reimbursement. Public expenditures may increase, and patient payments decrease, when an on-line communications network, or an up to date smart card, allows providers to immediately know whether to bill the government, the patient, or both. When the Saskatchewan drug program replaced patient reimbursement with its on-line information network there was an unexpected increase in costs.

Technology can reduce the administrative costs associated with reimbursement while reducing inconvenience for users. Blue Cross Atlantic has regional offices which are on-line with central adjudication and the regional offices can in a few minutes or seconds provide a customer with a reimbursement cheque.

Insuring against the cost of user fees

If users are allowed to carry insurance (private or public) to cover the costs of user fees then much of the population to whom the user fees apply will carry such insurance. Coverage will be almost exclusively through a work related and at least partially employer financed plan or through other group insurance. Such insurance will increase public costs because the effects of user fees on utilization will be lost.

If a universal public plan with user fees is introduced and users are not allowed to insure against the costs of the user fees persons who previously had 100% coverage will be unhappy. This population is made up largely of persons with first dollar insurance coverage through a work related plan.

The British Columbia drug plan has shown it is possible to provide everyone with good protection against health care costs without eliminating private insurance. This is done by offering public coverage which is not as attractive as that offered through private coverage, and by preventing private insurance coverage of the co-payments incurred by persons covered by the public plan. Persons with private coverage through work related or group programs keep their private coverage because the public plan is not as attractive as the private plan, whereas persons not covered by a private plan are protected against all costs except the user fees in the public plan. This option is in political terms a win-win situation although it has its own built in administrative problems and financial inequities.

Who should be exempt or partially exempt

Lower user fees, or full exemption from them, may apply to any population or service. Exemptions in public programs have in various jurisdictions been given to persons 65 or over, persons 65 or over and who qualify for the old age supplement, persons under 65 and on social assistance and persons receiving drugs through special drug programs such as those for sexually transmitted diseases, cystic fibrosis or dwarfism. Exemptions may also apply to very expensive services or services classified as life saving. Such an exemption is used in several European countries in their public drug programs and it is used in some ambulance services.

Most provinces exempt persons on social assistance from drug program user fees, but Saskatchewan for several years applied reduced user fees to this population. Most provinces initially exempted persons age 65 and over from user fees in drug programs, but in most provinces this exemption has ended. User fees for seniors may be lower than for those under age 65. Seniors who qualify for the federal Guaranteed Income Supplement are usually exempt from user fee payment, although in Manitoba's universal provincial drug program this population is not given special status.

The rationale for exempting seniors from user fees, especially those who do not qualify for the old age supplement, is unclear. It is a form of discrimination based on age, with the non-elderly being discriminated against.

SUMMARY

Users, either alone or collectively, are major players in the development of health care policy and in the delivery of care, and their roles are increasing in importance. As public funding decreases there will be greater competition for scarce dollars, and it is important that public rather than professional priorities establish the expenditure patterns.

Public participation is a complex task. If governments are serious about consultation they must expect new costs and new confusions as well as new and necessary points of view and different solutions to problems. Users should usually have the opportunity to choose the care they will receive, decide what risks to take, choose household companions and personal lifestyle when in long term care, choose between institutional and community based care, influence the mix of services to be delivered at public expense, decide whether or not to choose to stay in the queue for public care or buy the care privately, and decide whether to buy in the private market those services which have been deemed by the public system to be inappropriate. In all cases there should be taxpayer protection against user choices which are inappropriately expensive.

Despite the deep public resentment towards reduced levels of service, in health care and elsewhere, governments must cut back on health care spending in the 1990s with a vigor which would have been unthought of only a few years ago. Hopefully there will be a gradually growing public acceptance of this need to control spending on health care. This acceptance will, if it arrives, not be an easy one, especially for those who fear loss of access to necessary health care, but it is essential. Accurate, sensitive, planned and repetitive efforts by administrators, politicians, community leaders and health care professionals will be needed to assure the public that control of health care costs is a way to protect their health rather than endanger it. (Local Decision Making for Health and Social Services, Premier's Council on Health Strategy, Ontario, 1991)

Health care downsizing will be most successful, and reaction mildest, when everyone has access to all information, everyone is involved and the people whose health is at risk play a dominant role in deciding priorities. All provinces should support continuous and well financed public involvement programs to assist users to participate in policy development and personal health care decisions.

Learning about and adapting to the realities of resource shortages should begin in high school and never end. Public involvement will not end public abuse of political, public service and health care leaders, but it will mute the abuse and will result in more citizen support for the difficult choices which must be made.

The public may, in time, agree that although access to a broad range of basic health care should be guaranteed to everyone, the original Medicare model, in which everyone received everything health care professionals wished to deliver, is not only intolerably expensive, it is undesirable for other reasons.

Users are increasingly funding health care directly as well as through taxes, and the trend to greater private financing will continue. Consumers should be allowed to stay outside of the publicly funded system completely if that is their wish, or to supplement publicly funded care with additional privately funded care if that is their wish.

User fees are here to stay, and a more rational and participative examination of when they should be applied is needed.

Individual users should have significant control over the mix of services delivered to them at public expense. They should either have the opportunity to negotiate a mix of care different from that prescribed by professionals, although not at greater cost, or they should have direct control over some or all of the public dollars allocated for their care.

Users have a responsibility to respect the values and safety of those who deliver care, and they have a responsibility to contribute to the success of care. The public should be asked to discuss the role that user cooperation should have in resource allocation.

Users have a responsibility to accept publicly financed health care that is not 100% perfect by professional standards. Risk must be accepted by all users when the cost of eliminating the risk is poor value-for-money. Risk cannot be eliminated from any aspect of life, and threats during, or from, health care should be evaluated against the same criteria as are applied to risks elsewhere.

The public often sees the government as the boss and the boss gets blamed for everything. Occasionally it sees the government as a hired man, and when this is the case the hired man gets blamed for everything. Professionals can also be seen in both ways. In actual fact the government and the professionals are associates, partners and at times temporary bosses who are on a short term contract. The public needs to become much more involved in, and much more directly responsible for, many policy, administrative and health care delivery choices.

Chapter 13

Health Professions

INTRODUCTION

The supply of almost all types of Canadian health care workers has for decades been expanding more rapidly than the population, with nurse practitioners and dental therapists being perhaps the only exceptions. There is now a definite oversupply of physicians and dentists and probably of chiropractors, and an undersupply of midwives, nurse practitioners, well trained ambulance attendants, specialist clinical nurses and formally trained physiotherapy aides.

THE POLICY ISSUES

The primary human resource issue is how each type of worker is to be used. Decisions regarding the tasks which can reasonably be performed by each type of worker should be made before there is consideration of how many workers of each type are needed and how much the skills of existing workers need to be altered. If the optimal utilization of workers is understood then decisions can be made as to how to train or retrain each type of worker and how the supply of each worker type should be increased or decreased.

Many studies of human resource needs have been a waste of time because they assumed that the functions of key personnel such as physicians and nurses would continue in the patterns of the past. This assumption is not defensible in the face of the emergence of new independent professionals, the increasing superspecialization of physicians, new methods of payment for physicians, tools for control of total public payments to physicians, new organizational forms which do not use health care professionals in the traditional ways, and the financial crunch which will lead governments to search for better ways to use the various professionals and other health care workers.

Other policy issues relate to how the decisions will be made. Who should decide what types of workers will exist? Who will decide what each type of worker will do? Who will define the training/education processes through which each type of worker will be produced, and how aggressively should provinces protect employment of workers, including physicians?

THE OPTIMAL USE OF HEALTH CARE WORKERS

Optimal use requires that workers be competent to perform the tasks assigned, that the work be, as much as possible, performed by the least expensive worker who can do it, and that the tasks be performed at the lowest unit cost.

An examination of health care activities would identify some being done by persons inadequately trained for them, some being done by expensive workers when less expensive workers could do them equally satisfactorily, and some not being done by anyone. Tasks are left undone if they are not seen as the domain of anyone, if not enough persons feel competent to do them, if the tasks are not socially/culturally attractive and/or if payment mechanisms make them unattractive. One or more of these reasons has lowered the involvement of health care workers, in particular FFS physicians, in the care of addicts, the chronically mentally ill, persons with AIDS, the developmentally handicapped, some ethnic groups and street people.

Many services which were originally provided by physicians were later delegated to other health care professionals, for example, taking X-rays, performing injections and examining laboratory specimens. Many activities routinely performed by physicians to-day could be performed by others, and sometimes better. There are opportunities for many additional transfers of function.

A 1990 report (CJPH, March/April 1990) compared costs of immunization in Ontario, where many of the services are provided by FFS physicians, with those in Alberta, where the services are provided by public health nurses. The study estimated that costs per immunization were 2.9 times higher in Ontario. The vaccines are funded by the government in both provinces and this cost was excluded. The cost of the biologicals would also probably be higher in Ontario because of the low service volumes in some private offices. A low volume leads to vaccine wastage when the vaccine has a short shelf life. Distribution costs would also be higher when a large number of offices are involved, but the big cost disparity arises from the different personnel involved.

CHANGES IN ROLES AND SKILLS OF EXISTING WORKERS

Even when health services appeared to be quite stable, evolution was constant. When the status quo became unsatisfactory (and this continues to be the case) the rate of change accelerated. New workers, new roles for existing workers, new required skills in existing workers and loss of roles by existing workers are now the order of the day. It is difficult to find a health care professional whose future is fully predictable.

The tasks of all workers within the medical model have historically been determined by physicians, but new processes and legislation will increasingly place these decisions in the hands of publicly accountable agencies or committees. This transfer of authority will lead to decisions which reflect the public interest rather than the interests of physicians.

Many health care workers have expanded, or sought to expand, their spectrum of activities. Discussions of expanded roles usually centre on such groups as midwives, nurse practitioners and ambulance attendants, but physicians are the health care professionals who have most successfully expanded their roles in recent years. They have moved aggressively into all types of counselling (marriage counselling, family counselling), psychotherapy, the alternative therapies (hypnotherapy, musculo-skeletal manipulation and acupuncture), refractions and stress management. (In British Columbia in 1992-93 family physician billings for counselling rose 15% over the previous year.) Payment arrangements and legislation which gave physicians the right to do anything which appeared to be a health care activity, and be paid by third party payers for almost all of those activities, have promoted expansions in physician functions. Physicians offer almost all services without cost to the patient whereas the same services provided by other qualified (or even more qualified) professionals are often either not insured, as with private consulting dietitians, or are only partially insured (as with chiropractic services in Ontario). Physicians have also expanded opportunities for more than one physician to be involved where once there was only one, such as surgical assistant services and the presence of more than one physician at child birth.

The current milieu favors limitation rather than expansion of physician roles within publicly financed care. In the past when a function, such as immunization, was transferred out of the physician fee schedule the physicians merely found other services to provide. Their incomes did not go down. Now that the capping of total and individual payments to physicians has become routine, and with the limiting of billing numbers just arriving, the provinces have tools for reducing payments to physicians when functions are transferred.

If the function of geriatric assessment was transferred largely to public health nurses the government could fund the expansion of public health budgets from the physicians' budget. A few less billing numbers could be issued or income ceilings could be lowered. The same would apply if nurses became the primary providers of care in hospital emergency rooms or radiology technologists read many of the X-rays. Decisions regarding transfers of function should be made entirely on the basis of cost-effectiveness. Physicians' fees would often have to fall if they wished to continue to provide a service at public expense.

Physician roles are changing in other ways. Many family physicians are dropping their affiliation with urban hospitals, or are not seeking one. Specialists control beds in the urban hospitals, and there are few benefits to a hospital affiliation. It is more productive to spend the full day in the office.

NURSES

Nurses are the largest professional group in health care. There are about four nurses for every physician. Nurses will continue to be important, as they have been since the days of Florence Nightingale, but their future roles are perhaps the most unknown of any of the health care professionals. Will their educational programs continue to emphasize production of a nurse generalist who requires on the job upgrading before she/he can be confident and competent? Will the opportunities for new roles, most of which will require special skills, be missed, with the new roles being seized by persons other than nurses? Will the basic differences between pediatric nursing, long term care nursing, intensive care nursing and psychiatric nursing be recognized and action taken? Will nurses leave the determination of their future directions to others, or will they become more futuristic and imaginative than they have been in the past?

When Saskatchewan moved psychiatric care from institutions to the community in the 1950s community mental health nurses became the key personnel. Social workers also played a greater role. Psychiatrists became predominantly back-up personnel, a pattern which continues in programs such as the Greater Vancouver Mental Health service. These functional revisions should occur throughout health care.

Nurses in physicians offices have always provided substantial volumes of work for which the FFS physicians bill. Nurses in consumer sponsored health centres, in home care, in emergency departments and in public health provide a broad range of primary care and nurses in hospitals are highly skilled in patient assessment and care in their specialty area.

Nurses could, with specialization, be cost-effective primary health care providers in many parts of the health care network. It is not at all clear, however, whether nurses will take leadership in identifying exactly what they wish to do, how they will fit into new organizational and care delivery patterns, and how they will prepare themselves for new primary care roles. In 1993, nurses in Alberta asked the government to designate them as salaried primary care providers and the government has given them support, but this desirable objective is unlikely to be realized unless nurses become quite specific and realistic in goals and in the development of processes to achieve those goals.

Whether there has, in the past, been a shortage of nurses depended primarily on the strength of the economy and the extent to which hospital nursing positions were reduced in response to cutbacks. The determining factor in the future will be whether nurses assume new roles. Nursing organizations have recommended that all registered nurses have a baccalaureate degree, but there are associated financial and academic issues which remain partially unresolved. Considering the status and responsibility of nurses the wish for a university education is very reasonable, but a change in academic status will not in itself assure employment of generalist nurses.

The future of nurse practitioners is unclear despite the fact that they have established their ability to provide high quality care. Reestablishment of the nurse practitioner training program in Ontario has been approved but no start up date has been announced. Their future will depend partly on the willingness of governments to transfer funds from the global fund for physician services to practitioners who perform duties equivalent to those performed by physicians and partly on the new curriculum which is being developed. An assured supply of nurse practitioners is necessary if Community Health Centres are to offer the multidisciplinary primary health care for which they are noted.

The future of nursing personnel with less training than a registered nurse is also uncertain. Even the names continue to change. In Ontario, the Registered Nursing Assistant is becoming the Registered Practical Nurse, which is consistent with some other jurisdictions. The role of these workers in hospitals has been reduced, but their role in community nursing and in long term care institutions is secure and may expand.

PHARMACISTS

The roles of pharmacists are changing. If pharmacist expectations are fulfilled the future will see increased use of pharmacists as drug educators, more pharmacist involvement in lifestyle counselling and more use by pharmacies of a single wholesaler for all drug supplies. The majority of pharmacists believe that dispensary assistants should be permitted to fill prescriptions and hand them to patients when no patient counselling is needed. (Cockerill and Williams, 1989) Payment of a fee for advice given to users when a prescription is filled is currently not supported by at least some Colleges of Pharmacy, and in a 1992 survey over 80% of pharmacists in every province opposed a separate fee for advice. Advice is considered to be part of the professional service included in the dispensing fee. (Survey of Canadian pharmacists by Dr. Murray Brown, 1992)

An increased role for pharmacists will require greater pharmacist knowledge of the patient. In some parts of the United States outpatient information can be provided to the pharmacist without patient consent (as is the case in a hospital), and the back of the prescription is used to provide the pharmacist with relevant patient information. Patient information is available to a pharmacist in a hospital through access to the patient medical record, but such transfer of information from a privately practicing physician to a community pharmacist would, without patient consent, be improper in Canadian jurisdictions.

The advisory role of the pharmacist may increase as midwives, physiotherapists, clinical nurse specialists, nurse practitioners and others join the list of health care practitioners with prescribing privileges. New prescribing powers for additional professionals will bring both opportunities for better drug use and the possibility of greater drug abuse. The need for a central monitoring professional will increase and pharmacists are best suited for this role. To perform the new advisory functions more pharmacists will be on salary with community and regional agencies.

REHABILITATION PERSONNEL

Rehabilitation personnel appear to be in short supply, although the cost-effectiveness of many rehabilitation activities has not been established. Physiotherapy programs, as with many other academic fiefdoms, should be more flexible in the extent to which they acknowledge previous academic experience equivalent to parts of the physiotherapy curriculum. More flexibility would allow the same academic resources to graduate a few more needed professionals.

The skills of athletic therapists continue to be underutilized. They provide direct patient care in a variety of situations but are unrecognized in most jurisdictions. There are options which could legitimize these workers, including identification as a licensed profession or creation of greater liaison between athletic therapist training programs and physiotherapy programs. They represent a skilled and specialized work force with no established spot in the health care team.

Physiotherapists will almost surely become independent health care providers with the authority to prescribe prescription drugs and order diagnostic investigations. British Columbia began this process in 1991. Physiotherapists have recently, after decades of formal opposition, begun to support the production of a formally trained physiotherapy aide, and this worker is likely to appear. Change to an independent practitioner will be difficult for the physiotherapist who has for many years practiced a very limited type of physiotherapy, but the change is wanted by most physiotherapists and will add a new dimension to rehabilitation services.

MIDWIVES

Midwives are finally being legitimized in Canada. This responds to an often strongly expressed wish by women for options when seeking obstetrical services. (Stewart, P., and B. Soderstrom, Can Fam Phy, July 1991)

Midwives originally trained in other jurisdictions graduated from a special Ontario upgrading program in 1993. In September 1993 students entered new midwife training programs at three Ontario universities. Midwives began practicing as legal and independent professionals in Ontario when the Regulated Health Professions Acts were proclaimed as of January 1994.

Midwives formerly delivered about 4000 babies annually in Ontario. It is unclear how much this figure will change now that professional standards have been adopted, standards which many practicing midwives cannot meet. The role of midwives in a broader range of female health care (beyond obstetrics) has not yet been determined.

Physician response to expanded use of other health care professionals has sometimes been a reflection of self-interest rather than maturity. When the Minister of Health of Quebec announced in 1989 that there would be testing of the use of midwives the president of the Quebec Corporation of Physicians (a male) was quoted as saying *You might as well make prostitution legal. More people are asking for prostitutes than midwives.* The president of the Quebec Federation of General Practitioners (another male) was quoted as saying *It's like letting an apprentice pilot take charge of a Boeing 747 loaded with passengers.* (Pregnant persons have probably never been so publicly compared to a jumbo jet.) In most of the United States physicians have successfully obstructed midwife access to hospitals. (Knedle-Murray, M.E., D.J. Oakley, J.R.C. Wheeler and B.A. Petersen, "Production Process Substitution in Maternity Care: Issues of Cost, Quality and Outcomes by Nurse Midwives and Physician Providers", Medical Care Review, Vol. 50, No. 1, Spring 1993, p. 81-112)

Formal approval of midwifery is late but timely. Many specialist obstetricians/ gynecologists and family physicians are reducing their involvement in obstetrics. A lack of rural anaesthetic services and of physicians able to perform Caesarian sections, plus the rise in malpractice premiums (even although many provinces pick up some or all of the cost of malpractice insurance), have discouraged family physicians from practicing obstetrics. This has decreased rural access to local obstetrical services. The licensing of midwives may not alter the picture very much in rural communities. It can be argued that midwives should practice in locations where the surgical and other specialist back-up which was wanted by family physicians is available when needed.

The reduced involvement of family physicians in obstetrics is understandable, but the reduced involvement of specialists is surprising. A survey in 1988 indicated that over one-sixth of all specialist obstetrician/gynecologists had stopped practicing obstetrics in the previous five years, and another one-sixth had reduced their obstetrical practice. The changes were primarily because of a wish for a different lifestyle, with fears of malpractice claims being the second largest factor. (Hannah, W.J., "Report of a National Survey of Obstetricians and Gynecologists", JSOGC April, 1990) This change in specialist practice patterns will have its greatest effect in urban centres, locations in which midwives, if they are available in sufficient numbers, will be able to replace the physicians who withdraw from obstetrical care.

Midwives in Ontario will be on salary and will start at $55,000 per year. In Holland, where most births are in hospital but attended by a midwife, a midwife is expected to manage about 300 cases per year for about $40,000. (Medical Post, Jan 12, 1993)

The competition between midwives and physicians will increase as the number of midwives increases, as midwife services include more gynecology and as midwife costs are taken from the physician global fund.

PUBLIC POLICY AND NEW INDEPENDENT HEALTH CARE PROFESSIONS

Policy will determine the future authority and functions of existing and emerging professions. Options exist with respect to training, grandfathering, licensing, prescribing, ordering diagnostic tests, admitting privileges, relationships with other professionals, evaluation, methods of payment, amounts of payment, the breadth of approved services and limits on professional discretion.

Changes in professional functions, and the appearance of new professionals, are not new. In the middle and late 1800s nurses joined physicians and dentists. Chiropractors became well established in the first half of the twentieth century. In the 1950s and 1960s specialization of physicians, dentists and nurses became established, and new categories of workers appeared.

The creation of a new type of worker has in the past usually been initiated by health care providers rather than through a public policy initiative. Examples include pap smear technicians, respiratory technologists, the 50 plus types of medical specialists and the clinical nurse specialists. A few new workers have been a product of public policy, such as the introduction of Certified Nursing Assistants (which was opposed by nurses but supported by institutions and governments) and the Saskatchewan Dental Therapists, but these are exceptions.

The role of public policy has recently become more visible in the approval or in the expansion of the role of workers such as midwives, chiropodists and osteopaths. Legal support for professionals not endorsed by the physician fraternity began decades ago in most provinces when chiropractors became protected by law, but the granting of independence to practitioners who operate within the medical model did not become established in Canada until the 1990s. The independence of workers within the dental model, such as denturists, occurred earlier in most provinces.

When a new profession is created, policy establishes who will be recognized as a member of the profession. Grandfathering is the device by which persons without recognized qualifications but who are already working in a field can be recognized as members of a new profession, or as having specialty status, without having to undergo additional formal training. Recognition may be based on consideration of training in other jurisdictions and/or on years of acceptable practice in the relevant field and/or on the passing of examinations.

Licensure of new professionals may be by a professionally controlled licensing agency or by a public body. The pattern in Canada has been one of licensure by a legally mandated professional College.

Defining the range of services which can legally be provided by a given profession can be left to the profession or be spelled out in legislation or regulations. If the statutory route is chosen the approved services can best be described in regulations rather than in a statute. Statutes are difficult to amend.

Within the range of approved services there may be some which are, by law, restricted to one profession. Other services may be provided by a number of professions. New professionals, as with existing professionals, may in specified circumstances be obliged to refer the patient on to others with greater qualifications, or to ask for a consultation from an expert. This type of limit is commonly applied in hospitals to family physicians, and it could apply to midwives, physiotherapists, nurse practitioners and others.

216

If physiotherapists become private practitioners with their own case load, then consideration will have to be given to whether they will be authorized to order X-rays and other diagnostic tests, and whether they will be able to prescribe prescription drugs. There will be strong arguments in favor of both. Physician objections have to date prevented chiropractors from having their X-rays taken in hospital X-ray departments and in private physician owned facilities. It would seem reasonable for all professionals legally able to order an X-ray to have that X-ray taken in a publicly financed facility.

The question of whether new professionals, or existing professionals who are becoming more independent, should be able to refer to specialist personnel and receive reports from them also needs to be addressed, but legislation may not be the appropriate tool for the establishment of referral patterns. Chiropractors can refer to whomever they wish, but physicians may refuse to accept direct referrals and refuse to provide reports to chiropractors. Midwives may or may not be treated similarly. Increasing independence of such providers as physiotherapists, nurse practitioners, ambulance attendants and respiratory technologists will bring a need for clearly defined relationships between them and more specialized personnel, especially specialist physicians.

Many physicians have informally referred patients to chiropractors, but this has officially been a form of malpractice. Relationships with optometrists have also been considered unethical, but this silly rule has been ignored with impunity. Expansion of community based facilities such as community health centres in which a full mix of professionals can be on staff may in the future reduce the unhealthy isolation of some professionals.

A new health care worker may or may not provide publicly financed services. Dental hygienists and dental technicians, for example, were important additions to dental manpower and were financed almost entirely in the private market. Saskatchewan dental therapists, on the other hand, worked almost exclusively within a publicly funded dental program. To the extent that a new worker does provide publicly insured services the province may determine how the new worker will be paid. All payment options are available, but governments are unlikely to offer FFS to new professionals or to existing professionals who are not already paid in this way. This restriction will merely be a continuation of past patterns. Dental therapists (originally called dental nurses) entered the publicly financed work force in the 1970s on salary, as did nurse practitioners.

THE PRODUCTION OF HEALTH CARE WORKERS

Human resource policy includes decisions with respect to how workers will be trained/educated. There are several options.

The new worker can be someone with no previous health care credentials who is fully trained in a completely separate educational program. This model is used for most health care professionals and has been chosen for midwives in Ontario. When a new educational program is to be established a department of education or some other body with the appropriate jurisdiction will decide whether the program will be in a community college, a university or some other setting. Canada is much more likely to choose the community college option than is the United States, where laboratory technologists, radiology technologists, registered nurses and a variety of other health care professionals are routinely university graduates.

A new type of health care worker may also be someone who has already graduated as a health care professional and who takes additional academic training to acquire a new professional designation. This model is used in Canada for nurse practitioners, who must be a registered nurse before they can enrol in the nurse practitioner program, and for most formally recognized clinical nurse specialists who must have a B.Sc.N. to enter a masters program. It was also the model used for many years to produce public health nurses, a pattern now discontinued.

As another option for the production of a new category of professional, a person already graduated as a health care professional can receive additional training in a nonacademic setting. This model is used by physicians who wish to become specialists and by British midwives who are nurses before they enter the practise based midwifery program.

Occasionally there are training options available. Foot care is provided by chiropodists (2 years of training) and podiatrists (4 years of training). Ontario opted for the chiropodist. In midwifery there are the options of adding midwifery training to an RN qualification or establishing separate programs unrelated to nursing. For specialist clinical nurses the main options are a masters program versus a field based internship type of training. Policy choices will be affected by cost, the training capacity of the system, professional advice and experience in other jurisdictions.

THE IMPACT OF ORGANIZATION AND
METHOD OF PAYMENT ON WORKER UTILIZATION

Any organizational form which brings a broad mix of health care workers into the same organization has greater opportunity for worker substitution, for the creation of teams and for multidisciplinary treatment and prevention programs and plans. Examples include regional mental health programs, community health centres and Health Maintenance Organizations in the United States.

FFS impedes optimal worker utilization by restricting payment almost exclusively to work done by one worker, and this worker is usually the most expensive one. It is a poor method of payment when the services or activities involve many workers in unpredictable patterns. FFS does not interfere with optimal worker utilization if the fee is paid to an organization in which all workers are employed, as in a hospital financed through a prospective payment mechanism.

PHYSICIAN SUPPLY

Slightly less than half of all Canadian physicians are family physicians. Specialist supply varies greatly among provinces. Almost half of the medical graduates have, in recent years, been female, and in 1993-94 for the first time females were more than half of the new enrollees in Canadian medical schools. The existing total physician population is still three quarters male.

Primary health care delivered by specialists is significantly more costly than care of the same patients by family physicians. Some of the increased costs of United States health care are due to the delivery of most of their primary health care by specialists. (Bertakis, K.D., and J.A. Robbins, J Fam Pract 1989; 28:91-6) One of the devices for a lowering of the cost of primary care is greater use of health care professionals other than physicians, especially specialist physicians.

The first attempt at curbing the rate of growth of the number of physicians in Canada occurred in the middle 1970s when the federal government, at the request of the provinces, altered immigration procedures to reduce the arrival of graduates of foreign medical schools. (GOFMS) Despite this restriction, the number of doctors in Canada grew 3.5% per year from 1981-1987, years in which the general population grew only 1% per year. (Ont Med Review, Sept, 1991)

In 1992, in response to a report commissioned by them on medical education and manpower, (Towards Integrated Medical Resource Policies for Canada, the Barer-Stoddart Report), the Ministers of Health approved a 10% reduction in medical school enrolment. This decision assured a continuation of the downward enrolment trend initiated in 1984, a reduction in which Quebec and Manitoba led the way. Provinces moved quickly to implement the national consensus. First year medical school enrolment at the University of Toronto was reduced 30% in 1993. By the fall of 1998 the number of graduates from Canadian medical schools will be 14% lower than in 1985. (Association of Canadian Medical Colleges Forum, Oct./Nov. 1993)

In the absence of control of physician numbers, Canada could follow the path of the United States, where as long ago as 1980 an oversupply of 145,000 physicians was forecast for the year 2000. (USDHHS, Report of the Graduate Medical Education National Advisory Committee, 1980, and referenced in Lomas and Stoddart, "Estimates of the potential impact of nurse practitioners on future requirements for physicians in office based general practice", Can Journal of Pub Health, 76, 119-123, 1985) The oversupply will be caused by continuing overproduction, delivery systems and payment methods which require fewer physicians (capitation, prospective payment and worker substitution) and increasing identification of inappropriate care. Canada is fortunate in its ability to control the number of physicians who will graduate from our publicly funded universities. The United States does not have this ability.

The objective set by the provincial Ministers of Health is one physician for every 575 Canadians. (The physician to population ratio went from 1:656 in 1979 to 1:515 in 1989, a change of over 20%. (HWC, 1990) By the late 1990s there will probably be one physician for 450-475 Canadians. The exact figure is not very important, and certainly not worth the attention it receives. Whether the figure in Canada is 400 or 500 or 550 depends on what categories of physicians are included, for example, should physicians in administration be counted, should all physicians be counted or only those who are in active practice, and should physicians be excluded from the count if their annual earnings from clinical practice are below a specified figure. It has been estimated that 10% of practicing physicians do clinical work only part-time. (C. Woodward and O. Adams, CMAJ, 132:1175-1188, 1985). The figure is also unimportant because no-one knows what supply is best. In Britain the average family physician has 1900 persons on his or her roster. In Spain there are 3.7 physicians for every 1000 persons. Spain is probably no healthier.

However physicians are counted, and whatever figure is reported, the important question is, as was stated at the beginning of this chapter, whether health care in the future will be delivered as it was in the past. Will the roles of other health care professionals be expanded, and will the publicly financed system stop providing health care which is of little or no value? Will undesirable duplication of care or investigation be reduced, and will user responsibility be increased? Will care be designed to meet the needs of the patients and communities or the requirements and incentives of the providers?

There are several powerful reasons for reducing physician supply. Health care costs will be easier to control. It will be easier for provinces to expand the mix and responsibilities of other health care workers. Physicians will be less inclined to expand their activities into areas in which other workers are better qualified, and fewer physicians will be forced to make a living outside of publicly financed health care.

The supply of physicians is theoretically not a financial threat to government if total payments to physicians are capped. In practice, however, capping does not eliminate the efforts by physicians to maintain their incomes, nor does it prevent communities and physicians from wishing to keep their hospital beds open. Increases in physician supply may also be less financially threatening when the government limits the number of physicians who can bill the public medicare plan, but physicians working outside medicare will produce pressure for increased public expenditures on physician services.

The Canada/United States Free Trade agreement made it easier for professionals, including physicians, to cross the United States/Canada border. In 1992 there was a net migration loss of over 400 physicians. (Med Post, Dec. 21/93)

RESPONSES TO AN OVERSUPPLY OF PHYSICIANS

The question of whether there is an oversupply of physicians should not be debated. There is an oversupply. Attention should be focused on how to reduce the oversupply and what to do about the oversupply that already exists. Physicians wish to be employed, as do all other workers, while payers wish to control costs.

Licensing a physician has not in the past had the same financial implications to the province as has the licensing of a nurse or a policeman or an airplane pilot. Other recognized professionals must find a job, whereas until 1993 registration with any of the Canadian physician licensing bodies carried an automatic right to submit bills to one or more medicare agencies. The number of econo-mists or nurses or school teachers paid for out of the public purse is determined by the number of positions established, but physicians have historically not faced this constraint.

Reduction of the rate of increase of the physician population requires a knowledge of the sources of growth and of the techniques available to control growth. The possible sources and types of new physicians are Canadian residents who graduate from Canadian medical schools, Canadian residents who graduate from foreign medical schools, foreign residents who graduate from Canadian medical schools and then become Canadian residents, foreign medical graduates without Canadian or American specialty status who become permanent residents of Canada and foreign graduates who become residents of Canada after obtaining specialty status through training in Canada or the United States. The major tools available to control physician supply are reduction in domestic medical school enrolment (Canadian students and/or students in Canada on student visas) and more stringent require-ments for, or prohibition of, licensure of graduates of foreign medical schools (GOFMS).

RESPONSES TO A SCARCITY OF PHYSICIANS

Despite the existing oversupply of physicians taken as a group, there are regular claims that there are shortages of specific types of physicians.

Provinces or regions have faced perceived or real shortages of anesthetists, geriatricians, oncolo-gists, radiologists (diagnostic and therapeutic), emergentologists, psychiatrists and others. The tradi-tional responses have been to increase incomes, recruit from outside Canada or/and increase spe-cialty training spaces. Other more acceptable responses have received too little attention.

Duties could be transferred to other types of workers who are either in greater supply or are more readily produced. Using this solution a shortage of diagnostic radiologists could be relieved by training radiological technicians to read a chosen number of high volume X-rays such as ankles and forearms, a shortage of geriatricians could be relieved by the training of nurses in geriatric assess-ment, a shortage of physicians trained for emergency department staffing could be relieved by use of nurses or technicians to care for a variety of high volume emergency department cases, and a shortage of neonatologists could be relieved by expansion of the special skills already found in nurses who work in neonatology units. In emergency care the use of nurses is well established in agencies paid on capitation, such as Health Maintenance Organizations in the United States and the Sault St. Marie Health Centre.

When tasks are very specialized and relate to a narrow range of problems it is reasonable to assume that many of the clinical decisions would be as well made by, and many of the duties as well performed by, nonphysician specialists such as clinical nurse specialists as by physician spe-cialists or by physicians in training. Governments should be taking the lead in identifying clinical areas in which greater use of nurse specialists and other health care professionals would relieve a perceived shortage of physicians as well as provide care more cost-effectively. In the short run this move could avoid recruitment of physicians at a time when the physician supply is already too high. In the long run it would help establish a pattern in which less expensive personnel would replace physicians. Before total payments to physicians were capped the replacement of physicians by other workers was not financially tolerable, but replacement is now financially safe so long as the costs of the replacement workers are subtracted from the total pool of public funds available to physicians.

A perceived shortage of physicians could also be relieved by reduction in the volume of work. Studies of surgery have routinely found that many of the procedures performed cannot be justified. A reduction in surgical volumes would relieve a shortage of anesthetists and reduce requirements for surgeons, surgical assistants, operating room nurses and all other personnel involved in surgery.

Shortages of specialists could also be overcome by encouraging family physicians to acquire middle level skills in a field such as dermatology. One family physician with moderate dermatological skills could sharply reduce referrals to dermatologists from a group practice or a CHC. Upgrading family physicians within group practice settings would compensate for the increasing narrowness of specialization of specialists and would lower costs.

Family physicians and new graduates could be given incentives to enter specialty training programs in areas of perceived shortage, although these incentives are probably no longer necessary. The current physician oversupply, when coupled with changes in incomes and reduced access to billing numbers, is likely to see physicians anxious to enter fields in which there may be employment.

DEVICES TO INHIBIT INTERPROVINCIAL MIGRATION OF PHYSICIANS

The devices available to provinces who wish to be less attractive to physicians include limits on billing numbers, reduced rates of payment for new registrants, impediments to the granting of hospital privileges, special language or other requirements, lower than average physician incomes and administrative delays.

Controls designed to make a province unattractive to graduates of medical schools in other provinces, or to physicians practicing in other provinces, are now being put in place. These policies will be effective, but only until all provinces impose such disincentives. As access to public funds in one province disappears physicians will go wherever access still exists. Eventually all provinces will limit the number of physicians eligible to bill the provincial medical insurance plan, and the excess physicians will struggle to preserve incomes. New Canadian graduates will settle wherever they can make a living.

THE LICENSING OF GRADUATES OF FOREIGN MEDICAL SCHOOLS (GOFMS)

The number of GOFMS wishing licensure in Canada is large. In 1992 there were almost 900 in postgraduate training positions in Ontario, and these 900 are a minority among those who are unlicensed. (Members Dialogue, CPSO, May 1993)

GOFMS come to Canada as immigrants, refugees and Canadians coming home. They may, unless prevented or discouraged, arrive in Canada in increasing numbers as more European physicians are unable to obtain employment within the national health insurance systems of their home countries.

A province could decide to license all GOFMS. In the presence of a cap on total physician payments, especially if combined with limits on billing numbers, additional licensed physicians would not lead to increased public expenditures. Such a policy would, however, be as unreasonable as encouraging in-migration of any other worker who would arrive and find poor employment opportunities and whose training might not meet Canadian standards.

A province could choose to license GOFMS who demonstrate skills and knowledge comparable to Canadian graduates. This degree of restraint was the norm (with many variations) during the 1980s.

A province could license GOFMS willing to practice in underdoctored geographic areas and who satisfy other criteria as defined. This approach was used for decades by some western provinces and by Newfoundland to encourage physicians to locate in isolated communities. Within a similar pattern, provinces could license GOFMS with skills considered to be in short supply or who represent an ethnic or linguistic population without adequate access to physicians who understand the language and culture.

Provinces have the option of creating such major and insurmountable barriers to licensure that only a few GOFMS obtain a license. This has been the policy in most provinces for the last few years. Barriers have included sequential examinations, a requirement for one or more years of hospital training in Canada, and tight control of the number of internship and residency positions available to GOFMS who have resident status.

Provinces could place a statutory limit on the number of new medical licenses to be issued each year, and specify the priorities which are to apply to various applicants. The licensing body would be obliged to conform to the numbers and priorities identified in the statute. This option might be legally challenged as unconstitutional.

A province could also decide not to license any of the GOFMS. This would be within provincial authority and would not appear to offend the Charter of Rights and Freedoms.

Several problems have made it difficult to control the registration of graduates of foreign medical schools. GOFMS can, while in Canada on trainee visas, become trained to the level of Certification by the Royal College of Physicians and Surgeons (RCPS) of Canada, a certification which identifies them as fully qualified specialist physicians. They then can apply for permanent resident status directly or as a family member. After resident status is granted the provincial licensing body may have no basis for refusal to issue a license. This route to licensure could be closed by refusing to allow GOFMS to enter specialty training programs in Canadian hospitals, a decision which would be contrary to the Canadian wish to help train physicians from the developing world, or by setting up special training programs which do not make the trainees eligible for certification by the RCPS or the College of Family Physicians of Canada. The RCPS does not support the establishment of separate training programs.

GOFMS can also train as specialists in the United States, pass the Canadian specialty examinations, acquire permanent resident status in Canada and become eligible for a medical license. Prevention of this sequence will require alteration of the historical reciprocal acceptance of specialty training in the United States and Canada.

GEOGRAPHIC MALDISTRIBUTION OF HEALTH CARE PROFESSIONALS

Policy options which promote better geographic distribution of health care professionals include the use of lump sum bonus payments, fees or salaries higher than for the same services in areas which have more adequate supplies of personnel, student bursaries associated with a commitment to practice in underserviced areas, assistance with locums, payment schemes which link opportunities for income to service in less attractive locales and local or central assistance with the costs of housing, relocation and education of children.

The linkage of location with opportunities for income will be the technique of preference in the future. This linkage can be accomplished through limits on the number of workers (including physicians) who can find employment in the public system in a given region or location. The options are regional or district billing number quotas or province-wide use of capitation and/or salary, or some mix of the options. Part salary-part capitation was used in Britain in 1945 to successfully and quickly redistribute family physicians from the overserved south to the underserved central and northern regions. Use of a fixed number of hospital based positions accomplished the same redistribution of specialists. Once regional or community billing number quotas are established all other devices formerly used to promote better geographic distribution of physicians will be able to be dropped.

THE IMPLICATIONS OF SUPERSPECIALIZATION

The generalist specialists are being replaced by expensive superspecialists who provide care with respect to only a very narrow spectrum of problems. Superspecialization leaves a very large gap between the family physician, and other primary care workers, and the specialists to whom they refer.

Superspecialized physicians often create, or are created by, superspecialized technology. For example, as the technology for life support of very small infants has progressed the neonatologist has emerged and become a separate subspecialty. Very premature infants generate very high costs, and some of these costs arise from the high cost of the superspecialized pediatricians involved.

The number of consultations rises as specialists narrow their range of practice. The generalist specialist in internal medicine would provide care to a diabetic patient with arthritis and congestive heart failure, but now this patient may receive continuing care from three internists, one for the diabetes, a second for the arthritis and a third for the heart failure. There appears to be little data on the extent to which outcomes change with three internist superspecialists versus one generalist internist, but the costs are certainly higher.

Policy options include preserving the generalist specialist, producing specialist family physicians, producing specialist nonphysician professionals or allowing the current trends to continue. Preserving the generalist specialist is probably not possible, and allowing the current trend to continue is not in the interest of anyone except the superspecialists. The training of either family physicians or other personnel to perform many of the high volume tasks performed by specialists (in orthopedics, dermatology, anesthesia, trauma care, intensive care, obstetrics, oncology, psychiatry, gynecology and geriatrics) is a viable option which should be pursued.

SUMMARY

The spectrum of health care activities extends from the very nontechnological and human to the extremely technologically sophisticated. The evolution of health care professionals has not fully kept up with the needs of to-day.

There continues to be a need for a generalist gatekeeper and adviser who can both protect the taxpayer and see the user as a total person rather than a diagnosis or specimen, but there is an increasing need for inexpensive specialists who can provide the vast array of specific services now needed.

The family physician and the nurse practitioner appear to most closely resemble the gate-keeper and user adviser. The medical specialist is fully appropriate as the provider of highly sophisticated, often highly technological and almost always expensive care. There is, however, a need for an expanded array of semi-specialists, equivalent to the midwife and the physiotherapist, who can best and most cost-effectively provide specific types of services. Governments should move quickly to examine the optional ways in which family physicians or a variety of other workers can fill the void between generalist gate-keepers and superspecialists.

The roles and importance of health care professionals other than physicians should be strengthened. Statutory and other impediments to expanded functions for a variety of health care professionals should be removed. There should be establishment of, or expansion of, capacity to train nurse practitioners, physiotherapy aides, midwives and specialist clinical nurses.

There should be a search for services, in particular high volume and/or expensive services, which could be adequately provided by less expensive personnel than those who currently provide them. The search for functions to transfer should be most aggressively pursued in those areas in which the Canadian supply of physician specialists is thought to be deficient.

Continued control of medical school enrolment and of registration of graduates of foreign medical schools is needed.

Pharmacists should be designated as the major source of advice and monitoring of drug use.

Caregivers, especially nurses, should be assured that the demand for more health with fewer resources will not be met by expecting each caregiver to work faster and harder.

The production and utilization of health care professionals is still dominated by the patterns of yesterday. There is need for major revisions to reflect the financial and delivery requirements of the 21st century.

Chapter 14

Research and Information

INTRODUCTION

Both public and private policies affect the types of research which are emphasized, the amounts which are spent, the manner in which funds are dispensed, the selection of projects or centres to be funded, where the research is based, the extent to which private and public research spending is coordinated, how findings are disseminated and who owns the findings.

Research which is important to health is partly financed by Ministries of Health and by private agencies closely linked to health care, but most health related research is performed by and financed by other ministries and a broad range of private funding bodies with no direct connection to health care. Research performed by or financed by Ministries of Health and by disease related agencies and foundations, such as the Cancer Society or the Arthritis Society, tends to be directly related to the delivery of health care. Ministries of Health and disease related agencies spend very little on research into primary prevention.

Research in a multiplicity of Ministries other than the Ministry of Health examines the primary prevention of illness and injury. The topics studied in this health related research (but not health care research) are very diverse, and can include the use and disposal of pesticides (Departments of Agriculture), the impact of different income supplement programs (Departments of Finance or Social Services), the reduction of ground water pollution from garbage land fill sites (Departments of the Environment) or the prevention of injuries in the workplace (Departments of Labor).

Research spending which examines factors important to the health status of Canadians is not usually *health care* research, but is certainly *health related* research. A study in the late 1980s in British Columbia which reported slaughterhouse injury rates which were triple the industrial average is not health care research but certainly may have led to healthier slaughterhouse workers. (The Hamilton Health and Safety Centre, Dec. 1989) Similarly, some of the decline in the incidence of injuries in mining, logging and other industries will have been because of research.

Primary prevention research in all public and private departments and agencies could, so long as the findings are acted upon, save the lives of many of the more than 10,000 persons killed accidentally each year in Canada, and avoid many of the hundreds of thousands of injuries. It also could reduce the volume of illness that comes from our lifestyles and from our many environments. Most of this health related research cannot be performed by the researchers and institutions who perform health care research. This chapter makes no attempt to discuss all of the research which is important to health. It looks only at health care research.

Distinctions between categories of research are not clear, but in general terms health care research can be divided into clinical and nonclinical, with projects in each category being either basic or applied research.

BASIC RESEARCH

Basic research produces knowledge. It allows a better understanding of what is happening and why. Health and health care can be improved by basic research in almost any field, including chemistry, sociology, biology, psychology, administration, political science, demography, engineering, physics, social work and the health sciences. Basic research, whether organizational, biological, epidemiological, chemical, behavioral or anything else, is conducted primarily in universities and by the private sector but also, to a limited extent, by governments. Much of this research is not directly applicable to health care but it provides the understanding which allows improvements in population health and in redirection of health care resources.

Basic research includes health surveys, many of which have been done provincially and nationally in the past 15 years. These surveys have produced large quantities of excellent data. They should continue to be done in areas in which good baseline data are not yet available, and important surveys should be carried out at regular intervals. Smaller local and regional surveys should be carried out only when they serve a specific purpose for which national and provincial data are not adequate (and these data usually are adequate).

APPLIED HEALTH CARE RESEARCH

Applied health care research examines clinical and nonclinical problems associated with the operations of the health care network. Applied research can teach us how to alter care to reflect what is known, and it can improve the organization and delivery of that care. Applied research is commonly a part of Research and Development (R and D).

Private sector multiproduct industries with many clients and with complex and sophisticated production, distribution and marketing systems routinely spend 2-20% (17% in the drug industry) of their operating budgets on R and D. If they don't spend on R and D they cannot compete. They cannot compete because they become inefficient, out of date, out of touch with their clients and/or not cost-effective. In the process they become unprofitable.

Health care in Canada is an industry with all the above characteristics except the need for profit, but it spends almost none of its operating dollars on R and D. As a consequence it does not know as much as it should about the relative value of its many products or the wishes and needs of its users. It does not know whether its activities reflect the latest in knowledge, and it usually does not know the locations and providers whose decisions are most often appropriate or inappropriate. It therefore does not know whether it is delivering the greatest possible social benefit per dollar spent. This social benefit is, in publicly financed health care, the equivalent of profit in the private for-profit sector. Health care programs and institutions do not methodically and scientifically examine the alternative mechanisms through which service to the public can be improved, and therefore they do not know the most appropriate changes to make. These deficiencies mean health care is poorly prepared for the competition for public dollars which has now developed.

Health care institutions and programs have expected others to do their R and D. They have chosen to spend virtually 100% of their resources on delivering relatively unevaluated services through relatively unevaluated systems to users selected primarily by one of the professional groups within the system. The R and D has been left to academics and funded by government and private agencies. Neither the researchers nor the funds have done the job, nor can they do the job. If governments do not assure allocation of operating funds to R and D the inevitable restructurings and reallocations within the health care network will not be nearly as successful as they could be.

If governments wish to assure allocation of major funds to R and D then two options can be considered. Government may either transfer money from the operating budgets of all health care agencies to a ministry research funding budget, or they can require the operating budgets of health care institutions and programs to support R and D.

226

The first option will not work well. The field must dominate in selecting the applied research to be funded. The second will be badly received because it will require reallocation of global budget dollars from health care to what will be seen as administrative spending. The second offers the best hope, however, especially if the R and D in health care institutions and programs is part of an integrated province-wide, province led and decentralized program for better spending. (See Chapter 16) A combination of the two options may also be successful.

The study of the performance of the organization, and of ways to improve that performance, is apparently thought by health care administrators and planners to be *research* which should be funded by research funds and performed by *researchers*. This is quite wrong. Improving the performance of an organization is part of the responsibility of management. Those who plan, administer and deliver services should be in charge of R and D activities and fund them from operating budgets.

RESEARCH EMPHASES AND EXPENDITURES

Health care research represents less than 1% of expenditures on health care. Federal expenditures on research which can be classified as health care research are in the order of $300 million per year. Provincial expenditures are less. Almost all of the federal money is spent on basic or applied clinical research, with the provinces distributing their expenditures much more evenly between clinical research and projects which examine the way health care is organized and delivered. Special federal research funds are set aside for family violence, drug use by seniors, child sexual abuse and AIDS, but except for the latter the funding does not reflect the magnitude of the problems.

The federally funded Medical Research Council (MRC) in 1992 spent over $240 million on clinical research. Over ninety five per cent of the MRC funds are spent on research related to physical health. Mental health, health promotion, primary prevention, improved professional decision making and the involvement of the patient in clinical decisions receive little or no support. There should be greater public policy influence over the allocation of public research funds so that allocation better reflects current priorities. The priorities of the MRC have changed very little in the last 20 years.

The federal National Health Research Development Fund (NHRDP) spends about $30 million annually, mostly in research grants and mostly on projects closer to the clinical focus of the MRC than to the structural, financial, strategic, informational, evaluative and production questions so central to the future of Canadian health care. The physician/academic community quite easily and continuously captures the NHRDP funds as well as the MRC funds, leaving provincial governments as the major funders of policy research.

Foundations, societies and other private sources spend about $200 million annually on research. (Guide of Funding Sources for Health Research in Canada, HWC 1989) As with the Medical Research Council, greatest attention is given to clinical research, physical health and improved treatment. The private nonprofit research funding agencies and the centres funded by governments should review their allocation patterns to assure better balance between prevention and treatment, between physical, mental and psychosocial health and between basic and applied research.

In 1989, in response to a personal enquiry, the Princess Margaret Hospital (the dominant cancer hospital in Ontario and the centre performing a large part of the cancer research in Ontario) reported that it did not do any research into the cost-effectiveness of cancer therapy. If agencies such as this hospital cannot more appropriately balance their research spending then it is desirable that public representatives become dominant in determining how research dollars are spent.

Research priorities should not be static. A few years ago it appeared that measuring the value of specific health care activities should be a primary research emphasis in Canada. Events suggest that this emphasis is no longer desirable. It is more important now to emphasize research into how to change health care so that what is done reflects what is known to be most desirable. This includes research into how to identify inappropriate decisions at the moment they are being made (so that correction can occur before the decisions are final), how to replace the inappropriate decisions with more appropriate ones, how to implement policies known to be superior, how to identify the priorities and preferences of communities and individual users, and how to alter health care delivery to reflect the priorities of users and communities.

Other countries (United States, Japan and countries in the European Economic Community) are now spending hundreds of millions of dollars every year on cost-effectiveness research, mostly in large longitudinal, prospective and multi-centre randomized clinical trials. The most useful Canadian contributions to this research will be as partners in large multi-country projects.

The adequacy of the evaluation of different types of health care varies immensely. The expenditures on drug evaluations, and the thoroughness of these evaluations, are impressive compared to the expenditures on evaluations of other health care before it is accepted for general use. New studies of the cost-effectiveness of surgery, home care, emergency services and other health care will reduce the current imbalance.

Because of the volume of cost-effectiveness research now underway the body of cost-effectiveness knowledge will, in the near future, explode. The literature already is full of the findings from large clinical trials started in the last few years. Unless the art of responding to this information is mastered we will have a great deal more information but will not know how to alter the system and its decisions to reflect the new knowledge. Research which tells us (and the rest of the world) how to make use of information already available should become a primary focus of Canadian research.

Policy will determine the degree of emphasis which will be given to the funding of projects versus the funding of Centres of Excellence or persons of excellence. The Ontario Ministry of Health provides half a million dollars of core funding annually to the Centre for Health Economics and Policy Analysis (CHEPA) in Hamilton, plus project financing, and the investment has paid off handsomely. The same Ministry has more recently funded the Institute for Clinical Evaluative Sciences (ICES) at Sunnybrook Hospital. Manitoba funds the Centre for Health Policy and Evaluation in a similar way. The federal National Health Scientist and Health Scholar programs, and equivalent provincial programs, provide stable and ongoing funding to appropriate persons so that these persons may follow their own research initiatives. These persons are invited to devise their own research strategies, and funding is terminated or not renewed only if the output is unsatisfactory. The individuals involved have much more stable financing than would be the case if they were constantly competing for project funds.

Provincial governments have often tested new programs through the use of demonstration projects or pilot projects. These have sometimes been experiments, as with the Saskatchewan experiment with universal medical care insurance in the Swift Current region and the children's dental care program in Oxbow, but usually the pilot projects have merely been a device to spread the introduction of a new program (and the associated costs and political mileage) over many years. If an idea is fully tested in many other locations there is no need for local experimentation.

The federal government could usefully select new research emphases. Attention should be given to reducing the incidence of inappropriate decisions, performing Health Impact Analysis, involving consumers and communities more routinely in health care policy selection and the delivery of care, and evaluating the options available to policy makers, administrators and planners as they restructure health care.

GUIDELINES FOR RESEARCH SPENDING

A number of principles may be helpful as the funders of research examine their priorities and practices.

1. Do not endlessly count, sort and describe, and then do it again. Many descriptive data are collected with no particular planning or other purpose in mind. These data usually are not useful to those who must write policy or make other decisions. Descriptive research should usually be funded only when it is the clearly defined first step from which useful applied research will flow, and when information already available is not adequate for the problem solving which will follow. In many areas the volume of descriptive information is already more than is needed.

   As an example, a large Canadian study a few years ago documented the characteristics of hospital boards across Canada. The project, funded at over $100,000, documented board characteristics and habits. It provided detailed information which was of no value. The project made no attempt to identify which governance characteristics were desirable, or what effects flowed from different approaches to governance. The information merely led to what some would call *interesting* findings; interesting, but useless.

2. Do not fund projects which do not have the population base or the volume of resources necessary to study validly the selected question. Scientifically acceptable research is often not possible in one centre, in one year and with $50,000 or even $250,000. Good research may require millions or tens of millions of dollars, many years and many centres, often in a number of countries. Small projects should be supported only when there is assurance they will produce defensible information, or as the first phase of an already described larger project.

3. Do not study something about which we already know a great deal, especially when the system has not yet begun to respond seriously to what is already known. Further examination of small area variations in health care patterns falls into this category, as do most community studies of health needs. Community surveys to identify local priorities continue to be appropriate. Variations in health care utilization patterns by region or institution should no longer be documented unless the documentation is considered to be a necessary step within an already planned local, regional, institutional or provincial program to improve spending and allocate resources more equitably.

4. Do not study unimportant problems well. Study consequential problems even if methods and products are less than perfect.

5. Do not worry about wasting some money on research. Billions of dollars are wasted each year as a result of inappropriate clinical, policy and administrative decisions, and some research wastage should be tolerated.

6. Examination of costs and health care processes must often ignore the artificial boundaries within or around health care. The boundaries of research may need to be quite elastic if findings are to be useful.

For example, suppose the cost-effectiveness of the drug erythropoietin (EPO) in the control of anemia in hemodialysis patients is being evaluated. EPO markedly improves hemoglobin levels but costs $5-10,000 per year. (Other newer and similar drugs may be less expensive.) Offsetting benefits include fewer blood transfusions, less time off work due to fatigue and illness, fewer hospitalizations, less need for therapy for heavy metal accumulation and less use of steroids and other medications. A classical low cost research project would be unlikely to examine all elements of the cost-effectiveness equation, and yet without consideration of all elements the findings are likely to be misleading.

ISSUES AROUND INFORMATION

Policies determine what information to collect or not to collect, how and how often to collect it, who will have access to it, how it will be analyzed and by whom, the extent to which it will be protected, and how many data-bases will be integrated.

There will be no technical examination of health care information systems. They will be discussed only in terms of the questions which they must help answer, the information needed and the principles to be honored.

HEALTH STATUS INDICATORS

Measurement of health status is constantly being refined. Physical health status is measured through use of such indicators as length of life, prevalence of physical disability, infant mortality and the prevalence of disease. A nation's social health status can be measured through use of a social health index.

Such an index has been developed. It measures national performance with regard to seventeen social problems including child abuse, highway deaths due to alcoholism, the extent to which the elderly must pay for their health care, teen suicides, income support for low income families, adequacy of health insurance, adequacy of unemployment insurance, number of high school dropouts, number of homicides, unemployment level, percent of the elderly below the poverty line, percent of children in families with income below the poverty line, drug abuse, infant mortality, availability of affordable housing and poverty in general. In the United States the social index fell (the situation got worse) in 9 of the 11 years 1976-1986. Canadian data are not available.

THE NEED FOR BALANCE IN INFORMATION PRODUCTION

Provinces routinely compare the cost of various elements of care in one hospital with the cost of the same service elsewhere. Unfortunately few of the Management Information Systems (MIS) developed to date in health care have had the objective of measuring the appropriateness of the care which is delivered. The MIS which are in place are more helpful for cost control than for better spending. This data imbalance needs attention.

Some types of health status data are much better maintained than others. The Canadian Communicable Disease Surveillance system, for example, provides up-to-date information regarding selected diseases, most of which are communicable and are caused by microorganisms. Data appear to be more likely to be collected if a disease or condition is caused by bacteria than if it is caused by social pathology. Epidemiologists are more likely to document microorganisms than social stresses. There is national and usually mandatory reporting of such relatively unimportant infections and conditions as campylobacteriosis, listeriosis, Lyme Disease, cholera, chickenpox, botulism, and amoebiasis, but there is no similarly detailed and routine national attention to data on school dropouts, schizophrenia, urinary incontinence, drug abuse or family violence. This data-base imbalance should be addressed, partly by reducing the vigor with which there is reporting and surveillance of infectious diseases.

THE QUALITY OF, AND ACCESS TO, HEALTH CARE INFORMATION

Users, providers and policy makers do not have all the information they might like to have, but there is enough information to improve decisions in most situations and the supply of high quality information is expanding.

Data deficiencies arise from such factors as inadequate administrator skills, legal barriers, interprovincial variations (as in service definitions in fee schedules), the reporting of services by date of payment rather than date of service, identification of service by place of service rather than residence of the user, failure to use a unique patient identifier, fraudulent use of publicly financed health care, inadequate reporting, failure to report services which are privately funded, and inability to integrate different data-bases. Inadequate technical capacity is now seldom an acceptable excuse for inadequate systems.

Some health care information is not standardized across sectors, for example, unique patient identifiers are not commonly used throughout community health services, mental health services and social service agencies. Information may be stored in incompatible systems. It may be considered to belong to whoever collected it; parochialism begins at the program and institutional level. There may be constitutional or other legal barriers to transfer and integration.

Technology capacities are now excellent, but not all information needs can be met by sophisticated data systems. When users cannot understand the language, terminology and perceptions of professional advisors there is a need for either information interpretation or the presentation of information in a different form. The use of culturally and linguistically acceptable intermediaries may be useful. These intermediaries can alter demands, costs and user satisfaction. This applies to indigenous populations as well as to new Canadians. (Baker, F., CMAJ, Oct 15, 1984, p. 918)

Planners and administrators have often done a relatively poor job of identifying the most useful data for inclusion in major data-bases. Inadequate data selection is more likely to be due to errors by planners and administrators than by MIS staff. The functions of planners and administrators include selection of the data worth collecting. The main criterion when deciding what to collect must be cost-effectiveness.

The development and maintenance of data-bases is expensive, and expenditures on information systems come out of the general health care budget. To spend unwisely on information has the same effect as spending unwisely on anything else; there is less money for necessary services. To fail to spend adequately on the production of information, or on the use of information collected by others, can mean reduced positive impact upon the health status of individuals and communities than is possible with the resources available.

Information issues are receiving increasing attention. In 1989 the National Health Information Council was established in Ottawa. It established the National Task Force on Health Information, and a nonprofit Canadian Institute for Health Information (CIHI) with an independent board was created in 1994. This Institute integrates the former Hospital Medical Records Institute, The Management Information Systems Group and specific health information programs from Health Canada and Statistics Canada. These agencies will be useful if the provinces monitor and direct them sufficiently to prevent them from becoming technocratic self-sustaining cells of academic irrelevance, which they may become if not dominated by the ministries, agencies and communities which spend the money and face the problems.

When developing information systems the problems of those who must record the information must be considered. It is easy for a central agency to add unnecessarily to the tasks and costs of the field.

Information inadequacies occur at all levels in the system. Professionals have reported a lack of information. Over two thirds of physicians responding to a survey by a major pharmaceutical enquiry said they were not satisfied with their knowledge of drug equivalencies and nonpharmaceutical alternatives. (Lowy Commission, Ontario, 1989)

THE SHARING AND TRANSFER OF DATA-BASES

The transfer of information is now, for many business sectors, the third largest cost after capital and labor.

Sometimes data which are available have not been fully used. Nursing departments have for decades collected patient information every day or every shift. The information has allowed nursing staff to be allocated on the basis of expected work-load. This same patient information could serve the purposes of identifying patients who might be discharged, who warrant discharge planning, who are candidates for advance directives or no resuscitation orders or, perhaps at times, whose treatment plan merits review. The multiple uses are usually not considered; the information is collected by nurses for nursing functions and it stays in the nursing department.

The sharing and transfer of information produces conflicts. Decisions regarding access to data often must seek a balance between controlling costs, improving decisions and reducing health care abuse, on the one hand, and protecting the privacy of individual users and providers on the other. Regular access to data in which individual users can be identified should be limited to the user, the central paying agency and any department or agency which has been assigned special functions related to users. Routine access to information relating to individual providers should be limited to the provider, the paying agency(ies) and whatever agency or tribunal has responsibility for assessing that category of provider.

The balance chosen is likely to please no-one. There is inevitable continuing incompatibility between the wish to know what is going on in the system and the wish to protect personal files. There is a similar incompatibility between professional groups who do not wish external evaluation and users who wish to be able to evaluate those who are providing vital and expensive services.

Most analyses of collective data will be of consequence to users, providers and paying agencies. In keeping with the concepts of consumer participation, workers rights and taxpayer protection all parties should, if they wish, be represented in the process of data analysis. Some professional groups wish to be the custodians of, and the sole analyzers of, data pertaining to their members, but this would be inconsistent with contemporary values.

Some health care sectors have good information transfer arrangements within their sector. The Saskatchewan and New Brunswick records on prescribed drugs are, in both their completeness and their immediate access, an example of the future. Data will be increasingly centrally stored and able to be reported by region, institution, program, user, condition (disease, injury or prevention) and provider. Integration of data-bases will allow routine evaluation of the frequency with which investigation, prevention and treatment conform to what is known to be most cost-effective. Provinces will routinely report utilization and expenditures by region, type of service, type of provider and category of user.

Integrated information systems will allow identification of consumers whose pattern of use appears to be undesirable, for example, the use of multiple providers in the same provider category. Payers, providers and consumers who are anxious to improve the quality of spending and of care should search for these users. Review would be partly to hope for a lowering of costs and partly to see whether the patient has needs which are not being well served by the health care network. British Columbia and Manitoba have committees which examine the utilization of selected consumers.

Patients with a broad range of disorders or problems (such as panic disorders, chronic alcoholism, depression and spouse abuse) have been reported to often undergo many inappropriate investigations and treatments. Both the patient and the system would benefit from some form of review of the care provided. This review cannot occur unless there can be merging of information from data-bases currently stored in different departments and agencies.

DATA ANALYSIS: MAKING USE OF THE DATA SETS

The information available is, as has been described, in a number of different data-bases. To make use of this mass of information one must be able to not only integrate it, one must then understand how the various data-bases interact. When do cause-effect relationships exist, and to what extent is one data-base a function of another?

It is not very socially useful to know the size and nature of the health problems of a population, the services provided to the people with those problems, and the health status changes of the population over time, if there is a poor understanding of the extent to which the services contributed to the health status changes (the outcomes). The relationship between outcomes and resource consumption must be known if cost-effectiveness is to be known and if opportunity cost is to be estimated.

Unfortunately the relationship between the different data sets is not always well understood. There is, for example, a quite variable understanding of the extent to which various services contribute to improved health status. Sometimes the relationship is clear, for example, an appendectomy cures acute appendicitis. Sometimes the relationship is quite unclear, for example, what are the contributions of various forms and amounts of therapy to the control or cure of drug or alcohol addiction? The same applies to many cancer treatments, to treatment of middle ear infections in preschool children and to therapies for a variety of other mental, physical and psychosocial health problems.

The weakness of our understanding of the relationship between many of our health care activities and the changes in user health status means that it is often not useful to refine all data to any great extent. If there is only a poor understanding of how to treat alcohol addiction, and major disagreement regarding whether treatment should be daily or weekly, or inpatient versus outpatient, then there is little point in seeking perfect data on the number of alcoholics in the community. If the resources available to operate the treatment programs are also limited, and this is usually the case, then pragmatism will be likely to determine how many hours of counselling a week will be available per client.

THE IMPACT OF THE COMPUTER

The potential of computers is known, but many of their effects on health and health care are still to come. Present or future developments, which are discussed in many chapters, will often reflect ethical, legal, economic, cultural and practical considerations.

Computers allow on-line availability in professional work-places of user friendly information which will improve professional decision making. This information will improve the selection of drugs and their dosage, improve the selection of laboratory and other investigative tests, improve the establishment of diagnoses and improve the development of safe and cost-effective treatment plans. Software will contribute pre-packaged interactive information which will help users and providers understand the options available to them, and this assistance can be in many languages and adapted to many cultures. Large Area Networks (LANs) will allow the merging of information from many currently isolated data-bases. Prepackaged interactive material for use in schools, libraries and elsewhere will assist students, taxpayers and users to assess the policy options available to governments and health care agencies.

Computers will eventually allow comparison of individual, institutional, community and regional performance and experience, immediate evaluation of clinical decisions, immediate identification of a consumer who has already recently received identical or similar publicly financed care for the same problem from other health care professionals and, if desired, regular decentralized professional competency testing. (The data analyses possible in the future may make specific competency testing redundant. Analysis of actual professional decisions may allow a much more valid assessment of the adequacy of a professional than is possible with an examination.)

Health care may be able to use principles and practices now in common use in the private sector and in public sectors other than health care. The interactive computers in police cars provide police with information which allows them to quickly evaluate situations. This type of access to information would be equally useful in a variety of health care situations including emergency rooms and practitioners offices.

The automatic tellers used by banking systems allow users to deal directly with a machine rather than with a teller. There are similar opportunities for user interactions with a computer for such purposes as taking patient histories, providing patients with information regarding clinical options, giving patients access to information needed to understand their illness and giving patients access to advice from physicians and others. This latter advice is often not received when delivered orally to persons in situations of stress, but could often be easily provided on disk or in print in a personalized form if available technology is used.

Systems can now handle the integrated data-bases which are necessary if evaluation of service delivery and of outcomes is to be based on care provided in multiple locations. These systems are in place in large multiproduct industries who, as with health care, wish to know what is happening throughout the system and what products or producers are performing, or not performing, as expected.

SUMMARY

Health related research includes much more than basic and applied clinical research. It includes all research which is of relevance to health. Similarly, information relevant to health includes much more than information about health care.

Health care research includes much more than clinical research. Health care cannot be as cost-effective as it might be if there are deficiencies in professional use of available knowledge, in health care management, in human resource utilization, in organization, in the setting of goals, in the choosing of objectives and priorities and in many other aspects of the administration, planning, delivery and evaluation of services.

A network of laboratories and personnel exists for the conduct of clinical research. The beginnings of an equivalent network for research into health care policy, planning, delivery and evaluation have begun to appear at a small number of Canadian centres, but in light of the importance of these subjects this network needs significant strengthening.

In general, health care research should move (if it has not already moved) from individual care to population health, from small populations to large ones, from individual researchers or teams to multicentred projects, from retrospective to prospective studies, from short term to longitudinal, from small budgets to large budgets and from descriptive to analytical.

Public policy should determine the themes and subjects to be examined by research which is publicly funded. Options include the funding of clinical research, examination of the relative cost-effectiveness of the many activities and decisions which make up health care, the study of delivery changes which improve use of available knowledge, research into the nonclinical aspects of health care delivery, research into the impact on health of public policies in departments other than departments of health, the funding of projects versus the funding of Centres of Excellence or persons of excellence, and research into the implementation of Healthy Public Policies.

Supertechnocrats should not be responsible for deciding what data to collect. They, as others, tend to collect too much. If mistakes are to be made they should be made by those who use the information.

There are too many imbalances in our information inventory. Management information systems tend to accurately and immediately report whether expenditures are on target or below; there is no similar reporting of whether outcomes are on target or below.

Preamble to Part 3

Part one provided background to the issues of cost control and better spending. Part two looked at policy options, with special attention to issues of importance to cost control. Part three will continue the examination of policy options, but with special attention to how to spend our health care dollars better. Better spending is the second half of an essential duo.

The provinces have mastered the art of putting caps on expenditures. They now must master the art of better spending. Improved spending will allow Canadians to continue to receive a reasonable spectrum of cost-effective health care at public expense but with fewer public dollars.

If money can be spent better (and it can be) then reductions in the level of public spending on health care (and these will occur) will lead to only tolerable (if any) reductions in access to useful health care. Less public spending on health care could, in fact, mean greater protection of health if the same amount of useful health care continues to be available at lower than the current cost and the money saved is used to strengthen other public programs which also contribute to health. Governments and individuals spend money on health care on the premise that health care has a positive impact on health status. If the positive impact is not there, or is minimal per dollar spent, neither governments nor individuals should wish to spend. Governments, agencies and individuals are short of time, energy and money, but all should assign some of their scarce resources to the task of spending health care money more wisely.

Chapter 15 examines the tools and techniques which are available for improvement of the decisions made by providers, consumers, administrators and policy makers. Chapter 16 describes one approach to the implementation of a provincial program to improve micro decisions. Chapter 17 examines the question of how the general public might be made aware of the rationale which supports reduced public spending on health care, and of their role in better spending. Chapter 18 describes a province-wide program for more safe and effective use of pharmaceuticals. Chapter 19 examines the role of administrators and nongovernmental planners in better spending, and it describes some of the policy and process options which will be faced during implementation of some of the policy options discussed throughout the book. Chapter 20 examines a number of issues relevant to emergency health services, long term care, home care and other specific sectors. There will be no attempt to examine all of the issues in these various fields, but rather a commentary on selected issues and examples which appear to illustrate problems or opportunities.

Chapter 15

The Tools and Process of Better Spending

INTRODUCTION

The quality of spending is determined by the quality of the decisions made by individuals and executive bodies. The process of improving spending is therefore the process of improving decisions.

Inappropriate health care decisions may lead to spending on services which should never be delivered under any circumstances and on services which are inherently valuable but which were delivered when or where they should not have been. Decisions with respect to services which should never be delivered under any circumstances are easy. These services should be completely abandoned. Unfortunately the elimination of activities which are never indicated would have only a very small effect on health care delivery or cost. The handling of the second category is difficult. These are the health care decisions which lead to the use of a credible service or substance in a manner or situation which is inappropriate. The service or substance is inherently useful but should be used more selectively.

Appropriateness is particularly difficult to define when a service brings some benefits (even if small) but is expensive. The person(s) receiving the very small benefit are likely to believe that the spending is justified. Other persons who believe that they would receive greater benefit from the same spending will disagree, and those who are paying the bills and writing public policy may also disagree.

In June 1989 the National Health Policy Forum based at The George Washington University produced A Chart Book on the Appropriateness of Care. The introduction to the Chart Book states, in part, *"– a significant portion of current medical care is inappropriate. This statement is true whether we consider care provided in teaching or nonteaching hospitals, regions with high or low use of services, fee-for-service or non-fee-for-service physicians, or elderly or nonelderly patients. It is true in Canada, in Switzerland and in the United States, across many different kinds of medical and surgical procedures."* (This Chart Book was reproduced in the summer of 1990 by the Ontario College of Physicians and Surgeons and distributed on request to Ontario doctors. Over 1000 of them asked for a copy.)

Decisions which affect the quality of health care spending are made by many persons at many levels and places. The decisions range from public policies affecting millions of people to decisions made by one health care professional with respect to one patient and one portion of a complex package of care.

Decisions may affect efficiency or/and effectiveness. Thirty years ago evidence of inefficiency in hospitals was easy to find. In the last decade or two, however, the day to day management of health services, especially hospitals, has improved. The inefficiencies which remain are probably more prominent in the community health services sector and within the many interfaces between different components of the health care network than in hospitals. Inefficiency is not unimportant, but improving efficiency will not control global costs and it will not prevent the efficient delivery of services which should not have been delivered.

This chapter discusses techniques which identify and/or prevent inappropriate decisions, with special attention to better decision making at the time of delivery of care. It will look primarily at ways in which this micro level decision making can be improved.

EVIDENCE

Many different kinds of information suggest a need to be concerned about the appropriateness of professional decisions.

Large scale, randomized clinical trials (RCTs), usually prospective, longitudinal and multicentred, usually find that the therapies or procedures studied are either not useful, not as useful as was assumed or useful in fewer situations than was thought to be the case. These large scale RCTs have in the past usually assessed the effectiveness and cost of competing therapies or diagnostic procedures which are in general use. In the future they should be done before the therapy or procedure is in widespread use.

Regional, agency or provider comparisons have on many occasions shown large differences in the volumes of health care, and/or large differences in the processes of health care. Similar populations in different locations have on many occasions been shown to receive quite different volumes of specific types of health care, and there is usually no detectable improvement in health status when health care utilization is high. These comparisons do not establish which volumes or processes are most desirable, but in the absence of noticeable differences in outcomes it is reasonable to prefer the lower volumes.

National comparisons have confirmed the lack of correlation between total health care expenditures and the health status of the population. These data bring into question the desirability of spending more on health care, which in turn can lead one to be concerned about professional decisions.

Major professional differences of opinion exist with respect to the best way to handle many high volume conditions such as breast cancer, schizophrenia and control of cholesterol. Such large differences of opinion suggest that some of the professionals are wrong.

Other evidence has shown that the habits of professionals do not necessarily change when knowledge or professional consensus indicates that change is needed, and surveys have reported a significant number of professionals who do not feel sufficiently informed about the work they do.

The evidence which should be most respected is from the large prospective randomized clinical trials. The power of the information decreases as the trials become less scientifically defensible. Professional consensus which is not based on credible research should not be thought to be as good as scientific evidence. If scientific data are lacking, then professional consensus regarding cost-effectiveness should be respected, but this consensus should be reconsidered when objective evaluations have been carried out. Anecdotal experience (case studies) can indicate a need for further work, and in combination with other anecdotal reports can provide insight into rare conditions.

Despite the rapid growth in information which will improve clinical decisions, there are now and always will be many situations in which decisions will reflect values more than objective evidence. Values will at times dominate when society opts to protect one population ahead of another (the elderly vs the young), when choosing between present vs future benefit or when approving or disapproving of value laden services such as abortion.

There will, for the foreseeable future, be many clinical situations in which no valid evaluations have been carried out. In these areas society and health care professionals will continue to guess, but the presence of these unevaluated services should not prevent society from expecting the system to change when evidence indicates that change should occur.

Estimations have been made of the cost per additional Quality Adjusted Life Year for a number of policy and personal choice options. These estimates must be seen as very general. They change as perceptions of quality of life change and as a variety of direct and indirect costs change, but even with their crudeness they offer insights into the probable benefits of spending our money on specific programs.

Table 15.1 is a composite of data taken from a number of sources. Many other decisions and policies could be evaluated in the same way, including those originating outside of the health care arena.

WHY BETTER SPENDING SHOULD RECEIVE MORE ATTENTION

Few factors within health care could more quickly alter health care expenditure patterns without reducing consumer benefit than an improvement in the decisions made at the time of health care delivery. Some of the undesirable decisions are a product of a medical culture which teaches that doing something is better than doing nothing. Some of the decisions are made because professionals and users think health care can accomplish more than is actually the case. Some are caused by deficiencies in the information available to providers, while some are due to pressure from users and others are a product of a method of payment in which volume is necessary if incomes are to be maintained. Some are a product of providers who either ignore, or are unacquainted with, the findings of modern research. Whatever the cause, these inappropriate decisions are wasting 15-30% of our health care dollars. These wasted dollars should be spent on either useful health care or on the many activities in other social sectors which would cost-effectively improve health status.

Many professionals provide or authorize services in patterns and amounts which cannot be justified. This principle applies to physicians ordering diagnostic tests, home care case managers designing a care plan, nurses or physiotherapists in a geriatric day hospital designing a care and activity program for a patient and to every other type of professional performing virtually every other type of care. Professionals almost routinely prescribe or deliver more care than can be defended.

Spending wisely should not be seen as a response to the shortage of public money. Regardless of how much money is available for health care it is sensible to spend it wisely. Spending money better will reduce the number of premature deaths and improve individual and collective quality of life. It can mean better health care for individual patients as well as for populations and communities. The public will have reason to have greater confidence in the appropriateness of the health care they receive if they know that efforts are being made to reduce inappropriate decisions.

Health care institutions and programs which are publicly funded must make two related but also quite separate sets of decisions. They must decide how to stay within their allotted funds and must also decide how to spend the allotted funds. There is at times a tendency to give more attention to staying within budget than to spending money well, which is unfortunate. Both are essential.

Providers and consumers are in an era in which there is acute competition for a shrinking supply of public dollars. Everyone who wishes to spend a new dollar, or to keep all dollars they presently have, will do so by reducing the dollars that someone else can spend. In this environment the best protection of the funding of any provider and of the care of any consumer is to be able to prove that funds are being well spent.

Health care will, in the future, be forced to compete much more vigorously for public funds. If health care funds are spent more carefully then health care leaders will be better able to defend requests for money. Proof that non-cost-effective expenditures are being eliminated will strengthen the likelihood that necessary health care will be funded. Even if all useful care cannot be provided at public cost then good spending will reduce the impact of cut-backs. Services not available at public cost will be those which would have brought the least benefit per dollar spent.

Value-for-money attacks waste, the greatest single threat to universal access to useful health care. Avoiding unwise spending should allow less total public spending on health care, the funding of

Table 15.1

COST PER QUALITY ADJUSTED LIFE YEAR GAINED		
PROGRAM OR ACTIVITY	**COST***	**REF. NO.**
Screening for phenylketonuria	<zero (1986)	1
Post partum anti-depression therapy	<zero (1986)	1
GP (FP) advice to stop smoking	270+(1983)	2
MD advice re smoking cessation	700-9000 (1989)	5
Treatment of benign intracranial tumors	380 (1983)	2
Pacemaker implantation for heart block	1020 (1983)	2
Hip replacement	1200 (1983)	2
Ante-partum anti-depressant therapy	1480 (1986)	1
Coronary artery bypass for severe angina		
— left main vessel disease	1665 (1983)	2
Breast cancer screening — ages 50-70	3-5000 (1991)	3
Coronary artery bypass surgery for two		
vessel disease	3650 (1983)	2
Kidney transplantation (cadaver)	4800 (1983)	2
Coronary Artery by-pass surgery for left		
main coronary artery disease	5100 (1986)	1
Neonatal intensive care for infants weighing		
1000-1499 grams	5460 (1986)	1
Breast cancer screening	5600 (1983)	2
Low dose AZT for HIV positive		
asymptomatic persons	6-70,000 (1991)	4
Screening for thyroxine deficiency	7650 (1986)	1
Treatment of severe hypertension		
(diastolic >105) — men age 40	11400 (1986)	1
Hospital hemodialysis	22400 (1983)	2
Use of nonionic dye for highest risk		
population	23175 (1986)	1
Treatment of mild hypertension		
Treatment mild/moderate hypertension		
(age 55)	47000 (1990)	5
Estrogen therapy for postmenopausal		
women who have not had		
hysterectomy	32670 (1986)	1
Neonatal intensive care for infants weighing		
500-999 grams	28559 (1986)	1
Coronary artery bypass surgery for single		1
vessel disease in patients with		
moderate angina	44400 (1986)	1
Tuberculin testing in school	53000 (1986)	1
Continuous ambulatory peritoneal dialysis	57100 (1986)	1
Complete conversion to new contrast media	64000 (1986)	1
Hemodialysis in hospital	65500 (1986)	2
Malignant brain tumor	110000 (1983)	
Administration of nonionic contrast media to		
low risk patients	220000 (1986)	1

Table 15.1 continued

*costs expressed in 1986 US dollars. Some costs were in British pounds. They were converted at 1 pound equals $1.6 US

Sources for Table 15.1
1. Goel, et al., Nonionic contrast media: economic analysis and health policy development, CMAJ 140:393, 1989, as reprinted in Restructuring Canada's Health Services System, 1992, p. 248.
2. Culyer, A.J., Restructuring Canada's Health Services System, 1992, p. 322. Figures were adapted by Culyer from Williams, A., BMJ, 291:326-329, and Pickard, J.D. et al., BMJ 301, 629-635, 1990.
3. deKroning, H.J. et al., Int J Cancer, Oct. 21, 1991, 531-7.
4. Schulman, et al., Ann Inter Med, May 1, 1991, 798-802.
5. Rachlis, M., in Restructuring Canada's Health Services System, 1992, quoting various literature sources.

useful health care not being currently provided, the funding of other services also important to health and/or a lowering of provincial deficits. Greater attention to value-for-money will also make it easier for governments to control total expenditures on health care.

Health care financing by governments is already on its way down, and without attention to the quality of health care decisions the cut-backs will lead to reduced access to appropriate as well as inappropriate care.

THE PLAYERS IN A PROGRAM FOR BETTER SPENDING

Better spending can be encouraged and accomplished through the decisions and actions of the general public (as taxpayers, users, user advocates and user organizations), the health care professionals and other caregivers and their organizations, the policy makers, planners and administrators within government and throughout the health care network, the researchers, the Canadian Medical Protective Association (the physician operated medical malpractice insurance company) and the private sector. All of these players can promote better decisions during the planning, regulation, administration, evaluation and delivery of health care.

There will not be universal support for all actions in search of better spending, but support will be widespread. Physicians were at one time severe critics of devices which limited professional freedom, but they are now big supporters of attention to the quality of professional decisions and will probably accept other players as partners in the task of improving decisions.

Practitioners have a central role in better spending. Their biggest contributions will be in understanding the validity of the search for better spending, in cooperatively accepting the devices which will accomplish it and in participating in the introduction and evaluation of new processes.

The role of consumers in a program for better spending will at first be less well defined than the role of providers, but their participation is needed. An individual patient (or a patient advocate) decides whether to go to the doctor to-day, whether to question the purpose of investigations or therapies and whether to approve them, whether to make personal lifestyle choices which are healthy, whether to demand care which is not recommended, whether to contribute fully to the health care processes prescribed or selected and whether to encourage or discourage heroic measures for the dying. All of these user choices affect the quality of health care spending. In addition to the influence which each individual exerts over his or her use of health care, the general public also influences health care through influence over public policies.

PRINCIPLES FOR SELECTION OF PLACES FOR BETTER SPENDING

Efforts to improve spending must, as with other activities, be cost-effective. The cost-effectiveness will be greatest if efforts are targeted, planned and evaluated.

Several questions will assist in the selection of services or situations which merit consideration as sites for improved spending.

1. Have scientifically sound studies evaluated the service or situation? If the answer to the question is *no* then later questions become important. Services or decisions which have not been scientifically evaluated should be ignored either until they have been evaluated or until another rationale has been found to serve as a basis for policy or for provider choice.

   On the other hand, the answer to the first question may be *yes*. A service or activity may have been shown to have little or no value in specific and identifiable situations.

   It may be proper to allow people to buy services of no apparent value, or of very low cost-effectiveness, with their own money, for example, vitamin pills for healthy persons, but when public dollars are scarce the services of little or no value should be the first to be deinsured.

   When scientific evaluation has shown that different approaches to care for the same condition carry approximately the same costs and outcomes then professional and user preferences should determine which option is used.

2. Is there evidence of major utilization variation between sites and/or providers?

   Attention can be given to services for which there are poorly developed criteria of appropriateness but which are provided in very different quantities in different locations or by different providers. In the absence of evidence of improved health status when volumes are high it is reasonable to aim for the lower volumes of care. Hysterectomies, prostatectomies, cholecystectomies, amniocentesis, endoscopies and addiction treatment programs are examples.

3. Are there options with different costs but apparently similar outcomes?

   There are circumstances in which several different health care delivery patterns are all considered to be adequate, in which the options have not been validly assessed regarding cost-effectiveness, and in which the options carry different costs. In these situations it would seem logical to publicly finance only the least expensive option, or to spend only to that level, until research compares the cost-effectiveness of the options. There will be times when user preferences would mean higher costs but no proven increase in benefits. These expensive options should not be available at public expense.

4. Is the service, disease or location financially significant? Unless change is very easy to accomplish improvement should be given a low priority when the expenditure involved is small. A small number of clinical situations and procedures are financially dominant. In the United States twenty-three operations represent about 60% of major surgery, and about forty illnesses represent 70% of medical admissions to hospital. (Wennberg, J.E., "Improving the Medical Decision Process," Health Affairs, Spring 1988) High volume points of contact between users and providers also merit attention.

5. Can inappropriate care be identified before it has been delivered? Retrospective analyses are not a waste of time, but pay-off can be immediate if inappropriate decisions can be identified before they have been implemented. Pay-off can be immediate if decision makers can be informed of the best alternative before a choice has been made.

6. Is there a reasonable likelihood that the inappropriate care can be altered? If legislative or other forces make correction difficult or impossible the issue should be deferred until impediments to change are removed.

7. Are the decisions dominated by values and popular choice rather than data?

Decisions which are dominated by values or public opinion, as with abortion, care of premature infants and cancer therapy, are not the place to begin. Regardless of the statistical appropriateness of cancer therapy or the care of very high risk newborns it is possible that significant reductions in these areas of care would not be acceptable to the public at this time.

In evaluating the merit of action it is necessary to remember the breadth of the criteria and indicators which can represent important outcomes. Impact can pertain to mental ill-health (depression, anxiety, fear, abnormal behavior), wellness (happiness, optimism, a good self image), social well-being (personal relationships, personal networks) and physical health (disability, disease, pain, death).

DEVICES FOR BETTER SPENDING

Better spending can be promoted through the provision of information, the improvement of skills, the power of regulation, the influence of monitoring, the use of incentives or disincentives and the motivating effects of social benefit. The devices are organizational, motivational (behavioral), economic, technocratic and educational. In other words, the array of devices which can help spend our health care dollars better is immense.

Selection of the devices which can improve spending requires answers to questions such as which devices have been proven to be successful, which devices overlap or are the same, how do the devices interact, who can implement them, what opportunities and threats does each bring, who are the winners and losers from each of them, what are their strengths and weaknesses and how much have they been used, and by whom?

This and the following chapters will describe most of the devices which have been used and will offer a few which have not been used. Agencies and participants may, if they wish, add their own touches and wrinkles to the process.

Devices for better spending may be used at the discretion of the provider or they may be mandatory. If mandatory they may be demanded by a province, a professional association, a governing board, a regional body, a private payer or a user.

Some of the devices which can improve spending have been discussed in earlier chapters as tools for cost control. This may produce problems for persons who wish to spend money more wisely but object to cost control. (There may be a different response to a cost control objective than to a search for better spending.) The dilemma is not avoidable or solvable. Hopefully the majority of players will see both cost control and better spending as desirable objectives. All players should know that cost control will occur whether or not the available dollars are well spent.

The introduction of devices designed to improve decision making by providers on FFS will need to be sensitive to the relationship between patient turnover and income. This is another area of conflict that can be neither fully resolved or avoided. The capping of individual physician incomes will reduce conflict, but primarily with respect to the minority of physicians who are affected by the cap.

The most important tools and techniques for better spending are individually discussed in later sections.

LIMITS ON PROFESSIONAL DISCRETION

This subject was discussed extensively in Chapter 10 in the examination of issues and policies related to professional freedom. It also is very relevant to improved spending and some points are repeated here.

Professionals usually have considerable discretion as to whether to order another lab test, approve three versus six hours of homemaker service per week, order a drug three versus four times a day and for four, six or ten days, or use one-on-one counselling versus group therapy. Choices made on the basis of professional preference have immense impact on the quality and cost of health care.

Limits placed by colleagues on the choices (the degree of discretion) of professionals have existed at least since the Code of Hammurabi and the Hippocratic oath. Limits have became more common and more restrictive in the last half of the 20th century.

Limits on professional discretion and autonomy in Canada have been suggested or put in place primarily by hospital boards acting on the advice of a Medical Advisory Committees or by professional licensing bodies acting to fulfil responsibilities delegated by a legislature. Professional advice or action has provided the evidence and example which has led governments, third party paying agencies and other nonprofessional leaders to either introduce limits on professional discretion or consider doing so.

It was the examples tested and proven by professionals, supplemented by new data, which led to abandonment of the idea that only peers could evaluate and influence professional decisions. Clinical practice guidelines (clinical protocols), second opinion programs, daily assessment of the needs of patients in hospital, mandatory referrals, mandatory stop orders, mandatory substitution and limits on hospital privileges are amongst the devices which limit professional discretion and were developed by professionals or their associations. These and other devices can now legitimately be examined by governments and other external parties who wish to improve the quality of professional decisions.

The idea of users and buyers and their representatives being anxious to verify and approve the decisions of the providers (sellers) is quite rational. The users and buyers are the ones whose health and money are at risk. External review of professional decisions was not sensible when it was assumed professionals routinely made the best decisions possible, but it is sensible in light of current knowledge, consumer control and third party payers.

Mandatory substitution rules in a hospital or in a statute eliminate professional choice (discretion) in the interest of greater cost-effectiveness (improved quality and/or decreased cost). Policy may stipulate that a particular laboratory test which is out-of-date will, if ordered, be automatically replaced by a more cost-effective test. This substitution may occur with or without the permission or knowledge of the user or professional. The automatic substitutions occur on the basis of professional recommendations rather than as unilateral administrative or bureaucratic decisions, although actual authorization of the substitution is likely to be by an administrator, committee, board, public servant, minister or government.

Drug formularies, which can be regional and provincial as well as institutional, limit the extent to which providers and users have access to selected drugs. A drug may be excluded from the formulary because it is out of date and should not be used or because there are other drugs which are adequate and which cost less. Exclusion from a formulary may mean the drug is totally unavailable at public expense, is routinely available at partial public expense or will only be paid for after adjudication of arguments supporting its use.

Limits on the locations from which insured services can be received can reduce the number of professionals from whom insured services can be obtained, as with cancer chemotherapy (but usually not surgical treatment) and expensive drugs such as those for thalassemia, dwarfism and organ transplant follow-up.

Professional choice can be limited by surveillance as well as by regulation. Practice profiles change when it is known that someone is examining them. It is not always known whether the changes produce better spending, but they probably do. Elective surgical volumes at the Foothills Hospital in Calgary in the early 1990s dropped 30% after surgeons were asked to justify their surgery to their colleagues, and it can be assumed (but not known) that the social benefits per surgical dollar rose.

Limits on professional discretion may identify the proper thing to do or they may merely identify decisions which are inappropriate. The latter will be more common than the former. Professionals will still be left with a range of options, especially when costs and outcomes are reasonably similar, and within that range of options their professional judgment will determine which option to implement, but inappropriate choices will have been eliminated or at least made unavailable at public cost.

Some of the above limits are in place by virtue of a statute, regulation or by-law. All have been supported by, and usually requested by, professionals. All lead to better spending and all limit professional autonomy. Increased external intrusion into professional decision making, with an associated reduction in professional autonomy, is inherent in the concept of shared management of the planning and delivery of health care. It should be accepted by everyone as legitimate. All energies can then be directed to implementation of the most appropriate limits on professional freedom.

THE MONITORING OF PERFORMANCE

Regulations can place limits on the freedom of professionals to order or deliver care, but in the absence of monitoring, the recommended or required patterns of care may not be delivered.

Alberta, British Columbia, Saskatchewan, Ontario and Manitoba have introduced thyroid testing guidelines. These policies have led to a 20-40% decrease in the number of thyroid tests performed, but the full effect of these guidelines may vary with the extent to which the decisions of physicians are monitored. The next steps will be to identify individual physicians who are not following the guidelines and then use educational or regulatory devices to assure compliance.

Monitoring user compliance is worthy of study. Persons whose compliance is poor may be receiving no benefit from services which are consuming scarce resources.

CLINICAL PRACTICE GUIDELINES

Clinical practice guidelines (clinical protocols, standards parameters) are of interest to everyone and everyone should play a role in their production, evaluation and use. In response to a Canadian Medical Association poll in which Canadian physicians were asked what they would like to have, practice guidelines were at the top of the list. (J. Atkinson, speaking at the 1993 conference of the McMaster Centre for Health Economics and Policy Analysis)

Clinical practice guidelines bring to the practising physician the same types of information as are provided to medical students and internes. In medical school, and in all other professional schools, teaching is dominated by the belief that some clinical choices are better than others, and students are asked to learn which choice is best. In a given clinical situation there are examinations which should be done, tests which should be ordered and treatments which are likely to be the best. These preferred choices are the essence of medical education and of clinical practice guidelines.

Clinical practice guidelines may be quite general, for example, a patient history should always be taken, or may be specific to particular groups of patients, for example, a set of directions for the handling of a patient with chest pain or a protocol for immunization of infants. They can be advisory or mandatory, and conformity with them can be monitored or ignored. The American Medical Association has prepared clinical guidelines for hundreds of clinical situations, primarily in an attempt to prevent this function from being assumed by governments and other paying agencies.

Clinical practice guidelines are often said to be unrelated to financial control, but regardless of original intentions and regardless of the wishes of professionals who write them, these guidelines will inevitably, and desirably, include financial considerations. They will be used to help everyone spend money better.

Clinical practice guidelines can suggest only the most perfect care, without consideration of cost, or suggest care which is less perfect but represents better spending. Care which is more cost-effective, even although less than perfect, will, when resources are scarce, allow more people to be served and will produce more social benefit with the resources available. Guidelines can provide information regarding the cost-effectiveness of each component of a protocol. If this is done then as resources become more scarce the least defensible components of care will be the first to be dropped or reduced.

Practice guidelines should not be produced by the medical staff of every institution. The guidelines should be developed with multidisciplinary involvement and by central agencies or groups with general credibility. Agencies and programs, and their medical staffs, can then concentrate on assuring congruence between the guidelines and what is done rather than spend large amounts of time trying to write their own guidelines.

In the five provinces with guidelines for the use of thyroid function tests there was no local discussion regarding which tests should be promoted. There was strong professional consensus and provinces acted on this consensus. There was no need to collect data retrospectively to see who had misused tests in the past. Prescribers were merely informed that TSH was to replace T3 and T4 as the preferred screening test.

Fifteen years ago the Canadian Council on Health Facilities Accreditation replaced the old retrospective audit of patient's charts with the prospective audit. In this process clinical protocols or guidelines were to be approved by the medical staff of a hospital and the Health Records Department would then collect information which would allow a committee of the medical staff to assess the extent to which the guidelines were followed. The process was inefficient in that it promoted self generation of guidelines rather than the acceptance of guidelines produced by credible clinical leaders elsewhere, but it was an innovative and contemporary addition to a moribund accreditation process. Unfortunately it never became a keystone within the accreditation process and it was not followed by other processes which evaluated the quality of professional decision making and the impact of hospital care on community health status.

The Canadian Medical Association in the middle 1970s sponsored the Task Force on Periodic Health Examinations. This Task Force produced its first report in 1978 and has produced supplementary reports since then. This Task Force, as the name implies, makes recommendations regarding preventive activities and procedures which tend to be repeated. These recommendations are clinical practice guidelines, although not usually referred to as such.

Sweden experimented with clinical practice guidelines for 15 years and in 1990 reported they were being abandoned as a cost control device. This failure was predictable. Clinical practice guidelines support cost control but do not place limits on expenditures. They help reduce inappropriate care and they are a tool to help make choices between spending options, but they are not a substitute for direct cost control measures. Guidelines in the absence of ceilings can increase rather than decrease costs. Guidelines in the presence of ceilings can bring greater equity and improved cost-effectiveness.

The explosion of new drugs, tests and procedures, plus new information on the cost-effectiveness of specific elements of care, plus new regulations and programs, make it impossible for physicians and other health care professionals to be fully informed. The regularity with which patients are simultaneously under the care of several professionals makes it difficult for each caregiver to have full information on current investigations, therapies and advice. The requirements for informed patient consent, and for choices which reflect patient culture and preference, make it increasingly difficult for providers to perform the required roles.

In the presence of such difficulties there is great need for aids to decision making. Software to assist health care professionals in their decision making has been produced by a number of companies and health care centres and the material is being constantly improved and expanded. Clinical decision support systems, of which clinical practice guidelines are a part, will eventually be accepted as essential to good decision making. Computer assisted decision making will become routine and, in many situations, mandatory.

246

PREDELIVERY SCREENING, CERTIFICATION AND/OR JUSTIFICATION

Procedures which question or limit professional decisions have been used extensively by institutions, programs and insurance companies in the United States. The Peer Review Organizations (PRO) routinely preoperatively screen proposed elective surgery on federally insured beneficiaries, and similar presurgical reviews are common with private insurance carriers.

Precertification (prior approval) and fixed payments for episodes of care are significant components of *managed care. Managed care* has altered the mix of services being provided and reduced the cost of some services, but the degree of improvement in professional decisions is uncertain. In addition, continuing increases in costs of health care in the United States indicate that external monitoring plus cost ceilings on episodes of care cannot control total costs.

There has been almost no predelivery screening in Canada. It has been practiced to a limited extent in cancer control agencies and some drugs are insured only with prior approval. Blue Cross Atlantic has introduced predelivery approval for a number of services as part of its recent introduction of managed care.

SECOND OPINIONS

Long ago paying agencies discovered that the volume of surgery was sharply reduced when proposals for surgery were reviewed by a second surgeon chosen by the paying agency. The concept has been tested extensively since then. Results have varied, with the effects being much less impressive if the second surgeon is chosen by the first one.

In 1985 a report of a United States Senate Aging Committee estimated that a mandatory second opinion program within Medicare (the American version) would eliminate 17% to 35% of the nine elective surgical procedures studied. In the 1970s the Vermont Medical Society, in response to high regional variations in tonsillectomy rates, instituted a number of actions including the mandating of a second opinion as hospital policy. The tonsillectomy rates fell to 10% of the previous level. (Wennberg, J.E., "Dealing with Medical Practice Variations: A Proposal for Action", Health Affairs, Summer 1984, page 23)

The requirement for a second opinion has also been applied to the use of expensive drugs and investigations. In some hospitals these drugs and investigations can only be authorized by selected individuals or departments. For example, all physicians on staff may be able to order expensive antibiotics or a CAT scan but the requests will not be acted upon until approved by selected experts. Similarly, a physician may refer a patient to home care but a home care case manager usually controls access to most home care services. The case manager provides the second opinion. In these examples, the second opinion is provided by someone acting as a gatekeeper. Unless the gatekeeper gives approval the service is not provided.

These gatekeeper second opinions should not be confused with the many other situations in health care in which a second opinion is sought. Referrals to specialists are usually for the purpose of a second and more expert opinion and not for the purpose of establishing the insurability of services recommended by the referring practitioner.

A few second opinion practices are probably not cost-effective, such as the routine and usually mandatory referral of X-rays to a radiologist for interpretation when the X-rays have already been read by some other physician such as an orthopedic surgeon. A broken bone may be diagnosed and treated before the radiologist sees the x-ray, but a second opinion is routinely received whether it is needed or not.

The rationale for this second opinion is that occasionally the radiologist sees something the orthopedic surgeon or other physician has missed. If this logic was applied throughout the health care system many decisions would be checked by another professional, and the use of a second opinion in many of these situations would be much more defensible than in the radiology example given.

Second opinions should not be required or encouraged, and on occasion, not publicly financed, unless their cost-effectiveness has been established.

THE USE OF EXPERTS AS FIELD ADVISORS

The use of *anti-detail* persons has, in the field of drug use improvement, been shown to be able to counteract some of the undesirable overselling of drugs which characterizes the visits of drug company representatives to physicians. Professionals are influenced by one-on-one contact with respected colleagues. This one-on-one approach has also been effective in other clinical situations. It may or may not be as cost-effective as other less labor intensive options.

On-site advice from respected experts was shown long ago to be a very effective continuing education model.

UTILIZATION MANAGEMENT (UM)

Utilization Management is a more encompassing term than Utilization Review, but the two terms are sometimes used interchangeably. It is not yet clear whether both terms will be replaced by *outcomes management*, which appears to be an even more encompassing and desirable term. If it is process which is being altered (in the interest of improved outcomes) then UM appears to be an adequate term.

Utilization management is a process for better resource use. It incorporates many of the individual devices already discussed. It relies on communication, participation, proactivity, improved databases and action. It proposes that the best quality care consists of only those activities which are necessary to investigate, inform, involve or treat the patient adequately. The aim is improved efficiency and effectiveness. Inappropriate decisions and activities are identified and reduced or eliminated.

UM is (depending on your perception) equivalent to, a successor to, or a forerunner to such processes as Quality Assurance, Total Quality Management (TQM) or Continuous Quality Improvement (CQI). The many terms represent a reasonably natural progression from, and integration of, prospective medical audits, management by objectives, participative management, matrix management, decentralized responsibility, utilization review and a number of other phases in the evolution of modern health care and its management.

UM can apply to utilization of dollars, equipment, services provided, services generated and/or location and sequence of care. It is incomplete if it does not include consideration of both cost and effectiveness of care.

Hospitals have for many years used a variety of tools to examine and improve professional decision making or increase equity. These tools include admission criteria, autopsy reports, clinical rounds, medical audits, clinical practice guidelines, adverse drug reaction reporting, second opinion programs, requirement of justification for services proposed, automatic stop orders on drugs, automatic substitution orders, limits on who may authorize selected high risk or high cost items, automatic review of long stay or high risk patients, daily assessment of patients to determine staffing needs, the use of case-managers and the costing of activities and patients. These and similar activities can be part of utilization management.

Most elements of utilization management can be only as successful as the available information will allow. There may be a need for routine reporting of both direct and generated costs. There may be a need for comparison of unit and provider costs with the costs of similar units and providers, for on-line monitoring of professional decisions, for measurement of the degree of congruence between clinical decisions and the choices known to be most cost-effective, for linkage of pre, during and post hospital data to produce a more total picture of care and of costs, for identification of delays in service and for special attention to high cost cases. Much of this information is not routinely available.

248

Utilization management will, as time passes, increasingly be a prospective as well as a retrospective process. The retrospective approach will not disappear, and for the immediate future it will at times be all that is possible, but it will be joined by many more on-line real-time systems.

UM will be less useful (and could be harmful) if it is seen as primarily an externally initiated monitoring exercise. This is the undesirable pattern which has become dominant in some of the 'managed care' experiences of the United States. The desirable UM process may be initiated by senior management but it must be responsive to and operationalized by all management levels and by all providers. It benefits from the wisdom and energy of all administrative and clinical staff, and will increasingly involve users.

UM could increase costs unless combined with cost control measures. Optimal professional decision making can be interpreted to mean 'do everything which has any chance of being helpful', which would be expensive. Spending money on Utilization Management or other programs to improve cost-effectiveness can also increase cost unless the evaluation and improvement of care are funded from within global and sectoral caps.

Utilization management is said to lower United States hospital costs by over 10% and physicians costs by 6%. (Wickizer, et al., Medical Care, 27(6) 632-647, 1989) Another author reported an 8.3% decrease in annual cost with utilization review. (Feldstein, et. al., NEJM, 318(20) 1310-1314, 1988) The UM considered by these authors did not include significant attention to the quality of professional decisions, and obviously has not prevented continuing rapid escalation of United States expenditures on health care.

Utilization management and clinical practice guidelines are given major attention in the 1993 agreement between the British Columbia Medical Association and the Ministry of Health. Hopefully the process will include many players other than physicians and government.

INFORMATION AND ITS DISSEMINATION

Cost-effectiveness will not improve as much as it should unless information is collected better, used better and disseminated more widely. If there is to be broad involvement of everyone in the process of better spending there should be full access for everyone to whatever information is available, subject to constraints associated with privacy, confidentiality and legality.

Regional, agency, program, population, client and provider profiles will help identify users, providers, populations and health care components worthy of special attention. The profiles will show costs, trends, appropriateness of decisions and other outcomes. This information has been shown to affect patterns of care when fed back to providers. The impact of feed-back to users is less well understood.

Feed-back to practitioners should be personalized. It should describe what the practitioner did, compare performance to the performance of peers and to the most cost-effective care, and suggest changes. Providers usually have a poor sense of the extent to which their habits differ from others or from what is considered optimum, and the provision of this information may lead to improvement.

INCENTIVES AND DISINCENTIVES WHICH AFFECT QUALITY OF SPENDING

Some incentives and disincentives are not financial. The strongest incentive should be the social benefits which better spending brings. Awareness of the potential for improvement and of the successful techniques available may also provide an incentive for change. The opinion of peers, associated with a wish not to be seen as an outlier, can motivate some professionals to change.

Tangible incentives and disincentives also alter patterns of care. Changes in physician's fee schedules can encourage or discourage delivery of certain kinds of care, for example, after hours service and care of the elderly. Payment for specific services, as with selected preventive activities in Britain, increases the delivery of these services by capitated providers.

Budgeting practices also provide incentives. Sectors, agencies and departments respond better when they know that they will be the beneficiaries if they are able to make better use of available funds. Penalties and rewards associated with quality of spending should lead to better spending decisions.

Education can provide consumers with incentives for better use of health care and better protection of health status. User fees provide some consumers with incentives for altered use of health care, but not necessarily better use.

THE 'BAD APPLE' THEORY

Considerable attention has been given to professionals whose practices were noticeably different. These statistical outliers have been given special attention by paying agencies and professional associations on the assumption that the main body of professionals were performing in an acceptable manner. This assumption must be abandoned. Those whose practice profiles are unusual may or may not be providing less value-for-money. Certainly they do not represent most of the decisions which have been shown to be less than optimal.

Evidence has shown that the profiles which are the norm are not good enough. It is the *average practitioner* whose practice patterns must change if the cost-effectiveness of health care is to be significantly increased.

DECENTRALIZED BUDGET CONTROL

Participation is one of the devices to promote cost-effective realignment of resources. Global budgets for cost centres throughout a region, agency or institution are one of the vehicles which can involve everyone in the search for more value-for-money. With the decentralization of budgets there is a greater possibility that everyone will, if they wish, be able to become aware of where money is spent, by whom and for what. Everyone can then have the opportunity to be aware of the payoffs and the hazards, to them, of altered spending patterns. Resource allocation becomes the domain of the unit rather than the property of a distant and isolated *administration*. Fire-fighting may be less common and planning better. The decentralized units can learn that it is they who benefit from improved use of resources within the global budget.

Participative decision making should improve the quality of decisions and reduce opposition to the desirable changes. The process should be dominated by openness and may use the zero-base budgeting approach in which all activities are considered dispensable until proven otherwise.

Ownership of a sum of money can provide incentives for better spending. If more can be done with the same amount of money no group in the cost centre need be a loser and the users and communities are winners. Other cost centres are not losers unless the decisions of one cost centre bring new costs outside of the budget of that centre, but the regulations governing the decentralized budgeting should have anticipated this possibility and made sure that new external costs are charged against the appropriate unit.

THE LOWERING OF UNIT COSTS

The improvement of efficiency has been given more attention than the improvement of clinical decision making, but further improvements in efficiency should still be sought. The lowering of the costs of an episode of care may accrue from lowering the costs of individual components of care, for example, lower costs of individual laboratory tests or lower costs per operating room hour. Lower unit cost may also be achieved from fewer services during the episode of care. Fewer services may be accomplished without changing the general pattern of care (fewer laboratory tests) or by substitution of some different but acceptable form of care (caesarian section replaced by vaginal delivery).

Lowering unit costs often occurs independent of changes in professional decision making, but the two are so often linked that there should be little effort assigned to deciding whether the improvements are in efficiency or in effectiveness. The bottom line is more benefit per dollar spent.

ATTENTION TO PREVENTION

There are many situations in which prevention is more cost-effective than treatment. These have been extensively discussed in earlier chapters. They include prevention within health care, as with immunization and contributions to the prevention of fetal alcohol syndrome, and prevention throughout other social systems, such as fewer sports injuries and fewer highway accidents. For the immediate future the health care system and budgets should concentrate on internal allocation to prevention when that prevention is possible by health agencies and personnel. The bigger reallocations should also receive attention but they require different evidence and techniques and involve a broader set of players.

PARTNERSHIPS

Partnerships are a powerful technique for better spending but one of the most difficult to use. They should, in theory, not be difficult to create, but the system has been a top-down centralized operation for so long that few leaders, especially in the provincial bureaucracies, have experience with the sharing of power.

Partnerships can be very informal. In this case, there can be no binding commitments as players share information, resources and opportunities. Partnerships can be formal but voluntary. There is a contractual relationship which was entered into voluntarily by all parties with the aim of achieving some common objective. They also can be formal but mandated; 'work together or else'. Most external demands are now made by a province but the pattern was widely used 30-50 years ago by private funders of hospital capital costs.

Partnerships are consistent with a number of contemporary themes including local control, participative management, shared responsibility and decentralization. Partnerships can tackle problems that no-one can solve alone. They can identify win-win situations. They can meld the experience and wisdom of the leaders in the field with the regulatory powers of the province.

This chapter discusses only partnerships for improved cost-effectiveness, but partnerships can also be formed to implement regional budgeting, improve coordination, establish local priorities, increase local control and implement healthy public policy.

Partners at the provincial level can include various components within the Ministry of Health (the Minister's office, the Deputy Minister's office, the Assistant Deputy Ministers and the many directors, coordinators and managers), other representatives of government (such as the Premier's office, multiministerial secretariats, research centres, Ministry of Finance), regional agencies, provincial consumer, provider and diagnosis specific organizations and private sector representatives. Partnerships at the regional level are equally important, and the range of possible players is even more broad than at the provincial level.

The many possible partners each bring something that no other player can bring. Governments bring a special legislative and regulatory power. Consumers bring their own unique points of view and can bring a political legitimacy which encourages top level support. Professionals bring a special knowledge. Boards and Councils bring the collective concerns of the region or community and their own level of authority. All players can contribute energy, resources, leadership, creativity, experience and power.

There are many examples of successful partnerships. In many communities agencies and institutions which had been competitors became partners when Ministries made it clear that consensus was a prerequisite to Ministry generosity or action. Government/physician joint committees have made progress on areas of joint interest, although the history of these committees is too short to be sure they will survive. Partnerships formed to address a highly specific problem can be extremely successful, as with the Ontario network to improve utilization of capacity for coronary artery by-pass surgery.

There are many reasons for partnerships either not developing or failing to succeed after formation. Common reasons which are difficult to overcome include unreasonable expectations, mistrust among partners and covert or overt sabotage by powerful players. Other reasons for failure are more able to be overcome, for example, an inability to identify ways of accomplishing the selected goals, lack of financial support, lack of data, poor understanding of the processes of compromise and consensus building, and failure to proceed as quickly as expected.

When the objective is better spending there should be no expectation of sudden and lasting success of all partnerships. The objective is a paradigm shift, and the shift needed may not be fully understood or fully accepted even by those who know that something of this nature is required. There will be a great need for tolerance as almost everyone struggles to do things which often are not welcomed and which most participants have not done before. There will be many mistakes and many unfruitful efforts, but the overall impact will be steadily upward if people hang together. The thread which can be the tie which binds is the fact that there is no alternative which looks nearly as good as partnerships.

The process will be disrupted by those who think they know more than anyone else or who wish a process which is safe, perfect and painless. Many will feel insecure in the face of no neat blueprint and few role models. Bureaucrats may feel threatened by a process in which they are merely players, in which they will have few vetos and in which many of the other participants have more relevant ideas and experience. Many will long for the old ways of confrontation, blame and private decision-making. Being proactive and responsible can be a terrible burden.

A number of factors favor the development of successful partnerships. (Figure 15.2)

THE FUNDING OF VALUE-FOR-MONEY ACTIVITIES

Improving spending is a basic management responsibility. Processes which evaluate the quality of spending, and which improve it, should be regularly funded from operating funds.

A request for provincial assistance is justifiable only when an activity has provincial significance. Proposals to public or private research or charitable agencies are not improper but they perpetuate the idea that the promotion of better spending is outside of the routine responsibilities of management.

Those who are responsible for assuring taxpayers and health care consumers that public money and health are in good hands must understand that the pursuit of better spending will not come cheaply, and the expenditures will never end. There is an excellent theme in the title of the popular process of Continuous Quality Improvement.

THE WINNERS AND LOSERS

The users are the big winners if our health care dollars are spent better. More people will be able to receive useful care at taxpayer expense, more tax dollars may be able to be available for other necessary services, and/or fewer users will be placed at risk as they receive inappropriate care.

Taxpayers will probably not see much difference, although public deficits will be easier to control and that brings long term benefits. Policy makers will be less pressured to provide more money, and will have more supportive partners, if value-for-money is the responsibility of everyone.

Some providers, especially physicians, but also chiropractors, laboratories, drug companies and others, will be losers. Some duties will be transferred to less expensive providers, and some services

Figure 15.2

FACTORS FAVORING SUCCESSFUL PARTNERSHIPS

Perceptions

Recognition that there are problems no-one can solve alone.
Recognition of mutual advantage in the partnership.
A reasonable level of respect for others in the partnership.

System characteristics

A dispersion of power. All partners must have some.
Leaders willing to support shared decision making.
Common goals.
An appreciation of the environment.

Process characteristics

A clearly identified and accepted plan.
Identified and realistic short term goals.
Sensitivity to legal, economic, political and cultural constraints.
A search for solutions in which almost everyone benefits in some way.
Universal access to information.
Avoidance of problems on which agreement cannot be reached.
Emphasis on conflict resolution and compromise.

---

now being provided will be classified as inappropriate and will not be available at public expense. Monitoring will increase, and penalties for inappropriate practice patterns could emerge. The financial losses of physicians will be less if a privately financed health care system is allowed to fully develop. Providers will benefit if more clearly defined guidelines reduce the likelihood of inappropriate litigation.

A new cadre of consultants and researchers will emerge to contribute to the value-for-money program. They will be minor winners.

SUMMARY

In 1972 Professor Archie Cochrane proposed a number of principles to guide health care spending. (Figure 15.3) These principles are almost as relevant to-day as they were in 1972.

There should be widespread acceptance that inappropriate expenditures are the largest current threat to those medicare principles which Canadians hold dear.

Some improvements in spending will come from improved administration, planning and policy decisions, but the biggest short term improvements in spending will come from improvements in professional decision making. Some of the improvement in professional decisions will come because of good administrative and policy decisions, but most will flow from adjustments by individual providers.

253

Figure 15.3

THE COCHRANE TEST*
1. Consider anything that works.
2. Make effective treatments available to all.
3. Minimize ill timed interventions.
4. Treat patients in the most cost-effective place.
5. Prevent only what is preventable.
6. Diagnose only if treatable.

*Donald W. Light, "Effectiveness and efficiency under competition: The Cochrane Test", BMJ 1991:303, 1253-4.

Very few of the products and activities which make up health care should be illegal or abandoned, they should just be used more appropriately. New cost-effectiveness information will steadily appear, and it will contribute to better decision making, but a better understanding of how to change professional habits and processes, and an implementation of the necessary changes, are even more important.

Improved spending will minimize public discontent with cut-backs in health care. If inappropriate spending is curtailed quickly then the funds currently available will, for the next few years, allow access by everyone to reasonable quantities of care of proven cost-effectiveness.

Any suggestion that professional choice might be influenced or controlled by government was until a few years ago perceived to be inappropriate interference with professional freedom. This perception is out of date. Intrusion by governments and consumers into professional decision making is legitimate and required and it will increase.

When there is validated evidence as to which professional decisions are desirable it is justifiable for regulatory bodies to require certain actions and decisions. Whether the tools used are clinical practice guidelines, mandatory second opinions, Utilization Management or something else, they all are restrictions on professional choice. These restrictions are unlikely to lead to immediate or identifiable changes in total expenditures on health care in Canada, but they will, over time, reduce the volumes of inappropriate care. This, in turn, will reduce pressure on the system and indirectly assist in cost control while improving social benefit per dollar spent.

Better spending of health care dollars requires knowledge of the health care worth buying and actions which reflect this knowledge. These objectives hold true whether the dollars are public ones or private ones. For public dollars, social priorities and health status improvement or protection per dollar spent should determine what is bought. When private dollars are being used the choices can be as different as the buyer wishes.

Completion of the change from political intuition and professional preference to policies dominated by cost-effectiveness will not be immediate, but it will happen. Improved value-for-money through improvement of micro decisions can occur more quickly.

Involved persons, whether providers, patients, planners, policy makers or administrators, cannot improve spending unless, first, inappropriate decisions can be identified, second, inefficiencies in the system can be identified and, finally, the inappropriate decisions and the inefficiencies can be reduced.

The development and implementation of guidelines and policies which promote better spending will not be easy. There will be negative effects for some users and complaints from many providers. The objective must be to minimize the negative effects while reaping the massive benefits which will accrue from reduction of waste and improvement of priority setting.

"No matter how perfect we make our environments, no matter how perfect our lifestyles, no matter how perfect our public policies or how high our collective wealth, there will never be enough public dollars to deliver all of the health care for which at least a bit of justification can be found, and not enough justification to spend large sums of public money on health care rather than other areas of social need. This being the case, it is sensible to learn, and as quickly as possible, how to spend our money wisely." (Quote from an unknown source)

Chapter 16

A Provincial Program for Better Spending

INTRODUCTION

The previous chapter described tools and techniques which can improve spending. This chapter describes a provincial program in which all players work together to improve health care decisions, in particular the micro level decisions made at the time of delivery of care.

Many of the tools and techniques described in Chapter 15 show great promise. Many have been tested in institutions and in research projects, and a few are in fairly general use. What is needed now is a plan which builds on the many random experiences and produces a synchronised, rational and ongoing provincial program for better spending.

In the face of financial constraint the challenge is to sustain the current level of social benefit, or perhaps a higher level of benefit, with fewer dollars. The goal is saving medicare. Whether the process is called more for less, greater value-for-money, improved spending, the reduction of waste, greater cost-effectiveness, Continuous Quality Improvement or Total Quality Management is not of consequence.

WHY A FORMAL PROVINCIALLY SPONSORED PLAN IS NECESSARY

The informal uncoordinated approach to the goal of greater value-for-money has not worked. Ministers and Deputy Ministers have asked everyone to please spend better, and everyone likes the idea, but only bits of the job get done.

Good intentions and sincere wishes are not enough. Commitment and good process are also needed, and good process for the handling of a complex task requires good planning. Good planning, in turn, requires objectives, targets, work plans, task assignment, communication networks, schedules, budgets and staff.

Uncoordinated and random efforts, mostly by teaching hospitals and Health Maintenance Organizations (in the United States) but partly by government, have proven that money can be spent better. They have shown that the task is manageable and have demonstrated the availability of tools and knowledge, but these uncoordinated efforts have not led to the generalized changes which are necessary. A pooling of experiences, skills and resources within a formal plan offers the best, and perhaps the only, possibility of reasonable progress towards the stated goal.

Experience indicates that when any health care sector is financially squeezed it first puts major effort into finding new sources of revenue or finding ways to transfer costs to other programs. Next it improves efficiency. Equivalent effort is not put into weeding out health care which adds little or nothing to the health status of the community.

Millions of users and their associations and advocacy groups are worried about the possible effects of cut-backs. All will welcome, and most will cooperate with, a program dedicated to better spending. Almost all now know that there is no new money, and there will be none in the future. Better spending is the only way to sustain the present level of protection with fewer dollars.

A formal and province-wide program for better spending will bring benefits regardless of its form. Performance will improve when the program is announced. Unfortunately the impact of the program will be quite limited unless there is sustained and tangible provincial commitment to a comprehensive plan.

The sponsorship and design of the proposed program cannot be left to, or assigned to, any single sector, interest or profession, although physicians will wish to be in charge. Physicians will have an important role in the program, but the broader public interest and the interests of the many other professions and interests involved can only be served by an agency which has an interest in all populations and all professionals. Government fits these specifications best.

Governments have options regarding the vigour with which they pursue the objective of better spending. The options vary significantly in their commitment and cost.

A province can wait until other jurisdictions have developed ways to reduce inappropriate spending and then copy the model which appears to be best. In the meantime the province can continue to talk about the importance of the problem. In 1993 the Ministry of Health of Ontario released a major long term care reform paper which stated "it has been estimated that inappropriate or unnecessary treatment for seniors cost Canada $4 billion in 1989". The entire report then proceeded to say nothing about how to improve spending. (Partnerships in Long Term Care, Ontario Ministry of Health, April 1993)

A province can establish a Commission or Task Force to examine options, or hire a consultant to write an expensive report with recommendations. These will kill time without being committed to anything.

A province can also, if it wishes, create and fund a provincially endorsed program to actively promote better spending and get on with the job. This is the option being proposed.

Ministries of Health have a vested interest in, and a responsibility for, optimal use of public funds. They are actively pursuing a greater role in the management of health care. They are more accountable to the public than a special purpose body or a private nonprofit agency. They have the resources with which to fund the program and the regulatory back-up which will, on occasion, be necessary. The Ministry can assure encouragement and support for all who wish to spend better but do not know how to get started. Regardless of who is responsible for resource allocation decisions (province, region, agency or individual) there is a need for a coordinated and continuing program to assist in the making of the best allocations.

Politically the program is a winner. Any Ministry can safely pursue more benefit per dollar spent. All of the players, including consumer organizations, support that objective. No special knowledge or skill is needed to wish to be a better shopper. Thousands of health care providers, managers, trustees and planners would like to deliver more health care to the public for each dollar spent. Many are working at being more cost-effective, but all would benefit from working within a network devoted to the task. They need a major ally with muscle and money to motivate, provide leadership and assist with staff training, information production, information sharing and the control of opponents. The Ministry must be that ally.

Everyone supports the principle of better spending and is committed to it. When the general support for better spending is combined with a participative, Ministry sponsored and field dominated process the only way the program can be a partial failure is due to bad Ministry management. If the field is genuinely allowed to generate most of the ideas and is given a major role in development of incentives, disincentives and regulations then chances of moderate success are high.

The final reason for Ministry leadership of such a program is the lack of alternatives. The status quo is wasting a great deal of money, and the field wishes help in adapting to cut-backs. Unless a better alternative is offered the proposed program should be tried, and a Ministry of Health should sponsor it. The province is not only better equipped to generate and sustain such a program than is anyone else, there is no indication that anyone else intends to attempt the task.

THE IMPORTANT PARTNERS

The long term control of health care costs while continuing to provide the public with a reasonable level of publicly financed health care will be possible only if the leadership, experience and skills of the field are added to the leadership, funding and regulatory ability of government. Cooperation and advice from the providers, users and the nongovernmental boards, administrators and planners of health care are essential.

The program being proposed emphasizes changes at the micro level, a level dominated by nongovernmental decision makers. These nongovernmental decision makers are the persons who must implement change, and they will cooperatively and willingly implement only changes which are seen as sensible and practical. Changes are much more apt to be seen as sensible and practical if endorsed by the implementors ahead of time. The top-down decision making process will not work.

A partnership with providers, consumers, planners and policy persons in the field is essential to the success of the program. These partnerships can only be successful and sustained if the province offers the field opportunities for meaningful involvement with a high degree of decentralized pluralism and with a high degree of local and regional control.

The field has the leaders and providers with experience in implementing techniques for better spending. The field leaders will often know the literature relevant to their particular corner of the health services network, whereas the Ministry often will not. The art of improving spending is in its infancy, but to the extent skills and knowledge do exist they exist primarily in the field and the community rather than in the Ministry or the universities.

Users and communities have a particularly important role to play. Only the public, or individual users, can identify and rank their problems, fears and objectives. It is they who can identify the health care choices which most accurately reflect local values and preferences. If the users do not play a constant and important part in the process, then the choices will be made by professionals or bureaucrats, and history suggests that providers and managers do not see priorities in the same way as they are seen by users.

THE RATIONALE FOR PLURALISM

Many approaches to improved spending have been used, and many appear to be successful. In the absence of an understanding of which techniques work best, and in recognition of the fact that the preferred techniques change as the situations change, it would be unwise to design a standardized province-wide program. It is more rational, and certainly will be more acceptable and motivating, to invite professionals, agencies and communities to implement the approaches which are most appealing to them. As time passes, pluralism should not be lost but there may be less flexibility allowed in situations in which certain tools and techniques have been shown to be either successful or hopeless. Use of the successful techniques may become mandatory and public funding of useless techniques may end.

POSSIBLE GOALS AND OBJECTIVES OF THE PROGRAM

The mission of the provincial program being proposed is increased social benefit per health care dollar spent. Within that general mission the program should define goals, objectives and subobjectives. The options represent a spectrum from which each province and its partners should select those of interest.

One goal could be to promote a Ministry and industry culture in which policies and decisions are routinely evaluated in terms of value-for-money. It could aim for reductions in the volume of health care in places and ways such that the reductions will have the least possible negative effect on consumers and communities.

Another goal could be to sponsor, fund and coordinate a decentralized province-wide program for the purpose of bringing micro level health care practices and decisions closer to those which are known to be most cost-effective. The program would, to achieve this purpose, implement, or assist with the implementation of, strategies and techniques which improve micro level decisions and sustain and increase the improvement over time. In the process, agencies and providers would be helped to become aware of the extent to which their own decisions conform to current evidence and expert opinion.

The program could aim to assist individuals and agencies to deal with cost constraint, and to strengthen cooperation between the Ministry and the field. It could invite the participation of all who have an interest in better spending of health care dollars. There could also be incentives and disincentives which promote more cost-effective health care.

The program could wish to prepare, or assist in the preparation of, action plans tailor-made for specific activities and programs such as home care or laboratory tests. Strategies and techniques would be adapted to the milieu and characteristics of the many different types of health care and health care agencies. The program could seek to accumulate and distribute (as software, videos and printed material) information on relevant experiences in Canada and elsewhere, and to assist in the production of audio visual material for use by groups and agencies wishing to participate in the program.

The program could promote and support the creation of regional, local and provincial committees to strengthen the program. The committees could be sectoral and/or multidisciplinary. These committees, along with other structures, would be designed to assist communities and regions to identify their priorities and select processes to serve those priorities.

The program could (and should) apply the same monitoring and the same standards to resource allocation decisions within the Ministry as will be expected of the field, and it could seek to maintain balance in the attention given to regions, sectors, populations, professions and types of health care.

There would be a need to identify the barriers to better spending and assist in the development of responses to these barriers.

THE CHARACTERISTICS AND PRINCIPLES OF THE PROPOSED PROGRAM

The program will be participative and collaborative. Central sponsorship, funding and coordination will be combined with the enthusiasm, skills and experience of those who deliver, use and manage health care.

The program will be flexible and pluralistic. *"Unity of purpose, diversity of means"*. (Donabedian, A., Inquiry, 25:173-92, 1988) Initiatives by all manner of groups, associations, agencies and individuals will be welcomed, and the devices used will be chosen by the field, subject to the understanding that there will not be central funding for processes and techniques which have been shown to be ineffective.

The program will be considered to be an ongoing function of management. Its activities will be integrated into the day-to-day management and delivery of care. It will be seen as ongoing research and development.

Users and communities will be full partners in the program. When there is disagreement between providers and communities or users regarding the priority of a physical, mental or psychosocial outcome the opinion of the communities and users is likely to be given the greatest weight. Local groups will be encouraged to give earliest attention to activities or services which meet the criteria for better spending.

The program being proposed seeks only to apply what is known. It aims to bring actions throughout the system closer to those actions which are known to be best. Much of the good evidence pertains to micro level decisions and the micro level is the most productive place to start.

The search for better spending will include attempts (i) to reduce demand by the use of cost-effective prevention, (ii) to reduce unit cost through improved efficiency and (iii) to reduce service volumes by elimination of activities which are not sufficiently cost-effective.

The program is likely to emphasize decisions in acute treatment hospitals in the early months of the program. These institutions have the most experience with the tools of better spending, the largest pool of experienced and well trained leaders, strong affiliations with useful university departments and the largest body of literature to call upon. As quickly as possible emphasis will be equally distributed among all sectors such as mental health services, home care, emergency health services, public health and long term care services.

During the implementation of the program there will often be identification of desirable changes which are cost-effective but which will increase costs. These practices should be considered for implementation when cost reductions have made funds available. The exercise is one of trade-offs, and services being provided should routinely become less generously funded if services not currently being funded are more cost-effective.

The program will adapt constantly to feed-back and experience. Some agencies will give early emphasis to increased efficiency, others to better professional decision making and others to protection through prevention. As experience confirms which approaches are most successful in given situations the partnerships will be able to consider incentives and disincentives as tools to accomplish the selected goals.

AUTHORITY AND ORGANIZATION

If a province opts for the creation of a provincial program there are several organizational and authority options available. The province could delegate the program and function to some legislatively created body such as a College of Physicians and Surgeons, some private nonprofit agency such as a Public Health Association, or a consumer association. The program could also be fully decentralized to regions. The Ministry could also locate the program staff within the Ministry and maintain strong Ministry control over the program. It can also locate the program secretariat within the Ministry but invite regional and local structures to work in association with the provincial framework. This is the recommended option. An earlier section sets out the arguments in support of provincial sponsorship of a pluralistic and decentralized program.

The program may or may not require new statutes, new regulations under existing statutes or amendments to existing statutes. For example, if a province does not already have statutory authority for approval of payment for a service in only selected circumstances then this authority should be created. Public Hospital Acts may require the performance of routine laboratory testing or X-rays which are no longer indicated. Limits on the functions which can legally be performed by a variety of health care professionals may prevent sensible reallocation of function.

Responsibility for the new program within the ministry could be assigned to a new organizational unit or to an existing unit, or could be dispersed to many units. Because all parts of the ministry will be affected by the program, especially the operating units who deal directly with the field, there are arguments in favor of either a new organizational unit or location of the program within a unit with a staff function. Attachment to a strategic planning group might be appropriate.

RESPONSIBILITIES OF THE MINISTRY

The program will require Ministry commitment and support, especially from the Minister and Deputy Minister. The support should include funding of a broad spectrum of central personnel and activities, and of decentralized activities which cannot reasonably be considered to be the responsibility of a region, agency or program. The Ministry should fund think-tanks, workshops and provincial committees, central and regional information banks (including printed material, software and videos), vehicles for information transfer among regions and programs (newsletters, electronic mail, reports) and compilation of information relevant to the program (annotated bibliographies). The Ministry is also the agency best able to reward health care sources who move towards the goals of the program. Ministries are best able to use regulations as a tool for better spending.

The Ministry should provide, from provincial data sources, information which will support the program. These data could include regional costs by health service sector and, where appropriate, service volumes and costs by type, agency, department and provider. All information will not initially be available but to the extent it is available (subject to legal constraints) it should be given to all partners.

The Ministries can, and should, promote, and cooperate with, national initiatives which promote better spending, as when meetings of Ministers of Health consider changes in the criteria and priorities of national and voluntary research funding bodies so that the projects supported by these agencies contribute more fully to better spending.

It will be necessary for the Ministry to reorient provincial programs, practices and personnel to support the program. Research allocations, innovation funds, incentive funds, program evaluations, global funding guidelines, resource allocation patterns, support for new and expanded programs and guidelines to service and planning agencies should all be adapted to complement or supplement the program for better spending.

Planned and ongoing actions throughout the Ministry are necessary so that ministry staff will know what is going on and will be able to contribute. Staff throughout the Ministry will need to be able to offer assistance to the field as well as make appropriate changes in the processes and decisions within the Ministry.

The reorientation within the Ministry will require a plan and a program. Meetings, briefings, workshops and written material may be used to acquaint ministry staff with the information with which they should become familiar. They should be aware of the experiences of programs promoting greater value-for-money, especially within their own sector of health care. Staff may need assistance with the idea of inviting the field to provide much of the leadership. Considerable effort is likely to be needed to acquaint staff with what is expected of them, and to identify desirable changes in Ministry processes and programs.

EVALUATION

Evaluation should not be a significant element of the first phases of the project. The eventual need for comprehensive evaluation should be kept in mind but an evaluation master plan need not be in place before the project proceeds.

Evaluation will, when introduced, be built around two criteria, namely the degree of congruence between what is known, or what is thought to be best, and what is done, and the extent to which consumer and community priorities are reflected in the delivery of care. Success of the first will be reflected in the extent to which inappropriate care has been reduced.

BUDGET

Better spending will not occur without both effort and expenditure.

262

If the health care industry spent 2% on R and D, annual expenditures in Canada would be greater than $1 billion. Total expenditures on basic and applied health care related research in Canada by governments, voluntary agencies and foundations and private industry (mostly the drug industry) probably do not add up to $1 billion, and little of this is spent on the applied R and D which the recommended program represents. Evaluating performance, improving performance and identifying and conforming to community priorities receives little attention.

If 0.5% of annual expenditures on health care were spent on R and D related to the relatively unserved areas just described the budget for these activities would be $5 million per billion dollars of annual health care spending. This would mean annual expenditures of roughly $10 million in Saskatchewan or Manitoba and $90 million in Ontario.

If 0.5% of budget could eliminate non-cost-effective activities representing 5% of previous spending the system would have an additional $45 million per billion dollars to spend on useful care or on services outside of health care which are also essential to improved provincial health status. Elimination of $10 worth of inappropriate care for every dollar spent on the new program is a reasonable expectation.

Funds for the program should come from the regular budgets of the Ministry and of involved agencies and institutions. It may be possible to generate some outside funding from foundations or the private sector, but the program should be designed to be publicly funded from operating budgets.

All phases of the program should be assigned a budget and budget overruns should be as unacceptable as overruns anywhere else in the system. The schedule of workshops, the number of outside persons hired, the communications networks created and most other facets of the program will vary with the generosity of the budget.

The budget in the first year can be relatively small. In the absence of experienced staff, without well organized information, and with other obstacles to overcome, spending in the first year may be as little as 0.1% of the budget of the Ministry of Health.

Provinces will determine whether the budget of the program should include the incentive payments which will eventually be offered, or whether these incentive payments should be found within the operating budgets of the sectors within the Ministry or region.

The budget may include the distribution of block funds to groups who assume specific roles, especially if the groups have limited capacity to finance their activities. Block funding of professional associations would be less indicated. They are interest groups as well as participants in this program and also have their own sources of funds.

STAFFING

Staffing will, because there is no new money, be from within the Ministry and within the involved programs, or will be replacement staff. The program will eventually require new job descriptions. Some positions should be permanent although changes in organization and function will be the order of the day during the first year or two and opportunities for flexibility should be preserved. Many staff will be on short secondments to the program from operating units.

Regional leaders may be added to the Ministry staff in some capacity, probably part-time, during at least the initial months of the project. These persons can be *de facto* regional coordinators who will work with Ministry staff to promote regional networks and programs.

THE USE OF CONSULTANTS IN THE PROGRAM

Consultants may be needed because they bring special skills or knowledge not present in the Ministry or because there is a short term manpower shortage. They can be a blessing or an expensive interference. A number of guidelines can increase their usefulness.

One protection is to require that consultants work closely and constantly with Ministry and/or regional staff. Through this relationship the skills of the consultants can be observed and learned by Ministry staff and others. Ministry staff will, by virtue of their constant participation, have an understanding of, and a sense of ownership in, the product(s) of the exercise. Staff will be more likely to accept the outcome and act upon it. The involvement of the staff should also assure a product which reflects practicalities, statutes and other ministry programs.

Consultants in the proposed program will often be helpful as participants or leaders in workshops or brainstorming sessions, or as advisors to agencies in the field who have an idea and need help to get it off of the ground. Consultants should usually not be hired for large projects and then allowed to go away for 1 to 2 years and come back with a very large report. The fee will be large and the product probably not useful. Ceilings on daily fees for consultants are reasonable.

As much as possible the `experts' should be persons from within the province or region, although going farther afield will occasionally be justified. When outside technical consultants are to be used they will be best arranged for by the Ministry, preferably for coordinated use in a number of activities (conferences, workshops, think-tanks, brain-storming sessions).

STRENGTHS OF THE PROPOSAL

The program utilizes the universal consumer and provider support for the concept of greater value-for-money. It emphasizes action throughout the system rather than on pilot projects or special studies. The flexibility and decentralization will appeal to the field. The entire process resembles a consultation process combined with action. The program will develop the skills and structures which will allow decisions to change quickly when additional information becomes available.

It focuses on positive changes rather than being preoccupied with the negative impacts of cutbacks.

WEAKNESSES OF THE PROPOSAL

This program proposal is simple in concept but complex in implementation. Performance and impact may not meet expectations. The model is unproven. It may be seen by the field as presumptuous and by the experts as naive. It is recommended that initiatives be led by a Ministry, and the field does not hold most ministries in high regard. The promotion of cost-effective choices will be seen by some professional associations, and perhaps by many physicians, as an intrusion into professional territory. It challenges professionals in the very area where they have felt most secure - their clinical decisions. A thorough evaluation process has not been described.

Resource allocation between sectors is not being examined. The program will not examine the manner in which funds should be distributed to various Ministries or to various sectors within health care. This may be seen as an avoidance of examination of senior staff and policy makers while there is scrutiny of the decisions of those who are daily in the trenches.

IMPLEMENTATION STRATEGIES

Implementation processes will have to be tailored to fit the budget, to the amount of opposition met or support offered and to the preferences of a Minister or Deputy Minister, but a few comments may be sufficiently generic to usually apply.

Don't be immobilized by the complexities and difficulties of the task. Begin quickly and simply. Paralysis by analysis will be a hazard. Aim for early successes, even if small ones. Do not think everything must be able to be started before anything is started. Be active on many fronts. Keep lots of balls in the air at the same time. Some initiatives will die and the losses will be more easily handled if other initiatives are making progress.

Work almost exclusively in friendly environments. Go where the program is welcome. This may mean working initially with only some of the hospitals, with only one department in a hospital, with only a few of the CHCs in the province and with some professional associations more than others.

Give first attention to high volume high total cost services for which there are identified criteria for appropriateness and for which there is evidence of inappropriate patterns of care. Every service area should examine its own spectrum of services to find activities in this first category. Next highest priority should be given to high volume and high total cost services for which there are poorly identified criteria of appropriateness but which are provided in very different quantities and/or at very different costs in different regions or institutions. It is reasonable to aim for the lower levels of utilization and/or costs when there is no evidence in favor of the higher levels.

Repetition will be much more important than innovation. Copy what has worked somewhere else. Within the guidelines of the program, support people in what they prefer to do.

Keep adaptations in the Ministry as advanced as in the field. This will require a specific strategy and plan to alter decisions and processes in the Ministry, and a schedule which is tight and honored. Do not have a long range master plan. Establish general goals but operationalize the program in modules of 4 to 8 months and adapt constantly to new ideas and new obstructions.

Emphasize appropriate use of useful and completely accepted investigations and therapies rather than the elimination of investigations and therapies which are never appropriate.

Stay at the micro level as much as possible. Avoid attempting to use the program as a source of advice regarding resource allocation at the macro level. Do not expect regulation to be a prominent part of the program in the early months, or even the first year. It will become an important tool when consensus in the field begins to strengthen and the field supports use of more than the voluntary route to change.

The program will need a name, preferably one with a catchy and appropriate acronym. Better Health through Better Spending (BH through BS) might not be a good one. There is also a need for a decision on whether or not to use the term cost-effectiveness. If it is to be used, and it is a good term, then definitional confusion should be anticipated and clarification prepared.

PHASE ONE OF THE PROJECT

Phase one will be completely within the Ministry. It will begin with discussion of the desirability of such a program, and will end quickly if the decision is negative. If it is decided that some type of program should be implemented then there are a number of strategic, tactical, legal, political, communication, organizational, financial and personnel decisions to be made before the Ministry announces its intentions to proceed. This preannouncement phase will need to consider many of the options raised in this chapter and identify policies around which the program will evolve.

During this phase detailed plans will be made to allow rapid contact by the Minister, the Deputy Minister and other senior officials with a broad range of consumer and provider agencies and groups as soon as the program is announced. A communication plan will be developed. Answers will be prepared for questions which are likely to be asked, and media kits will be prepared. Lists will be made of all agencies or groups who will, as soon as the program is announced, receive a customized or standard information kit and an invitation to participate.

Packages of material can be prepared, or begun, for later distribution to specific sectors, agencies, professions or clientele. The information packages should describe the principles and rationale of the program, the kinds of assistance available from the Ministry, examples of the actions agencies and individuals can take to increase the quality of spending and examples of the networks which will be created in the province to allow everyone to know what others are doing.

The program will need to be reasonably well described so that it may be presented to cabinet, the Department of Finance or others from whom approval must be obtained. Preparation of the program will require decisions regarding such policy areas as program budget, the extent to which funds will be spent outside versus inside the Ministry, the roles of outside agencies (including the extent to which professions will be represented centrally by the provincial professional associations versus colleges) and the extent of funding of outside agencies and groups.

There will be identification of the staff in the Ministry who will be part of the initial program complement. The Ministry will begin the compilation of a library of relevant data, software, articles, reports, videos and any other relevant material. This activity will continue in later phases.

Work will begin on advisory kits specific to selected activities or agencies such as CHCs, community mental health programs, prenatal care, emergency health services and diagnostic imaging. These aids to action will continue to be refined for many years, but a beginning should be made immediately. The aim will be to provide the field with a shopping list of devices and techniques which have been shown to improve cost-effectiveness of health care and to identify the places where these tools have been used. This activity could be deferred to Phase Two to allow early involvement of the field.

There will be partial development of the agendas and participants for sectoral or regional workshops or conferences through which the partners can become acquainted with the program. There will be identification of the resource persons who will be asked to play central roles in various task forces, discussion groups or other projects. Most of these persons will be from outside the Ministry.

Phase One should not be allowed to take more than 4 to 6 months. It could end as soon as cabinet and other approvals are received, in which case some of the activities in Phase One would begin in Phase Two.

PHASE TWO

Phase Two will begin with an announcement by the Minister that a provincial plan for better spending of health care dollars is to be implemented. This phase will be dominated by meetings, workshops, interviews and publicity designed to acquaint everyone with the general nature of the program and of their roles in it.

Phase Two will concentrate on finding allies, creating networks, identifying locations, groups and individuals who are anxious to proceed and isolating or satisfying those who are uneasy about the program. There will be discussions with agencies, groups, associations, educational institutions and local governments. Discussion will be for the purpose of soliciting partners, receiving advice, identifying persons and agencies who have a plan for action and providing and receiving advice and information.

Discussions with universities and colleges will include faculties, departments and programs of medicine, nursing, pharmacy, physical and occupational therapy, dentistry, chiropractics, optometry, social work, health administration, chiropody, respiratory technology, ambulance attendants, laboratory technologists, health records librarians and others. Contact will also be made with many associations including those representing health care professionals, the umbrella consumer organizations (such as those representing seniors, the physically handicapped, the psychiatrically disabled and children), and disease specific organizations.

Phase Two will include formally organized activities within the Ministry, and perhaps in more than one ministry, to allow public servants to understand and adapt to the new program. Some of the internal discussions might precede the announcement of the program. These discussions will acknowledge actions already underway in the Ministry whose objectives support the program and will introduce the necessary changes in many Ministry programs, documents, processes and guidelines. They will consider the impact of this program and its organization on established programs and on agencies such as regional planning bodies.

During this phase the active and competent supporters of the program will be identified, as will some of those who do not approve. There will be creation of many provincial, regional and local committees. These committees may be sector specific, disease specific or service specific, and most should include both providers and users. These committees will be important vehicles for transfer of information upwards, downwards and laterally as well as a source of ideas for action. Staff support for many of these committees should, at least initially, be funded by the Ministry.

Phase Two will include a number of workshops and the planning of many more. These workshops may be local, regional or provincial. They will be most productive if they deal with highly specific services or clients, and as much as possible they should utilize local experts. The main objective of the early workshops will be to identify the experiences and interests of a broad range of consumers, providers and policy people and reiterate the central theme of improved professional decision making. Selected and locally identified persons will respond to such questions as `What have you done in the last year to decrease unit costs and improve clinical decisions, especially the latter, and what do you think can be done in the near future?'.

As time passes the workshops should have more and more tightly controlled agendas and topics and should deal with only one or two specific questions or problems. Even with a tight agenda the average group will spend part of the time rehashing the problems of the world, blaming everyone else for them and emoting on favorite topics.

The minimum practical lead time for a workshop or conference of 25-150 people is six weeks, but this time frame is realistic so long as plans for the workshops are well developed before they are announced.

During Phase Two agencies will be encouraged to develop and test processes for the identification of the extent to which their practices differ from preferred practices. This information will help agencies to select activities most worthy of early attention.

By the end of Phase Two the province-wide exchange of information should be underway, and the communication and information dissemination vehicles should be available. A pattern of feedback, follow-up and information sharing should have begun to appear. During this phase there will be many examinations of the quality and volume of data, and there will be a need for attention to data deficits which emerge.

There will be a need to discourage, and not to fund, projects or activities whose purpose is the assessment of the cost-effectiveness of health care services and activities. To give emphasis to this area of basic research would be contrary to the main goal, which is to reduce the incidence of decisions which do not reflect current knowledge or professional consensus.

Phase Two is likely to take less than a year and will merge imperceptibly into Phase Three.

PHASE THREE

Phase Three will see the beginning or strengthening of the locally selected activities which will proceed with the help of centrally provided information and mixed central and local funding. The details of Phase Three cannot be known until earlier phases have been partially implemented.

PROBLEMS AND COMPLAINTS WHICH WILL BE MET

Professionals and users will raise serious concerns. There will be complaints regarding concept, process, technique and resources. Some professionals and professional associations will reject the idea of involvement of outsiders in the monitoring of professional actions, and will even more strongly reject the participation of outsiders in the development of constraints on professional decisions. Real or imagined surveillance will meet resistance.

The program will be seen by some as *another excuse for not providing necessary care -just another cost cutting exercise*. This criticism may arise especially when the appropriate professional decision is to recommend no action at all. The idea of doing nothing, even when there are no useful actions to take, is not always acceptable to providers or to users.

Users will at times wish to receive services which are not considered to be indicated. They will complain about being inadequately served, and may complain about their inability to buy unavailable hospital and physician care with private funds.

There will be concerns regarding the legal consequences of withholding care which is not considered to be cost-effective. There will be demands that services known to be cost-effective and not now available be immediately funded. There will be professionals who disagree with the findings of research or with professional consensus.

The program will be called doctor bashing. Some changes will decrease provider incomes, especially the incomes of some physicians. The changes made will affect some providers and users more than others and will be seen to be unfair.

The transfer of funds from care delivery to the program for greater value-for-money will be seen as another example of putting administrative jobs ahead of the delivery of care.

Methods used within the program will be crude and therefore vulnerable to criticism. Instant experts will be everywhere. They will create confusion and make change more difficult. Some academics will wish to be involved and will ask for processes more valid than can be implemented at this time. They may seek a level of methodological perfection not possible, and issues of terminology may assume undesirable proportions.

There will be a tendency to see change as all or nothing, whereas the usual change will be one of degree. There will be problems of time. The program will lengthen the working day of many professionals, administrators and others.

Many of the participants will not be well supplied with the necessary skills. They will have little experience with networking, outcome measures, user participation, defence of budgets and shared decision making.

As the program unfolds attacks will accelerate. Losers will become identified. Their resistance will be strengthened by the inevitable mistakes that will be made. There will be demands that the process *be reviewed*, *go more slowly* and *be properly evaluated*.

Some problems may arise from jurisdictional disagreements between professions or within professions. Within professions the struggles for influence are likely to be between the Associations (the union organizations) and the Colleges. The Colleges have been assigned statutory responsibility for the quality of performance of the profession, but the Associations frequently wish to have control over professional quality matters.

RESPONSES TO THE PROBLEMS AND COMPLAINTS

Response to the problems and complaints which are met should, if possible, be thoughtful rather than defensive. The program will survive best if it is characterized by adaptability and sensitivity associated with persistence.

Despite the inevitable legitimacy of some criticisms of the program, and despite the inadequacies which will appear and many will see, the participants in, and leaders of, the program need not be apologetic. The alternative to the proposed program is to continue present practices. An imperfectly performed effort to reduce unproductive spending, and to make decisions based on evidence or consensus, is better than a continuation of resource allocation on the basis of power, tradition, convenience and intuition. The best defence of the proposed program lies in the inadequacy of present practices and the lack of other alternatives for future action.

The program can admit its lack of skills and experience but defend the attempt being made. The necessary new mind-sets and the necessary new skills will not evolve unless a start is made.

The risks of the system as it now operates should be described to those who fear that some persons will die or suffer because of the new program. The expenditures on the new program can be justified by comparison of these costs to the costs of delivering inappropriate care. Concerns regarding the process by which care is declared inappropriate may be difficult to deal with because the process will be imperfect. Concerned individuals should, when possible, be invited into the process so that they may appreciate the difficulties.

Persons concerned about the current nondelivery of useful care can be told that if the program is successful there may be funds to provide some services not now available at public expense, although this assurance cannot be firm.

THE PREREQUISITES TO SUCCESS

Prerequisites to success include immediate, unequivocal and ongoing support at the top, adequate funding and staffing, competent staff, acceptance of nonministry leadership, the cooperation of a significant number of providers, provider organizations and consumer groups, ministry changes which reflect the themes of the program, primary attention to the reduction of inappropriate care, avoidance of an interest in finding out what is cost-effective and avoidance of too much attention to efficiency.

SUMMARY

This chapter describes a provincially sponsored, decentralized, pluralistic and ongoing program for better spending. The improved spending will be through greater efficiency, improved clinical decision making and attention to prevention, with greatest emphasis on improved clinical decision making. This program can be part of the transition of government from a funder of health care to a major player in the management of health care.

Agencies and individuals who wish to spend their health care dollars better need help. They usually do not have the ability to proceed alone. Ministries should earmark substantial funds within the health care envelope to support those who wish to spend smarter and spend less. This improved spending will make long term cost control much easier.

The program which has been described is not presented as a blueprint, although it could serve as one if any province or other jurisdiction so wished. It is rather a number of ideas from which any jurisdiction can pick what it wishes and which can be embellished and expanded in many ways. It is offered in the hope that it may assist someone to spend better.

The proposal builds on the experiences of the private sector which have demonstrated that corporate performance can improve when the talents of everyone are fully used. The program for better spending can be successful in provinces of all sizes, and will be effective regardless of the extent to which the planning and management of health care is decentralized. Decision making in organizations and regions of all sizes will be improved by the presence of a coordinated and provincially promoted program. Communities and individuals will also be assisted in their wish to influence policies and resource allocation.

Incentives and disincentives should encourage proof of cost-effective spending. Financial penalties should be applied to health care delivery sites which do not actively demand professional and administrative decisions which reflect what is known. If only 1/4 of health care has been evaluated, then with respect to that 1/4 the decisions made by health care professionals and by users of care should, when the care is being paid for with public funds, be consistent with current knowledge. Allocations of resources should favor providers who prove their clinical decisions are consistent with current wisdom.

The proposed program should not be confused with programs in other jurisdictions, in particular the United States, whose mandate is to accelerate assessment of the cost-effectiveness of health care activities. These other programs will continue to expand the body of advice which will allow health care dollars to be better spent, but the program proposed in this chapter has the goal of learning how to alter health care to reflect what is already known.

Evidence has confirmed clearly, and future evidence will confirm again, that professionals faced with similar situations implement quite different investigative and treatment routines with quite different costs and outcomes. These variations often continue to exist whether or not a preferred approach has been identified. The program proposed in this chapter aims to recruit all sectors of society and of health care into an integrated but decentralized program in which everyone seeks to eliminate the clinical choices which are not cost-effective.

The proposed theme and culture, with the related new mood and purpose, will be no challenge to agencies and hospitals who long ago accepted the basic premise of the program and who have been experimenting with the tools and processes of better spending, but the proposed program will be a major and difficult departure for many workers and agencies. There will at times be chaos, instability, misunderstanding and anger. These cannot be allowed to prevent progress. The community is entitled to a successful effort.

The theme of this chapter is not new. Writing in *Health Affairs* in the 1984 summer volume John E. Wennberg, in an article titled 'Dealing with Medical Practice Variations: A Proposal for Action', said:

"— doctors and their professional organizations ... can be expected to assume leadership roles in projects that deal with the cost and medical outcome implications of the variation phenomenon. But the feasibility of the plan will depend ultimately upon broad-based support from the private and public sector, including government."

We concur, but propose an even more central role for government.

Chapter 17

The Marketing of Change

INTRODUCTION

A provincially sponsored public participation program has many of the operational characteristics of the program described in Chapter 16, but the two programs have one fundamental difference. While Chapter 16 described how the public can be a partner in accomplishing a preselected goal, this chapter describes a program which invites the public to choose its goals. Both programs are pluralistic and ongoing but the difference in objectives is significant.

This chapter describes activities which will help individuals and communities to understand the changes in the health care environment and in health care, and to indicate their support or opposition to various policy options. All of these activities could be fully integrated with the program described in Chapter 16, and integration is an attractive operational option, but a province could decide to sponsor a public participation and information program without embarking on a major program for better spending.

Health reform faces a major dilemma. Canadians still expect unlimited access to at least physician and hospital services at public expense. Many health care professionals would like to give unlimited amounts of health care at public expense. Governments cannot finance this volume of care and, even if they could, they believe maintenance of high levels of health care spending is not the best way to protect the health status of communities.

Citizens should be given the opportunity for informed comment on a variety of policy issues such as the extent to which reductions in public spending on health care should be opposed or supported and where spending should be increased or decreased. The informed comment and opinion are only possible if the public is aware of the implications of spending in one place versus another. Understanding the options available to every province and every community requires information and a process for access to, and use of, that information. This chapter discusses the kinds of information needed by individuals and communities if they are to be informed partners, and it discusses the processes by which individuals and communities might be helped to understand and use the information and then convey advice to governments.

The program described in this chapter is meant to identify the priorities and preferences of consumers and communities. This is social marketing in which the marketer tries to find out what the customer wants. The term social marketing does not refer to the sale of health care by for-profit providers of care, nor to the processes through which a hospital tries to convince its region or community that it is better than other hospitals. It also does not refer to the process through which a hospital or any other institution or program recruits the public as allies in an effort to get more money from the government or collect more charitable dollars from the public. Social marketing refers to the process of working with consumers so that policy can reflect consumer choices and the trade-offs they prefer.

Marketing is, in this chapter, not used in the sense of the hard sell or of manipulation of the public. It is used in the best sense, that of providing users with accurate information so that they may, both individually and collectively, make the decisions which are best for them. There is a thin line between information and propaganda, and between brain-washing (which is feeding people a particular line until they believe it) and giving people nondirective assistance so that they may make up their minds. The aim is to stay on the side of information and nondirective assistance.

Marketing with the purpose described is an essential part of the modern consumer era. Governments and experts wish to see changes in publicly financed health care, but the public loves some of the system as it is. Should the politicians push through the changes and politically survive if they can, or should they spend public money on a program of information and involvement which will allow consumers and taxpayers to be knowledgeable about what is happening and then decide for themselves whether to accept, encourage or oppose some or all of the changes?

The proposed program is an exercise in community development. It is a program to assist people to find and pursue their common interests. A community development exercise does not presume to know what direction will be chosen by the community. It seeks to help the community identify common goals and then work to reach them. If the community development approach is used well, then one can hope that the public will decide reduced spending on health care is a good thing, and hope that they will accept the idea of fewer physicians providing publicly financed care, but it should be understood that these may not be the positions which are chosen by communities and tax-payers.

THE PUBLIC HAS A RIGHT TO FEEL CONFUSED

Consider some of the confusing challenges and changes presented to the public by a myriad of authors, bureaucrats, politicians, professionals and other leaders.

After decades of believing that physicians and other health care professionals give reliable advice and appropriate care the public has now been told that a significant percentage of health care is not worth what it costs and often may bring more hazards than benefits. After a period of open-ended spending associated with the promise of unlimited access to health care the public is now told there will be, and should be, tight caps on public spending on health care. They have been asked to believe that the spending restraints do not represent a threat to health. Having become accustomed to the idea that health care is extremely important to good health, the public is now told that they will live longer and have a higher quality of life if some health care dollars are spent on job creation, divided highways, the environments and community protection. They have been told there are too many doctors, but they still sometimes cannot see one when they wish to and some families cannot find a physician who will make them part of his or her case-load. Having for generations been taught that physicians were the most important health care workers the public now see, or will soon see, an expanding number of professionals with the ability to prescribe, order laboratory tests and X-rays, and see patients without referral from a physician.

Canadians have been told that it is their right to decide what health care they wish to receive, but most have lived all of their lives believing that the health care decisions will be made, and ought to be made, by a health care provider. They have been told, and most believe, that user fees for physician and hospital services are terrible, while at the same time they know that other important health care services are not be available at all at public expense. The public is constantly told by politicians that medicare is sacred and will not be tampered with, but in every province there are overt and covert decisions and policies which reduce access to some element of health care. Physicians and nurses regularly spend large sums on media campaigns describing how the health care system is falling apart and must be better funded by government, but the government and a vast array of experts say there is enough money in the field. How do Canadians know who to believe?

Having become convinced that physicians and hospitals are central to good health the public now has deep concerns about reduced access to these services. Hospitals, which were and to many still are, the temples of the system, have been replaced by community care as the area of growth. The health care system is being called the sickness system, with health being the responsibility of all departments, governments, agencies and individuals rather than the exclusive domain of Departments of Health.

The public have not yet been involved in widespread and organized discussions of the changes which have occurred and of trade-offs which now must be made. Having been told that 15 to 30% of health care is either useless or of very little value, the public has not yet been told which part is useless or of very little value. They may or may not know that the gap in health status and life expectancy between upper income and lower income populations has increased rather than decreased since the introduction of universal health care insurance in Canada and Britain.

The public cannot be expected to assess the importance of the many changes and opinions, and understand their implications, unless they have more reliable access to understandable information and are offered organized opportunities to discuss the changes and options.

ISSUES

Public discussion of policy options could assist the public to develop their own answers to a number of questions such as:

a) Should governments spend less on health care? People are more likely to support reduced spending on health care if they believe they can receive essential health care with less spending. If they become convinced that less health care can protect their health just as well as the amount being delivered now they will know that some of what they got before should not have been provided. If they believe they were provided with health care that did not need to be delivered they will know that some of the professionals who provided the care made inappropriate decisions. Perhaps this line of reasoning will lead the public to support less spending on health care.

b) Should our health care system be one tiered or two tiered? Should the amount of health care a person receives depend partly on publicly funded institutions and programs and partly on the amount of private money a person has to spend?

c) Is too much money spent trying to delay unavoidable death?

d) Is too much money spent trying to prevent a death due to imperfections in publicly funded health care? A death is just as final when caused by a preventable cave-in at a mine as when caused by failure to obtain a heart or kidney transplant. In each case additional public spending might have prevented the death.

e) Should there be greater autonomy for health care professionals such as physiotherapists, midwives and nurse practitioners?

f) Should some health care dollars be transferred to other areas of social spending?

g) Should only a limited number of physicians be able to provide insured services? Is it desirable that all physicians be able to send bills to the public medical care plan?

h) Is it essential that everyone be able to go and see any doctor they wish at public expense?

i) Should there be regional or local health care budgets which are under the control of local governments or organizations?

The answers preferred by the public will not be known unless the public is given information and is given the time and opportunities for open discussion of the information.

SHOULD GOVERNMENT SPEND MONEY ON PUBLIC PARTICIPATION?

If the answer is *no* then this chapter is irrelevant. If the answer is *yes* then the question is *How?*.

When deciding whether to invite the public more fully into the policy selection process governments may choose to consider philosophical, political, tactical and economic consequences. To a centralist the idea of increased public influence over policy is philosophically unattractive. To a centralist a government is elected to govern and it should get on with it. In terms of tactics, there are significant obstacles. How can the public be involved, and how much should be spent on that involvement? Speaking economically, participation comes with a hefty price tag.

Depending on the level of government commitment, there may or not be a formal plan for public involvement. If the process is considered to be of high priority then someone will prepare a plan. If lip service is unavoidable but the idea is unattractive, or if the idea is attractive but of low priority, there will be no plan. If a formal plan is considered desirable it can operate independently or be merged with other activities. A government could decide that the public information objectives will be adequately met through implementation of the program described in Chapter 16 (the involvement of the public in a program to promote greater value-for-money). The value-for-money program could be seen as the best vehicle through which the public will become aware of the changing face of health care and of the trade-offs which need to be made. This is a viable option and may be the best one. It is contingent upon the provision, by the Minister and the Ministry, of the funds, the commitment and the leadership required by the program proposed in Chapter 16.

Involvement of the public in a discussion of health care priorities can also be piggy-backed on almost any other public consultation. Any government/community examination of the clean-up of toxic dump sites, the use of pesticides or herbicides, the building of a new airport or the community use of schools can quite appropriately look at the implications of the choices to the health of the community. Examination of all of these issues is more complete, and the perspective of the audience better preserved, if there is comparison of all the social benefits and costs of the various alternatives. Government can also decide that there should be a separate program to assist the public to arrive at a more informed opinion regarding its choices for the future of health care.

Government could believe that increased public understanding and comment on the issues is important but does not need any formal program. This is the current choice in those provinces which sincerely like the idea but assign no resources to it. This choice is inexpensive and not controversial. It does, however, leave the public to receive its information from the media campaigns of physicians, hospitals and other providers with money to spend and self interests to protect, or to other sources which may or may not provide the types or quality of information needed. Whether there is a plan and a budget will say a great deal about whether there is sincere interest in increasing the degree of public awareness of the issues in health care and of their implications, and whether public advice is wanted.

THE TECHNIQUES OF MARKETING THE NEW HEALTH CARE

The central tools and techniques are information, organization, planning, community development, funding and pluralism. A well funded and well planned program will be adapted to many levels of sophistication and education, many different age groups, many different disease and disability related advocacy and user groups, and many cultural groups. Presentations will have to be customized to the many audiences. The program will utilize the full spectrum of communication devices. There could be the fullest range of involvement of service clubs, community groups and associations and athletic, occupational, cultural, ethnic, religious, political, educational and other organizations.

The program is likely to be multi-ministry. It will involve at least health and education, and would benefit from the participation of municipal affairs, social services, recreation and culture.

RELEVANT INFORMATION

Many members of the public are already acquainted with much of the descriptive information in earlier chapters, such as that on primary prevention. There will be less awareness of the policy options which need to be considered so that trade-offs can be selected.

It is reasonable to regularly remind taxpayers and users that governments can only spend each dollar once. Everything is a trade-off. Opportunity costs must be known before the desirability of a particular expenditure can be known. Sensitive and tolerant foster homes may be very important to the future (and to the health) of unwanted or disturbed children, but foster homes are funded from the same financial pool that funds health care. Should expenditures on foster homes be reduced so that more funds are available for physician and hospital services, or should priorities be reversed? These choices should reflect public rather than provider priorities.

Information for individuals and communities should as much as possible be expressed to reflect local realities. Real numbers can be used to illustrate the magnitude of local spending on each component of publicly financed health care. Local health care expenditures can be compared to spending on snow clearance or interest on debt or police services or education. This type of information will allow people to visualize the losses and benefits of decreasing and increasing spending in various areas. Citizens and communities have a right to know what savings would be associated with various service cut-backs such as a 5% reduction in the number of physicians or a 5% reduction in snow clearance, and the hazards and benefits of each. Description of local events which have led to recent deaths, illness and injuries, and of expenditures in the community on various programs and types of persons, may be more meaningful than national or international ratios and quantities. Every province should describe to its people what can be done with $5 million or $25 million or $100 million. What impact would reduction or expansion by these amounts have on home care, community mental health services, specialist physician services, public housing, subsidized day care, divided highway construction or community safety, and what impact would the changes in the various programs be likely to have on the health of the population of the province?

The program can compare the impact of various programs in which additional public spending could have saved a life or have improved quality of life. Recognition should be given to the fact that persons killed, injured, made ill or placed at risk outside of health care are usually fully healthy, whereas the ones who are damaged or allowed to die because of a deficiency in health care may already be seriously ill or injured. Information presented within this perception of risk will inevitably make the public aware of how seldom people die because of an absence of access to health care, but how often they die, are injured, become ill or suffer a decreased quality of life because of deficiencies in other public policy sectors.

The public could be presented with the kinds of benefits which come from different services and should be asked to indicate which general categories of benefits should be partially or fully paid for with tax dollars, or which should not be paid for at all. Anecdotes and individual cases may not carry much statistical weight but they are understandable to everyone and should often be used to make a point

A public information program can have both an ongoing information function and a fire-fighting responsibility. Ministries and planning councils are not always well prepared for the headline creating events which occur or are manufactured, and a regional or provincial unit with a great deal of information at its fingertips could be useful to keep isolated events in perspective.

Discussion of the factors affecting quality of life, and of what should be done about them, is much more value dominated than discussion of deaths and injuries but should not be avoided because of this. Many of the solutions involve culture and ethics much more than the spending of public money, for example, child rearing practices, the role of women in society and the environment in classrooms and workplaces. These discussions can reinforce the general knowledge that secure, confident children grow into stable productive adults, and that happy supportive households have less stress, violence and social pathology of all kinds.

There will be a need for curriculum material appropriate to elementary, intermediate, high school and post secondary education. The presentation of information, concepts and options should begin in elementary school and continue indefinitely.

HAZARDS AND PITFALLS

Although information is essential to participation, information transfer is not the objective. A public participation program should not be allowed to concentrate on describing the system, its costs, its statutes or any other feature. The objective is to involve the public in the making of choices, and information is provided only so that the choices can be better understood. The choices themselves, the options, must remain front and centre.

Individuals and groups should, as much as possible, be obliged to make choices. Persons who want more of the services that are important to them, or who do not wish to see reduced spending in the areas of specific interest to them, should routinely be asked to indicate who should be the losers. Opinion polls have shown that the public may ask for no user fees, no reduction in the number of physicians, no reduction in the range of insured services and no limits on treatments. At the same time they may support more spending on health promotion, more attention to prevention, higher levels of community safety, better public education and control of deficits. They should routinely be asked to indicate whether health care money should be transferred to other activities or vice versa, and they should be given access to enough information to indicate the opportunity costs of their choices. The information need not be detailed but it must be as honest as generalizations will allow.

Audiences may at times be single issue oriented, especially if meetings or hearings are convened specifically to discuss health care. Whenever possible a mixed audience should be sought, This is most assured if other factors dominate in determining who will be in the audience, as when the audience are members of a service club or an academic class. In a mixed audience the persons who wish savings at the expense of someone else will be less likely to be able to avoid making their recommendations in the presence of those who will be affected. The confrontations may at times be acute, but these confrontations will illustrate, to the public, the difficulties facing governments.

Some of the public will place a strong emphasis on saving lives without giving similar attention to protecting or improving quality of life. This emphasis on life saving may also be promoted by some health care professionals, and preservation of balance may require a planned effort to assure participation of persons to whom housing, transportation, income and preservation of the family unit are essential to health.

There are unlikely to be any meaningful measurable outcomes from a public participation process, and therefore there can be no defence of the spending other than a basic belief in the concept. The extra-parliamentary process must be believed to be one which strengthens democracy, reduces public apathy and reduces disrespect for government or it will not be seen as worth beginning or preserving.

It would be wrong to think this type of public participation program will go smoothly. The first sessions in most communities will be 95% government bashing. If, however, those responsible for the program can hang in for a while the venom may gradually become mixed with a serious wish to understand and to contribute. The process will move on to less anger and a different set of community spokespersons.

At early meetings the microphones and the discussions will be dominated by the bombastic demanders, but later leaders will often be persons who appreciate the gravity of the situation and who appreciate the opportunity to participate. They will, at least sometimes, wish to assist government in its desire to escape the task of doing everything for everybody, and the current fiscal environment will promote reality. In some communities, and with some consumers and providers, the phase of general abuse will never end.

The purveyors of descriptive data will be a menace. They will wish to enmesh all participants in such an overload of descriptive information that the policy options will be lost. Trees will be endlessly dissected but the forest will not be seen.

Controlling spending (staying within budget) will require care. Community studies can easily cost $10 to 20 per capita annually, and this does not finance any of the province-wide infrastructure which will be needed if there is to be good sharing of information and the development of the various sources of information.

THE COST OF A KNOWLEDGEABLE PUBLIC

Few things that are important are cheap.

The staffing and other costs associated with better information for communities and for specific user groups can be at whatever level a province or region desires. Something good should come from any well thought out program. In the absence of clearly established and measurable outcomes from public participation it would be best to merely budget a percentage of health care spending (for example, 0.2%) and learn from experience.

There can be an expanded federal role in the funding of public participation programs. The experience and tools developed in any province will be of national relevance.

SUMMARY

Opinion polls provide a picture of public wishes and feelings, but they do little to provide the public with information. The information which has led governments to wish to reduce spending on health care has not been effectively presented to the public. The public cannot be expected to contribute to the debate over the future of publicly financed health care unless they are offered a concerted, organized and understandable presentation of the policy options and of the implications of the options.

It is clear that many Canadians wish to have access to endless physician and hospital care at public expense, and that they do not expect similar access to drugs or dentists. It is not clear whether they are aware of the practicality of reducing the volume of unproductive health care. It is not clear whether they might, if better informed, support less spending on health care. There has been little organized public discussion of the circumstances under which the public supports a requirement for personal sharing in the costs of health care, of the degree of public expenditure which is appropriate for the moribund patient, or of the desirability of allowing people to buy additional care with their own money when they consider the care available at public cost to be inadequate.

The third annual Vienna Dialogue on Health and Social Policy (WHO Regional Office for Europe) in 1989 asked governments at all levels to directly support activities which allow communities to share information and actively participate in policy development. A provincially coordinated and financed program can support such activities and sharing.

Organized and sustained public discussion may strengthen acceptance of the fact that improvements in health come from better schools, highways, workplaces and homes as well as health care, and that death or lower levels of health caused by hazards in our physical, economic and psychosocial environments deserve the same attention as similar hazards which arise from inadequacies in health care.

Chapter 18

Controlling Drug Utilization and Public Spending on Drugs

INTRODUCTION

Chapter 15 described devices which improve the quality of our health care spending. Chapter 16 described a provincial plan to improve spending, and how that plan might be implemented. The contents of Chapters 15 and 16 apply to the pharmaceutical sector as well as all other health care sectors, but expenditures on drugs offer such special opportunities for better spending and for provincial leadership that they have been given a chapter of their own. Concepts and techniques described in Chapters 15 and 16 have been modified in this chapter to reflect the special challenges and opportunities associated with pharmaceuticals. This chapter should be read in combination with Chapters 15 and 16.

Inappropriate drug use occurs when a drug is used when no drug is indicated, when use of a drug is indicated but the wrong drug is used, when the best drug is used but for the wrong period of time, in an incorrect dosage, in the incorrect form or with an improper schedule, when the drug used is clinically appropriate but is less cost-effective than another available drug, and when the drug used is normally appropriate but is inappropriate in combination with other drugs or substances being used.

Whether or not a province decides to implement a program for improved spending throughout the health care network, every province should invest in a major effort to improve drug use. A province could even use a general program for better drug use as the introductory phase of a program for better spending throughout the health services network.

WHY THE COSTS AND UTILIZATION OF PRESCRIPTION DRUGS ARE OF CONCERN

Canadians consume more drugs than the residents of most other industrialized countries. (Carruthers, G., T. Goldberg, H. Segal and E. Sellers, Drug Utilization: A Literature Review, Toronto 1987) The universal drug plan in Saskatchewan in 1986-87 processed about six prescriptions per beneficiary. (Pharmacoepidemiology Unit Information Package, 1988) The elderly population, which grows at two to six percent per year (depending on the province), has the highest drug utilization. When the Saskatchewan drug plan was universal, and with user fees for all age groups, senior citizens utilization represented 39% of total consumption. (Globe and Mail, May 1/92) In Ontario in 1990-91 the provincial drug benefit plan paid for about 27 claims per senior citizen. The insured claims per person had been as high as 28.5, but this was before preliminary tightening of payment for nonformulary drugs.

Total public and private spending on prescription and nonprescription drugs represented 14% of Canadian health care expenditures in 1990. (HWC, provisional estimate, 1991) Three years earlier the figure was below 12% and in 1980 was below 10%. The costs of public drug programs have been rising at 15-20% per year. This increase occurred despite provincial efforts to control expenditures on drugs. A decade ago, expenditures on drugs were divided rather equally between prescription and nonprescription items, but the prescription component is now dominant.

Expenditures in Canada on prescription drugs rose from $1 billion in 1988 to $1.9 billion in 1991, and the extension of patent protection will maintain, if not accelerate, this rate of increase. The patent extending legislation of 1993 (Bill C-91) was even more damaging because it was retroactive to 1991. The many applications for the licensing of generic drugs which were submitted while the legislation was being developed were lost when Bill C-91 was passed.

Drugs are not targeted for increased public spending. Most governments have stated a wish to increase spending on community health services, long term care, health promotion, mental health services and primary prevention, and the drug budget is one of the places governments wish to find dollars for transfer to areas of higher priority.

Prescription drugs are overused and overpriced. No government need feel unfair if it develops devices to lower the cost of drugs or reduce expenditures on drugs. The generic drug manufacturers have reported that the average price per pill for new drugs coming on the market (from the brand name manufacturers) rose from $1 per pill in 1987 to $3 per pill in 1991. The prescription drug industry regularly reports profits two to five times that of other industrial sectors, and it reports these profits despite spending $10,000 per year per doctor on marketing. Within the pharmaceutical industry return on equity rose from 12% in 1977 to 27% in 1987. (Statistics Canada)

The costs of drugs have become even more difficult to control as the ownership of drug companies has moved to large multinational conglomerates who see drug portfolios as one of their most reliable profit centres.

THE COSTS OF PROVINCIAL DRUG PROGRAMS

The big determinants of expenditures by public drug plans are the number of persons covered, whether or not there are user fees, the range of benefits, the amount of effort being put into improving prescribing, and the average cost per prescription filled.

Per capita costs vary significantly among provincial drug plans. (Table 18.1) If Ontario had in 1990/91 implemented the Manitoba level of patient co-payments and used the Manitoba list of insured drugs, and if the Ontario use of drugs had been comparable to the experience in Manitoba, Ontario could have insured the entire provincial population for about half of what was spent providing deluxe first dollar coverage to 20% of the Ontario population.

WHY DRUG USE IMPROVEMENT EFFORTS WILL SUCCEED

Health care institutions, faculties, professional associations, professional colleges, consumer groups, commissions and task forces, and the drug industry, have all expressed support for

Table 18.1

PER CAPITA COSTS OF THE MAJOR PUBLIC DRUG PROGRAM IN THREE PROVINCES, 1990/91			
	Saskatchewan	**Manitoba**	**Ontario**
% people covered	100%	100%	20%
Per capita costs per person covered	$90	$49	$475+

280

Table 18.2

	Provinces without copayments		Provinces with copayments	
PUBLIC EXPENDITURES ON DRUGS FOR SENIORS IN FOUR PROVINCES 1990/91				
	Ontario	**Quebec**	**Manitoba**	**Saskatchewan**
Per capita cost	$570	$447	$194	$257

improved drug use. Many of these, especially teaching hospitals, have their own programs for improved drug use. Any government which chooses to give a high priority to improved drug use will have many allies.

The misuse of drugs occurs as a result of inadequate professional and consumer decisions rather than from deficiencies in the products. Drugs are evaluated much more thoroughly before entry to the market than are equipment, diagnostic tests and surgical procedures. Changes in decision patterns should be made easier by the inherent quality of the drugs themselves.

There have been many trials of many techniques to improve drug use and improve spending, and many of the techniques have been proven to be useful. There is a large literature on drug utilization review (DUR) and drug utilization management (DUM), and rapid benefits will accrue if the current dispersed and usually unrelated efforts to improve drug use can become more coordinated and widespread.

The fiscal impact of Drug Utilization Management (DUM) programs is impressive. Savings may be as high as 20 times the costs of the program. Implementation of a DUM program for antibiotics alone would save Ontario hospitals $24-30 million annually. (Third submission of the Canadian Society of Hospital Pharmacists, Ontario Branch, to the Pharmaceutical Enquiry of Ontario, July 1989)

WHY PROVINCIAL LEADERSHIP IS NEEDED

Hospitals, Health Maintenance Organizations, the Veterans Administration in the United States, community health centres in Canada and other agencies and programs have demonstrated the extent to which drug utilization can be improved. There is, however, no indication that the experiences of these agencies will significantly alter community drug use, no indication that the isolated efforts will coalesce into a comprehensive and sustained network, and no organizational or financial base from which comprehensive and integrated drug utilization management might flow.

There is a need for an umbrella agency able to promote the transfer of information, the production of regional, provider, agency and user drug profiles, the production of integrated and on-line data-bases and the participation of a broad mix of users, providers and payers. If this umbrella agency is to be accepted by all players it should not be dominated by any one of them. A public agency is most likely to have stable funding, and a public agency has the capacity to use regulatory powers to supplement other efforts when there is a consensus that regulation is indicated. When public funds are being used to pay for drugs there is an added incentive for public sponsorship of a multi-party DUM program, but there is merit in the public sponsorship, coordination and partial funding of such a program even when drug costs are borne primarily by private payers.

The great majority of individuals and agencies are likely to be overwhelmed by the task of identifying and correcting misuse unless generously assisted and encouraged to change. The frequency of misuse, and the many ways in which it can occur, demand a coordinated program. The province is the only player able to lead the kind of coordinated, communicative and pluralistic program needed. The province on its own cannot do much about misuse of drugs, but provincial sponsorship of a program in which everyone participates could convert local successes into province-wide successes. Provincial sponsorship is desirable because there are no promising alternatives. Decentralized activities without coordination and regulatory back-up have brought only limited results.

Provinces have every reason to provide leadership in the search for better drug use. This leadership is consistent with the current theme of an increased role for the provinces in the management of health care. Improved drug use programs will complement cost control efforts and will blunt public and professional objections to cost control. They will confirm government interest in quality of care as well as cost control. They will reduce the negative impact of reduced availability of resources.

Provincial intervention is also needed to counteract the overzealous marketing practiced by brand name drug companies and their agency, the Pharmaceutical Manufacturing Association of Canada (PMAC). A study described in the Annals of Medicine, June 1, 1992 reported that 50% of drug advertisements would, if followed, lead to inappropriate prescribing. The industry is not only inefficient and manipulative in its manufacturing and informational practices, it regularly abuses the concepts of honesty and public interest.

Higher drug expenditures can mean poorer health care. Drugs with very similar outcomes for similar conditions may be very different in price, and when the higher priced drugs are used the waste affects all health care. Inappropriate drug use also leads to avoidable health care costs. Adverse drug reactions cause up to 20% of acute care hospital admissions of the elderly. (The Drug Report, Ontario Medical Association's Committee on Drugs and Pharmacotherapy, Nov. 1993, quoting from a Canadian Medical Association Policy Statement) An earlier report by the Canadian Medical Association Task Force on Caring for Seniors had suggested that the figure was 30%.

THE INTERACTION OF COST CONTROL AND IMPROVED SPENDING

Cost control and improved spending can be sought independently, but many tools and techniques serve them both. Governments have tended to concentrate on cost control, whereas the field, in particular hospitals, has sought to accomplish both cost control and better spending. Governments have shown they can often lower prices, whereas the field is best at reducing misuse. Because opportunities for cost control often overlap with opportunities to lower the level of misuse of drugs it is efficient to simultaneously seek both objectives.

The fact that cost control and better spending are often symbiotic does not mean they cannot proceed separately. They can, but opportunities are lost. The devices which relate primarily to cost control are limits on the classes of persons who will be insured, lowering the price of drugs, lowering dispensing costs, substitution of lower cost equivalents, transfer of costs to users, applying penalties to physicians whose drug costs are high and placing ceilings on annual liability per beneficiary. Improved professional and user decisions (for which there are many techniques), limits on the range of items covered, limits on the situations in which drugs are covered, limits on the persons and locations from whom drugs can be obtained, and greater emphasis on nonpharmaceutical therapeutic options can contribute to both better decisions and to cost control.

PHARMACEUTICAL INFORMATION

Information can contribute to drug assessment and comparison, to consumer participation, to negotiation with pharmacists, to day to day operations and to long range planning. Information for all of these purposes must not only contribute to those purposes, it must do so cost-effectively. The usefulness of each data set, and the cost of its production, should be estimated before the data is collected.

In most provinces the largest single pool of information on drug utilization is in the files of the major provincial drug insurance programs. These programs know, with respect to every claim paid, the drug involved, who prescribed it, the amounts prescribed, the cost of the drug, the cost of the dispensing, the pharmacy or other place at which the drug was dispensed, the date of the dispensing and the person for whom the drug was prescribed. With this information it is possible, if the plan so wishes, to report costs and utilization by province and region and by physician, pharmacy, drug and beneficiary.

This provincial data-base could be expanded. A province could require provision of the same information with respect to all dispensed prescription drugs regardless of payer. This is easiest for the dispenser if the province has an on-line provincial network linking dispensers and the Ministry. This network would desirably include pharmacies, hospitals, cancer clinics, psychiatric programs, health centres, physician's offices, penitentiaries and public health clinics (if they dispense as well as prescribe). It could include information with respect to drugs administered by injection in offices, dispensed at the time of a home visit or given in the form of free drug samples. The data-base would then encompass almost all prescription drug use in the province.

Small diagnostically specific drug programs, of which most provinces have a number, often have their own reporting systems and their data may not be able to be integrated easily with other data-bases. Some programs do not store cost data and sexually transmitted disease clinics do not record recipient. Serious consideration should be given to integration of these isolated data-banks with the large provincial data base, recognizing that the extent to which the various data-base extensions would be cost-effective has not been determined.

Currently available data-bases can, for those drugs paid for by public insurance plans, identify use of hazardous drugs, use of hazardous drug combinations, totally inappropriate dosages or durations and users who are double doctoring. These data-bases cannot, however, evaluate the appropriateness of most prescriptions. This evaluation requires an ability to relate drugs to diagnoses and to a treatment plan. Neither drug program information nor the information on claims submitted to medicare by physicians is sufficiently accurate or complete to allow evaluation of most drug use.

Data derived from the payment of claims allows only retrospective evaluation of drug use. Retrospective evaluation can lead to improved drug use, as shown by the effects of the evaluations in hospitals and through the Saskatchewan provincial data-base, but maximum improvement may require that information be available to prescribers at the time drug selection is being made. Several companies are working on software for prescribers. Information to assist in decision making should accommodate the pressures of fee-for-service practice.

INFORMATION FOR STAYING WITHIN BUDGET

If a cap is placed on total drug program expenditures there are new information requirements. Program administrators must be prepared for mid-year program adjustments if expenditure trends indicate a budget over-run. These adjustments can be made only if managers have up to date information on expenditures to date, a sense of the magnitude and trends of costs associated with various cost centres, populations and drug categories, and a knowledge of expected new brand name or generic drugs. Information must be adequate to reasonably accurately estimate the impact of various policy changes so that actions with the correct impact can be implemented.

Program changes which might be used to stay within budget include delisting of drugs, decreased access to some drugs, introduction of ceilings in drug groups, lowering existing ceilings, increasing user fees or lowering prices. Programs for improved drug use are unlikely to give the rapid responses necessary for short term cost control.

INFORMATION FOR NEGOTIATIONS WITH PHARMACIES

Prescription costs have two components, the drug cost and the dispensing cost. These two costs are usually negotiated separately. The dispensing fee can be set arbitrarily by the province or can be a product of negotiation. In recent years many provinces have frozen or rolled back dispensing fees. In Canada the dispensing fee is usually between $6 and $10. (In some United States programs it is as low as $2.) For many low cost drugs the dispensing fee is the largest part of the cost of a prescription.

Governments do not know the level at which a pharmacy breaks even on the dispensing fee, and they often do not know the real cost to the pharmacy of the drugs being dispensed. Manufacturers offer many discounts, rebates and other benefits and perks, and governments can only estimate their value. In addition, the income produced by a prescription is only partly generated by the prescription. Purchases by persons who come to the pharmacy for drugs increase sales in all departments of the pharmacy, and the volume of these increased sales is difficult to bring into negotiations.

Dispensing fees can vary with volume. The pharmacy is an essential health care component which may need subsidy in communities where the volume of drug sales is marginal and no alternative dispensary exists. Quebec has a higher dispensing fee for the first 20,000 prescriptions per year per pharmacy.

Dispensing fees may not be a fruitful place to look when seeking significant reductions in the costs of most prescriptions. User fees, drug utilization review programs and increased availability of drugs without a prescription will lower the number of prescriptions filled. The lower volume of prescriptions will only be of consequence to the smaller community pharmacies, but there are many of these. Record keeping may become more complex and patient and prescriber advice may demand more pharmacist time. The usual dispensing fee may be appropriate when each prescription is individually prepared, but the same fee may not be appropriate for drugs which can be prepackaged. It is with respect to this type of prescription that dispensing costs are most likely to be lowered.

Average cost per prescription might go down if opportunities for nonpharmacy dispensing of high volume drugs are increased. Birth control pills, for example, could be more routinely dispensed by nurses or nurse practitioners in community health centres and in family planning clinics.

Mail order dispensing of drugs in long term use represents as much as 10% of total dispensing in some parts of the United States. Mail service is appropriate for users who have stable long term drug use patterns. Ontario has announced it intends to begin mail order dispensing in 1994.

Pharmacy profiles could be of some use when negotiating dispensing fees. Profiles can compare the frequency with which patients on long term medications have their prescriptions refilled at specific pharmacies. When dispensing practices are inconsistent with peers it would be reasonable to work with the industry and the Colleges of Pharmacy and Physicians to select methods to assure economical dispensing habits.

One way to assess the potential for reductions in dispensing costs would be to tender and see how low prices would fall.

INFORMATION FOR LONG RANGE PLANNING

Knowledge of costs and cost trends by major drug category, by diagnostic category and by population group will help planners estimate the expenditures associated with different levels of coverage. Estimation of the effects of various changes in access and user fees is necessary. Planners should be aware of which drugs might be transferred from the prescription to the nonprescription category and what new drugs are in the pipeline (although they can only guess at whether the drug will be approved and what its starting price will be). Planners can know well in advance which drugs will be losing patent protection and will be available in generic form.

INFORMATION FOR PHYSICIANS AND OTHER PRESCRIBERS

Information needs can be met by profiles, software, on-line systems, text, continuing education or consultant advice. Information will be of highest quality and be best received if prepared in conjunction with relevant professional organizations and specialties.

Computer assisted decision making can be useful in many clinical situations but has special applicability to the use of drugs. Computer assistance should become routine at the time physicians and others are writing prescriptions. This assistance will provide more complete knowledge of drug incompatibilities, dosage, preferred therapy(ies), alternative therapy(ies), cost, and whether there are rules governing public payment for the drug. This information will help both physicians and patients in their decisions. It has been estimated that 80% of undesirable reactions to drugs were predictable and therefore avoidable.

Printed materials, in particular the *blue book* (The Compendium of Pharmaceuticals and Specialties which is provided free to every physician), are used regularly. The blue book may be the most comprehensive source of advice currently available, and it is now on disk. It would be preferable if information designed by and financed by drug companies were not the only, or the most convenient and inexpensive, source of advice.

One on one advice from professionals who are not working for a drug manufacturer (anti-detail persons) has been proven to alter prescribing but it is labor intensive and the labor is expensive. Regional and local workshops, conferences, clinical rounds and other continuing education devices also provide information. All material should routinely consider economic as well as clinical and social factors.

Consulting pharmacists are in common use in hospitals and can also be effective sources of advice in community care. Their cost-effectiveness is proven in hospitals, and community usefulness should be equivalent. The experiences of the regional pharmacy services in Ottawa, Toronto, London and Peterborough, as well as the service operated by the University of Toronto School of Pharmacy (and probably other Faculties of Pharmacy) suggest there is a need for such advisory centres and persons.

A consultant pharmacist service is unlikely to be successful unless the pharmacists are paid on some basis other than fee-for-service. In a minor exception, Quebec pays a fee to a pharmacist if a prescription is not filled because of a pharmacist intervention.

On-line access to patient drug profiles alters dispensing. The on-line network in Saskatchewan led to the cancellation in 1990-91 of more than 30,000 prescriptions which represented inappropriate drug use (Saskatchewan Department of Health Annual Report).

INFORMATION TO ASSIST USERS

Information to users can alter utilization of most health care, including drugs. Information can be general, for the purposes of a better informed public, or can be to assist a user who wishes to understand the therapeutic choices of the moment. To be of help to users at the time drugs are being prescribed or dispensed information will need to be available in physician's offices and in pharmacies. General information should be part of educational curriculums as well as in libraries and elsewhere.

The Canadian Pharmaceutical Association (the pharmacists of Canada) produce a Self Medication Text. The information is now being put on compact disc and will be updated regularly. This text provides both background knowledge and information for users at the time of service. The United States produces a text *USP — DI* (dispensing information) which sets out the information a pharmacist should give a patient about each drug being dispensed. As pharmacists become responsible for providing patients with more information they will almost surely begin to make greater use of informational and interactive videos which the patient can screen in the pharmacy, as well as printed material.

At the time a drug is prescribed and/or dispensed a user ought to be informed with respect to the therapeutic options which are available (pharmaceutical and nonpharmaceutical) and the advantages, disadvantages and costs of each. The user should be informed regarding the amount of user payments associated with various therapeutic options and, in general terms, the public costs of the alternatives. The options may include an interchangeable drug which is less expensive. Patients should be helped to understand the implications of not using the drug and not using it properly. The users should be aware of the manner in which the drug should be stored and of its shelf life, as well as the nature and probability of adverse reactions from each drug and from any combinations of drugs and other substances being used.

A well informed user is probably more likely to use a drug correctly, although many factors affect compliance including the information given at the time of prescribing or dispensing, the clarity of the labels, the use of special aids such as drug calendars or unit dose packaging, follow-up visits or other contacts from the prescriber or other health care professionals, involvement with self-help groups, the general level of understanding of the patient of the hazards of drugs and the willingness and abilities of the patient.

ATTENTION TO SPECIFIC USERS AND PROVIDERS

An adequate data base can identify physicians whose prescribing patterns are expensive when compared to those of similar physicians serving similar patients. It can, for example, identify physicians who routinely use calcium channel blockers (expensive) and seldom use beta blockers (less expensive) in the treatment of various cardiovascular conditions.

Categorization of physicians by drug costs per patient is common in United States hospitals and Health Maintenance Organizations (HMOs). Physicians whose drug costs (or other health care costs) consistently exceed the costs generated by other physicians caring for similar patients are a threat to the financial viability of the hospital or HMO. These physicians are likely to be pressured by colleagues and by the hospital or HMO to alter their prescribing habits, and they may eventually lose their hospital privileges or HMO employment if drug costs (or other costs) remain above an acceptable upper limit.

The situation in Canadian hospitals on global budgets is analogous, but hospital response has not been the same. Physicians whose drug use patterns are consistently more costly than other physicians serving the same kinds of patients reduce the ability of the hospital to serve its community, but drug costs by physician are not commonly known. Unserved patients, and their physicians, are the losers, and probably without benefit to anyone. Higher expenditures on drugs may not mean better outcomes. In a search for equity and better spending hospitals should know the generated costs of their physicians, including the cost of drugs, and act to at least evaluate the habits of expensive physicians.

There has to date been little attention to users whose outpatient drug utilization appears to be excessive, possibly because most of the experience with drug utilization management has been in hospitals. Blue Cross Atlantic is introducing user surveillance as part of the responsibilities of its Managed Care Division.

A patient drug profile is usually a description of the prescription drugs being used by a patient. A patient drug profile could, however, also include a record of nonprescription drugs, of prescriptions written but not filled, of toxic substances at work or at home which might alter drug effects, of patient compliance, of failed therapeutic trials and of adverse drug reactions which have occurred, but this complete profile does not appear to be a practical expectation.

A complete physician or user profile requires integration of information from a number of sources. At the moment there is seldom even integration of information from such providers or payers as hospitals, public and private drug programs, cancer clinics, public health services, psychiatric institutions and programs, Workers Compensation and Department of Veterans Affairs, and these are the data-bases which would be easiest to integrate. The addition of information regarding nonprescription drugs and occupational chemicals would be more difficult.

It is possible that the drug profile of the future will be on a plastic card in the possession of the user. The card will store health and health care information including information on drug use. The strength of the Smart Card is its ability to be up to date and immediately available to, and updated by, pharmacists, physicians and others, and to contain more than just drug information.

A provincial data-bank is best suited for the monitoring of trends, the identification of populations with specific drug use patterns, assistance to physicians and pharmacists when evaluating the insurance status of the patient or a drug, and the conducting of research.

Both smart cards and on-line systems will identify patients who are seeing two or more physicians for the same problem (double doctoring). Studies done by Green Shield in New Brunswick and in Sudbury have shown that one prescription out of thirty is a duplicate of another prescription written on the same day by another physician.

Triple prescription programs are another device for user and provider monitoring. First introduced in Alberta, and now in place in several other provinces, these programs were developed primarily to allow the province to monitor the use of addictive drugs. In these programs the patient takes one copy of the prescription to the pharmacist, the physician keeps one copy and the third copy is sent to the Ministry. These programs identified a number of physicians as overprescribers and identified many users who were receiving identical drugs from two or more physicians. The programs helped establish the effectiveness of drug use monitoring as a tool for the improvement of prescribing habits and the identification of drug abusers.

A province with a complete central drug data-base can produce information equivalent to that from the triple prescription program without the costs and hazards of a special prescription pad. The prescription pads, or even single pages from the pad, are valuable street items.

The inadequacy of Canadian data bases suggests that for the foreseeable future the most productive efforts will be those which target specific problems rather than seek to assess overall prescribing patterns. Hospitals are an exception to this general statement. They have a broad and integrated data-base which includes clinical, personal and pharmaceutical information and they can much more fully evaluate drug use.

DRUG COVERAGE IN ONLY SELECTED CIRCUMSTANCES

A drug which is insured in a public drug program is usually available in whatever situation, whatever quantity and for whatever duration the prescriber chooses. This is a pattern which will gradually change as tight ceilings on public expenditures on drugs become the norm and as these ceilings are lowered. If public liability becomes tied to outcome per dollar spent many drugs will be available at public cost in only selected circumstances and some will be available only at the expense of the user.

It is now common for a drug family, such as calcium channel blockers, antihistamines, nonsteroidal antiinflammatory drugs (NSAIDs), beta blockers, platelet aggregation inhibitors and nonionic contrast media, to include ten or twenty or more regularly used drugs. There is often an even larger menu of drugs available for treatment of a particular clinical condition such as depression, hypertension, infection, pain or schizophrenia. Within these drug families or groups prices can vary by as much as 1000% or more, and effectiveness does not usually correlate closely with price. (Table 18.3 and 18.4)

It is common for public drug plans to refuse to pay for an expensive brand name drug when a less expensive identical generic drug is available. There has, however, not been enough study of the collective benefits of refusing to pay for expensive drugs when less expensive but different drugs produce outcomes which are almost the same. Should the public plan refuse to pay for the *best* drug or drugs when the additional benefits are small and the price is much higher. There is a high opportunity cost associated with paying $200 a month for a drug when $30 per month will bring 90% of the benefits. That difference of $170 per month is lost to populations who would appreciate having some of whatever they can't have because public dollars have been spent bringing the last 10% of benefit to someone else.

Dr. Gordon (Table 18.4) calculated that if all elderly patients with hypertension were on one of the low cost drugs the annual savings in Ontario would be at least $30 million (at 1987 prices). Complete substitution is not clinically desirable, but the savings would be large even if all patients who obtained satisfactory results with the lower cost drugs were kept on them. This substitution of lower cost drugs would become even more possible if nonpharmaceutical anti-hypertensive therapies such as weight loss, exercise and stress management were fully exploited.

There are strong arguments in favor of limited access to selected drugs. Limited access for some users will allow other persons to also have access to a reasonable mix of drugs at public cost. Limiting access to expensive drugs within a particular drug group will give the manufacturers of the more expensive drugs an incentive to lower their prices. This device is one of the few that offers the possibility of lowering the prices of drugs still under patent.

Lower priced drugs often bring the same level of benefit as more expensive drugs. In this situation lower cost will not reduce outcome. Propranolol is not tolerated well by all persons but is tolerated well by the majority of persons. For those who tolerate it well it is an effective beta-blocker and it is 1 to 2% of the cost of the expensive beta-blockers.

On the other hand, sometimes the expensive drug is very much better than the options, and the consequences for the user will be serious if the expensive drug is not provided. The money for the essential drugs which are expensive is more likely to be able to be found if costs are reasonably constrained where constraint brings few if any hazards.

Arguments against the concept of limited access are substantive. Limited access will at times mean patient inconvenience, expense and/or risk, and will at times increase physician paper work. It can be bureaucratic and therefore a cause of conflict between users, prescribers and the plan. It rejects the popular proposition that the insurer should always pay for whatever drug is best. There will definitely be a greater drug selection available to those with greater incomes, which will be objectionable to those who wish everyone to have access to the same level of health care. It will be difficult to develop consensus on relative cost-effectiveness, and therefore difficult to decide what expenditure ceilings are appropriate within drug groups or specific clinical situations.

Despite these arguments limits on access should be considered for drugs which are therapeutically similar to other less expensive drugs as well as for drugs whose use tends to be well understood by a limited number of prescribing persons or clinics. Limited access should also be consid-

Table 18.3

A COMPARISON OF PEPTIC ULCER DRUGS (Ontario Drug Benefit Plan Prices — 1991)		
Drug	**Daily cost (drug only)**	**Cost for 2 weeks (drug plus disp. fee)**
Cimetidine (generic)	0.35	11.40
Ranitidine (generic)	1.10	21.90
Famotidine (Pepcid)	1.30	24.70
Sucralfate (Sulcrate)	1.76	31.14
Misoprostol (Cytotec)	1.40	26.10
Antacids	0.10 to 1.00	1.40-14.00 (no disp. fee)

Table 18.4

RELATIVE COSTS OF ANTIHYPERTENSIVE AGENTS (excluding dispensing fee)	
Drug	**Monthly Cost**
Nifedipine (a Ca channel blocker)	
Adalat PA 20	$18.30
Captopril (an ACE inhibitor)	
Capoten 25 mg one daily	13.50
Capoten 50 mg one daily	27.00
Enalapril (an ACE inhibitor)	
Vasotec 10 mg one daily	24.00
Vasotec 20 mg one daily	29.10
Propranolol (a beta-blocker)	
Inderal 10 mg one daily	0.60
Inderal 20 mg one daily	0.90
Hydrochlorothiazide/triamterene (diuretic)	
Apo-triazide	1.36
Hydrochlorothiazide 25 mg one daily (diuretic)	
Hydrodiuril	0.15

*Ontario Drug Benefit Plan prices 1987

Ref: Gordon M., Hypertension in the elderly, Can. Fam. Physician, Dec, 1989

ered for drugs with a record of significant misuse, and drugs which do not tend to be effective unless there is full patient compliance.

Initial or continued access to specific drugs may require proof of failure of other less expensive drugs and therapies, proof of presence of specified diagnoses or hazards and/or proof of user compliance. The Estraderm patch is insured by the Ontario Drug Benefit Plan only where *"a less costly estrogen product is contraindicated or has been tried and has caused an adverse effect"*. Ciprofloxacin is covered only *"for culture proven gram negative bacterial infections —- for which no alternative therapy is available and which would otherwise require hospital treatment"*. Similarly, ticlopidine (Ticlid) *"is restricted to eligible patients with transient cerebral ischemia due to embolization of platelet thrombi, who continue to have events while taking ASA, or who cannot take ASA because of true gastrointestinal intolerance or allergy."* (The Drug report, Ontario Medical Association, Dec 1993) These kinds of constraints, which have been used extensively in some provincial plans, can lead to bureaucratic and inefficient processes, but they will at times be the best choice.

A limit on public liability for drugs within a drug group would not prevent anyone from having access to some of the drugs at either no cost or at reasonable cost. Persons wishing to use more expensive drugs would, depending on the policy of the insurance plan, pay either the entire cost or costs beyond the established limit .

Support for use of the less expensive drugs is found in strange places. In the Compendium of Pharmaceuticals and Specialties, the *blue book* in which manufacturers describe their drugs (and a book referred to daily by physicians) the manufacturers of sucralfate (Sulcrate) state that in comparative studies of cimetidine and sucralfate there was no statistical difference in the healing rates produced by the two drugs. Since sucralfate costs several times as much as cimetidine it would appear that the public plan should not usually pay more than the cost of cimetidine.

Very expensive drugs merit special attention. These drugs cost $5,000 to 25,000 per year or more, are often used for years and are rapidly increasing in numbers. One of the drugs for Gauchers Disease (Ceredase) costs hundreds of thousands of dollars per year. Often there are no adequate substitutes, as in thalassaemia or dwarfism. Expenditures on these very expensive drugs are growing at 25 to 50% per year, and this rate of increase will continue if the new and useful drugs are covered. In Ontario the total costs exceeded $100 million in 1991. (Table 18.5)

These very expensive drugs were in the beginning primarily a problem for hospitals, but two factors have moved the problem into the community. First, there has been a shift in emphasis from institutional to community care and this has moved the use of many hospital drugs into the community, as with clozapine for schizophrenia. Second, the drugs are increasingly used for persons who are not ill and therefore are quite naturally cared for in the community, as with dwarfism and thalassemia.

Coverage of, and therefore the costs of, these programs for special high cost drugs vary greatly from province to province. Reasonably extensive coverage in 1991 represented $8-12 per capita (total population). To keep these costs in perspective, note that the per capita costs of the universal drug programs in Saskatchewan and Manitoba were, in 1990, $90 and $50 per capita respectively.

If governments withhold payment for the very expensive drugs they may be severely criticized, as was the Ontario Ministry of Health when it delayed the financing of clozapine for schizophrenics, and some users will be exposed to avoidable hazards and ill health. If, on the other hand, governments pay for these drugs whenever physicians or users deem them to be needed the costs will rise rapidly. Controlled access is the preferred policy.

The process through which very expensive drugs should be assessed is the same as for all other drugs. Patient co-payments should be applied to the same extent as to other drugs. The cost-effectiveness of the expensive drugs should be evaluated in the same way as the cost-effectiveness of other drugs is evaluated. Public programs should pay only for less expensive alternatives when they are adequate. Drug family price ceilings should be put in place when alternatives are considered to be adequate. Criteria for access to the drugs at public expense should be reasonably stringent. It has been estimated, for example, that erythropoeitin (EPO) is needed by only about 1/3 of all patients on dialysis. (Quebec Ministry of Health, 1990). There should (at $10,000 plus per year) be firm guidelines governing when and how the drug is prescribed, plus ongoing monitoring to be sure the guidelines are followed.

For provinces without a reasonably generous universal basic drug program the preferred alternative appears to be universal coverage of catastrophic costs. This would allow limited access by everyone to very expensive drugs without having to deal with them outside of the general program. Everyone could, for example, be protected against drug costs beyond $1000 or $2000 per year. It is difficult to see equity in a situation in which a single expensive drug may be fully paid for with public funds but a person who requires several moderately expensive drugs may receive no public assistance. This is the case in several provinces.

Very expensive drugs are also of financial significance to hospitals. Intravenous antibiotics represented 27% of the total drug expenditures in the Lions Gate hospital in British Columbia in the late 1980s. One drug (cefoxiten) was the dominant item. (Sonnichsen, D., and R. Nakagawa, "A DUR of Surgical Prophylaxis in Obstetrics and Gynecology", Can J of Pharmacy, Dec 1990)

Access to very expensive outpatient drugs may be only through designated offices or clinics. This approach has been used for patients with thalassemia, cystic fibrosis, dwarfism (growth hormone),

Table 18.5

Diagnosis	Cases per 100,000	Cost/yr pr case (or total cost)	Cost per million pop'n
DIAGNOSTICALLY SPECIFIC OUTPATIENT DRUG PROGRAMS (Ontario experience, 1990/91)			
Cancer (chemotherapy)	not available	(28M total)	3,000,000
Organ transplants (cyclosporine)	20-25	5-8,000	1,000,000
Dwarfism (growth hormone)	2	20,000	400,000
End stage renal disease (erythropoeitin)	10	5-10,000	700,000
AIDS — AZT	25	3-5,000	1,000,000
AIDS — Pentamidine	15	6-900	100,000
Cystic Fibrosis (many drugs)	3	10,000	300,000
Thalassemia (many drugs)	1	10-20,000	1-200,000
Hemophilia (blood products)	not available	(11M total)	1.2,000,000
Inborn errors of metabolism (PKU, etc.)	360	500	25,000
Tuberculosis and leprosy	716	1,500	120,000
Hyperalimentation (TPN)	not available	(10.5M total)	1.1,000,000

organ transplants (cyclosporine), dialysis (erythropoietin), AIDS (AZT, pentamidine, acyclovir) and other severe infections (ceftrioxone and a number of other antibiotics).

Many devices implement the idea of careful description of the clinical situations in which a drug is to be prescribed and of the dosage(s) and methods of administration which are to be used. These concepts all would be part of a comprehensive drug utilization management program which gives attention to limited access.

GENERIC DRUGS

A generic drug is a chemical copy of a patented drug. Almost all of the generic drugs used in Canada are produced in Canada by Canadian owned companies. In 1989 generic drugs represented less than 10% of the dollars spent on prescription drugs in Canada but 20% of prescriptions filled. Generic drugs are routinely less costly than the equivalent brand name drugs.

With the extension of patent protection to 20 years and the elimination of mandatory licensing of generic copies the opportunities for the introduction of new generic drugs has been sharply reduced. The reduced opportunity will persist until drugs begin to lose patent protection after 20 years. This will begin early in the next century. Fortunately, a drug which is a significant improvement when it is first released will often still be a clinically satisfactory drug when the 20 year patent period ends. The drug can then be marketed by the generic manufacturers.

Ministries should be certain that they are helpful to the generic drug manufacturers so that generic copies can be on the market as soon as possible. Preparation for approval of a generic drug should begin long before a patent expires so that the drug can be on the market the day the patent expires.

Consideration should be given to incentives for rapid entry of generic copies. Rewards could be offered to the generic manufacturer who is the first to offer a new drug in generic form, perhaps with a guaranteed market share for a period of time so long as the price is significantly lower than the price of the brand name equivalent. There should be no demand for clinical trials of generic equivalents, although this decision is outside of the control of the provinces. Chemical equivalence is all that is needed, but the new Canadian legislation which extended patent protection also introduced a requirement for clinical trials of generic equivalents. In the United States new clinical trials are not required. The legislation introduced by the Mulroney government was designed to serve no-one but the brand name manufacturers. The requirement for clinical trials will unnecessarily increase the price of generic copies and delay their entry to the market, and the Federal government should remove this requirement from Bill C-91.

After a patent expires some brand name manufacturers market the drug under two different names and at two prices. The lower price clone is offered in competition to the generic drugs and the higher cost equivalent is kept available for use when it is prescribed. When this double pricing occurs provinces should pay only the lowest cost for both products.

Generic drugs should be encouraged. The use of cost ceilings within drug groups with similar functions will favor generic drugs, as will a mandatory therapeutic trial with lower priced similar drugs before more expensive drugs become available at public expense. Co-payments which are a percentage of the prescription cost also encourage the use of lower cost drugs. Both the user and the insurance plan are winners when a lower priced drug is used. If a user wishes to be provided with a more expensive drug than is deemed appropriate then the extra cost should be a personal responsibility. New Brunswick has this policy.

AUTOMATIC STOP ORDERS AND PRESCRIPTION CHANGES

Policies which authorize or instruct pharmacists to change selected physician prescriptions are now widely used in hospitals. The list of circumstances in which these automatic changes occur is likely to lengthen and be extended to community use.

Examples include mandatory substitution of the lowest cost product when products are chemically identical. The lowest cost equivalent drug is automatically dispensed when a more expensive equivalent is prescribed. Usually a generic drug is substituted for a brand name drug. Historically mandatory substitution did not apply when a physician requested *no substitution*, but in many hospitals and most provinces the request for *no substitution* is now either routinely ignored or ignored unless supported by an acceptable explanation. Allowing a physician to generate additional cost for little or no gain is not sensible. The patient should usually be aware of substitution so that she/he can choose to buy the higher priced alternative at personal expense if so wished. Involving patients in a discussion of substitution will consume the time of pharmacists, physicians and nurses but the payoff will be a more informed and cost-sensitive public and lower public cost.

Automatic substitution can go beyond the substitution of products which are chemically equivalent. There can also be replacement of a prescribed drug by another with the same therapeutic objective but which is chemically different. In 26 hospitals in Ontario there was, in 1991, automatic interchange of aminoglycoside antibiotics. In nine hospitals an order for ranitidine (Zantac), cimetidine (Tagamet) or famotidine (Pepsid) was automatically filled with whichever of these drugs was in stock. There also may be an automatic change of parenteral administration to an oral form, as with ranitidine.

Regulations can alter the amount or duration of payment for a drug. Extended use of many drugs is not recommended, and public responsibility could be limited to the recommended maximum usage. Some tranquilizers should not be used for more than three or four weeks. In hospital this principle is inherent in the use of mandatory stop orders. Orders for antibiotics, for example, may automatically expire after a certain number of days.

THE PRICE OF DRUGS

A shortened patent protection and mandatory licensing of generic competitors kept Canadian drug prices low until 1986, when patent protection was extended in return for industry promises of increased research spending and limits on drug price increases. Industry spending in Canada did increase, but mostly on clinical trials and on new jobs in sales and marketing. (Federal government document quoted by the Canadian Medical Association, 1992)

The extended patent protection was opposed by the provinces, the general public and the health care industry. One of the responses of the federal government was creation of the Drug Prices Review Board (DPRB) to monitor and control drug price increases. The DPRB was given the authority to require price roll-backs when increases exceeded the allowable levels, and it rolled back the prices of many products of many companies.

A prices review board is a device worthy of consideration by any country, but its importance should not be overstated. The Canadian DPRB has not affected the price at which new drugs enter the market, and the industry therefore is able to easily defend itself from later price control by establishing high initial prices. Monitoring and regulating the price increases of drugs after they are on the market does not appear to offer as many opportunities for cost control as are offered by an improvement in the way in which drugs are used and by greater use of the powers of a competitive marketplace.

Provinces can unilaterally establish the drug prices their provincial drug plans will pay to a pharmacy, and several provinces have frozen drug prices or rolled them back across the board. A manufacturer has the option of lowering the prices charged to pharmacies or of letting the pharmacist be the loser.

Methods of payment by provincial drug plans to pharmacies for dispensed drugs include the Best Available Price (BAP) and the Actual Acquisition Cost (AAC). The BAP ought to produce the lowest costs. Under BAP the drug plan automatically pays the pharmacy the lowest price quoted for a multiple source drug, and it automatically lowers the payment to all pharmacies for a given drug whenever it is known that that drug has been delivered to any pharmacy at a lower cost. The AAC method requires that the plan pay for identical drugs at different prices, and provides fewer incentives for either the pharmacist or the manufacturer to lower price.

The price of drugs may be altered somewhat by the distribution systems used. Provinces should encourage the use of drug wholesalers rather than direct sales to pharmacies by manufacturers. The use of wholesalers makes it easier to monitor prices, increases the efficiency of the system (especially for smaller community pharmacies) and reduces manufacturer opportunities to manipulate pharmacists. Dealing with manufacturers is attractive to the large chains and to all pharmacies when discounts and other promotions are offered. These discounts and promotions do not lower prices to insurance plans or users.

One of the policy options available to a province is to operate its own drug distribution program. Since 1959, Ontario has operated a drug and medical supply system which serves psychiatric hospitals, public health units, provincial laboratories, penitentiaries, some long term care institutions, some rural hospitals and some physicians offices. This service was started when there were no hospital group purchasing plans, no public drug insurance programs and no drug wholesalers comparable to those in existence now. Despite recommendations that the provincial distribution system be either abandoned or overhauled, and despite requests from psychiatric hospitals and others that they be allowed to obtain drugs through other vehicles, the program continues. It handles about $30 million of goods annually.

CONTINUING EDUCATION AND RESEARCH

Centres for drug use research have been suggested. It would be useful to establish such centres, but they should not be seen as a substitute for the participative and decentralized drug use improvement programs which have been described. The changes which are most needed will take place in the field, and academic centres are more likely to bring international recognition and sophisticated publications than early and widespread changes in the field.

The same applies to conferences. Large international meetings with expensive speakers are fun, but changes will come when the conferences are local, open to all who make on-the-spot decisions and geared to how to improve decisions at the point of delivery of health care.

RANGE OF BENEFITS

Products covered by a drug insurance program can include prescription drugs, nonprescription drugs, oxygen, special diets and medical supplies such as those associated with ostomies and incontinence. Some public programs have in the past covered a broad range of nonprescription items and medical supplies so long as a physician ordered them. Many prescriptions were written for nonprescription items, which increased the cost of these items. Extensive coverage of nonprescription items is not defensible and is decreasing, but there are arguments in favor of access to a few nonprescription items at public cost. Coverage of some nonprescription drugs can prevent substitution with more expensive prescription items.

Shortening the list of insured drugs will, if substitution with other insured items is possible, have only a modest effect, if any, on the number of prescriptions written. Substitution will occur. Provincial costs go down only if the expensive drugs are delisted or only partially covered. A significant decrease in costs occurs if a total group of drugs, such as antihistamines, is delisted.

Reducing the list of insured or fully insured drugs in the interest of cost control will almost always be seen as arbitrary, simplistic and unfair, and the criticism will to some extent be valid. Many items have in recent years been excluded from the list of insured products in various jurisdictions, including all nonprescription items (many jurisdictions and plans), Rogaine, Talwin Compound 50, contraceptives (Spain), appetite suppressants, nicorettes, Mycostatin, Septra, Betnovate cream, Kenalog cream, Elavil and Haldol. Nonprescription products which have been delisted include cough and cold products, laxatives, travel sickness medications, mouth washes and gargles, skin cleansers, surgical supplies, sugar substitutes, salt substitutes, nonmedicated shampoos, infant foods, lozenges, diagnostic aids, items for lens care, antihistamines, multivitamins, calcium preparations and dietary supplements. Many combination and delayed release (long acting) medications have also been deinsured. These compounds tend to be more expensive and/or to contain ingredients which are unnecessary or hazardous. Every shortening of the list of insured items is accompanied by complaints that the decreased access will be damaging to someone's health. These complaints should be evaluated within an understanding of how most of those items became insured in the first place.

The range of items insured by some provincial drug insurance plans has in the past reflected the feeling that whatever a physician prescribed for the health of the patient should be provided. Carried to an extreme the things which should or could be prescribed in the interest of someone's health include winters in Arizona, a better house to live in, a safer or different job, or just any job. It is now

294

clear that if these very necessary *prescriptions* cannot be insured then the provision of marginal medications, or of shampoos and lozenges, at public expense should certainly be questioned.

Drug plans are moving towards payment for only cost-effective prescription drugs. There is no pretence that other items are unimportant, but there appears to be an acceptance that a drug program is not the device by which an endless array of items should be available at public expense. Items will be excluded from the list of benefits either because they are a bad buy (they are useless or hazardous or opportunity costs are too high) or because they are not seen as an item that ought to be provided by a drug insurance program.

THE DRUG REVIEW PROCESS

The federal Health Protection Branch controls entry of drugs to the Canadian market. Once this Branch issues a Notice of Compliance (NOC) and a Drug Identification Number (DIN) the drug can be legally sold in Canada, sometimes with restrictions.

Drugs are classified as either prescription drugs or as belonging to one of two classes of nonprescription drugs. Some nonprescription drugs are able to be sold anywhere (subject to more restrictive provincial legislation) whereas other nonprescription drugs are only available through direct request to a pharmacist. Pharmacists do not usually enter sales of the monitored but nonprescription drugs onto the patients computerized drug record. It is unclear whether pharmacists are responsible for appropriate use of these drugs, or how many drugs will eventually be in this category. (Editorial, Ontario College of Pharmacists Journal, Jan. 1992)

A few drugs go through the licensing process twice. A drug which has been approved for use for only specific diagnoses or conditions may be later found to have other uses. This can lead to new clinical trials, after which the drug may be given a second identification number and sold under a new name and perhaps at a significantly higher cost. This manipulation rewards the manufacturer but its merits are difficult to see. A new number and name should not be assigned even if new clinical trials were performed and new uses approved.

The approval of a drug by the federal department does not mean it will be insured by a provincial drug program although some provinces insure all federally approved prescription drugs. The federal evaluation does not assess cost-effectiveness relative to other competing drugs or nonpharmaceutical therapies. It does not ask *'is this drug therapeutically better than existing drugs, and, if it is, does the therapeutic gain justify the increases in cost which may occur?'*. Some provinces wish to insure only drugs which are more cost-effective than other therapies already available and these provinces have established committees to make recommendations to the Minister regarding the insurability of new drugs, the conditions under which the drug should be insured and the desirability of continuing coverage of old drugs.

These committees can save provinces money and improve drug use, but they can also become large, inefficient, expensive and closed. These deficiencies can lead to delays in addition of generic equivalents, delays in removal of drugs no longer cost-effective and unnecessary administrative expense.

Drug review committee members may be technocrats or consumer representatives. Technical experts may reasonably be dominant in technical decisions, but the setting of priorities and the limiting of access should be dominated by consumer representatives. Whether the extra benefits available from a given drug are worth the extra cost is a very value-laden decision and therefore should be made by the users and payers rather than by technical experts. How much public money should be spent to obtain a 10% improvement in half of the acne patients or a reduction in a nonlife threatening side-effect of a drug? How important is pharmaceutical relief from abdominal discomfort, painful feet, insomnia or tension headaches?

Evaluation of drugs could be a two stage process, with the technical advisors evaluating the usefulness and safety of a drug and consumer representatives advising with respect to the extent to which the drug should be available at public expense. Separation of the two levels of decision making will become more necessary if any province opts for global regional health care budgets in which regions, within their fixed expenditure ceilings, can opt for different drug insurance coverage. It would be unwise to make technical decisions at the regional level, but regional populations might quite reasonably differ in their health care priorities.

Drug evaluations in one country are not necessarily accepted in other countries. The most widely used oral contraceptive in the world (desogesterel — Desogen, representing 15% of world consumption of oral contraceptives) has been used in Europe since 1981, was not approved for use in the United States until 1993 and is currently still being evaluated by Canada. In November 1992, in a news release, the federal Minister of Health announced an intention to explore *'international harmonization of the drug review process'*.

There have been suggestions that the testing of drugs should not be left as fully under the control of drug companies as has been the case in the past, and that either national or international testing agencies should be created. Certainly some drug companies have, in their submissions in support of licensing, demonstrated enough deceit to merit closer surveillance of their drug testing than is now the case. A number of major companies have been cited for fraudulent submissions.

Prelicensing research does not identify all adverse drug reactions or other hazards or deficiencies. New postmarketing surveillance programs, plus large randomized clinical trials early in the life of the drug and preferably before final licensing, would more effectively detect low volume but often highly risky side effects of drugs and confirm or dispute original perceptions of efficacy.

At least eight drugs have, because of side effects which appeared after they had been on the market for significant periods of time, been taken off the market since the thalidomide tragedy. Some of these, such as triazolam (in all strengths or only in higher dosages, depending on the jurisdiction), have been removed only after their use by millions of patients. (Strom and Carson, "Use of automated data bases for pharmacoepidemiology research", Epidemiologic Reviews, 1990)

Other drugs originally released for unrestricted use have, after postmarketing surveillance, remained on the market but with warnings regarding use. The antihistamines Hismanal and Seldane were after many years identified as hazardous to some persons. This led to transfer of these drugs from open pharmacy shelves to storage behind the pharmacist (which led to advertising which made no mention of the reason for the move but which announced `you don't have to look for your Seldane any more, it can now be obtained directly from your pharmacist'). The question of who will finance additional long term postmarketing research is not settled.

A PROVINCE-WIDE OR REGIONAL
DRUG UTILIZATION MANAGEMENT PROGRAM

If a province or region implements a comprehensive program for better spending of health care dollars then that program would encompass the use of drugs, but if a comprehensive program is not launched the same principles and activities could apply to a provincial or regional program for the better use of drugs.

The principles governing such a program would be similar to those described in Chapter 16. There should be central sponsorship and coordination but participative, collaborative, flexible and decentralized implementation. Because there is only a fuzzy understanding of the relative cost-effectiveness of the many drug use improvement devices the program should be pluralistic.

Local and regional differences within the provincial program should be welcomed. Agencies and regions should, with some limitations or understandings, be free to use whatever drug use improvement devices they feel are most appropriate. The province should not help fund activities proven to be ineffective, some provincial regulatory constraints would apply universally and not be subject to local amendment, and regions or agencies would not be allowed to implement policies contrary to provincial objectives.

There should be central funding of core activities and agency or regional funding of decentralized activities. The program should be funded from operating rather than research budgets, and it should be established as a permanent cost centre in agencies, regions and provinces. Users and communities should be full partners.

Incentives and disincentives would be developed to encourage improved drug use. Documentation, monitoring, analysis and assistance should almost always invite change rather than demand it, fully recognizing that at times consensus will support use of regulation and disincentives. First attention would be given to areas of major expenditure in which there has been identification of abuse.

A drug utilization management program will on occasion support drug use patterns which increase cost, but these instances of increased cost will be few compared to the frequency with which expenditures will go down. Better use of drugs will both lower costs and improve health care.

If a government wishes to implement a major drug utilization management program there are a number of tasks to be undertaken. The roles of the ministry(ies), the professional Colleges (of Pharmacy, Physicians and Surgeons and Nurses), the professional associations, the hospitals, other health care associations, other providers, consumers and the drug industry will need to be clarified. An organizational framework and a budget will have to be selected. An action plan will be needed, as will policies regarding allocation of funds to various activities, groups and regions. Data-bases will need to be evaluated and plans made for upgrading where indicated.

Because improved spending will occur best in the presence of tight global cost control, a global public expenditure cap for drugs should be chosen if not already in place. Measures for protection of the cap should be identified and implemented quickly if necessary. Legislation should be reviewed to identify impediments to improved spending and to cost control, and revised as necessary. Changes in legislation may be necessary to protect evaluators, protect privacy, provide the necessary legal base for decisions which are likely to be challenged by drug companies and provide broad authority for drug utilization review.

The statutes and regulations required to legalize a broad program of improved drug use are much more encompassing than is legislation which authorizes the operation of a drug plan which merely pays for a list of identified substances. To forestall successful court challenges the enabling legislation must allow the Ministry to delist drugs for defined reasons, to limit access to specific drugs, to pay different percentages of the cost of different drugs, to vary payment and access with changes in diagnosis or user characteristics, to use different pricing strategies for different drugs and different situations, to alter public payments and limits on access with respect to any drug at any time, to establish relative cost-effectiveness as the primary criterion for policy choices and to give preference to one drug over another. These powers will not assure avoidance of court challenges but are the necessary legal foundation. The operation of the plan and the making of decisions within the legislative framework will require equitable and open processes which can be defended as consistent with due legal process. Written, public and understandable criteria should govern decisions which are made. Appeal mechanisms should be created, and the legislation should provide protection for external advisors who make recommendations to the ministry.

The first phase of the program would be internal and private. Basic policy questions need to be answered so that when the program is announced the Ministry can indicate how much it will cost, what groups will be consulted, what effects are expected, when it will start, what units within the ministry will be responsible for the program, who will be the senior Ministry administrator and, perhaps, whether there will be block funding of major organizations, what criteria will be used to allocate funds and how funds will be distributed among professional groups and user groups.

Announcement of the program ought to be followed immediately by action. Delays will invite scepticism and encourage power struggles. Early meetings with all major players to seek involvement and advice, and to disseminate answers to operational questions, will establish the seriousness of the Ministry.

This introductory phase will merge imperceptibly into a phase in which the field begins to request assistance with specific projects, regional and sectoral workshops begin to be held and regional and provincial networks begin to form. The province can be happy if the program is reasonably in place by the end of the first year with most of the start-up conflicts and uncertainties resolved.

ADMINISTRATIVE COSTS

Administration costs as a percentage of total program costs are not a fully reliable indicator of the adequacy of administration. These costs, both in total dollars and in percentage of program costs, will rise if there is major attention to improved drug use. If programs operate the drug use improvement programs that they should, and if they produce the data and data analyses which are necessary, and if total program costs are constrained as they should be, administrative costs may be 3-4% of total costs and still be cost-effective.

Administrative costs of the Ontario Drug Benefit Plan were estimated by the Lowy Commission (1989) to be about 1% of total costs. The Plan estimated them at 0.5%. These low costs were at least partly a result of an almost complete absence of activities to improve drug use combined with a very high level of total spending.

THE ROLE OF BIOTECHNOLOGY

The financially frightening but clinically promising part of future drug therapy is biotechnology. Its miracles are just emerging. It has been predicted that by the year 2000 biotechnology firms may generate one third of all drug costs. (The Economist, Oct 5, 1991) Examples of this new category of drugs include tPA (the anti-clotting agent that turned out to be usually no better than streptokinase, which costs one tenth as much), erythropoeitin (Epogen, the drug which reduces the threat of anaemia in patients on dialysis — $1 billion in sales in 1991), Neupogen, which stimulates the production of white blood cells after the use of chemotherapy, Centoxin, a monoclonal antibody which is used to treat septicemia (at $6000 per treatment — 1991), and a new drug for cystic fibrosis (by Genentech at $10-20,000 per year).

DRUG MANUFACTURING IN CANADA

Brand name drugs are usually either manufactured abroad or are manufactured in Canada from imported raw materials. Most of the active ingredients are manufactured within the parent multinational companies but outside Canada. The active ingredients and other raw materials can be imported at inflated prices, assuring maximum profits in jurisdictions with low tax rates (transfer pricing).

In the period 1983 to 1990 Canadian imports of pharmaceutical commodities grew at an annual rate of 9.7%. In 1990 pharmaceutical imports exceeded exports by $712 million. (Pharmaceutical Industry Study, Ontario Ministry of Industry, Trade and Technology, 1991) In recent years the percentage of drugs imported fully manufactured rose from 9% to 18%.

Time will tell whether the commitments made by the brand name companies in return for longer patent protection will improve the industry trade balance or merely lead to higher prices and more marketing jobs in Canada.

PREFERENTIAL PURCHASING POLICIES
WHICH FAVOR DRUGS PRODUCED IN THE HOME PROVINCE.

Quebec policy assures preferential pricing up to 10% for selected drugs manufactured by companies based in Quebec. This policy appears to have been attractive to drug companies. Research and

Development expenditure growth in Quebec in recent years has been three to four times that in Ontario.

The question of the extent to which Canada, or individual provinces, should trade higher drug costs for more economic activity in the province is one to be made by cabinets and legislatures, with the advice of the economic and industrial ministries, rather than the Ministry of Health.

SUMMARY

Regulation is the only sure way of staying within selected expenditure ceilings, but regulation alone can only modestly improve the way drugs are used. Partnerships of governments, consumers, professionals and health care agencies offer the best chance for improved prescribing, improved user compliance and multi-party cooperation in the selection and implementation of high quality pharmaceutical policies. The desirable partnerships are unlikely to develop or flourish unless the provincial ministries of health provide leadership, resources and encouragement, assist in the development of the necessary data-bases and encourage regional, agency, provider and user leadership and responsibility.

Provincial drug programs should pay for only those drugs which have been adequately evaluated before release, which are more cost-effective than the available alternatives and which are being used in appropriate circumstances and ways. Provincial drug program expenditures should be held at less than increases in inflation, and user fees should be seriously considered where not already in place.

Many of the policy options relevant to public expenditures on drugs are value laden. Many policy choices should therefore reflect consumer preferences before professional values, and this requires the creation of permanent vehicles for public participation in policy development and program review.

Provinces should clarify their intentions with respect to a number of central questions. Is there to be reasonably equal access by everyone to necessary and cost-effective drugs? Is there to be capping of total provincial expenditures on drugs? With what degree of vigour will appropriate drug use be pursued? Will there be user fees? Will a greater role for consumers and communities in drug use review and drug policy development be actively supported? Will data-bases be developed to support chosen objectives?

Drugs are more systematically screened before availability to the public than almost any other health care component, but they are remarkably abused once they have been licensed. Better drug use (improved pharmacotherapy) will mean better health care at lower cost, an attractive combination.

Future use of drugs, and public payment for them, offers many challenges. The use of mood altering drugs, for example, has entered a new phase. The barbiturates and amphetamines have been replaced by newer drugs with fewer side effects, and the specificity of these new drugs will increase as the chemistry of the brain is better understood. Millions of adults are taking Prozac entirely to allow them to have a happier day.

Chapter 19

Practitioners and the Policy Process

INTRODUCTION

Most of this book has concentrated on the policy choices of governments and boards, but important choices are also made by the policy implementators. The skill with which policies are implemented often determines their success or failure, and implementation responsibilities rest with the operational planners and administrators throughout the system.

Administrators are largely responsible for the management philosophy of organizations. They largely determine the degree of managerial openness, the degree of support for public participation efforts and the response to public and provider involvement. They largely determine the extent to which decisions are decentralized, the degree to which accountability is encouraged, the mix of creative versus traditional solutions, the extent to which change is approached vigorously versus timidly, the way agencies respond to financial constraint and the extent to which an agency seeks or avoids collective versus parochial action. Higher level policy makers may support creativity, partnerships, openness, accountability, innovation and courageous decision making, but these directions are unlikely to be represented by actions in the field if administrators and planners have insufficient talent or prefer other emphases.

Those who do the implementing have many options. Many of these options are specific to one health service sector. Other choices pertain to process. Short case studies in Chapter 20 will frequently demonstrate some of the options which routinely are available to operational planners and to administrators.

INNOVATION VERSUS REPLICATION

The importance of innovation has been overestimated, especially at the macro policy level. It is far more important to adapt the ideas and experiences of others to the local scene than it is to look for original ideas. It is difficult to find ideas, activities and options which have not already been expressed and tested by others.

In 1989-90 British Columbia established a fund to provide seed money for hospital projects which would reduce hospital expenditures. The funds were granted on the basis of a business plan which identified benefits and defined a pay-back period. There was no requirement that the idea be absolutely new, a requirement which had made the innovation funds in Ontario largely ineffective. The British Columbia program was oversubscribed. The Ontario Innovation Fund placed such emphasis on innovation that it excluded local testing of options already tried somewhere else. It had trouble finding useful projects to approve.

SUPPORTING ACCOUNTABILITY

Accountability does not just happen. Supportive structures and environments are needed.

Provider accountability to users is most likely when providers voluntarily accept the concept and when legislation establishes the supremacy of user preferences and the obligation of providers to assure user access to relevant information in an understandable form. Accountability is improved when providers are skilled in transmitting information to users, when payment mechanisms encourage providers to communicate with users and respect their wishes, when there is user control over regional/local boards and councils, and when appeal mechanisms include, or are dominated by, user representatives.

Provider accountability to payers is increased when the payer has access to profiles describing individual providers and provider groups by region, institution, type of service and type of user. Established standards of expected/preferred practice allow evaluation of the profiles. Use of the profiles depends primarily on processes created by operational staff.

Payer accountability to users is increased by openly established and understood priorities, by good public access to information on services and costs (including expenditures on administration), when decisions are made by democratically elected persons and when advisory committees representing population groups such as seniors, the physically disabled, the chronically psychiatrically disabled and ethnic and cultural groups are regularly consulted.

User accountability to payers and other users is increased by acceptance of the idea of user responsibility for many utilization decisions, by production of user profiles, by mechanisms for review of user profiles, by mechanisms for monitoring user cooperation in responsible use of health care and by the provision to users of information on costs and on their patterns of utilization of health care.

AGGRESSIVE CHANGE VERSUS TINKERING

It is the implementors who, through their advice to higher level policy makers and through their implementation choices, largely determine the rate and courageousness of change.

Many social systems are resistant to change. Users and providers tend to resist change unless it appears to be immediately favorable to them, and many of the desirable health care changes do not meet this criterion. If the planners and administrators join the opponents of change then the changes become much more politically and operationally difficult, if not impossible. In this situation tinkering is all that will happen.

An incrementalist process has led to significant changes in health care, but the change has usually been slow. Some of the changes needed now cannot wait for another twenty years. The support of leaders in the field is essential to provinces who know change should occur but who are having trouble getting on with it.

OPTIONS FOR INTRODUCING NEW PROGRAMS

New programs may be introduced experimentally, incrementally or completely. The new programs can be limited in terms of the populations involved, the geography involved, the costs covered or the services covered. When Saskatchewan first contemplated universal medicare they established a true pilot project in one region (Swift Current). This pilot project was copied 15 years later when the program was expanded to cover the entire province.

A similar sequence was used for children's dental care. A program of dental care delivered by dental workers other than dentists was tested for three years in one Saskatchewan locality (Oxbow) before being established as a province-wide program. The dental care program was then planned to grow incrementally as providers became available. The program began when the first class of dental therapists was graduated.

302

The program was offered in the first year only to children born in 1968 because of the limited supply of dental therapists. The program expanded at the rate of graduation of new therapists. The program was a model of good planning and good implementation, and was a tribute to the planners in health care and in education. The government decided there should be a children's dental care program, but it was the quality of the implementors who made it a success.

SUPPORT FOR PARTNERSHIPS

Participation leads to a sharing of power. The leaders in the field can accept that participation either sincerely or reluctantly. There are many who are unable to openly oppose the consumer era but who do not approve of the peasants as partners. Administrators and other leaders can obstruct the development of partnerships or provide support and resources. Leaders can carefully select the issues which will be discussed (usually for the purpose of retaining central control) or allow agendas to be prepared in consultation with all participants. The process can be controlled by those who organize the program or it can operate within principles consistent with the process of Community Development.

Issues in participation include its purpose, the items under review, who controls the process, the extent to which there will be full dispersal of information and the activities which will be promoted or allowed. The options chosen will be determined far more by bureaucrats than by policy makers.

IMPLEMENTATION OF HEALTHY PUBLIC POLICIES (HPP)

Health impact analysis (HIA), which is a component of social policy analysis, can only be carried out to the extent that the skills and intentions of policy analysts and administrators allow. Unless health impact analyses are carried out HPP is merely a dream.

Health impact analysis is only one part of the policy analysis process. Other components include estimation of economic impact (including impact on employment, tax revenues and foreign investment), political impact, environmental impact (predominantly the physical environment), cultural acceptability (which could be seen as part of political impact) and impact on national or provincial image.

HIA will be made difficult by problems of turf. Health care leaders, especially those in Ministries of Health, may wish to be the dominant players, and if they do the process will not be as productive as it should be. Ministries of Health should not expect to have ownership of the HIA process. To seek this ownership would be a mistake. Other ministries have used HIA more routinely than ministries of health. Policy analysts in all departments, and planners and administrators throughout the system, should see HIA as one of their responsibilities.

The process of health impact analysis will be complicated by the many definitions of health and by disagreements over the indicators, measures and standards which should be used. Leaders in the field, and bureaucrats in health ministries, can use the difficulties inherent in the task as an excuse for inaction or they can accept the desirability of the process and contribute to the development of it.

Prerequisites to successful implementation of HPP include support at the top (the premier, prime minister, mayor or chairman of the board), a sense of ownership in all ministries and throughout the health service network, and funding from operating budgets. Public interest groups will be natural allies of HPP. The turbulence associated with the introduction of health impact analysis will be lessened by acceptance of the infancy of the process, by noticing the difficulties associated with other policy analyses such as environmental impact, and by recognition of the extent to which nonhealth departments have pioneered use of the concept.

RESPONSE TO COST CONSTRAINT

While governments matured in their understanding of how to keep the lid on total spending, health care agencies were going through a number of stages of learning to live with less. The oil crisis of the early 1970s precipitated the first major hospital cut-backs. Construction projects were cancelled across Canada, regional cooperation became mandatory rather than voluntary and there were significant reductions in the number of beds in many hospitals.

Despite the industry outcry there were no noticeable effects from the first round of bed closures. Referrals to home care did not increase, waiting lists did not increase and administrators reported little or no need to lay off staff. (Sutherland, R., and D. LeTouze, "Review of 10 Ontario hospitals who reduced their bed complement by at least 10%", 1974). The period of rapid growth had produced such slack in the system that closure of 10% of the beds with an associated budget decrease produced nothing but lots of noise from hospitals and physicians.

Later budget restraint, in association with provincial refusal to cover deficits, once again caught hospitals unprepared. Response tended to be random and reactive. Deficits were prevented through the use of such devices as across-the-board cuts to all departments, a hiring freeze, cancellation of travel and education funds and staff reductions without reduction in volume of activity. Supplies became scarce, red tape increased and workers had no idea what would happen next. Little if any information was provided to workers, and few if any of them were involved in the response to cut-backs.

Many reactions were based on the premise that the right arguments or the right amount of political pressure would produce more money. Hospitals in particular, and their provincial associations, became expert at producing expensive reports designed to prove that the budget assigned was unfair, that money could be found, that somebody else was getting more, that the cut-backs would lead to community catastrophies and/or that political retribution was just around the corner if more money was not found. Unfortunately, more money often was found. Blackmail was in style.

Another commonly used device for staying within budget was, and is, to provide less care. Fewer hospital admissions and fewer services to the home mean fewer expenditures. If this option is chosen, and if the system continues to operate as it did before, the volume of both appropriate and inappropriate care falls and the community is less well served. The publicly funded system becomes smaller but little else changes. This response requires few management skills. It also is undesirable.

As cut-backs in hospital budgets continued in the 1980s some hospitals announced they would not allow government to dictate hospital spending limits. In Ontario a group of large hospitals announced that they intended to budget for huge deficits ($17 million at the University Hospital in London, Ont.). Governments responded by giving the Minister of Health the power to immediately take over the operation of any hospital that refused to operate within the funds allocated, and this power was used a number of times in B.C. and Ontario before hospitals realized they could not rewrite the constitution or fail to respect the resource allocation decisions of elected governments.

The revolts were highly unintelligent given the assumed quality of hospital leadership, and can be explained only by a health care culture which thought health care services were central to community health status and also too politically sensitive to be constrained. The ability and willingness of government to take over the duties and responsibilities of hospital boards and hospital administrators who defied government policy was quickly established and now seldom needs to be demonstrated.

Those who are feeling the pinch may quite reasonably let off some steam, but they are paid to do better. It is much more useful to put almost all available energies into figuring out how to serve communities best with the resources available. Blaming current politicians for economic events which are the products of earlier domestic choices, choices which are now unaffordable because of international events over which Canada has no control, should be left to reporters. Administrators and planners should now search for solutions rather than look for someone to blame.

Efforts to increase nonpublic revenues are another common response to reduced funding. These revenues can be charitable dollars or income from rentals or business ventures. Increasing revenue has received a disproportionate degree of attention, especially in agencies or institutions with good fund raising potential, such as children's hospitals. Better spending should get more attention.

Until the 1990s the usual responses to cut-backs were annoyance, scepticism, anger, revolt, a search for more money and a search for someone to blame. Hospitals and physicians have been most undisciplined, although Manitoba nurses performed poorly in 1993 with their demands for continued high spending on health care. The amount of the noise does not necessarily correlate with the amount of abuse. In 1992 several British Columbia hospitals and their communities screamed loudly when hospital budgets were decreased. A team of union, physician and administrative representatives studied these hospitals and reported that they were more generously funded than many other hospitals and that effects of the cut-backs on the community could be zero by implementation of some of the many solutions already in place in other British Columbia hospitals.

Hospital responses to cost constraint have not changed quickly. A survey by the Ontario Hospital Association in 1988 showed that hospitals, in order to adapt to new restrictions on deficit recovery, had reduced costs by (a) reducing services, (b) improving staff productivity, (c) closing beds (which was reported separately from reduced services) and (d) controls on purchasing and consumption. The hospitals did not mention reducing the delivery of inappropriate health care.

There are many useful ways in which an institution and its leaders can respond to budget constraints. The system can emphasize lower unit costs. This has been the emphasis of the last two decades. It lead to increased use of outpatient and day surgery, the rationalization of specialty services, improved productivity, preoperative work-up before admission, admission on the morning of surgery rather than the night before, better operating room scheduling and regional approaches to laundry, purchasing, dietary and other hotel and administrative services.

Improved efficiency has often been combined with raising the threshold for service. Individuals must be more seriously injured or ill before they are admitted to hospital, and discharge occurs at an earlier stage in recovery. These approaches do not significantly alter the mix of patients cared for but they allow community service to be maintained despite resource reductions.

Other devices include administrative economies. These include a flatter organization chart with fewer middle managers, fewer other administrative staff, a decentralization of budgetary control and responsibility, a freezing of salaries and forced or arranged mergers of two or more hospitals or of several health care sources.

An agency can also stay within budget by emphasis on reduction of inappropriate clinical decisions. This option is difficult, but it offers the greatest potential. It challenges the status quo much more than other options. It requires fundamental behavioral adjustments as well as technical adjustments. It has not as yet received the attention it deserves.

The concept of making choices on the basis of cost-effectiveness (opportunity cost and trade-offs) has not yet fully arrived. A new institutional or program expense still can produce a knee-jerk request to the Ministry for more money rather than a search for reallocations within existing spending. If low value services are identified they can be discontinued, or given fewer resources, so that higher value services can be preserved.

The problem solving approach can help those who don't know what to do. Identify and evaluate the options. Develop a strategy that reflects the best option. Such a strategy could include working with the appropriate constituency and forming alliances with parties with similar objectives. This strategy will be more widely accepted if based on proof of cost-effectiveness and consumer priorities rather than on precedent, institution or program protection and provider priorities. It will be more successful if it abandons the expectation that there will be new money. Certainly there should not be new money without proof of the cost-effectiveness of what will be done with that money. Even retaining current funding may require proof of positive impact. This strategy will require examination of what is being done now to see if it is consistent with the current state of knowledge.

Cost control by lowering the volume of care and/or by increasing output per employee, with little or no attention to the possibility that some care is of greater value than other care, has been shown to reduce the volume of appropriate as well as inappropriate care. If money is to be better spent so that the community is optimally served with whatever resources are available the issue of cost-effectiveness must become important. If cost control devices do not improve the mix of care provided then the community is the loser.

Although most hospitals have given minimal attention to better spending there are important exceptions. Some hospitals, mostly teaching hospitals, have tested and implemented devices to improve professional decisions, and their successes point the way for the entire health services network.

Some responses to cut-backs are not yet clear. How, for example, will physicians respond as more and more of them are affected by individual income ceilings? Only Quebec has long term experience in this area. What services will the physicians choose to give, and which ones will be dropped? Will the adaptations chosen by the physicians be acceptable to Ministries of Health, and, if not, what steps will be taken to protect the public interest?

The processes and principles of better spending are equally applicable to all health care agencies. Hospitals have been emphasized, but only because they have illustrated both the best and the worst of responses and they have the bulk of the reported relevant experience. (Collins, A.L. and R. Noble, "Hospital Rightsizing: In line with Long-Term Strategies and Economic Realities", Healthcare Management Forum, Spring, 1992)

In responding to cut-backs agencies should give emphasis to creating *do* lists, not wish lists. Make value-for-money a part of every clinical and administrative discussion. Involve all personnel in the search for ways to spend money better. Transfer money and functions to other agencies if they can do the same thing for less money. Stop spending money on accreditation surveys unless they become relevant to the 1990s. Don't expect someone else to solve the agency problems. Stop concentrating on that part of the solution which can only be implemented by someone else and give full attention to those parts of the response which are under in-house control.

As programs examine their costs and outcomes they will inevitably look at the originators of those costs, and physicians will experience the greatest scrutiny. Whether Canada will extend physician comparison and evaluation to the levels now present in the United States is not known, but increased surveillance is certain.

SUMMARY

Those who implement the strategic choices of others, and who must continue to serve their community but with fewer resources, should know now that there are no simple solutions to complex problems. They should not expect anyone else to solve their problems, although help should be available.

There should be no belief that the economic constraints will go away. They will not. They will, instead, worsen. The extent to which the economic constraints affect the outcomes of health care depends largely on the wisdom, commitment and courage of those who control the day to day operations of health care.

Health care agencies faced with cut-backs can complain, get mad, document the perceived abuse, prove more money is needed, predict catastrophy, ask everyone for more money or work with all affected parties to do the best possible with the resources at hand. Only the last response is acceptable.

Chapter 20

Sectoral Policies

INTRODUCTION

Earlier chapters have looked mostly at policies and policy options pertaining to the entire system. The chapters on physicians and on drugs are exceptions. This chapter looks at a random mix of policy options relevant to only one sector such as long term care, emergency health services, public health, home care and mental health services.

The discussion and examples in this chapter do not begin to expose the total spectrum of sectoral policies. A separate book could, and should, be written examining the strategic and operational policy options in each sector of Canadian health care. The purpose of this chapter is to illustrate a few of the sectoral issues and some of the opportunities which exist for better sectoral spending.

LONG TERM CARE (LTC)

Throughout LTC, major options exist regarding user involvement, the role of the for-profit sector, the degree to which resource allocation is on the basis of cost-effectiveness and the role of institutions.

Clients can have a limited role or a dominant role in designing a care plan and determining which needs are to be met first. Client involvement in chronic care is easier to implement and more necessary than in acute care, partly because many of the services are easy for users to understand, partly because values dominate when selecting services which best preserve quality of life, partly because providers routinely deliver services to users which are not of high priority to the user and partly because the care plan applies in the long term and user/provider partnerships are easier to establish and maintain. When cost constraint prevents all services from being delivered the available funds should be used to deliver those services most important to the user. Experimentation with user control over resource use should be accelerated.

In some provinces LTC leaders have been slow to relate services to outcomes. Resource shortages are accepted (they have always been a feature of this sector) but resource allocations too often reflect intuition rather than analysis. The *principles* listed in the 1993 Ontario LTC reform document *Partnerships in Long-Term Care* do not include serious mention of cost control, cost-effectiveness, better spending or any similar themes. These desirable concepts appear to be seen as impediments rather than as goals. Trade-offs are not discussed, and not enough effort is made to reduce the delivery of services which are *nice to receive* but which have not been shown to have a positive effect on outcomes.

The role of institutions is not always clear, and the quality and amount of care which should be delivered to various categories of patients who are institutionalized is even less clear.

Society needs to be involved in a continuing discussion of the extent to which resources should be allocated to persons who may or may not fall easily into one of the following indistinct categories.

One category of users is permanently cognitively disabled and without significant response. These are the decerebrate or almost decerebrate. Their deficits may be the result of a head injury, stroke, cerebral destruction from anoxia or a toxin, or the failure of the brain of a newborn to develop (the anencephalics). They may also be the end stage of a degenerative disease such as Alzheimers. Except for the anencephalics, whose life expectancy is short, these persons can be maintained for long periods of time in a vegetative state.

Another category of user has major permanent cognitive deficits but has an identifiable level of human response. They may or may not have physical disabilities. The causes of the cognitive deficits are the same as for the decerebrate group but the effects are less severe.

Another category has severe physical disabilities and significant communication deficits but relatively intact cognitive function, for example, some cerebral palsy patients. Another category are severely physically handicapped but with normal cerebral function and normal communication skills. This category includes persons on respirators, severe arthritics, persons with advanced muscular dystrophy, advanced ALS (Lou Gehrig's disease) and quadriplegics. The seriously psychiatrically disabled with intermittent intervals of improvement and an uncertain future, such as severe schizophrenics, are a category who receive long term care but are not cared for in the LTC system.

A final category, a category also not usually classified as receiving LTC, consists of persons who are oriented and who have no major physical disability but who are permanently socially unacceptable or unable to cope. These persons include some long term substance abusers who have lost most of their potential, and others who cannot cope with life.

The above groups all usually require significant social support. All except the last group have, in the past, been institutionalized. Only a few individuals in these categories have enough personal or family resources to finance the types and volumes of long term care which public systems currently provide. Public policy in a general way determines the extent to which social resources are assigned to each of these groups, and determines who lives in an institution and who lives in the community, but administrators and operational planners have more influence on the services available than do any other of the players.

Current deinstitutionalization practices include a number of apparent inequities. For example, many quadriplegics now live in the community but most people on respirators do not, and opportunities for living in the community are much more developed for younger populations than for equivalent older populations.

Criteria for allocation of public resources in LTC

The LTC sector has not emphasized quantification as a component of priority setting. Costing is often weak. Information systems may be rudimentary. The relative desirability of various trade-offs is often not well examined. Intuition and its associated cliches are often still generously used, although there are exceptions.

Allocation of LTC resources ought to be based on the same factors as those which dominate in other social sectors, including evidence that services do or do not contribute to health, estimation of cost per year of life saved, cost per year of quality life saved and/or cost per year of improved quality of life, the degree of cooperation of the user, and the priorities of communities and users. Indicators useful in LTC priority setting might include potential for increased independence, degree of cerebral capacity, degree of effect of the services on client, family and community health status and sensitivity to culture.

There is a need for policies governing what is to be done when the wishes of a user or family are more expensive than an option considered adequate by the public decision makers. Should user wishes be ignored, should additional public funds be made available, or should more expensive care only be available if personally financed. The last should apply.

There is room for more discussion of health care prior to death and of the distinction between premature and expected or appropriate death. These discussions may alter the role of acute treatment hospitals in the care of the dying and may lead to greater use of living wills and other forms of advance directives which allow providers to terminate services in defined circumstances.

The role of the private for-profit sector

Ideology has to date largely determined the priority to be given to profit, private nonprofit or public sectors in the sponsorship and management of LTC programs and facilities. There is little if any evidence of better management in profit organizations. There has been little comparison of outcomes from care by profit versus nonprofit agencies, but the objective of increasing client independence appears to be best served by nonprofit agencies.

One policy option in need of consideration is the use of private capital and ownership to produce forms of integrated housing in which institutional levels of care can be delivered to persons or households living in the housing they prefer and can afford.

The importance of age

Age sixty-five has to date been treated as though it was significant when calculating LTC needs. It is often the boundary of eligibility for programs. Should this artificial separation of populations be continued? Persons in the age group 65 to 74, and certainly 65 to 69, are more like younger than older populations.

If the age boundary was discarded then disability, potential for life improvement and other indicators unrelated to age would govern LTC planning, service development and eligibility for service. Abandonment of the artificial boundary between the elderly and those less elderly would encourage abandonment of vocabulary which classifies the elderly as a separate species, as in the common phrase *elderly people and adults with disabilities*.

EMERGENCY HEALTH SERVICES (EHS)

EHS are another sector in which trade-offs and cost control are still not in the sectoral vocabulary. Examples will illustrate how attitudes and traditions lower the wisdom with which money is spent, and how regional leaders often fail to act in the best interests of their communities.

For a number of years, a lobby in Ottawa headed by an emergency room physician and a municipal politician pressed for ambulance personnel with advanced life support skills (paramedics). In 1993, in the presence of zero growth in the budget of the Ministry of Health, the lobbying accelerated and was supported by the regional planning agency (the District Health Council — DHC). The Ministry of Health was told that for approximately $1 million the necessary upgrading of manpower and equipment could occur, and without the expanded service many people would die.

Pressure on the Ministry was immense and sustained. The paramedic service had been established in some other Ontario centres when funds were more available. The Ministry initially refused the funding but did not support its refusal with credible arguments.

The Ministry had several options. It could have decided to study the idea, which had some merit so long as the study was an examination of the relative cost-effectiveness of this extension of service versus other ways of spending the EHS dollars. The Ministry could have provided the $1 million per annum from its contingency reserve, from the EHS envelope in the Ministry budget, from the EHS allocation by the Ministry to the Ottawa region or from the funding of some other health care sector. To fund the program with new money would send a signal that budgetary allocation depended mostly on the power and persistence of the lobbyists. The Ministry opted for an operational trial using new provincial money.

The preferred option for the Ministry was to provide the District Health Council and all other interested parties with a breakdown of all EHS spending in the Ottawa region and invite the community and the DHC to indicate which EHS activities should have their allocations lowered so that the paramedic program could be funded without new provincial dollars. The DHC could have been reminded that its mandate included the task of examining opportunity costs.

The Ministry could also have widened the opportunities for regional decision making. It could have provided the region with information regarding provincial health care spending in the region, including information on spending by sector and program. The DHC could have been invited to indicate which health care services within the region should receive less money so that the paramedic program could be funded without new provincial dollars.

Either of the last two options would have made the region struggle with its own allocations, and would not have threatened the provincial global budget for health care. The $1 million only represented about 0.05% of the expenditures on health care in the Ottawa region, and finding the $1 million would have been easy if the region had chosen to search.

In agreeing to fund a trial of paramedics the Ministry accepted responsibility for a decision which should have been made by the region. The Ministry decision reflected a centralist mentality in which decisions were considered to be the responsibility of the Ministry, even if the Ministry didn't have the foggiest notion what to do and had no money to do it with. With health care spending capped no consideration should be given to requests for new spending, especially requests from planning agencies or funded programs, unless the request indicates which local budget should be reduced to fund the new services.

A second example also illustrates the unreasonable pressures which the media and the industry can mount, and the unwillingness of regional providers to deal with regional problems.

In the late 1980s a rural Ontario resident drank a fatal caustic product. The physician who first cared for her tried to send her to Toronto but was initially unable to find a hospital with a bed available. She died shortly after transfer. This inevitable death led to, or at least contributed to, the appearance of a Central Resource Registry which documents the bed status of all Toronto hospitals, knows the operating status of 28 emergency departments, can direct ambulances to an emergency department able to receive the patient and can quickly find a bed when one is urgently needed. The Registry has a full-time central staff in one hospital and every hospital provides bed status information on a regular basis. The central office reports regularly on the frequency of closure or semiclosure of each emergency department in the city.

A central bed registry has many merits. In some form it is needed when the emergency response network is large. The issue is whether ministries should have to be responsible for the planning or the new costs associated with a problem which should have been solved by the hospitals of the region.

The demand for additional funds and for provincial leadership for the establishment of the bed registry illustrates the inability or unwillingness of hospital administrators, boards and clinical leaders to work together to address a regional problem. Action was absent until there was special government funding. The budgets of the institutions concerned represented 5% or more of the total provincial health care expenditures. All institutions knew they were each at times unable to respond adequately to emergencies, but they were unable or unwilling to work together to reduce the impact of the unpredictable distribution of emergency demand. They refused to collectively serve the community by using their global budgets to solve a visible community hazard. The problem was not dealt with until the Ministry provided extra money.

As a third example, in the early 1990s a Regional Emergency Health Services Planning Committee in Ontario recommended provincial funding of over $900,000 per annum for a neonatal transfer system in the Ottawa Region. The report recommending the funding presented no evidence of undesirable effects on infants from the existing transport arrangements. It gave no data on the probable impact of the new service on outcomes. It did not calculate costs per case for the new service. It did not note that this new 24 hour standby system would move about one baby per day, that 60% of these would be transfers between Ottawa hospitals, and that 30% of the Ottawa transfers would be between connecting hospitals (the baby would be wheeled down a corridor).

It is a terrible commentary on the leadership in the field that such an undocumented and preposterous proposal would be forwarded to a Ministry by a committee composed of senior health care administrators. This example indicates the extent to which the highly paid experts in the field can choose to provide no leadership and then complain loudly when a much smaller mass of less highly paid public servants don't provide everything asked for. What would have been the response of the committee to such an incomplete and indefensible proposal if the only possible source of funding was a regional global budget for all health services or a regional global budget for all emergency health services? Hopefully they would have studied the proposal and then rejected it.

The general principles illustrated by these examples are not unique to emergency health services. They illustrate a mind set not ready for cost constraint. Perfection is the preferred standard, there is limited self evaluation, there is minimal evidence of resource allocation based on relative cost-effectiveness, there is an expectation that outside experts will solve local problems and there is a belief that more money can be found.

In these cases it is the administrators and planners who lacked the problem solving skills and/or the leadership to fulfil their mandate of service to their communities. They should, when policy is required, present options to the policy makers. They should, when they have the authority to act, evaluate options and proceed with the one which is most cost-effective and most consistent with the missions of their agencies. They should, when giving advice, be prepared to give the advice they would like to see implemented rather than scratch each others back. The province cannot, or at least should not, pay attention to irresponsible advice. It is entitled to better advice from health care administrators and planners than is often received.

Emergency health services need to begin to examine the impact of alterations in service levels such as increasing or decreasing ambulance response times by one minute, or reducing or lengthening ambulance travel time by five minutes. It is time to replace *if this isn't done someone will die* with *if this is done, will fewer people die?*.

The role of EHS systems in prevention

The EHS network should not be considered to be a major player in primary prevention. Its primary function is to care for emergency victims. Rehabilitation services (tertiary prevention) for trauma victims should also not be primarily within the purvue of the EHS system.

Prevention is the role of everyone. When education is the tool the prevention is usually best done by educational systems. Prevention in athletics is usually best done through recreational programs, and prevention of highway trauma is accomplished best through departments of transportation and law enforcement. Actions in each of these arenas will reduce the demand for emergency services, but emergency health services personnel cannot be responsible for the actions.

The separation of primary prevention activities from rehabilitation and from treatment does not suggest that the systems should not collaborate on all aspects of prevention, care and follow-up. It does mean that each has its own particular emphasis. To leave the prevention function in the hands of a network whose orientation and preoccupation is the short term initial care of the injured and acutely ill means prevention will be the primary focus of nobody. The glamour and crises of response to tragedy will eliminate attention to prevention.

A 1990 British Columbia report on trauma services described the sources of trauma and included prevention and rehabilitation in its mandate, but the major recommendations were directed to the transportation and early treatment of trauma victims. It is difficult for preventive and rehabilitative services to seriously catch the attention of persons dedicated to finding, moving and caring for the seriously injured. A Critical Care Hotline is discussed in detail and is recommended by the B.C. report. There is no examination of spending to reduce injuries.

A 1989 report to the United States Congress estimated that it costs approximately $2 million of EHS expenditures to save one life. Only 8-10% of the deaths following trauma can be prevented by optimal health care. For the remainder, primary prevention is the only hope. (Rice, MacKenzie and Associates, Costs of Injury in the USA — A Report to Congress, Johns Hopkins, 1989)

The lack of attention to injury prevention is unfortunate. The most ideal and expensive trauma network could not have duplicated the positive effects of the use of seat belts, nor can emergency services have the positive impact on community health status that would result from fewer drinking drivers or enforcement of speed limits.

Standards and guidelines

These tend to still be written in the language of yesterday. The EHS guidelines in Ontario were rewritten in 1991 but remained a description of what were considered to be desirable inputs and processes. There was no mention of outcomes as a measure of adequacy, and no attempt to use outcomes research and literature as a basis for deciding what level and quality of resources (inputs) and of processes (throughput) could be defended. In addition, the guidelines made little if any mention of response to psychiatric emergencies or to the special needs of victims of family and sexual violence.

EHS should operate in ways which respect the general proposition that when all services cannot be provided (and this is the usual situation) then all types of cases should face approximately the same level of inadequacy in the services they receive. Guidelines should be designed to improve equity and cost-effectiveness rather than be unrealistic wish lists.

Emergency services in hospitals

The first EHS policy question with respect to any hospital is whether that hospital should have an emergency department. Except for some urban hospitals immediately adjacent to other hospitals there should be one, but only a minority of the departments should offer 24 hour service and be prepared to receive major emergencies. The key policy questions for those hospitals who offer emergency services are what range of services, for how many hours a day, with what types of on-site and on-call personnel and with what forms of liaison with other hospital emergency departments and other sources of ambulatory care. Physicians would add method and amount of payment of physicians as another major policy issue.

Most of the same policy questions apply when public funds pay for emergency services in locations other than a hospital. Quebec has opted for the use of CLSCs as major sources of care of minor emergencies, a choice which is convenient for the user. A similar policy will not work well in provinces which have not put a complete network of community based ambulatory care centres in place.

The preferred choices are somewhat different for urban versus rural care. In urban centres only a very few hospitals should have 24 hour emergency departments. Whether other hospitals should provide 15 to 18 hour walk-in emergency care will depend largely on whether alternative sources of care have been developed at other sites in the community.

COMMUNITY HEALTH SERVICES (CHS), INCLUDING PUBLIC HEALTH

One policy question is whether all ambulatory care should be brought under the public planning umbrella. Should the functions and working relationships of private practitioners, social support services, consumer sponsored sources of ambulatory care, hospital outpatient departments, occupational health services and public health departments be defined by public planning bodies? Private practitioners and occupational health services are usually outside of public planning, and other CHS may be.

The role of CHCs is unclear except in Quebec. In other provinces there appears to have been no estimation of what it would cost if all of the province were served by a CHC, no plan for geographic placement of CHCs in multi-centre communities, no mandated or suggested interaction of CHCs in communities with more than one of them, and no clear identification of the populations which are to be served.

It is likely that community health services will eventually be given a global allocation of public funds. Every component of this sector will then be able to receive additional funding only at the expense of other components. If expenditures on physicians services grow at a rate greater than the rate of growth of the sectoral envelope then other components will see their allocations shrink. If new community based and independent workers appear (midwives), or if the roles of some of the existing workers are expanded (physiotherapists or nurses), and if the expansions bring new costs, then someone must get less. The sector is not developing the data and the rationale to assist Ministers of Health and community planners to be ready for regional or community global budgets when they arrive.

Public health programs

There may still be, in some public health programs, more discussion of preventive programs against hepatitis B, hemophilus influenza or bacterial pollution of swimming locations than against family violence, sexual abuse, highway violence, spinal cord injuries or emotional disturbances in teen-agers. Public health has been a vigorous opponent of smoking and heart disease but quality of life has seldom joined protection of life as a central theme.

At the Second National Conference on Immunization in Toronto in 1992 the Ontario Chief Medical Officer of Health said that where immunization was concerned money should not be an issue. It is unlikely that the same position would have been taken at a conference on social pathology, despite a rapid increase in the incidence of violence and other anti-social behavior by youths. It has been estimated that six percent of Ontario children suffer from clinical levels of behavior disorders. (Dr Dan Offord, Ontario, 1992) Senior public health officials should aim for immunization against anger, insecurity, loneliness, abuse and fear as well as the hazards of microorganisms.

Community health services are not immune from undesirable responses to financial constraints. In 1993 an eastern Ontario health unit, when faced with a budgetary squeeze, cancelled school immunization clinics. The community was informed that the central immunization clinics would continue to operate in the early afternoon as usual, and school children who wished to be immunized should come there. Since the clinics were during school hours and were not adjacent to the schools the change in policy effectively moved the immunization of school aged children from the public health program to physicians offices.

This change represented use of one of the classical devices for operating with less money, transfer the costs to someone else. It did not represent a change which was in the interest of the community and it produced inconvenience for the community. It moved immunization from a low cost setting to a high cost setting, and from a setting with a reputation for good record keeping to one whose immunization records are less integrated and continuous. It was a change which did not support the wish to use health care dollars better.

The future of public health programs and of other community health services may vary with the skill with which they consolidate ownership of traditional and appropriate services. Giving these services away will not help.

Control of the cost of care at home

Two general approaches have been recommended. One is the global budget approach in which home care costs are capped. The other is the slots approach, in which the number of persons allowed in the program at any one time is fixed. The global budget approach is the one most commonly used.

Either model will work. Both leave admissions and discharges under local control. Both have disadvantages. A global budget may discourage service to very expensive clients, whereas limiting the number of persons under care does not put a cap on total costs. In the 'slots' model the control could extend to the placing of limits on the numbers of persons who could be receiving specific types of care. The global budget is simpler, more financially predictable, gives the local managers the greatest flexibility and requires much less monitoring by the ministry.

Home care programs will eventually be obliged to respond to the many large and well performed randomized clinical trials which could not prove that home care had a significant effect on outcomes. Large populations who had received home care did not appear to be any different from similar populations who did not receive home care. As proof of impact becomes routinely demanded the home care sector will have to disprove these findings or lose funding.

If a user living at home wishes to supplement publicly financed services with additional services bought with private funds, or available under private insurance, this option is open. Community care is, therefore, a two tier system in which the range and volume of services received can vary with the user's ability to pay. This arrangement works well and should be seen as an indication that public and private health care can co-exist to everyone's benefit.

Community mental health services are, as with some other community based services, not sufficiently concerned with opportunity costs. In 1991 a presentation at a monthly meeting of Friends of Schizophrenia in Toronto described a 24 hour 7 day a week community based program for the care of severely disabled schizophrenics. The program, operated by a private group, had been in operation for about a year and was undergoing its first evaluation by the Ontario Ministry of health. It had a case-load of less than 40 and an expected future case-load of 60. The program had 7 full-time professional staff plus a part-time psychiatrist whose function was to support and advise staff.

Evaluation of the agency was based on client and family satisfaction, qualifications of the personnel and the range of services offered. The evaluation included no consideration of outcomes and no mention of cost. To a question concerning costs per year or other financial measures the respondent indicated that money was not a consideration.

Rough calculations indicated a per diem cost of $300-450 per day per client, with an additional estimated $60-150 per day for a variety of forms of social assistance and for the costs of care outside the program, including FFS private psychiatric care and medication costs. Costs of $100,000 to $200,000 per year would fall by one quarter to one third if the case-load expanded to sixty with no increase in staff.

The client centred orientation and the enthusiasm of the leader of the program were evident, but the deficiencies in the evaluation were equally obvious. The staff of the program and the attitudes of the public service evaluators represented a too common perception in community based programs. Money is a dirty word. This program, and all similar programs, should be obliged to immediately begin to justify expenditures on the basis of outcomes compared to the outcomes when other forms of care are used.

Balance in mental health services

Policy will determine the balance between care of the seriously mentally ill and of the walking worried, care in institutions and care in the community, and care by psychiatrists versus care by other personnel. A fourth required balance might be between one-on-one care and group therapy or counselling.

In most major mental health reports improved care for the seriously mentally ill has become the starting point. (Macnaughton, E., "Canadian Mental Health Policy", Canada's Mental Health, March 1992) In the absence of new money, where will the funds for improvements in the care of the seriously mentally ill come from? Some of the needed funds could come from reductions in payments to psychiatrists who provide counselling and stress management assistance which can be equally well provided by less expensive professionals. More emphasis on outpatient treatment of alcohol and other addictions would also reduce costs.

The potential for savings in payments to fee-for-service psychiatrists may be large. In 1993 Ontario proposed a limit of 100 hours of individual psychiatrist counselling for any one patient, and there were howls from the psychiatrists. If cost-effectiveness becomes a routine measure of the desirability of expenditures it seems likely that $10,000 in psychiatrist fees for one patient in one year will be often indefensible when compared to the options available.

PREVENTION

Prevention can be practiced everywhere and by everyone. Policy analyses of opportunities for prevention therefore cannot be narrow if they wish to find the most cost-effective options. To try to prevent something that cannot be prevented is a waste of money. To fail to try and avoid serious risks which can be avoided is to waste money on the avoidable sequelae. Breast cancer kills 5,000 women annually but there are no credible and routinely available preventive strategies available. Prostatic cancer is similar, as is diabetes. But the same is not true of lung cancer, coronary artery disease, accidents and suicides.

When prevention policies are being developed there is no shortage of examples. Alberta has tested a community cancer prevention program, many communities have tested or implemented accident prevention programs and many have implemented programs to reduce the incidence of heart disease and strokes.

Some of the prevention options with great impact cost nothing or almost nothing. The volume of infant deaths from Sudden Infant Death Syndrome (SIDS) falls by half if babies sleep on their backs rather than their stomachs. This change will prevent several hundred infant deaths in Canada each year (more than die from almost any other cause). A campaign to prevent diving head first into unknown water will prevent 30-50% of the broken necks caused by diving into shallow water. A program to reduce checking into the boards from behind during hockey will prevent another 3 to 10 quadriplegics per year. Mandatory roll-bars and seat belt use on all-terrain recreational vehicles will reduce the injuries caused by unsafe use of these vehicles, especially by children. Daily use of small doses of acetylsalicylic acid (ASA) by persons with atherosclerotic arterial disease markedly reduces the incidence of heart attacks and strokes.

Choice of the techniques of prevention which should be used is not always easy although there have been many successes. Iodized salt eliminated common goitre, and mandated vitamin D supplementation in a variety of foods eliminated the common form of rickets. Advising people to eat low fat, high fibre diets is inexpensive. Use of regulations and market influence to promote these diets is more controversial and can be more expensive. These diets lower the risk of heart disease and colon cancer, and perhaps prostate and breast cancer, but how should they be promoted?

Some prevention options provoke violent opposition. The usefulness of a sharply lower intake of red meat is clearly proven, but the beef lobby is powerful. The violence in hockey could be ended quickly but the owners of the teams know the audience likes rough play. It is difficult to know whether to blame the fans or the owners for the sequelae of the rough play. Many procedures with preventive potential bring too many negative effects and/or too little impact per dollar spent to be performed at public expense, as with repeat colonoscopy to find early bowel cancer. Other policies which have been described as preventive have, when assessed, not been proven to be so, as with regular home visits by public health nurses to elderly persons. (van Rossum, E., C. Frederiks, et al, "Effects of Preventive Home Visits to Elderly People", British Medical Journal, 307:27 1993)

Some prevention programs will of necessity be multidepartmental, multilevel and complex, as with the *Better Beginnings, Better Futures* programs in Ontario. These collaborative programs are attempting to lower the incidence of emotional and behavioral problems in children.

Some prevention policy choices will use technology. The development of small and inexpensive devices to measure sound levels will assist businesses and users to identify sound levels above 85 decibels, the level at which hearing loss can occur. This level is often exceeded in cars, video arcades and when using walkman radios and tape players.

BLOOD TRANSFUSIONS AND PRODUCTS

The Canadian Red Cross, under a mandate from all provincial governments and monitored and funded in recent years through the Canadian Blood Agency (which represents provincial Ministers of Health), provides blood and blood products to Canadians. Canada is self-sufficient in most blood products but still spends $100 million per year buying foreign blood fractions including albumin, immune globulin and coagulation factors 8 and 9 (for hemophiliacs). (Jacobs, Turner and Saunders, "Economic Costs of Self-Sufficiency in Blood Products: The Case of Albumin", in Restructuring Canada's Health Services System, 1992, p301-305)

Blood product policies are currently under review, and the options are being hotly debated. The debates relate mostly to the extent to which Canada should be self-sufficient in blood products, the methods by which self-sufficiency might be attained if it is desired as a goal and the extent to which power will rest with the Canadian Board Agency versus The Red Cross. The vigor with which the Red Cross is objecting to accountability to a public body is anachronistic. Public representatives should monitor and set policy with respect to any agency which spends several hundred millions of public dollars per year.

One issue is whether Canadians should use any blood fractions extracted from blood collected outside Canada. Blood collected outside Canada is, because of the 1200 persons infected with the AIDS virus through receipt of a blood product, considered to bring an increased risk, but the likelihood is weak if present at all. There are small and currently unavoidable risks with both Canadian and foreign blood and blood products.

A second issue concerns the extent to which the processing of Canadian blood should be performed in Canada versus outside Canada. Canada currently does not have the facilities required to produce several important plasma factors. These factors are currently produced in the United States either from Canadian plasma or from foreign plasma.

Canada could decide that foreign processing of blood collected in Canada is acceptable but that use of blood fractions extracted from blood collected outside Canada is not. This policy, if adopted, would require either increased blood collections in Canada, decreased whole blood use in Canada, the importation of blood for transfusions so that more Canadian blood could be exported for processing or some combination of the three options. The option of importing whole blood is unlikely. It places far fewer persons at risk than does the importing of blood fractions produced from foreign blood but would significantly increase total costs.

In late 1993, The Red Cross and Miles Laboratories decided that all blood processing should be carried out in Canada. Halifax was selected as the site for a new fractionation plant. By early 1994, conflict still surrounded this choice. Canada almost surely has, or could quickly develop, the scientific and technical skills required to operate the plant. The employment associated with the facility would be in Canada and there would be fewer Canadian dollars exported to the United States, but several factors make this option unattractive.

Canada uses twice as much Factors 8 and 9 as can be produced from blood collected in Canada. Producing a plant to do the fractionation will not increase the supply of collected blood. Assessment of the desirability of domestic production is made more difficult by the probability that manufacturing in Canada might be under the control of the Canadian Red Cross. The senior management of this agency has on occasion been seen to be less than adequate and it may be unwise to extend its management responsibilities into the complexities of more sophisticated blood fractionation. Of even greater importance is the probability that genetic engineering will produce Factors 8 and 9 in the near future. An expensive fractionation plant might be at least partly unneeded by the time it is built.

The tragedy of AIDS in hemophiliacs is already reducing the consumption of Factors 8 and 9, and the demand will continue to fall as one third to one-half of all hemophiliacs die from AIDS contracted from contaminated blood products in the period 1983-1985. This tragedy has encouraged the move to Canadian self-sufficiency, but a new plant will not protect against a repetition of the tragedy. Use of genetically engineered products will be the safe option.

The question of creation of new sources of employment in Canada is important, but many kinds of manufacturing or other value-added processes would bring new employment. Selection of areas for Canadianization should include consideration of many factors and be based on examination of many employment alternatives, and whether blood fractionation would be selected is unknown. A careful look at utilization of whole blood for transfusions is the first and most desirable step, as is evaluation of the probability of early availability of genetically engineered Factors 8 and 9.

SUMMARY

These sectoral policies illustrate a number of hazards and opportunities as well as the need for books which thoroughly examine sectoral policy options in Canada.

Chapter 21

The Future

INTRODUCTION

This book has explored policy options for spending smarter and spending less. It has offered an overview of the health care policies which will hopefully dominate for the remainder of the 1990s. The policies discussed are general. They will need to be customized to fit the diversity of situations found throughout the health care system and among the provinces.

Policy preferences have often been identified throughout earlier chapters. The policy preferences, when taken together, have three general objectives, namely to assist governments in their efforts to reduce spending on health care, to improve decision making (especially at the micro level) so that public funds which are available will bring the highest possible level of population health and to involve all major players, especially the public, in all processes in the hope that everyone will contribute to cost control and better spending. A subsidiary theme in the search for better spending is the transfer of duties to less expensive providers.

The remainder of this final chapter is a summary of significant policy preferences also found in earlier chapters. It describes where health care should be by the twenty-first century, and what steps may result in the desirable targets being met.

Public institutions, in particular Ministries of Health, should assist in the evolution of new societal and health care perspectives (a new culture) in which the role of health care in preserving and restoring health is seen in a balanced rather than an exaggerated way. Improvements in health due to better schools, highways, workplaces and homes should be seen as just as valuable as better health arising from health care. Death or lower levels of health caused by inadequacies in our physical, economic, emotional or social environments deserve the same attention as death or lower levels of health which arise from inadequacies in health care.

Priority setting in health care should first of all aim for a population characterized by a healthy state of mind. Quality of life is what makes life worth living. The preservation of physical health is important but only because physical health is often a prerequisite to quality of life.

All sectors, agencies and groups should be routinely involved in the development of the policies which affect them, including health care policies. There should be ongoing and welcomed local/regional involvement in the planning and administration of health care networks. This partnership approach may lead to intellectual, prospective and continuing processes of strategic realignment of resources rather than crisis reactions.

The new process should be dominated by openness, with everyone having access to most information. The resource allocation process should utilize the zero base budgeting format in which all programs and activities are considered dispensable until proven otherwise. Programs and activities should be preserved only if, and to the extent that, positive impact justifies the cost. All policy, administrative and clinical decisions should be examined and reexamined.

As health care funding is decreased the priorities of the public should be sought and, if reasonably validly identified, should be honored.

Decentralization should occur. It should be characterized by regional, sectoral, program and institutional global budgets. Choices will be decentralized, subject only to general provincial constraints.

Nonprofit boards of health care institutions and programs should move from the parochial agendas of yesterday to the community service agendas now needed. There should be less talk about the responsibilities of others to solve problems and greater assignment of energy and resources to finding and implementing solutions.

Macro level decisions regarding which health care is to be fully or partially available at public cost (the explicit rationing decisions) should be determined by public policy. Allocation decisions at the micro level, allocations currently made almost exclusively by health care workers (the implicit rationing decisions), should be the product of a combination of professional preferences, user preferences and public policy.

Preferred organizational and payment arrangements will be those which reward physicians and other providers who have attractive service profiles. Policies should avoid reduction in the provision of cost-effective care as health care funding is reduced.

The five basic principles inherent in Canada's current medicare system should be endorsed but with some modifications. All Canadians should have reasonable and reasonably equitable access, primarily at public expense, to a broad range of cost-effective preventive, investigative and reasonably treatment services. This does not mean that all useful services in endless quantity should be available at full public cost. User fees should not be automatically prohibited for any services. Portability cannot be fully assured because levels of public coverage will continue to vary from province to province, but provinces should work together to assure as much portability as possible. Public administration should be preserved.

The trend towards greater government influence in the design and delivery of health care should continue, but the dominant future theme should be partnerships before regulation.

Canadians should, for all forms of health care including hospital and physician services, routinely have the opportunity to choose to stay in the queue for public care or to buy the care privately. They should routinely have the opportunity to buy additional care beyond the amount approved for public funding if they so wish and can afford it. They should be able to buy services which are legal and which have been deemed by the public system to be ineligible for public financing. A one tier health care system is not in anyone's interest. The privately financed second tier of health care services could be delivered through a public system or a regulated private system.

Users should have full access to their files, subject to the decision of a court that such access should not be granted.

All Canadians should have relatively equal protection from financial ruin arising from a need for useful health care. There should be reasonably equitable access for all residents, at public cost or with public assistance, to health care which has an acceptable and affordable level of cost-effectiveness. Equitable protection of everyone against major direct expense for health care of high relative cost-effectiveness is more important than special protection of any population group against all health care costs. First dollar coverage will often not be possible if equity is given a high priority. Drug plans which discriminate on the basis of age, and the excessive preferred accommodation charges in some provinces, will have to change.

Persons with similar degrees of probable benefit from health care should have relatively equal likelihood of receiving publicly financed care. When care cannot be optimal, all users facing similar degrees of risk should receive approximately the same level of service.

320

Those receiving publicly funded care should be discharged from such care, or receive less care, as soon as the hazards of discharge or of reduced levels of care are less than the hazards faced by those who are waiting for publicly financed care or who are receiving inadequate care.

Restricted access, and less than perfect services, will inevitably be present throughout the system if equity and tolerable levels of public spending on health care are to exist.

Criteria for receipt of a specific type of service should be reasonably equal across the system. The Ontario province-wide criteria for coronary artery by-pass surgery are a good example.

There should be increased attention to interregional equity of per capita funding for health care. The funding should be adapted to reflect selected regional and population characteristics. The attention to regional equity may or may not lead to regional budgets.

Ministries of Health should sponsor, lead and partially fund continuing programs for better spending (Chapter 16), public involvement (Chapter 17) and better drug use (Chapter 18).

Provinces and agencies should encourage self help groups and provide support when impact is proven. These groups can be an integral and low cost part of the social support system.

The emerging ability to identify genetic abnormalities will, unless public paying agencies move quickly, become a source of great cost without gain in most circumstances. Policies in this area are urgently needed.

There should be decreased spending on services to persons with permanent loss of cognitive response, on heroic measures to delay imminent, unavoidable and expected death, on care outside of Canada and on services of little or absent cost-effectiveness, and reduced payment to expensive caregivers when less expensive alternatives exist or can be developed.

The important current activities are rigid capping of costs, major sustained province-wide efforts to improve micro level decisions and limited user access to services of relatively low cost-effectiveness. Capitated agencies in the United States and Canada should be examined for experiences which can be applied by the provinces as they seek better spending. Changes in method of payment of physicians is not as urgent as was formerly thought.

It is difficult to know whether AIDS is consuming more or fewer resources than it merits. Certainly AIDS caregivers on fee-for-service are underpaid, but the need may be for better use of money rather than more of it. Certainly the international conferences with 20-50,000 registrants (which are regularly held) are a waste of scarce resources which would be better spent on local dissemination of the latest information and on the care of patients. There may also be excessive use of expensive and unproven or disproven drugs. AIDS will consume many more resources in the future, particularly as the number of intravenous drug user adolescents who are HIV positive become young adults with AIDS and as HIV infection moves steadily into the heterosexual population. One truly frightening science fiction prospect is the evolution of an equally fatal and infectious agent which is spread by droplets rather than the transfer of body fluids.

The twenty-first century, and the final few years of the twentieth century, will bring many opportunities. There should be new levels of public benefit per public dollar spent. The impact on health status of public policies, personal choices and health care should become better understood. Health care decisions should become more appropriate and health care policies should support better spending. New partnerships should bring new levels of cooperation between providers and government, communities and governments and providers and communities. Providers of all types should be invited to prove their usefulness, with rewards for those who can. Providers and users should become more involved in policy development, a role which will require a greater understanding of government and of how public policy is created and influenced. All players will become more skilful at networking, alliance building and the art of compromise.

The changes which are occurring will inevitably lead to unexpected new dilemmas and issues. A reporting of the total public expenditures on addicts may, for example, lead to a massive public rejection of these expenditures. Quantification of the benefits from health care spending versus other social spending may indicate that there should be reduced public spending on health care, which may bring emotional and psychosocial overreaction. Significant substitution of other health care professionals for physicians will lead to serious disruptions in the lives and the psyche of physicians and some users.

In the next century many things will still be the same. Others will have evolved slowly. A few will be quite different. (Figure 21.1)

A number of events and changes provide the rationale and legitimization of the new paradigm. These include the continuing disintegration of the medical model, an expanding cadre of independent health care professionals with private patients and authority to prescribe and/or admit, and health care in which self diagnosis will be much more common. Health policy will not mean health care policy, health impact analysis will be a respected although often primitive process and the federal domination of provincial health care policy will be gone.

WHAT TOMMY DOUGLAS WOULD DO TO-DAY

Many of the elements of our current medicare were first put in place by Tommy (T.C.) Douglas as Premier of Saskatchewan. He is a hero of many, and was a very wise man. He was so wise that he would have the same objectives to-day as he had in 1945 but he would do quite different things to achieve them. (Figure 21.2)

The current policies of health care do not adequately reflect the knowledge of our times. In an era in which *efficiency and effectiveness* are the credo of everyone, the system continues to deliver services whose value is poorly known. Even worse, the system continues to produce and deliver much that is known not to be appropriate. We treat and investigate and raise funds as if activity was all that counted; impact is often unmeasured and/or ignored.

The next era should be one in which there are rewards for greater positive impact on health status per dollar spent. Better spending will allow reallocation of funds to high priority activities.

Figure 21.1

THE HEALTH CARE PARADIGM OF 2001

1. Resource allocation will be on the basis of impact on health status. Evidence will replace opinion, intuition and preference as the basis for individual and collective decisions.
2. Governments will use all of their departments and policies to protect and elevate the health status of their citizens.
3. Health care will either justify its expenditures or lose funds to other activities which prove they improve health status.
4. Society and its policy creators will write the rules: professionals will advise.
5. Communities and regions will have increased control over their expenditure priorities.
6. Equitable and cost-effective access at public cost will have replaced the goal of unlimited care. Public administration will survive throughout health care.
7. Accessibility and portability will be limited.
8. Competition for health care dollars will be intense.
9. A second tier of privately financed health care will be in place.
10. Alternative therapies will have increased in importance.
11. Self diagnosis will be much more common.
12. There will be greater government/practitioner/agency collaboration.
13. Government policy will protect population health before individual health.

Figure 21.2

WHAT TOMMY DOUGLAS MIGHT DO TO-DAY IF THE CURRENT HEALTH SYSTEM WAS NOT IN PLACE AND HE WAS A BRAND NEW 35 YEAR OLD PREMIER

WHAT HE DID 1945-62	WHAT HE MIGHT DO 1994-2010
He sought equal access to the best health possible.	No change.
He acted on the belief that hospitals and doctors were central to good health.	He would know doctors and hospitals are not central to good health.
He built a hospital in every hamlet and introduced universal hospital and medical care insurance.	He would assure universal access to health care that is cost-effective compared to other forms of social spending.
He left doctors in charge of medical decisions because he thought only they could decide which care was appropriate	He would monitor professional decisions, would expect conformity with current wisdom, and would cap health care spending.
He encouraged an increase in doctor supply.	He would cap the amount of money that would be available to spend on physicians, and would prevent growth in doctor supply.
He built a University hospital and established a Faculty of Medicine in Saskatoon.	No change.
He increased the supply of psychiatric beds to 6/1000.	He would (as he eventually supported) decrease psychiatric beds to less than 0.5/1000
He improved rural transportation, provided rural electrification, assured rural telephone service and promoted rural utilities.	He would do all these but would call them Healthy Public Policies and would do them because they protect health

---

The 1990s will reject some of the perceptions which dominated health care as late as the 1980s. The old argument to the effect that *I need more because I can spend more* will be forgotten because any fool can spend more. The proposition that *I can do more if you give me more* will be equally ignored. Almost any fool can do more if given more. These cliches will be replaced by the requirement that an equal amount of social good be produced with fewer resources. Poor spending will be the enemy, and it will be attacked.

The changes required in the 1990s are more likely to occur if everyone appreciates the need for their participation in the changes. All players have much to contribute and a responsibility to contribute. Players must seek solutions which affect everyone rather than only the solutions which affect everyone else.

Pogo said *"We have seen the enemy and they is us"*. This could describe the attitudes and perceptions of the public and of health care providers with respect to health care. In the demand for more care there may be the genesis of less health.

It has been postulated that extinction of the human species may be necessary if other life forms on the planet are to survive. This book neither accepts or rejects that proposition, but it does suggest that human health, and perhaps survival, requires less spending on health care so that there can be more resources available to support the many activities which are, especially in the long run, more central to population health.

There are already many signs of the changes which will become solidified in the future. If Pogo was to make another pronouncement on health care he might say *"The future is here but we ain't seen it yet."* Another old chestnut states that *"the more things change the more they stay the same".* In health care it is *"the more things change the more they change".*

This book does not offer simple solutions for complex problems. Rather, it offers ideas for new partnerships, better use of evidence and a new health care culture. There is no assurance that all of the proposed difficult and sometimes poorly understood solutions will work. There is assurance that continued use of the old processes will not work.

To some this book may recommend too many changes. It may in fact, not offer enough. There has been no consideration given to the possible effects on the health status of Canadians of a tripling of the world's population, of global warming, of artificial intelligence, of international economic feudalism, of a rapid expansion of the number of countries with the nuclear bomb or of the probable separation of Quebec from Canada. These are all real possibilities, and all will, when or if they happen, affect the health of Canadians and the ability of Canada to protect that health. But some are beyond our comprehension and all are outside of the scope of this book. We have dealt with only imminent and comprehensible factors.

Some of the preferred policies recommend significant change. This should not be taken to mean that the authors believe the current health services network is in chaos. Our position was well expressed by Maureen Dixon from Britain at a conference in 1990 (and quoted in the book Restructuring Canada's Health Services System, How do we get there from here? 1992, p. 314).

"In conclusion, it is worth remarking on the excellent relative position of the Canadian Health System. There is lots of money in the system, services are of high quality and generally accessible. If Canadians cannot get anywhere from here, the rest of us have little chance."

We agree. Despite the need for change and progress, the existing health services network is an excellent platform from which to build. It does, however, have a number of features which must be directly confronted as policies are amended to suit future realities.

At a conference in Washington D.C. in November 1993 Dr. Bob Evans of Vancouver said: *"Man never reads the writing on the wall until his back is to it, and perhaps it is, and perhaps we will."*

Perhaps this entire book is about whether Canadians and their leaders will courageously and intelligently manage the changes which are inevitable, or will we just muddle through. Will we be unable to see the writing on the wall because our back is to it?

Appendix I

Evidence Suggesting a Need
to Review Clinical Decision Making

This annotated bibliography is material which proves or suggests that health care decisions within the health care system could be improved.

References are not of equal value. Some do not pass a rigorous examination of their methodology. The quality of economic analyses in randomized clinical trials, for example, has been examined and found to be almost universally inadequate. (Adams, M.E. et al., Medical Care, Mar 1992, 231-43; Udvarhelyi, I.S. et al., Ann-Intern-Med Feb 1 1992, 238-44; and Ganiats, T.G., and Wong, A.F., Fam-Med Aug 1991 457-62)

The literature search was not exhaustive. Each department, clinical area or other operating unit seeking to evaluate the adequacy of their own decisions, and to improve them, should become acquainted with many more useful sources of advice than are listed. The material is meant merely to establish that there is a significant volume of literature to aid those who wish to make appropriate professional decisions, and to discourage those who wish to delay change until more information is at hand.

1. MEDICINE (general and subspecialties)

1.1 Cardiac antiarrythmia drugs

Arrhythmias after myocardial infarction (MI) can be suppressed by a variety of drugs but two of three widely used drugs tested in the Cardiac Arrythmia Suppression Trial (CAST) actually increased mortality. The other had no effect. This large double-blind multicentre randomized clinical trial (RCT) has been reported in many places, e.g. American Heart Association, 1991.

1.2 Acute myocardial infarction

a) For treatment of acute myocardial infarction tPA is no better than streptokinase unless streptokinase has been used in the previous year, but tPA costs 10 times as much. Many European and North American references, including GISSI 2.

b) The preliminary report of the Stroke Prevention in Atrial Fibrillation Study showed ASA 325mg and Warfarin reduced strokes similarly and with a comparable incidence of bleeding episodes, but ASA is much less expensive.

c) Acetylsalicylic acid (ASA) if regularly used at onset of MI would save 5-10,000 lives annually in the United States. It is the single most cost-effective therapy available. (Survival and Ventricular Enlargement Study, as quoted by Dr. C. Hennekens in Medical Post, Feb 4, 1992)

1.3 Antibiotics; antifungals

Oral quinolones (synthetics) are said to be as effective as IV third generation antibiotics and are 15-20% of the cost.(Kibsey P., Can Fam Phys, Nov, 1990)

1.4 Cholesterol lowering drugs

a) The Toronto Working Group on Cholesterol Policy (whose recommendations were accepted by the Ontario Task Force on the Use and Provision of Medical Services) supported the position that treating hypercholesterolemia with drugs was a less cost-effective way to reduce the hazards of coronary artery disease than a number of other strategies such as smoking cessation and diet with less fat. (in the report Detection and management of asymptomatic hypercholesterolemia, Ontario, 1988)

b) Nineteen thousand persons over age 65 are on lipid lowering drugs paid for under the British Columbia Pharmacare program ($8 million per year) despite lack of evidence in support of use of this treatment in this age group. (McCormack, J., in the Medical Post May 12, 1992, p55)

c) Review article. Cholesterol lowering medication is cost-effective only in high risk persons and the cost-effectiveness varies significantly with the cost of the drugs. Data on the elderly and on women is still inadequate. (Goldman, L., et al., Circulation, May, 1992, 160-8)

1.5 Arterial insufficiency

A Danish randomized double-blind study of chelation as a treatment of atherosclerosis found EDTA (edetate) to be less effective than a placebo. (The Journal of Internal Medicine, March, 1992, 231-267.)

1.6 Osteoporosis

A fluoride-calcium regimen is not effective in preventing fracture in post-menopausal women. (Riggs, B.L., Hodgson, S.F., et al., NEJM, March, 1990)

1.7 Hypertension

a) "Randomized clinical trials have shown that, after three years of treatment with a placebo, the blood pressure of nearly 1/2 of those diagnosed with mild hypertension was below the treatment threshold." (Leenen, F, Cardiac Care Update, Ontario Medical Review, Jan 1992, p25)

b) A workplace blood pressure control program reduced employer health care costs by 2 to 3 times the cost of the clinic. (JAMA, Mar 13, 1991, 1283-86)

1.8 Isotretinoin (Accutane)

This drug which is likely to produce fetal deformities has been found to be commonly prescribed to females in their child bearing years and who are not on birth control. In one study 38% of users were females 13-19 years. 2/3 of these patients were on no birth control or were already pregnant when the drug was prescribed. This prescribing pattern occurs with family physicians and with dermatologists. (Hogan, D.J., Strand, J.M., and Lane, P.R., CMAJ, Jan 1, 1988; and Lammer, Chen, et al., NEJM, 1985, 313:837-841)

1.9 Intermittent Positive Pressure Breathing (IPPB)

A large 1983 RCT indicated that IPPB was not useful. (Duffy, S.Q. and Farley, D.E., "The Protracted Demise of Medical Technology: The Case of IPPB," Medical Care, August 1992, 718-736)

1.10 Anxiety/anxiolytics

Sixteen thousand patients in Saskatchewan receiving triazolam (Halcion) were reviewed. Over 5% were on the drug for a full year at greater than the recommended dosage. Ten percent of those on higher than recommended dosage were over 65. (Report of the Saskatchewan Drug Evaluation Unit)

1.11 Alcoholism

a) A review article of program assessments. The general pattern seemed to be that the higher the cost the lower the effectiveness. (J Stud Alcohol, Nov. 1991, 517-40)

b) A one year follow-up of graduates of an outpatient alcohol recovery program showed only 23% with major relapses and sustained lower use of health services. (Perspectives, Royal Ottawa Hospital, Oct 1991)

c) Survey article. Some studies reported that outpatient programs which include family support are at least as effective as inpatient programs and cost only about 1/3 as much. (CMAJ, June 16, 1986)

1.12 Search for a primary tumor

A comprehensive search for the primary tumor was calculated in 1983 to be $2,000 to $8,000, and 10-20% of the primary tumors would be identified. Most of them would not be treatable except for palliative purposes. (CMAJ, November 15, 1985, 977-987)

1.13 Cost of chemotherapy

The cost-effectiveness of two drugs which both bring complete remissions in acute myeloblastic leukemia showed that the most expensive drug (idarubicin) was associated with much lower total costs. (Lobo, P.J., et al., BMJ, Feb. 9, 1991, 323-6)

1.14 Holter monitoring (HM)

a) HM should not be used to assess the frequency of irregular heart beats (ectopic beats; premature ventricular systoles) because there is now no proven treatment for the arrhythmias. (Ruskin, J., American Heart Association annual meeting, 1991; Med Post, Jan 7, 1992)

b) Continuous ambulatory ECG monitoring should often be replaced by patient activated intermittent recording. It is less expensive and just as good. (US Task Force Report; reported in J Am Coll of Cardiology, Feb 1989)

2. LABORATORY TESTS

2.1 Thyroid function tests

The use of multiple tests for initial thyroid assessment is not cost-effective. The most appropriate first test is the sensitive thyrotropin (sTSH). Only high risk groups should be screened including the elderly, post-partum, menopausal and those with a strong history of thyroid dysfunction. (Report of the Ontario Task Force on the Use and Provision of Medical Services, 1990)

2.2 Examinations of cerebrospinal fluid (CSF)

Analysis indicated no value in doing additional routine studies if pressure, WBC and protein are normal (American Federation for Clinical Research, Annual Meeting 1986)

2.3 Preoperative screening

Preoperative screening laboratory tests in asymptomatic healthy patients undergoing elective surgery were discontinued after assessment of their usefulness in all patients in 1988. (Narr, B.J., et al., Mayo-Clin-Proc Feb 1991, 155-59)

2.4 With use of anticonvulsants

Regular platelet counts, SGOT and CBCs are not necessary on children on long term anticonvulsants. Only initial baseline values are needed. Undesirable changes will occur in one out of 20 to 50,000 patients, but they are accompanied by clinical signs and can be picked up then. Study of 200 patients for 2 years. (Camfield, C., Annual meeting of the American Academy of Pediatrics, 1986). (Note: A RCT to validate this study would take one million cases followed for several years.)

3. USE OF TRANSFUSIONS

A survey article reported on nine methodologically acceptable studies of the use of red cell transfusions from 1986 to 1989. The studies used very different criteria for appropriate use. Three studies found levels of appropriateness of 88-99%. Five studies reported inappropriate use of 18-57%. Conclusion: high rates of inappropriate blood use are continuing. (Hasley, P.B., J.R. Love and W.N. Kupoor, "The necessary and unnecessary transfusion: a critical review of reported appropriateness rates and criteria for red cell transfusions", Transfusion, Feb 1994)

4. PEDIATRICS

4.1 Acute otitis media

European experience shows outcomes are the same whether antibiotics are used initially or withheld for 2-4 days and then used only in those cases that do not spontaneously resolve. Also, the use of 10 days of antibiotics (the North American practice) shows no improvement in outcomes over 5 days (United Kingdom practice), and neither show better outcomes than 2-3 days treatment, especially in children after second birthday. (Dixon, T., International Approaches to Otitis Media, Can Fam Physician, Sept 1990)

5. IMAGING

5.1 Routine chest X-rays

At least 100 Quebec hospitals, including some teaching hospitals, still do routine chest X-rays before anesthesia despite consensus that this is not cost-effective. (Conseil d'évaluation des technologies de la santé, 1992 report: Med Post, Feb 11, 1992)

5.2 MRI vs CAT scan

a) A review article reported on 54 articles on MRI versus CAT scan. None of the articles provided scientifically acceptable data to support use of the more expensive technology. (Can Fam Phys, Mar 89)

b) MRI may eventually be found to lead to better outcomes in specific circumstances but at the moment this has not been proven. (Kent, D.L. and E.B. Larson, Annals of Internal Medicine, 1988:108: 402-424, a survey article with 393 references)

5.3 X-rays of anxle

50% of x-rays of ankles would be avoided if done at first visit only when there is swelling, bone tenderness and inability to weight bear. (Beaulieu, Corriveau and Nadeau, CMAJ, Nov 1, 1986)

5.4 Low vs high osmolality contrast media

a) The low osmolality nonionic agents bring benefits to both low and high risk patients (Preston, M., Amer J Roentgenology, Aug 1990)

b) the safety of nonionic agents is great enough to warrant use despite the increased cost (Dawson, P. and D.J. Allison, Br J Hosp Med, Nov 1989)

c) Patient questionnaires indicated they would not pay $50 to avoid the nonlife threatening effects of ionic contrast media; income class determined whether they would pay the $50 so as to avoid the small additional risk involved with the older contrast media. (Appel, L.J., et al., Med Care, April 1990)

d) A large scale prospective study (337,647 patients) compared ionic and nonionic contrast media. The frequency of adverse drug reactions was 12.66% versus 3.13% respectively, with severe reactions being 0.22% and 0.04% respectively. There was one death in each group. (Katayama, H., et al., Radiology, June 1990, 621-8)

e) In a randomized double blind trial of patients undergoing cardiac angiography high osmolality agents produced three times as many moderate adverse reactions but no more severe reactions than low osmolality agents. All severe reactions were in persons over 60 or with unstable angina. They recommend use of the more expensive medium only in selected high risk patients. (Steinberg, et al., New England Journal of Medicine, Feb 13, 1992, 425-30)

5.5 Use of intravenous pyelograms (IVP or IV urogram)
Many imaging services can be of assistance in deciding how to deal with benign prostatic hypertrophy, but the practice of a routine IVP (IVU) is not necessary or desirable. (McClennan, B.L., Uro Clin N Amer, Aug 1990)

5.6 Colon screening
A comparison of barium enema and colonoscopy showed them to be equally able to demonstrate polyps but colonoscopy could not reach the cecum in 10-36% of patients and barium enema is therefore most cost-effective and preferable. (MacCarty, R.L., Mayo-Clin-Proc, Mar 1992, 253-7)

5.7 Cancer of rectum
Ultrasound and magnetic resonance screening are not yet able to accurately estimate whether or not there has been extension of rectal carcinoma to lymph nodes. They cannot reasonably accurately identify patients who might benefit from presurgical radiation or who will require a particular type of surgery. (de Lange, E.E., "Staging Rectal Carcinoma with Endorectal Imaging: How much detail do we really need?", Radiology, March 1994)

5.8 Exercise radionuclide angiography
A Mayo clinic study concluded that this angiography is no better than a supine exercise ECG to establish presence of severe CAD, and the ECG is less expensive.

6. SCREENING

6.1 Electrophysiology testing
Routine use of screening with electrophysiology testing after MI is opposed unless rigid criteria are used including low ejection fraction, an abnormal signal averaged ECG and high grade ectopy on Holter Monitoring. (Dr. Ruskin, American Heart Association, reported in Med Post, Jan 7, 1992)

6.2 Screening for prostate cancer
a) Routine use of ultrasound or other imaging is not recommended. Many cancers would be aggressively treated which would never become clinically important, especially in older men. The use of the lab test for prostate specific antigen (PSA) is not useful for screening. (Annual Review of Medicine, 1991, Vol 42)
b) The American Cancer Society recommends use of prostate serum antigen plus transurethral ultrasound and rectal exam as cost-effective in looking for prostatic cancer. (Medical Post, Jan 12, 1993)
c) 8-10% of untreated stage one cancers of the prostate progress (to later stages) in 10 years. This information should be known to patients with stage one cancer before treatment is considered. The information will especially change patient choices when average life expectancy is less than 10 years. Autopsies of men aged 40-49 showed 34% with focal cancer of the prostate. (Williams, R.D., "Radical Prostatectomy for early stage cancer of the Prostate", Urology, February 1994, and Chodak, G.W., R.A.T. Thisted, et al., "Results of Conservative Management of Clinically Localized Prostate Cancer", New England Journal of Medicine, Feb 1, 1994)

6.3 Screening for osteoporosis
Bone mass measurement is accurate as a measurement of bone density but there is no valid data confirming that increasing bone density lowers the incidence of fractures. (Melton, L.J., et al., Ann Intern Med 1990, 112:516-528)

6.4 PAP smears

a) There are two sets of current guidelines. Both recommend smears commencing with sexual activity. One recommends smears once annually for three years, then, if normal, every 3 years to age 69. The other recommends annual screening to age 35 then every 5 years. (Carmichael, J., JCME, April 1990)

b) An evaluation of Manitoba PAP smears found 40-50% inappropriate (Cohen, M., 1989)

c) Despite the array of cytotoxic drugs that have been evaluated in the treatment of cervical cancer, none have as yet had a major effect on advanced disease. Early diagnosis is the only effective protection. (Omura, G.A., "Chemotherapy for Cervix Cancer", Seminars in Oncology, Feb 1994)

6.5 Endometrial and ovarian cancer

There are no practical screening tools. Screening with ultrasound or laparoscopy costs $1.5 million per case found, and outcome changes are unknown. Antigen screening is still experimental. (JCME, April 1990)

6.6 Congenital Ricketts

Screening is cost-effective in a ratio of 7:1. (Quebec study 1980-82.)

6.7 Neuroblastoma in infants

Urine screening will find cases early and at low cost. Early treatment extends life but does not cure. (CMAJ, May 1, 1987)

6.8 Colorectal cancer

a) Fecal occult blood screening not recommended. No RCT evidence of reduced mortality although some cases are found earlier. (CMAJ, Oct 1, 1985, and Can Fam Phys, May 1990).

b) Occult blood screening produces 20-30 positive results per 1000 screenings, and 1-2 of these will have subclinical carcinoma. There is as yet no proof this screening improves mortality although it lengthens the interval between diagnosis and death. Controlled trials are under way. Justification equivocal. (United States Preventive Services Task Force, 1989)

6.9 Galactosemia in newborns

At $1 per infant and one case found per year in British Columbia it is very cost-effective.

6.10 Open neural tube defects

Prenatal screening can be cost-effective in highly selected cases. Criteria include willingness to abort. (CMAJ, Feb 1, 1987)

6.11 Sexually transmitted diseases

In a routine testing of all first trimester abortions for chlamydia and hepatitis B, 3.6% were found to have chlamydia and 0.3% Hep B. Screening was considered to be worthwhile but there was no discussion of costs or of whether this would be the best or only population to screen. (Can Weekly Diseases Report, Dec 8, 1990)

6.12 Upper GI endoscopy

a) Routine endoscopic screening of patients with Barrett's disease of the esophagus is probably not justifiable considering the low frequency of malignancy and the high morbidity and mortality of esophagectomy. (Michieletti and Simon, Can J of Diag, Oct 1989)

b) Endoscopic screening of patients who had gastric surgery 15-20 years earlier is probably not justified. Recent studies show there is only minimally increased risks of cancer in these patients. (Michieletti and Simon, Can J of Diag, Oct, 1989)

6.13 Mammography for breast cancer

a) The Canadian National Breast Screening Study, an $18 million study involving 90,000 women, took place in 15 centers between 1980 and 1988. The Canadian screening study reported a 40% reduction in breast cancer mortality in women 50-64 years but no change in the 40-49 year group. (CMAJ, Nov 1992)

b) The American National Medical Roundtable of Mammography Screening Guidelines (representing 11 US medical groups) has recommended that routine screening should begin at age 40, as has the National Cancer Institute

c) The United States Preventive Task Force in May 1992 recommended screening begin at age 50.

d) A University of Toronto study reported no proof that mammograms lengthen life. The diagnosis is definitely made 2-4 years earlier in post-menopausal breasts but this study said there was no proof life is lengthened. (CMAJ, Nov 15, 1992)

e) The Ontario Breast Screening Program began in 1990-1992. In the period July 1990 to December 1991 16,000 persons were screened and 161 cancers identified (a positive rate of 1%). The 16,000 women represented only 15% of the 50-69 year old females eligible for screening. Some of the screening centres "encountered total unawareness, indifference, and even hostility from some of the practitioners in their area". (Dr. Leo Mahoney, Chairman of the Ontario Medical Association Committee on Breast Cancer, Ontario Medical Review, December 1992)

6.14 Thalassemia

Very expensive to treat. Screening is inexpensive. Montreal has the only screening program. Fetal diagnosis through chorionic villus sampling or amniocentesis is possible but expensive and hazardous and should be used only after the possibility of a fetus with thalassemia has been established. (Chui, D.H.K., Wong, S.C. and Scriver, C.R., "The Thalassemias and Health Care in Canada", CMAJ, 1991: 144[1])

7. OBSTETRICS

7.1 Caesarean sections (CS)

a) "... the rupture of a lower segment caesarian section scar (during a trial of labor) carries a lower maternal mortality than that associated with a repeat caesarian section. Furthermore, provided the diagnosis of rupture is not delayed the perinatal mortality is not altered." (Allardice, J.G., JSOGC Jan 1992)

b) Effects of education on use of trial of labor (TOL) after CS.
A RCT involving 3552 cases, 76 physicians, 16 community hospitals. Physicians in 3 groups; controls, physicians whose work was audited and feed-back provided, and physicians who received Opinion Leader Education (OLE). In the group who received OLE the use of TOL was up 46%, LOS in hospital went down and vaginal birth after CS was up 85% (and CS rate therefore down). CS rates in the other two groups were unchanged or higher. (Lomas, J., et al., CHEPA WP 90-16)

c) The CS rates of 11 physicians in a community hospital were compared. Rates ranged from 19-42% for affluent women of low obstetrical risk. (Goyert, G.L. et al., "The Physician Factor in Caesarean Birth Rates", NEJM, 320:706-09, March 16, 1989) The CS rate in Denmark is 2% and they have very low maternal and neonatal mortality rates.

7.2 Routine fetal monitoring

Routine fetal monitoring for the purposes of assessing fetal risk during or prior to labor is not justifiable. It has not been assessed through RCTs. Interpretation is difficult. The monitoring when used by competent persons in selected cases and in conjunction with other testing procedures can be useful. (Parboosingh, JSOGC, June 1990)

7.3 Preterm rupture of membranes

In the absence of fetal/maternal pathology conservative treatment is indicated. No evidence to support induction. No RCT examination of the use of antibiotics and steroids.

7.4 Prevention of premature birth

a) "There has been no evidence provided of any benefit of hospital rest in prevention of preterm birth in uncomplicated twin pregnancy." (Young, D.C., JSOGC, Jan 92)
b) a drug which has been extensively used to reduce premature deliveries has been found to delay delivery by not more than 1-2 days. A seven year multi-centre Canadian study. The drug is justified only if the 1-2 days of delay of labor will lead to transfer to another centre, or if it serves some other purpose. (NEJM, July 1992)
c) There is "no evidence of effectiveness" of parenteral progestins or oral beta-adrenergic agonists. (Young, D.C., Journal SOGC, Jan 92)

7.5 Handling of low risk pregnancies

a) Family physicians vs specialists.

	Fam Phys	Specialists
Spont vag delivery	68%	55%
Induction of multigravidas	5%	15%
Low forceps and vacuum ext'n	10%	19%
Episiotomy	39%	57%
Outcomes	the same	

(Anthony Reid, U of T, 1990)

b) Shorter LOS
Comparison of outcomes from use of a new birthing centre with post-partum LOS of 1.6 days showed no change. (Mil Med, Nov 1991, 583-84)
c) Comparison of three prenatal care models for poor women showed care by nurse specialists to be equal in quality and less expensive. (Am J Public Health, Feb 1992, 180-84)

7.6 Routine use of ultrasound (US)

Five RCTs have shown better dating of pregnancies and better prediction of baby size with use of US. One RCT showed fewer inductions of labor. None of the RCTs showed significant improvement in outcomes. (Young, T.K., J. Horvath, E.K. Moffatt, CJPH ,July/Aug 1989)

7.7 Drugs to prevent habitual abortion

"*proper studies on treatment efficacy are lacking*" (Daya, S., JSOGC, Jan. 1992)

7.8 Infertility

A randomized clinical trial showed that none of the therapies currently in use for control of endometriosis as a cause of infertility is effective. (Obs. Gyn. Surv., 1986, 41:538, used in a presentation to the Royal Commission on Reproductive Technologies.)

7.9 Amniocentesis

From 1973 to 1983 one Ontario hospital performed over half of the amniocenteses in the province. By 1987, 2 hospitals, one a community hospital, accounted for 53% of the provincial total (32 and 21%). (McDonough, P., "The diffusion of Genetic Amniocentesis in Ontario: 1969-1987", CJPH, Nov/Dec 1990)

7.10 Maternal Serum Alpha Fetoprotein Screening (MSAFP)

Screening volumes vary from low to routine, with testing being routine in Manitoba and some parts of Ontario, and in many part of Europe. (JSOGC, Feb 1992 63-71)

8. SURGERY (including surgical diagnostic procedures)

8.1 Carotid endarterectomy

a) Carotid endarterectomy is the treatment of choice in patients who have had a Transient Ischemic Attack (TIA) or a non-disabling stroke in the preceding 4 months, who have a 70+% stenosis on the side causing symptoms and who are having their surgery done in a centre with a perioperative rate for stroke or death of less than 6%. There is no evidence to support surgery in the patient with asymptomatic stenosis (bruit), and therefore no need to refer these patients for evaluation of the degree of stenosis. (The North American Symptomatic Carotid Endarterectomy Trial {NASCET}, many references including Patient Care Jan 1992 - What's new in stroke prevention)

b) Two carotid endarterectomy analyses deemed 55% (salaried physicians - VA patients) and 35% (Medicare FFS patients) of the surgery to be appropriate (45% and 65% inappropriate) (Winslow, NEJM, March 24, 1988)

c) A 1981 study found over 50% of carotid endarterectomies probably inappropriate (along with 10-15% of angioplasties and 20-25% of G.I. endoscopies). A follow-up study in 1987 found little if any change in the clinical choices. (Chassin, et al., RAND Corporation, JAMA, Nov 13, 1987)

d) Evaluation of a random sample of 1300 carotid endarterectomies resulted in 35% being considered appropriate, 32% equivocal and 32% inappropriate. Almost 10% of patients suffered death or a major complication within 30 days of surgery. (Winslow, C.M. et al., NEJM, 318:721-727, 1988)

8.2 Surgery for stage one and two breast cancer

In the period 1985-1990 there was a decrease in the use of surgery which preserves the breast, despite the publication of a major study in 1985 recommending lumpectomy instead of mastectomy. (two papers in JAMA in late Dec 1991, reported in The Wall Street Journal Dec 26, 1991)

8.3 Routine review of surgical necessity

a) In two Calgary tertiary care hospitals (Foothills and Calgary General) surgeons are asked to justify their reasons for elective surgery. There has been a 25-30% drop in the volume of elective surgery. (Dr. Robert McMurtry, Chief of Surgery)

b) 88 male patients recommended for coronary artery by-pass graft were reviewed by a second surgeon. The second opinion recommended that 74 (84%) be maintained on a medical regimen. 28 months after the second opinion was given 70% of those on the medical program were actively employed, compared to only 45% of those who received surgery. 14 of those not recommended for surgery were later (within the 28 months) approved for surgery. Outcomes with deferral of surgery appear to be better than would have been expected if all patients had been treated surgically. (Graboys, T.B., et al., JAMA, 258:1611-14, 1987)

8.4 Hysterectomy

a) Saskatchewan had high hysterectomy rates in 1964-1971. A surveillance program by the College of Physicians and Surgeons led to a 32% drop in frequency and the lower rates have persisted through the 1980s while rates in other parts of the country, in particular in the Atlantic provinces, remained high. (Report of the Working Group on Quality Assurance and Effectiveness of Health Care, HWC, 1990)

b) The annual rates for hysterectomy per 100,000 population for the five year period 1984-1989 varied from 263.6 in Prince Edward Island to 536.4 in Newfoundland. Quebec was second highest at 396.2 and Saskatchewan second lowest at 309.8.

c) Male physicians are twice as likely to recommend hysterectomy as female physicians. (Chronic Diseases in Canada, May-June, 1992, p40)

8.5 Prostate surgery

Postoperative mortality rates in the 90 days after surgery for both complete prostatectomy and transurethral resection (TUR) are about 2.5% (one patient in 40). Rates for men over 75 years are five times those of younger men. Because of the likelihood of a second operation when a TUR is performed (15% vs 4%) the risks to the patient are higher with the TUR. This information is quite different from the common appreciation of the relative risks of these two procedures. (Shapiro, E., Manitoba Health Care Studies and their Policy Implications, 1991, p19) (Roos, N.P., et al., NEJM, 320:1120-1124, 1989)

8.6 Cardiovascular surgery

a) Invasive versus conservative therapies have the same outcomes for myocardial infarction (MI), i.e. surgery or angioplasty did not improve outcomes. (The Thrombolysis in Myocardial Infarction Study Group, 1989; NEJM, Mar 9, 1989; A Chart Book — Appropriateness of Care, Brook, R.F., and Vaiana, M., National Health Policy Forum, George Washington University)

b) An assessment of coronary artery by-pass (CAB) in 3 hospitals found 14% inappropriate and 30% questionable. (Winslow, C.M., et al., JAMA, July 22-29, 1988). In one hospital only 35-40% were deemed appropriate, in another 78% were deemed to be appropriate.

c) The Survival and Ventricular Enlargement (SAVE) study allowed comparison of the outcomes of care in Canada and the United States. Outcomes were similar except there was a 6% increase in residual activity limiting angina in Canada. United States care included 80% more surgery, imaging investigations and drugs. (NEJM, March 18, 1993)

8.7 Pacemaker implantation

An assessment of pacemaker implantations found 20% not indicated and 36% questionable (Greenspan, A.M., et al., NEJM, Jan 21, 1988)

8.8 Vascular surgery (excluding cardiovascular)

a) A Mayo clinic study of surgery on asymptomatic patients with aortic stenosis indicated surgery should be delayed until symptoms appear. The risks of the surgery outweigh the risks of the stenosis until symptoms develop. (J of Am Coll of Cardiology, April 1990)

b) Carotid artery by-pass surgery was performed on thousands of persons over two decades before analysis confirmed that persons who had the surgery had 14% more strokes than those who were treated nonsurgically. (NEJM, 1986)

8.9 Orthopedics

a) Tennis elbow.
A review of all articles 1966-1988 was reported to show no clear scientific basis to support any of the treatment modalities routinely used. There were 14 randomized trials but none of high quality. (Labelle, H., Annual Meeting of the Canadian Orthopedic Association, 1989)

b) A study of patients with low back pain compared chiropractic care to hospital outpatient management. Improvement was greatest with chiropractic care, but the great majority of patients were helped very little by either type of care. (Meade, Dyer, Browne et al., British Medical Journal, 300:1431, 1990)

c) Chiropractors manage injured workers with a history of low back pain better than physicians, and return them to work more quickly. (Nyiendo, J., J-Manipulative-Physiol-Ther, May 1991, 231-9)

8.10 Cholecystectomy

Asymptomatic patients with gallstones should be left alone — a risk benefit analysis. (Johnston, D.E. and M.M. Kaplan, "Pathogenesis and treatment of gallstones," NEJM Feb 11, 1993)

8.11 Vasectomy

Ontario could achieve over $4 million in savings if vasectomies were performed in offices rather than hospitals. Costs per procedure varied by over $300. (Goel, V. and W. Young, Institute for Clinical Evaluative Sciences, Sunnybrook Hospital, 1993)

9. COMMUNITY CARE (including Health Promotion)

9.1 Anti-smoking programs

Three different evaluations of the "Time To Quit" (TTQ) smoking cessation program all reported no discernible effects from the program. (Davies, et al., CJPH, Jan-Feb 1992)

9.2 Home Care

There is very little evidence that spending on community services in the United States improves outcomes or is more cost-effective than institutional care. Life was not lengthened by home care, and activity skills did not increase. Health care costs were routinely increased. The studies could not identify the patient characteristics which caused a patient to be high or low cost. The profiles of patients costing $600 a month looked about the same as the profiles of patients costing $60 per month. (Weissert, W.G., "Cost-effectiveness of Home Care", in Restructuring Canada's Health Services System, U of T Press, 1992, 89-98)

9.3 Hospital in the Home

Evaluation of Verdun Hospital in the Home recommended no further similar programs until further study. (Stuart, N., Proceedings of the First National Home Care Conference, 1989)

9.4 Home care for the terminally ill

Total costs were 18% lower using home care instead of hospital care. (Hughes, S.L., et al., Health Services Research, Feb 1992 801-17)

9.5 Prenatal care

A community based program of prenatal care for adolescents reduced costs by 40% compared to care through a traditional medical center, with no change in outcomes. (Kay, B.J., et al., Medical Care, June 1991 531-42)

9.6 Profit vs non-profit

A comparison of home care delivered by commercial and nonprofit agencies in Calgary in 1985-86 reported that the commercial agencies delivered 36% more nursing care to comparable patients and also kept clients in the program longer. The commercial care cost 48% more per equivalent case.

10. NONSURGICAL GYNECOLOGY

10.1 Estrogen replacement therapy

There are no satisfactory randomized clinical trials of the use of replacement hormone therapy at menopause, and there is not enough evidence to know when to use estrogen versus progesterone, or how much or for how long in those cases in which it is indicated. (Prior, J., Med Post, Feb 11, 1992)

11. LENGTH OF HOSPITAL STAY

11.1 Use of case managers

Case Managers (CM) followed the care of patients over 65 with fractured hips. There was marked improvement in the percentage discharged home, fewer patients died, length of stay was shortened and mobility status improved. (Ogilvie-Harris, The Toronto Hospital, Ontario Medicine, Mar 9, 1992)

11.2 Obstetrics

The LOS of uncomplicated obstetrical cases in many parts of the world is 2 days. Outcomes are no worse with shorter LOS and costs are lower. (CMA Task Force Report, 1985)

13. LONG TERM CARE

13.1 Tube feeding

Tube fed patients are often on DNR orders and are often unresponsive or semi-responsive. There often has been no discussion with families regarding the continuation of tube feeding, and no apparent relationship seen between the DNR order and the tube feeding. (Wilson, D., Can J on Aging, Vol 10, No. 4, 1991)

13.2 Per diem costs in homes for the developmentally handicapped

Minnesota costs of these residential facilities were lowest for units with 13-16 beds or over 65 beds. The most expensive were 6 or less beds, or 33 to 64 beds. (State of Minnesota Policy Analysis paper No. 15, 1983)

13.3 Factors important to quality

The weight of the evidence supports the following. The least effective interventions in nursing homes are the formal therapies such as reality orientation, reminiscence therapy and pet therapy. Improvements in the milieu pay off in well-being. Breaking down barriers between the nursing home and the community increases well-being. The more that residents perceive they have choices and control over their lives, the better are both their physical and psychological outcomes. (Kane, R.A. and R.L. Kane, Inquiry, 25:132-46 1988) (The last finding is uniformly and impressively shown, as in Hall, N., De Beck, D.J., et al., Can J on Aging, Vol 11, No. 1, 1992, 72-91)

13.4 Geriatric Day Hospitals

Geriatric day hospitals are not a cost-effective way to use scarce health care resources. (Eagle, D.J. et al., Restructuring Canada's Health Services System, 1992, 285-299)

14. NURSING

14.1 Nurse endoscopists

Nurses who are trained for 3-5 weeks can carry out flexible sigmoidoscopy as accurately and safely as experienced gastroenterologists. (Maule, W.F., "Screening for colorectal cancer by nurse endoscopists", New England Journal of Medicine, Jan, 24 1994)

15. MENTAL HEALTH

15.1 Schizophrenia

A one year follow-up of schizophrenic patients discharged in Vancouver B.C. and Portland, Oregon showed fewer readmissions, higher levels of well-being and higher employment rates in Vancouver, which has a much more extensive community psychiatric network. No cost data. Only about 1/3 of the discharged patients in each city were able to be followed. (Am J of Psychiatry 142:1047-1052, 1985)

15.2 Sex offenders

A long term follow-up of sex offenders treated at the Penetanguishene Mental Health Centre showed the persons treated did more poorly that persons not treated. (Marnie Rice, speaking to a conference on forensic psychiatry, June 19, 1989, reported in Toronto Star June 20, 1989)

16. PRIMARY PREVENTION (in health care)

16.1 AIDS in health care workers

Three approaches to the protection of health care workers exposed to blood which could carry AIDS were compared. (Allen UD and others, Clinic-Infect-Diseases, April 1992, 822-30) AZT may be a cost effective protection if used for workers injured by needle-stick and the patient is HIV positive. (Ramsey, S.D. and Nettleman, M.D., Medical Decision Making Apr-Jun 1992, 142-8)

16.2 Wellness programs

Work site wellness programs aimed at hypertension, obesity and cigarette smoking and consisting of health education, follow-up counselling and plant organization for health promotion were cost-effective in terms of reduced risk and the costs of those risks. (Erfurt, J.C. et al., J-Occup-Med Sept 1991, 962-70)

16.3 Immunization for Hemophilus Influenzae b

a) A universal immunization program brings societal savings 50% greater than the cost of the program, but most of those savings do not occur in health care. Society gains but health care loses. The cost-benefit picture changes markedly with changes in the price of the vaccine and the cost of administration. (Ginsberg, G.M., I. Kassis and R. Dagan, "Cost benefit analysis of Hemophilus Influenzae type b vaccination program in Israel", Journal of Epidemiology and Community Health, Dec 1993)

b) In Arkansas there was a 90% decrease in the number of cases of hemophilus meningitis almost immediately after immunization at 2 months of age of less than 50% of children. Cases which did occur were almost entirely in unimmunized children. (Buchanan, G.A. and T. Darville, "Impact of Immunization Against Hemophilus Influenzae Type B on the incidence of HIB meningitis Treated at the Arkansas Children's Hospital", Southern Medical Journal, January, 1994)

17. REGIONAL OR PROGRAM VARIATIONS IN HEALTH CARE

a) Canada's rates of gallbladder surgery are the highest of the 24 members of the Organisation for Economic Cooperation and Development (OECD) despite similar rates of gall-bladder disease. (OECD report; Measuring Health Care p117, 1985, as quoted by M. Rachlis May 5, 1989 MRG)

b) The rates, for the elderly, of coronary angiography, carotid endarterectomy and upper G.I. endoscopy in different regions of the United States were found to vary up to 130%, 400% and 45% respectively. (Chassin, et al., JAMA 258:2533-37, 1987) Appropriateness of care was also studied. Levels of inappropriate care were higher in high use than in low use regions.

c) The Swiss Canton of Bern had a hysterectomy rate over 50% higher than that of Canton Tocino. (Domenighetti, Lancet, Dec 24/31, 1988, and the National Health Policy Forum Chart Book, 1989)

d) A resident of Boston is twice as likely as a resident of New Haven to receive a carotid endarterectomy. The same resident of Boston is half as likely to have a coronary by-pass operation as a resident of New Haven. Other surgical procedures also showed unexplainable differences in volume. (Wennberg, J.E., "The Paradox of Appropriate Care", JAMA, Nov 13, 1987) Boston hospital costs per capita were also almost twice those of New Haven. (Wennberg, J.E., Freeman, J.L. and W.J. Culp, Lancet, 1:1185-89, 1987)

e) High risk patients (over age 85 or having multiple diagnoses) have surgical rates up to 50% higher in some regions than others. (Shapiro, E., Manitoba Health Care Studies and their Policy Implications, 1991, p13)

f) Utilization rates of Medicare beneficiaries for 123 procedures were studied in 13 United States regions representing all of the country. Sixty-seven of the procedures, after adjustments for age and sex variations among the regions, showed at least a threefold difference in rates between the lowest and highest use areas. (Chassin, M.R., et al., NEJM, 1986, 314:285-315)

g) By the age of 55 an Alberta women has a 38% probability of having a hysterectomy, a figure equivalent to the lifetime risk in Australia and the United States. (Svenson, W.L. et al., Chronic Diseases in Canada, May-June 1992) The lifetime risk of an Alberta female is 49%.

h) A comparison of hospital LOS by diagnosis showed no institutional pattern. A hospital could have a low length of stay for one diagnosis or department and a long LOS for a different department. The variations appear to suggest physician dominance rather than institutional culture or bed supply. (Shapiro, E., Manitoba Health Care Studies and their Policy Implications, 1991)

i) Studies have demonstrated that shorter LOS are not associated with worsening of outcomes. (Cleary, P.D., et al., JAMA, 1991 266:73-79, and Mannheim, et al., Inquiry 1992 29:55-66)

18. PHYSIOTHERAPY AND OCCUPATIONAL THERAPY

18.1 Osteoarthritis of the knee

"The efficacy of strength training for treating osteoarthritis of the knee has not been clearly demonstrated." Six out of seven studies reported decreased pain and improved function but none were methodologically sound. (Marks, R., "Quadriceps Strength Training for Osteoarthritis of the Knee, A literature review and analysis," Physiotherapy Jan 1993.)

18.2 PT for burns of hands

A survey of 22 pediatric burn units in Britain showed great variability in treatment philosophy and process, some completely contradictory to others. (Raeside, F., Physiotherapy, December 1992.)

18.3 Electrical neuromuscular stimulation (ENS)

a) ENS had no demonstrable effect on spasticity or active movement or function in patients with multiple sclerosis. Single blind trial in 40 patients. (Livesley, E., Physiotherapy December 1992)

b) Patterned neuromuscular stimulation should not be used outside of a research setting. 'Trophic stimulation' has become a buzz-word. The usefulness of the technique has not been confirmed by RCTs. (Howe, T., et al., Physiotherapy, October 1992)

18.4 Manual hyperinflation (MH)

MH is widely used, especially in ICUs, but there is no conclusive evidence of its value. Throughout the UK there is great variability of both when and how it is used. A literature survey. (King, D., and A. Morrett, Physiotherapy, October 1992)

18.5 Hip replacements

Costs of Occupational Therapy for hip replacement patients was reduced by one third with no change in outcomes when group therapy replaced individualized therapy as the main method of service delivery. (Trahey, P.J., Am-J-Occup-Therapy, May 1991, 397-400)

19. OPHTHALMOLOGY

Costs per year of ocular beta-blockers (glaucoma medication) varies over 500% depending on the drug prescribed and the size of the bottle. (Ball, S.F. and E. Schneider, Arch. Ophthal., May 1992, 654-7)

20. EXAMPLES OF STUDIES AND EXPERIENCES OF QUESTIONABLE CREDIBILITY

20.1 Studies which examine intermediate effects rather than patient outcomes

A paper proposed use of 24 hour ECG monitoring to identify persons having silent ischemic attacks. Persons having these attacks have 2 to 3 times the risk of dying in the next 2 years as do persons without these episodes. (Circulation, March 1990) The defect in this study is that no evidence is provided to suggest that knowing about the ischemic attacks alters patient outcomes.

20.2 Studies whose findings may be the effects of factors not examined in the study

A study reported by staff of the Royal Ottawa Hospital on the cost-effectiveness of treatment for Multiple Personality Disorders followed progress over a number of years and assumed all improvements were the product of health care when many other factors were at work.

20.3 Studies which examine what is already understood and do not build on what is known

A randomized trial of a Health Promotion program showed that if people are given more emotional support at home, and more control over their lives, they can stay at home longer and they live longer. (Can J of Aging, Vol 2 No. 1, 1992) This study proved what has been already proven and confirmed the desirability of policy directions already in place, but it did not measure costs and did not compare anything with anything. A follow-up study, preferably multi-centred and long term, might examine the outcomes (per dollar spent) from various combinations of traditional health care and the activities central to the first study.

20.4 Studies which merely prove more can be done if more is spent

A study showed an expanded home care program can serve patients better. No costs were provided. (Can J of Aging, Vol 2 No. 1, 1992)

20.5 Studies which use inferior research methods when better methods are available

The United States News asked 1500 physicians to identify the best hospitals in the United States. Governments and consumers should ask for objective evidence.

INDEX

344

household caregivers 140
human resources (see also professionals and specific headings) 211-223
— optimal use of 211-212
— policy issues 211
hypertension 47, 240, 326
hysterectomy 16, 40, 242, 333

I.

illness, changing patterns of 9
imaging 16, 42, 121-122, 128-129, 143, 150, 156, 240, 328-329
immunization 46, 53, 98, 142, 153, 182, 313, 337
— costs 212
impact (see outcomes)
inability to cope 308
inappropriate health care 325-338
— avoidance of 228
— identification of 242
— evidence of 238-239
— magnitude of 53, 239
— types of 237
incentives 135, 182, 249
income
— general population 13, 24
— importance to health 13, 18-19
— health care professionals 89
incontinence 41-42, 230
independence 84-86
— of agencies and sectors 84
— of provinces 95-96
Independent Health Facilities Act (Ontario) 86, 99, 121-122
inequity (see equity)
information 229-234
— access to 232, 233, 319
— causes of deficiencies in 230-231
— deficiencies in 230
— dissemination of 210, 246, 249
— effects on utilization 196
— expenditures on 231
— impact of 194
— needed by individual users (see also users) 275-276
— needed by communities (see also public participation) 275-276
— overrefinement of 233
— sensitive to culture and language 195, 231
— sources of 274
— transfer of 231-232, 281
— utilization of 231
information systems 230
— on-line 208
informed consent 60
injuries
— cost of 41, 312
— from bicycle accidents 52
— from motor vehicle accidents 9, 41
— from sports 9, 40-41
— incidence of 9
— mortality from 12
— prevention of 52, 311-312
— spinal cord 12, 41, 315
input 2-3
innovation 47, 265, 301

Institute for Clinical Evaluative Sciences 228
insurance (see also provincial drug programs) 96-101
— administration of 96
— claims review process 202
— importance to health 19
— loss of coverage 153
— mixed public/private 76, 97, 108, 209
— number of carriers 97-98
— one tier vs two tier 75, 96-101
— operation of the second tier 101
— policy issues 96
— premiums 96, 97, 135, 152, 203
— private versus public 163-164
integration 84-86
— disadvantages of 86
— of data-bases 125
— of medicare and WCB 101-102
— of sectors 84
— of service delivery 84-85
intensive care 43, 240
Intermittent Positive Pressure Breathing (IPPB) 153
international forces 80-81
Internet 196
in-vitro fertilization 153
iodine, in salt 127
ischemic health disease (see coronary artery disease)
Israel 54, 99

J.

Japan 9, 18, 24, 35, 131, 194, 228
Joint Management Committee 74
joint ventures 137, 139-140

K.

Kaiser-Permanente 151, 171, 196
Kids Help Line, Toronto 196

L.

labor legislation 14
laboratories 159, 162
— private 150, 153
— regulation of 86, 122, 149
Laboratory Centre for Disease Control 67
laboratory services 41, 76, 327
laboratory technologists 217
large area networks (LANs) 125, 233
law of diminishing returns 45-46
leadership
— from government 31, 63-64
— from the field 73
lease-back arrangements 75-76
libraries 196
licenses (see federal government)
licensure standards 95
life, definition of 51-52
life expectancy, determinants of 9
lifestyle 66, 126, 194
Lions Gate Hospital, Vancouver 290
literacy 208
living wills 197
local government 80, 87

T.

Task Force on Periodic Health Examinations 155
tax rebates 66
taxation, by regions 88, 138
taxes 163
— funded 135
technology 15
— costs 156
— evaluation of 39, 95, 127-128
— outside health care 10
Technology Evaluation Council (Quebec) 39
teen-agers (see adolescents)
tendering (see competition)
terminology 95
— economic 2
— financial 134
— of consumerism 189
— of disability and chronic illness 42
— of organization 83
— of planning and policy analysis 47, 115-116
— of user fees 202
(the) Territories 17
thalassemia 155, 244, 290, 291, 331
thyroid testing 245, 327
The Hospital For Sick Children 52, 142
tonsillectomy 247
Toronto 111, 159
Toronto Hospital, the 103
total parenteral nutrition (TPN) 136, 291
Total Quality Management (TQM) 3, 124, 248, 257
trade-offs 45, 49, 205
transfer of funds as costs move 141-142
transfusions (see blood products)
triple prescription program 287
trustees, functions of 77-78, 126, 132
two tiered health care system 30, 96, 97, 98-101, 148, 273, 314, 320

U.

ultrasound 332
Une Reforme Axee Sur le Citoyen (Que) 114, 179
unemployment (see employment)
unemployment insurance 6, 33, 66
United Kingdom (see Britain)
United Nations Charter on Children's Rights 112
United States 22, 54, 65, 97, 103, 128, 131, 140, 157, 185, 292
— administration costs 43
— capitation in (see Health Maintenance Organizations)
— expenditures on health care 18, 35, 40, 151
— physician supply 80
United States Foundation for Informed Medical Decision Making 198
universality 18, 69
— definition 25
— degree of presence 58
— options for attainment of 180
University of Alberta Hospitals 159
University of Toronto 218
university teaching units 173
unpaid caregivers (see voluntary caregivers)
user fees 16, 95, 109, 120, 135, 138, 202-210, 272

— administration of 208
— changes in 203-204
— effects of 205, 206, 207, 282
— exemptions from 209
— impact of illiteracy 208
— insurance against 208-209
— objections to (includes disadvantages of) 203, 205-206, 208
— rationale for 139, 203, 204-205, 207
— types of 26, 149, 206-207
— utilization of 162, 203
— variable with user cooperation 56
user friendly services 84
users 189-210
— choices of 20, 55, 198-199, 200-201
— compliance of 199
— confusing issues faced 272-273
— control of decisions 56, 140, 191, 200, 201, 207, 209
— control over funds 60, 140-141, 210
— direct advertising to 198
— effects of 201
— impact of illiteracy 195, 197
— information needed by 193, 194-195, 233, 275, 277, 285-286
— limits on control of 198-199
— penalties for lack of cooperation 55, 202
— priorities of 29, 60, 271
— protection of 58, 100
— responsibilities of 210, 241-242
— rights 20, 56, 232
— roles of 110, 189, 195, 202, 232, 259
— sources of information for 184, 233
— techniques for involvement of 196-197
— unhealthy choices of 199
utilization review (see utilization management)
utilization management 248-249, 254
— of drugs 200, 296-298
— provincial and regional programs 198
— role of users 202
utilization of health care
— factors affecting 10, 16
— effects of culture 8
— variability 242, 337-338

V.

value-for-money (see cost-effectiveness and better spending)
values 49-62, 242-243, 299
— effects on policy 49, 238
Victoria, B.C. 10
Victoria Health Project 85, 141
videos 196, 262
violence 7, 28, 38, 52, 54, 67, 227, 230, 276, 313
visible minorities 57
voluntary agencies (see private nonprofit)
voluntary caregivers 201
volunteers 86

W.

waiting lists 183-184
walk-in clinics 105-106, 129, 160
wealth (also see determinants of health)
— national/provincial 24, 306

Y.

Z.